The Politics of Crime

CLARENDON STUDIES IN CRIMINOLOGY
Published under the auspices of the Institute of Criminology,
University of Cambridge, the Mannheim Centre, London School of
Economics, and the Centre for Criminological Research,
University of Oxford.

GENERAL EDITOR: ALISON LIEBLING (*University of Cambridge*)

EDITORS: MANUEL EISNER AND PER-OLOF WIKSTRÖM
(*University of Cambridge*)

PAUL ROCK, JILL PEAY, AND TIM NEWBURN
(*London School of Economics*)

LUCIA ZEDNER AND IAN LOADER
(*University of Oxford*)

Recent titles in this series:

Bouncers: Violence and Governance in the Night-time Economy
Hobbs, Hadfield, Lister, and Winlow

Policing and the Condition of England: Memory, Politics, and Culture
Loader and Mulcahy

The Criminological Foundations of Penal Policy:
Essay in Honour of Roger Hood
Zedner and Ashworth (eds.)

CCTV and Policing: Public Area Surveillance and Police Practices in Britain
Goold

Prisons and their Moral Performance: A Study of Values,
Quality, and Prison Life
Liebling

Constructing Victims' Rights: The Home Office, New Labour, and Victims
Rock

Desisting from Crime: Continuity and Change in Long-term Crime
Patterns of Serious Chronic Offenders
Ezell and Cohen

Courting Violence: Offences against the Person Cases in Court
Fielding

Bar Wars: Contesting the Night in Contemporary British Cities
Hadfield

The Politics of Crime Control

Essays in Honour of David Downes

Edited by

Tim Newburn

and

Paul Rock

OXFORD
UNIVERSITY PRESS

OXFORD
UNIVERSITY PRESS

Great Clarendon Street, Oxford OX2 6DP

Oxford University Press is a department of the University of Oxford.
It furthers the University's objective of excellence in research, scholarship,
and education by publishing worldwide in

Oxford New York

Auckland Cape Town Dar es Salaam Hong Kong Karachi
Kuala Lumpur Madrid Melbourne Mexico City Nairobi
New Delhi Shanghai Taipei Toronto

With offices in

Argentina Austria Brazil Chile Czech Republic France Greece
Guatemala Hungary Italy Japan Poland Portugal Singapore
South Korea Switzerland Thailand Turkey Ukraine Vietnam

Oxford is a registered trade mark of Oxford University Press
in the UK and in certain other Countries

Published in the United States
by Oxford University Press Inc., New York

© The various contributors, 2006

The moral rights of the authors have been asserted
Database right Oxford University Press (maker)

Crown copyright material is reproduced under Class Licence
Number C01P0000148 with the permission of OPSI
and the Queen's Printer for Scotland

First published 2006
First published in paperback 2009

All rights reserved. No part of this publication may be reproduced,
stored in a retrieval system, or transmitted, in any form or by any means,
without the prior permission in writing of Oxford University Press,
or as expressly permitted by law, or under terms agreed with the appropriate
reprographics rights organization. Enquiries concerning reproduction
outside the scope of the above should be sent to the Rights Department,
Oxford University Press, at the address above

You must not circulate this book in any other binding or cover
and you must impose the same condition on any acquirer

British Library Cataloguing in Publication Data
Data available

Library of Congress Cataloging in Publication Data
Data available

Typeset by Newgen Imaging Systems (P) Ltd, Chennai, India
Printed in Great Britain
by
Biddles Ltd, King's Lynn

ISBN 978-0-19-920840-1
ISBN 978-0-19-956595-5 (pbk.)

1 3 5 7 9 10 8 6 4 2

General Editor's Introduction

Clarendon Studies in Criminology aims to provide a forum for outstanding empirical and theoretical work in all aspects of criminology, criminal justice, penology, and the wider field of deviant behaviour. The editors welcome excellent PhD work, as well as submissions from established scholars. The *Series* was inaugurated in 1994, with Roger Hood as its first General Editor, following energetic discussions between Oxford University Press and three Criminological Centres. It is edited under the auspices of these three Criminological Centres: the Cambridge Institute of Criminology, the Mannheim Centre for Criminology at the London School of Economics, and the Oxford Centre for Criminology. Each supplies members of the Editorial Board.

In order to celebrate David Downes' distinguished contribution to British criminology, the editors are proud to add *The Politics of Crime Control: Essays in Honour of David Downes*, edited by Tim Newburn and Paul Rock, to the series. David contributed hugely to what the editors call social democratic criminology throughout a period during which the social and intellectual composition of criminologists has changed dramatically. David's work and teaching have been part of a 'great social science tradition', which is celebrated here.

This book constitutes a *festschrift* in honour of David Downes, but it also constitutes an important contribution in its own right. Newburn and Rock have brought together an outstanding selection of essays on the politics of crime control by colleagues, friends, and students of David's. It serves as a useful reminder of the roles of social structure, class, and economics in crime causation, and of the importance of humanistic values in its control.

The editors welcome this important addition to the *Series* in its own right and as a most fitting tribute to the work of our eminent colleague.

Alison Liebling
Cambridge, March 2006

Contents

Notes on Contributors ix

1. David Downes: An Introduction
   Tim Newburn and Paul Rock 1
2. Beyond Risk: A Lament for Social Democratic Criminology
   Robert Reiner 7
3. Dangerous People: Beginnings of a New Labour Proposal
   Andrew Rutherford 51
4. With Respect to Order, the Rules of the Game have Changed: New Labour's Dominance of the 'Law and Order' Agenda
   Rod Morgan 91
5. East Ending: Dissociation, De-industrialization, and David Downes
   Dick Hobbs 117
6. Opportunity Makes the Thief-Taker: The Influence of Economic Analysis on Crime Control
   Lucia Zedner 147
7. Contrasts and Concepts: Considering the Development of Comparative Criminology
   Frances Heidensohn 173
8. Historicizing Contrasts in Tolerance
   Nicola Lacey 197
9. Contrasts in Intolerance: Cultures of Control in the United States and Britain
   Tim Newburn 227

10. Governance and Restorative Justice in Cali, Colombia
   Declan Roche   271

11. Neither Honesty Nor Hypocrisy: The Legal Reconstruction of Torture
   Stanley Cohen   297

Index   319

Notes on Contributors

STANLEY COHEN is Emeritus Professor of Sociology, London School of Economics and Political Science.

FRANCES HEIDENSOHN is Visiting Professor, Department of Sociology, London School of Economics and Political Science, and Emeritus Professor, University of London.

DICK HOBBS is Professor of Sociology, London School of Economics and Political Science.

NICOLA LACEY is Professor of Criminal Law and Legal Theory, London School of Economics and Political Science, and Adjunct Professor of Social and Political Theory, Research School of Social Sciences of the Australian National University.

ROD MORGAN is ex-Chair of the Youth Justice Board and Professor Emeritus, Faculty of Law, University of Bristol.

TIM NEWBURN is Professor of Criminology and Social Policy, London School of Economics and Political Science.

ROBERT REINER is Professor of Criminology, Department of Law, London School of Economics and Political Science.

DECLAN ROCHE is in private legal practice in Wall Street.

PAUL ROCK is Emeritus Professor of Sociology at the London School of Economics and visiting Professor of Criminology at the University of Pennsylvania.

ANDREW RUTHERFORD is Emeritus Professor of Law and Criminal Policy, University of Southampton.

LUCIA ZEDNER is Professor of Criminology in the Faculty of Law, Corpus Christi College, Oxford.

1
David Downes: An Introduction
Tim Newburn and Paul Rock

David Downes was born in 1938 in Sheffield, read Modern History at Keble College, Oxford, and then found himself stumbling into criminology, as so many criminologists do, when, 'not even knowing of the existence of the subject',[1] he applied to enter the London School of Economics (LSE) hoping to become a social worker and was told about how 'people [studied] such subjects as drug taking, white collar crime and delinquency'.[2] He was pointed towards research and the Sociology Department, came under the supervision of Terence Morris and Eryl Hall Williams, and received a doctorate, published in 1966 as *The Delinquent Solution*, on anomie, delinquency and the dualities of social class in the East End of London.[3] It disclosed how class in England brought its consolations to the young men he studied: to be working class was not a matter of shame, and it tempered aspirations, but there were frustrations none the less which sought outlet in hedonistic forays into petty delinquency. The research and the book mapped the interplay between biography, class, and social structure, relations which had long intrigued him, and it confirmed David Downes as a 'Left Realist' *avant la lettre*.

David Downes began teaching at the School in 1963, and there he remained until his retirement forty years later. The

---

[1] D. Downes; 'Predictive Value of Social Theories', in S. Holdaway and P. Rock (eds.), *Thinking about Criminology*, UCL Press, London, 1998, p. 101.
[2] ibid, p. 101.
[3] It should perhaps be noted that the book reflects David Downes' intellectual parentage in Terence Morris, who has been concerned always with delinquency, injustice, and the iniquities of punishment in an unequal world.

conventional British criminology he at first encountered was thin and under-populated (a 'mish-mash of cod psychology and social factor theory'[4]), and, like many other younger sociological criminologists of the time, he was obliged to be an autodidact. His thesis was perhaps the last major criminological study in the anomie tradition of Merton and Cloward and Ohlin.[5] But there were also to be seen the first stirrings of the reformation induced by the new interactionist sociology of deviance and its emphasis on process, meaning, and ethnographic method,[6] and that novel sociology left its mark: his inclinations, he said, lay 'with Weber rather than Marx, and with interactionists rather than functionalists'.[7]

Criminology endlessly reinvents itself, and the interactionism of the 1960s lost some of its immediate panache, giving way to radical or Marxist criminology in the 1970s, and then, in a predictable dialectical turn (the two contenders having been reconciled) giving birth to Left Realism in the 1980s before being swamped by new fashions blowing in from France in the 1990s. Over the duration of a long career, a career that paralleled the coming of age of British criminology itself, David Downes showed at once a responsiveness to all that change as well as a remarkable intellectual consistency.

He took to criminology principally as a spirited political project,[8] a way of understanding and perhaps amending structured inequities of power, wealth and life-chances. But he was never a polemicist, and his work has been moderated always by academic rigour, openness and the scepticism of an independent mind.[9] Crime and punishment importantly reveal to him the

---

[4] D. Downes; 'Predictive Value of Social Theories', n.1 above, p. 101.

[5] See R. Merton; *Social Theory and Social Structure*, Free Press, Glencoe, 1957, and R. Cloward and L. Ohlin; *Delinquency and Opportunity*, Free Press, Glencoe, 1960.

[6] And particularly H. Becker; *Outsiders*, Free Press, Glencoe, 1963.

[7] Preface to D. Downes and P. Rock; *Understanding Deviance*, Oxford University Press, Oxford, 1982, p. viii.

[8] See his 'What the next Government should do about crime', *Howard Journal*, 36:1, 1997.

[9] Demonstrated powerfully in his 'Praxis Makes Perfect: A Critique of Critical Criminology', in D. Downes and P. Rock (eds.), *Deviant Interpretations*, Martin Robertson, London, 1979.

inner workings of an unequal society.[10] Take his lament about the condition of England at the turn of the century: deliberately induced changes, he said, had brought about 'the erosion of...safeguards—the "Welfare State", working-class community, middle-class ideals of service and upper-class *noblesse oblige*—and the headlong pursuit of prosperity above all else, involving...*more* economic inequality and social polarization...'.[11] That has the marks of a passionate engagement with a world in which the institutions and procedures of criminal justice are failing, crime soars, people are excluded, communities are fearful and delinquents treated over-harshly. 'The criminal justice system in Britain is in deep trouble', he wrote in 1992. 'The crime rate has risen eight-fold since 1950 and...the resulting decline in the quality of life in worst-hit areas is cumulatively severe. The causes of this marked deterioration arguably lie in deep-seated social, economic and cultural trends beyond the reach of, though in their turn affecting, criminal justice processes.'[12] He sought aid in models of practice elsewhere, in Holland for instance, where things appeared to be done better.[13] Alone,[14] and then with Rod Morgan, he scanned and compared developments in the evolution of the public politics of crime and punishment in England and Wales, and saw little to reassure those who desired more tolerant, less repressive,

---

[10] He lists his interests and experience on the LSE website as comparative sentencing and penal policy; crime and the labour market; and theories of crime and delinquency.
[11] Introduction to D. Downes (ed.), *Crime and the City*, Macmillan, Houndmills, 1989, p. 8. And take his observation written ten years later that 'Since 1979, the pillars of the welfare state have been systematically and severely eroded. The components of a kind of market fascism have been assembled: through job destruction policies and the growth of job insecurity; through regressive taxation; through growing disenchantment at local level by the weakening of local authorities; through the increase in poverty, inequality and social exclusion...' 'Predictive Value of Social Theories' (n.4 above), p. 102.
[12] Introduction to *Unravelling Criminal Justice*, Macmillan, Houndmills, 1992, p. xii.
[13] See his *Contrasts in Tolerance: Post-war Penal Policy in The Netherlands and England and Wales*, Clarendon Press, Oxford, 1988 and 'The Case for Going Dutch: The Lessons of Post-war Penal Policy', *Political Quarterly*, 63:1, 1992.
[14] See his *Law and Order: Theft of an Issue*, Fabian Society, London, 1982.

and less strident policies.[15] A review of the work of the first New Labour administration concluded quite characteristically that 'Its newfound ... image, that it is "tough on crime", has been bought at a considerable cost in terms of civil liberties and the humane justice and penal policies that Labour espoused in the 1980s.'[16]

His work and teaching have in short been part of a great social science tradition, Fabian in much of its colouring, which marries an interest in scholarship with an equally large if not a larger interest in social improvement effected through research and education. He would have liked to improve conditions for the young—and would warm to phrases like 'teen canteen'; to improve conditions for the incarcerated, and *Contrasts in Tolerance* is a plea for what some would have called an enlightened approach to penal policy; he has deplored what has befallen British drugs policy, deeply critical of our veering towards a war on drugs that can never be won;[17] and he has argued again and again about the consequences of increasing social inequality for crime and delinquency. It is perhaps not remarkable that his writing has been tinged always with a sadness at the way in which, in Tuchman's phrase, there has ever been a march of folly in penology and criminal policy.[18] The new populism and the new *liberalismus* are not congenial to him or to the Fabians or to anyone, inside or outside government, who believes in the triumph of reason.

It should now be apparent why we chose to title this *Festschrift The Politics of Crime Control* and why the chapters it contains should dwell on the themes of comparative penal policy; the politics of crime; and subcultural theory and youth, the object of Downes' original research, which pointed to the manner in which delinquency takes form within the framework of class inequalities.

---

[15] See D. Downes and R. Morgan, 'Hostages to Fortune? The Politics of Law and Order in Post-War Britain', in M. Maguire *et al.* (eds.), *The Oxford Handbook of Criminology*, Oxford University Press, Oxford, 1994.

[16] D. Downes and R. Morgan, 'The Skeletons in the Cupboard: the Politics of Law and Order at the Turn of the Millennium', in M. Maguire *et al.* (eds.), *The Oxford Handbook of Criminology* (3rd edn.), Oxford University Press, 2002, p. 317.

[17] See 'The Drug Addict as Folk Devil' in P. Rock (ed.), *Drugs and Politics*, Transaction, Rutgers, 1977.

[18] See B. Tuchman, *The March of Folly*, Michael Joseph, London, 1984.

The Politics of Crime Control arose out of a one-day conference devised in June 2003 to celebrate David Downes as a scholar and a man, and it reflects more than a simple admiration for his ideas. David Downes must be one of the very nicest men to have worked in a university. He has always been a delightful colleague and teacher: modest, unassuming, helpful always, inclined to say 'yes' when asked to do anything, never visibly irascible or mean, concerned to make peace, to care for friends and associates, modest to a fault, concerned about injustice, pretending to be a pygmy standing on the shoulders of giants, and on the shoulders of Richard Titmuss as perhaps the largest giant of all.[19] Those asked to speak at that conference and contribute to this book did so with eagerness, saying 'anything for David', and a project can rarely have been sustained with such good will. We hope that this book will serve to commemorate, extend, and amplify what he began.

Bibliography

Becker, H. (1963) *Outsiders* (Free Press: Glencoe).

Cloward, R. and Ohlin, L. (1960) *Delinquency and Opportunity* (Free Press: Glencoe).

Downes, D. (1979) The Drug Addict as Folk Devil, in P. Rock (ed.), *Drugs and Politics*, (Rutgers: Transaction).

—— (1979) Praxis Makes Perfect: A Critique of Critical Criminology, in D. Downes and P. Rock (eds.), *Deviant Interpretations* (Martin Robertson: London).

—— (1982) *Law and Order: Theft of an Issue* (Fabian Society: London).

—— (1988) *Contrasts in Tolerance: Post-war Penal Policy in The Netherlands and England and Wales* (Clarendon Press: Oxford).

—— (ed.) (1989) *Crime and the City* (Macmillan: Houndmills).

—— (1992) The Case for Going Dutch: The Lessons of Post-war Penal Policy' 63 *Political Quarterly* 1.

—— (1992) *Unravelling Criminal Justice* (Macmillan: Houndmills).

---

[19] He had displayed in his room at the London School of Economics a photograph of Titmuss, and much admired his *The Gift Relationship*, Allen and Unwin, London, 1970.

Downes, D. (1997) What the Next Government should do about Crime 36 *Howard Journal* 1.
—— (1998) 'Predictive Value of Social Theories' in S. Holdaway and P. Rock (eds.), *Thinking about Criminology* (UCL Press: London).
—— Morgan, R. (1994) 'Hostages to Fortune? The Politics of Law and Order in Post-War Britain' in M. Maguire *et al.* (eds.), *The Oxford Handbook of Criminology* (Oxford University Press: Oxford).
—— —— (2002) 'The Skeletons in the Cupboard: the Politics of Law and Order at the Turn of the Millennium' in M. Maguire *et al.* (eds.), *The Oxford Handbook of Criminology* (3rd edn, Oxford University Press: Oxford).
—— and Rock, P. (1982) *Understanding Deviance* (Oxford University Press: Oxford).
Merton, R. (1957) *Social Theory and Social Structure* (Free Press: Glencoe).
Titmuss, R. (1970) *The Gift Relationship* (Allen and Unwin: London).
Tuchman, B. (1984) *The March of Folly* (Michael Joseph: London).

2
Beyond Risk: A Lament for Social Democratic Criminology
Robert Reiner*

Introduction

This chapter will examine one aspect of the profound changes in crime, control, and criminal justice over the last thirty years, the mysterious disappearance of social democratic criminology. This was a way of understanding and responding to crime that was widespread, perhaps dominant, for much of the twentieth century. Was its disappearance due to death by suicide, murder, or natural causes—or is it still alive and capable of returning?

In the next section I will define what I mean by 'social democratic' criminology. I shall then chart and analyse its virtually complete replacement by a variety of perspectives to which I shall give the general label 'contrology'.[1] The conclusion will argue that without a return to social democracy—however remote this may seem—the future directions of crime and control are grim.

Social Democratic Criminology

The term 'social democratic criminology' has been used before (e.g. Taylor 1981: ch. 2), but it has never been a self-espoused label. What I mean by it is a set of assumptions about the nature

---

* The arguments in this chapter are developed more fully in Reiner 2007.

[1] The term 'contrology' was coined by Jason Ditton in his book with that title (Ditton 1979). He used it to refer to a thorough-going formulation of 'labelling' theory, seeing crime as shaped by control. I have not only slightly shortened the word, but am using it in almost the opposite way. By 'contrology' I mean the variety of fundamentally conservative criminologies that are concerned with the pursuit of direct crime control rather than analysing causes of crime or criticizing criminal justice.

of human action, ethics, and political economy that broadly corresponds to the most common meaning of the term 'social democratic'.

Social Democracy

'Social democracy' has been used as a badge by many very different political movements. In the late nineteenth and early twentieth centuries the label 'Social Democratic' was espoused by Marxist parties, such as Hyndman's Social Democratic Federation in England and Kautsky's German Social Democratic Party (Sassoon 1996: ch. 1). Trotsky once declared that his nationality was 'Social Democratic' (Figes 2005: 10).

After the First World War, with the establishment of Bolshevik government in the Soviet Union, the term 'social democracy' came to be contrasted with communism. Social democracy signified at the very least a distinction of means from Bolshevism—the parliamentary road to socialism—and for many a change of ends too, reform of capitalism rather than its overthrow. Perhaps the culmination of this evolution was the founding of the British Social Democratic Party in 1981 as a breakaway from what was perceived as an unacceptably militant Labour Party. But for most of the twentieth century 'social democratic' referred to a wide variety of socialist viewpoints distinguished from, on the left border, Soviet communism, and on the right, the 'new' liberalism inspired by T.H.Green and his disciples in the late nineteenth and early twentieth centuries (Clarke 1978).

Its intellectual centre of gravity was the English tradition of ethical socialism (Dennis and Halsey 1988), the quintessential exemplar of which was R.H.Tawney but which also included such thinkers as Graham Wallas, Hobhouse, and T.H. Marshall. The 1990s' 'third way' of the two Tonies, Blair and Giddens, explicitly sought to triangulate this 'social democracy' and neoliberalism. 'Social democracy' was always a species of socialism, but it was itself a 'third way' between two poles—communism and liberalism. It was not, however, a presentational splitting of the difference, but an anguished and internally contested terrain, an intellectual and moral Buridan's ass, torn between the powerful pulls of justice and liberty. There were of course many attempts to synthesize the two poles. The most fully developed of these, John Rawls' magisterial *Theory of Justice* (Rawls 1971), appeared just as the political and social influence of social democracy was about to dip below the horizon, a paradigm example of Hegel's owl of Minerva spreading its wings at dusk.[2] 'Social democracy' as an intellectual discourse, and *a fortiori* actually existing social democratic parties and governments, encompassed a wide variety of viewpoints and programmes. In the middle of the twentieth century, the heyday of European mixed economy welfare states and the Rooseveltian New Deal in the United States, it stood for a broad consensus, albeit with vigorous opposition from unreconciled free marketeers, old conservative nostalgists, and most Marxists.

This consensus also tacitly underpinned the analyses of crime and strategies for reform developed by most criminologists (Garland and Sparks 2000: 195), despite sharp conflicts over specific issues, notably capital punishment (Ryan 1983; Morris 1989: 32, 77–85). The quintessential expression of social democratic criminology is Robert Merton's seminal formulation of anomie theory (Merton 1938), probably the most quoted article in criminology, and arguably one of the most misrepresented (Reiner 1984: 186–94). In Britain its clearest exponent was Hermann Mannheim. But beyond specific exemplars there was a deep structure of shared assumptions that could be characterized as social democratic. This was shown by the quiet confidence of policy-makers that, for all the problems of wartime and post-war crime, social progress would resolve these (Morris 1989: chs. 2, 3, 6; Bottoms and Stevenson 1992). Social democratic criminology as an ideal-type can be characterized, I believe, by the following ten dimensions incorporating the key themes of social democracy in general.

Social Democratic Criminology: An Ideal-type
The problem of crime
Social democratic criminologists were well aware of the difficulties in conceptualizing crime,[3] and did not simply take for

---

[2] Rawls is normally seen as a liberal theory, but its arguments for principles that balance liberty and equality offer a powerful case for the values underpinning social democracy.
[3] Henry and Lanier 2001; Lacey *et al.* 2003: Chs. 1, 2; Zedner 2004; Chs. 1, 2; Hillyard *et al.* 2004; Morrison 2005 are recent analyses of the vexed issues in conceptualizing crime.

granted the categories of criminal law. Legal definitions of crime embodied power rather than morality, so they inadequately reflected the gravity of different forms of antisocial or harmful behaviour.[4] Mannheim's *Criminal Justice and Social Reconstruction*, for example, offered a critical analysis of criminal law, assessing its appropriateness for curbing the most harmful forms of antisocial behaviour in the post-war period. It was particularly concerned about the inadequate definition and enforcement of the law against dishonest and harmful business practices. Weak policing of white-collar crime was not only problematic in itself, it called into question the moral integrity of criminal justice and undermined its ability to deal with routine crimes such as theft and burglary (Mannheim 1946: 119). In the United States, Sutherland had launched his pioneering attempt to bring white-collar crime within the ambit of criminological concern in 1939 (Sutherland 1983), for which Mannheim thought he deserved a Nobel prize (Nelken 2002: 848). Merton's pivotal theory of anomie was explicitly intended as an analysis of deviance, not limited to legal or criminal justice categories (Merton 1938). It is commonly criticized for adopting the official picture of crime as primarily a lower-class phenomenon, ignoring white-collar crime. However Merton began with an analysis of how a culture that defines success in purely financial terms is prone to anomie at all levels, because there is no inherent end-point to the goal of monetary gain. He explicitly applied this to crime in the suites as well as the streets (Merton 1938 [1957]: 131–44).

Social democratic criminologists realized that the powerful and privileged often perpetrated far greater harms than did ordinary crime, usually escaping criminal labelling or even its possibility.[5] Nonetheless, like subsequent 'left realism' in the

[4] Social democratic definitions of crime sought to combine the two elements of harm and official enforcement. An example is Bonger's definition of crime as 'a serious antisocial act to which the State reacts consciously by inflicting pain' (Bonger 1936: 5).

[5] Expressed in Anatole France's much quoted aphorism about 'the majestic impartiality of the law, which forbids the rich as well as the poor to sleep under bridges, to beg in the streets, and to steal bread' (*Le Lys Rouge* Paris 1894). Jock Young's recent reformulation of the golden rule puts this even more pithily: 'it is the people with the gold who make the rules' (Young 2005: vi).

1980s (Lea and Young 1984), social democrats viewed routine crime as harmful and problematic—especially to the most vulnerable in society—however much they may have been sympathetic to the plight of offenders. Social democratic criminology (like all criminology prior to the paradigm shift associated with the 'labelling' perspective of the 1960s) was primarily concerned with developing causal explanations of crime, with a correctionalist ambition of reducing offending.

Primacy of the ethical

In current political debate the language of morality has been captured by the religious Right in the United States, and by *Daily Mail* reading or fearing circles in the United Kingdom, restricting it to an extremely narrow conception of 'traditional family values'. This blots out much broader conceptions of the moral, governing all spheres of human activity, that used to be the focus of both religious and secular philosophies, on the left as much as the right of politics. As Michael Walzer put it recently 'For rightwing intellectuals and activists, values seem to be about sex and almost nothing else; vast areas of social life are left to the radically amoral play of market forces. And yet they "have" values, and we [the liberal left] don't' (Walzer 2005: 37). Especially in the wake of George W. Bush's second Presidential election victory,[6] attributed by many analysts to the 'values' issue above all (Frank 2004), there has been much discussion of the need for the left to recapture the language of ethics and passionate commitment to justice.

The left has often been uncomfortable with discussions of morality. Marx is said to have roared with laughter when he heard talk about morality (Lukes 1985: 27). He and Engels castigated ethically derived versions of socialism as 'utopian', rejecting them for a 'scientific' materialism (Marx and Engels 1848: 72–5; Engels 1880). This 'obstretric' view of history, in which socialists act merely as the midwives of communism, which will inevitably be born after the revolution generated by the contradictions of capitalism, has been a deadly illusion (G. Cohen 2000). It fatally underestimated the huge moral transformation that needs to

---

[6] Perhaps 2004 should be called his first election victory in the light of the still contested legitimacy of the 2000 result (Palast 2004).

anticipate and accompany political and economic change if it is to not to produce new forms of tyranny in the guise of liberation. It is also arguably a misreading of the depth of Marx and Engels' own moral sensitivity to the evils of industrial capitalism, which paradoxically underlay their rejection of moralism in favour of the wishful thinking of an inevitable progression to communism.

The non-Marxist left has always been clearly driven by moral concerns. Social democracy, in particular, was fundamentally idealist. The ends that social democratic political action aimed at, and the means adopted for their pursuit, were derived from and subject to explicitly espoused ethical values. Secular or religious, social democrats espoused the fundamental equality of value of individuals, the ancient Golden Rule embodied in the Biblical injunction to love your neighbour as yourself (Leviticus XIX: 18). Shorn of its religious cloak, this principle continued to underlie most modern (and arguably some post-modern) conceptions of morality and justice. This is most evident in Kantian formulations of the ethical as the universalisable (Kant 1785). But it is also implied in utilitarianism, usually regarded as a fundamentally opposed perspective which, at least as a starting point, treats every individual's utilities as equal inputs into the felicific calculus.[7]

Nietzche in the late nineteenth century, and some post-modernist and Foucauldian approaches in the late twentieth century, expressly reject both traditional religious and Enlightenment versions of universalist ethics as restrictions on human autonomy and diversity, advocating instead an aesthetic ethics and politics (Nietzche 1885; Rose 1999: 282–4). However, rejecting the claims of transcendental moral codes, and of any absolute epistemological foundations for ethics, does not entail the rejection of the value of the Golden Rule. Several attempts at developing post-foundational ethics—for all their differences—nonetheless seem to echo the principle of what Dworkin calls 'equal respect and concern for

---

[7] Kantians stress that utilitarianism does not respect the specificity of persons, so is compatible with outcomes that sacrifice individuals for the greater good of the majority (Rawls 1971; Hudson 2003: 19). This tyranny of the majority problem was recognized by utilitarians like John Stuart Mill early on, and their more sophisticated formulations attempt to cope with it (Reiner 2002).

Beyond Risk: A Lament for Social Democratic Criminology 13

others' (Dworkin 2000). Boutellier has made an impressive attempt to develop criminal justice ethics from Rorty's pragmatic conception of liberal irony (Rorty 1989, 1999; Boutellier 2000: ch. 6). Rorty argues that the ironist, who recognizes the contingency of her convictions, can still be a 'liberal', including among their 'ungroundable desires their own hope that suffering will be diminished, that the humiliation of human beings by other human beings may cease' (Rorty 1989: xv). This is paralleled by Bauman's attempt to develop a post-modern 'morality without ethics', 'resurrecting the consideration of the Other temporarily... suspended by the obedience to the norm' (Baumann 1995: 7). This also recalls Levinas' notion of the ethical as the obverse of 'egology'—the assertion of the primacy of the self. 'We name the calling into question of my spontaneity by the presence of the other ethics' (Levinas 1969: 33).

Some liberals and social democrats may have thought their values were grounded in the self-evidence of intuition, scientific knowledge, the ineluctable march of history, or the will of God. But for many it was clear that there are no indubitable Archimedean points on which to ground ethical commitments in an objective, unanswerable way. This does not mean, however, that the values espoused by social democrats—liberty, equality, fraternity, in the now hallowed formula of the French and other democratic revolutions—were unreasonable or that there were not arguments that could be marshalled for them. But these arguments were always essentially contested and potentially endless.

Ethics were also primary for social democrats in considering legitimate means. Good ends did not justify dirty hands (Sartre 1948). Violence in particular could not be adopted as a tactic of choice, however noble the cause pursued, but only defensively, of necessity, and proportionately. The use of morally dirty means was not only wrong in itself but also counter-productive. It corrupted the users and frustrated the achievement of ethically desirable goals.

Social democratic criminology is often associated with explanations of crime in terms of economic factors (poverty, inequality, unemployment). But it was much more than just criminological Clintonism ('it's the economy, stupid'). Social democratic criminology was primarily concerned with ethical issues, not least in its attempts to explain crime. In the first place crime, criminal justice, punishment, and antisocial behaviours (at all levels of the social hierarchy) were problematic because they were sources of harm and suffering. Not only victims of crime but also perpetrators and the social conditions that ultimately underlay crime were all matters for ethical concern.

More specifically it is important to stress that economic factors like poverty, inequality, or unemployment were seen as leading to crime primarily because they weakened support (in general and in potential offenders) for morality, in the sense of concern and respect for others. Bonger's work, for example, is usually characterized as the most thorough-going example of Marxist economic determinism applied to crime (Taylor, Walton and Young 1973). But Bonger analyses the inequities of capitalism as criminogenic not in themselves but because they stimulate a culture of egoism.

Merton's anomie theory, the paradigm social democratic account of crime, is often reduced to a simplistic explanation in terms of structural inequalities in legitimate opportunities. But moral factors are basic to Merton's analysis. Merton stresses that a materialistic culture, in which success is primarily defined in money terms, encourages deviance at all levels of society. This is because monetary aspirations are inherently unlimited and prone to anomie. The materialist ethos also prioritizes goal attainment over the legitimacy of means, and in itself erodes social and ethical controls. Merton's central typology of deviant reactions to anomie does indeed stress the significance of an unequal structural distribution of legitimate opportunities. However, this produces a strain towards deviance in cultures (like that of the United States) which stresses an ideal of equal opportunities. The key variable is the ethic of meritocracy, rather than inequality of opportunities *per se*. Mannheim's analysis of how wartime and post-war conditions generated crime, inextricably mixed together economic and moral issues (Taylor 1981: 45). The 1964 Labour Party study group document *Crime: A Challenge For Us All*, which informed the Wilson government's criminal justice agenda, adopted Tawney's analysis of the 'acquisitive society' to explain how Conservative economic policies had emphasized individual economic success thus 'weakening the moral fibre of individuals' (Labour Party 1964: 5).

Critique of capitalism

Social democrats saw capitalism as having systemic flaws that could be mitigated but were intrinsic to it. Its productive capacities were of course recognized. To ethical socialists like Tawney, however, economic growth was a means to desirable ends such as the relief of poverty, not an end in itself. Indeed material affluence posed moral dangers as it stimulated acquisitiveness and egoism (Tawney 1921).

Whatever its virtues, however, capitalism had several fundamental problems. Whilst differing from Marx's diagnosis of possible end states and how to achieve them, social democrats largely endorsed his critique of the pernicious consequences of market anarchy. The operation of unregulated markets inexorably generated inequality. Whilst growth offered increasing capacity to alleviate poverty there was no automatic trickle-down. Indeed the market price valuations that underpinned measures of economic growth reflected differential economic power. Price was determined by effective demand (desire backed by the ability to pay) not social need.[8] Capitalists' pursuit of their own economic rationality could produce external diseconomies, wider social costs such as pollution, which did not figure in their own private calculations of efficient productive methods. The neo-classical economists, such as Marshall and Pigou, who demonstrated that free market systems led to 'Pareto-optimal' allocation of resources in which (in the language of welfare economics) the 'gainers could over-compensate the losers', agreed with these criticisms. They endorsed political action to correct market dysfunctions. Capitalism also suffered from macro-economic fluctuations, the cycle of depression and boom, which, following Keynes' arguments in the 1930s, required government regulation to alleviate the ensuing misery. Social democrats' criticisms of capitalism were not only aimed at its economic consequences but also at the culture of amoral and possessive individualism that it accentuated.

---

[8] It is this point that has stimulated the New Economics Foundation and others to explore alternative measures of economic welfare and growth, building in estimates for social costs of conventional economic activity, and forms of wellbeing that do not command an adequate market price (Jackson 2004).

The economic dysfunctions of capitalism that social democracy identified were seen by criminologists as leading to crime, albeit not straightforwardly but mediated by intervening factors (such as their effects on morality, family life, and informal social controls). This has produced a plethora of research on the possible links between economic factors and crime, which will be considered later in the chapter. The results of this research are complex, but there can be no doubt that the political economy plays a significant, if not straightforward, part in the explanation of crime. Certainly the turbo-capitalism of the Thatcher–Reagan years has been a major causal factor in rocketing crime rates, and its slight attenuation under New Labour has contributed to recent falls in crime (Downes 2004; Hale 2005a).

Gradualism

Despite the critique of capitalism offered by social democrats, they did not advocate its overthrow. Specific reforms aimed at alleviating particular problems were to be argued for through the democratic process, and implemented gradually. For many social democrats the accumulation of such reforms was intended to result ultimately in a qualitatively different social order—socialism. But for many social democrats capitalism was seen as beneficial, or at any rate inevitable, so that perpetual struggle was required to alleviate its egregious failings. Gradualism was favoured in part to ensure by cautious experimentation that reforms worked without unintended negative consequences. But most fundamentally it was the necessary price of seeking to proceed democratically, by building consent, rather than through coercion.

The psychic cost of gradualism was living with a world of injustice and suffering, albeit one that was improving in stages. This required patience, fortitude, stoicism in the face of indefensible evil. Piecemeal reform aimed at little dollops of jam today, rather than vats of it after the Revolution. Social democracy sought gradual improvement in a forever messy and conflict-ridden world. As Kolakowski once put it: 'The trouble with the social democratic idea is that it does not... sell any of the exciting commodities which various totalitarian movements... offer dream-hungry youth... It has no prescription for the total salvation of mankind... It believes in no final easy victory over evil. It requires, in addition to commitment to a number of basic values, hard knowledge and rational calculation... It is an obstinate will to erode by inches the conditions which produce avoidable suffering, oppression, hunger, wars, racial and national hatred, insatiable greed and vindictive envy.' (quoted in Jenkins 1989: 142).

Social democratic criminologists sought not only to understand and reverse the macro causes of crime through economic and social policy. They were extensively involved in research and reform interventions aimed at effective (but humane) penal practice. The charge levelled both by Conservatives and by Left Realists in the 1980s that radical criminology was preoccupied with ultimate causes, not practical interventions to control crime, may have been true of the 'left idealism' of the 1970s. But it was certainly not true of social democratic criminologists, although they were concerned as much with the humanity and fairness of penal intervention as with 'What works?'.

Equality AND democracy

Social democracy sought equality through democratic means. There are of course extensive debates about how to interpret equality and democracy. But most social democrats subscribed to a fundamental principle of treating everyone with 'equal concern and respect' (Dworkin 2000). Rawls' two principles of justice—equality of basic liberties, and equality of material distribution (subject only to departures if they raise the position of the least well-off, the 'difference' principle)—expressed most explicitly the values of most social democrats.

Social democracy saw equality and liberal democracy as mutually reinforcing rather than in tension. In societies split by hierarchies of class (and gender, and ethnicity), equality was in the interest of the majority, so that ultimately the democratic process would produce a consensus for egalitarian measures. Conversely, in a highly unequal society, it was only possible to have the 'best democracy money could buy' (Palast 2004). Substantive democracy is incompatible with gross inequalities.

Social democrats certainly believed that the slow incorporation of all sections of society into civil, political and social citizenship (Marshall 1950) would achieve social order. The experience of the second half of the nineteenth century, during which recorded crime rates declined and then remained stable until after the First World War, seemed to confirm this (Gatrell 1980; Radzinowicz and Hood 1985). The 'dangerous classes' of the early Victorian period were progressively disciplined by the physically gentler, quotidien 'dull compulsion of economic relations' (Marx 1867: 737). Formal social control in the early twentieth century moved towards a more individualized, reform-oriented penal/welfare complex, informed by criminological research on the causation of offending and the requirements of rehabilitation (Garland 1985).

Quiet optimism

Until the early 1970s social democrats shared a tacit Whig theory of history. Without postulating any iron laws, there was a sense of continuing, if sometimes broken and tentative, progress towards equality, liberty, and democracy. This rested implicitly on a sense that there was a substantive historical agent, the working class, who constituted the majority of society and were receptive (if initially for self-interested reasons) to the ideals of social democracy.

Social democratic criminology shared this quiet optimism. However, this was challenged by the increase in recorded crime in the late 1950s. The rise in crime rates during a period of unprecedented mass affluence seemed to refute the expectation that crime would reduce with better social conditions. Jock Young famously called this an 'aetiological crisis' for social democratic criminology (Young 1986). But it is important to stress that social democratic criminology did not postulate a simple relationship between economic conditions and crime. This is not just re-interpretation with the benefit of hindsight. There are many examples of predictions by social democratic criminologists in the early 1960s of rising crime rates, due to the acquisitiveness, anomie, and relative deprivation sparked by the new consumerist culture (Labour Party 1964: 5; Downes 1966, 1988: 103–9).

Dimensions of justice

Essentially creatures of their time, most social democrats did not speak of other dimensions of inequality or oppression, such as gender, ethnicity, or sexual preference. There were isolated examples who did, of course. John Stuart Mill (a liberal but with views that became close to social democracy) was a famous early champion of the rights of women. As criminologists we can be proud of the example of Willem Bonger, the Dutch Marxist, Social Democratic Party activist, and academic criminologist, who championed the rights of gay people, and in the 1930s of Jews, ultimately committing suicide in despair when the Nazis invaded Holland (Bemmelen 1960; S. Cohen 1998). Certainly the principles of social democracy demanded justice for all forms of oppression, not just economic.

Social democratic criminologists primarily thought of issues of crime and justice in terms of class. The hope was that the gradual emancipation of the working class would alleviate progressively the problems of criminal justice. There was certainly recognition of the age dimension, and much work on juvenile delinquency. But differences of gender, race, and sexual preference were largely outside their attention until the 1970s. However, the general principle of equal concern and respect underpinning social democracy certainly lends itself to incorporating these dimensions of inequality and injustice into the analysis of crime, victimization, and criminal justice. It is also important not to neglect the continuing importance of class and economic inequality, not only in itself, but also as an underlying element in racial differences in crime and criminalization (Fitzgerald 2004).

The state as instrument of justice

Social democrats saw the democratic state as the primary means of achieving greater equality and justice. This is not to say that they were not acutely aware of the dangers of state power. The two most widely celebrated novels about the dangers of totalitarianism, *Animal Farm* and *1984*, were written by a social democrat (however idiosyncratic), George Orwell. There were always currents in social democracy that espoused non-state forms to achieve justice, such as the co-operative movement, the Friendly Societies, and versions of syndicalism and communitarianism. The 'local state' was also, in theory and in practice, an important agent of social democracy. Social democratic criminology saw the liberal democratic state's criminal justice agencies as fundamentally benign, although there was an agenda of reform to make them representative of, and responsive to, working-class concerns. But it was only from the mid-1960s that empirical socio-legal and criminological research began to focus on the way that policing and other parts of the criminal justice system discriminated in terms of class, age, gender, race, and sexuality (Bowling and Phillips 2002; Gelsthorpe 2002; Heidensohn 2002). The state-centred character of social democratic criminology has been called into question more recently by the proliferation of non-state modes of control (Jones and Newburn 1998), and of theoretical perspectives critical of state domination of criminal justice (Johnston and Shearing 2003).

Science

Social democrats viewed science as a positive force. Physical science offered the prospect of reducing the economic pressures underlying human drudgery and servitude. Piecemeal social engineering and the regulation of markets required social science to analyse problems systematically, and to predict the probable consequences of policies.

This did not entail the simplistic positivism that has become a crude term of abuse by many contemporary sociologists. Social democrats recognized that observations were theory-laden, that values affected the choice of study and the application of results, and indeed were hard to separate from the process of research. For the most part they saw human behaviour as a dialectical outcome of structure and action, people making their own histories but not under conditions of their own choosing. But they would also have accepted that there are regularities that can be discerned in social interaction, even if these are probabilistic and not the product of iron determinism. Knowing and understanding as much as possible about these was necessary to guide practical reform. Whilst a vital element of the liberal democracy that social democrats believed in was tolerance, this did not entail relativism with regard to either 'facts' or values.

There can be no question that social democratic criminology was broadly 'positivist' in its approach to social science, in that it felt it important to research as rigorously as possible the causes of crime and the effectiveness, humanity, and justice of crime control policies. Occasionally they even used numbers in their analyses! But for the most part they would not have been guilty of the accusations routinely hurled at a straw person version of positivism by subsequent critics. They did not think that social science results could be regarded as absolute truth, completely objective representations of reality, or that they could resolve all issues. Most would have accepted Weber's analysis of the problems, limitations, ultimate impossibility, and yet importance and desirability as an ideal of value-freedom in science (Weber 1918). Whilst they regarded it as useful to formulate and test empirical generalizations, few saw these as laws that determined individual behaviour. Merton's analysis of deviant reactions to anomie has been criticized as a deterministic account that gives no space to individual interpretation of meaning and autonomy (Taylor *et al.* 1973: 108). However, it intended only to suggest probabilities, not certainties (Merton 1995), and raises rather than forecloses exploration of why people in similar structural situations develop different reactions (Reiner 1984: 191–2).

Modernism

The values of justice and liberty, central to social democracy, have ancient origins. Many perceived a long chain of inspiration going back to antiquity—the Hebrew Prophets, Socrates, Jesus, Spartacus. The chain continued through the Middle Ages and early modernity—John Ball ('When Adam delved and Eve span who was then the gentleman?'), Wat Tyler, Jack Straw, and other leaders of the Peasants' Revolt, Thomas More's Utopia, the Levellers.

The distinctly modern element in social democracy was the belief that these values were not a millenarian dream, but capable of implementation as a practical political project. This was not necessarily part of a modernist 'grand narrative', though it was often tied to a view of history as (probably) progressive.

Social democratic criminology, and its penological counterpart the rehabilitative ideal, were quintessential elements of 'penal modernism' (Garland 2001). However, the label 'modern' implies that they are discredited, dead, in an era of 'post' or 'late' modernity. The rest of this chapter will be concerned to examine this, by analysing the eclipse of social democratic criminology, and assessing the possibility and desirability of resurrecting its core elements.

The Rise of Contrology

This section will analyse the displacement of the social democratic perspective. It will focus on six dimensions of the complex patterns of change.

Trends in crime and disorder

During the last quarter of the twentieth century crime and disorder increased to unprecedented levels. In the early 1950s the police recorded less than half a million offences per annum. By the mid-1960s this had increased to around 1 million, and by the mid-1970s 2 million. The 1980s showed even more staggering rises, with recorded crime peaking in 1992 at over 5.5 million— a tenfold increase in just under four decades (Barclay and Tavares 1999: 2). By 1997 recorded crime had fallen back to 4.5 million. Counting rule changes introduced in 1998 and 2002 make comparison of the subsequent figures especially fraught, but on the new rules (which undoubtedly exaggerate the increase) just under 6 million offences were recorded by the police for 2003/04 (Dodd et al. 2004).

There are of course enormous problems in interpreting recorded trends in crime (Maguire 2002; Hope 2005). It is impossible to determine with certainty how far the statistics track changes in offending, as distinct from shifts in reporting and recording practices by victims and police, and alterations in counting rules. The introduction of the British Crime Survey in 1981 does, however, cast light on a major aspect of the problems, variations in the propensity of victims to report crimes and of the police to record them. The General Household Survey in the 1970s had included questions on burglary victimization, so we also have some insight into reporting and recording changes in that crucial decade. During the 1970s a substantial proportion, but certainly not all, of the rise in recorded crime was due to increased reporting by victims. This was probably driven in large part by the spread of household contents insurance. Extrapolating back, the same may well be true of the 1960s.

However, during the 1980s police and survey recorded crime rose roughly in parallel. In the mid-1990s the two series diverged, with the police statistics registering falls. The British Crime Survey (BCS) by contrast found that victimization was still rising, but that the reporting and recording of crimes were falling. Since 1997 precisely the opposite has occurred. Above all because of counting rule changes, the police recorded statistics have recently started to rise again, whilst the BCS continues to record a decline in victimization[9] (Dodd *et al.* 2004). For the last quarter of a century, recorded crime has been at the highest levels since national statistics began to be collected in the 1850s. Victimization has become a normal phenomenon that most people have experienced.

Public disorder has also become a significant issue in a way it had not been at least since the 1930s. There was a clear resurgence of violent disorder and of militaristic policing in political and industrial conflict during the 1970s and 1980s, and in a variety of leisure contexts (Jefferson 1990; D. Waddington 1992; P.A.J. Waddington 2003 offer contrasting accounts).

Politicization of law and order

In the last quarter of the twentieth century the issue of law and order achieved an unprecedented prominence in Britain, following a similar politicization in the United States (Beckett 1997; Downes and Morgan 2002; Hale 2005b). A break becomes apparent around 1970, as shown most clearly by Downes and Morgan's analyses of election manifestos (Downes and Morgan 2002). Until then, crime and criminal justice had not been party political issues.

During the 1970s and 1980s partisan conflict on law and order became intensely heated. Margaret Thatcher's 1979 election victory owed much to the prominence she gave to the issue, and for most of the 1980s the Conservatives attacked Labour relentlessly on crime, gaining considerable electoral advantage (Downes 1983). The parties began to converge in the late 1980s. The Conservatives, embarrassed by the huge rise in recorded crime, moved to a more nuanced approach. This emphasized community crime prevention, and sought to reduce rising imprisonment in the 1991 Criminal Justice Act (Reiner and Cross 1991). Labour for its part began to distance itself from the

---

[9] This has made for an interesting politicization of the debate about crime statistics, especially in the context of the 2005 General Election. The police recorded statistics make Michael Howard's period as Home Secretary in the mid-1990s appear a success, and the post-1997 Labour government look bad. Conversely the BCS punctures the apparent Conservative success, and suggests that Labour has presided over a record fall in crime. So each party's electioneering focused on the deficiencies of the statistics that flattered the other.

image of being 'soft' on law and order (Downes and Morgan 2002: 290).

1993 marked a new watershed in law and order politics, with the advent of Michael Howard as Home Secretary and Tony Blair as his Shadow. A new 'second order' consensus on law and order emerged, based on a shared commitment to toughness (Downes and Morgan 2002: 295–7, 317–18; Ryan 2003). Subtle differences remain, and opportunism has brought about some odd temporary reversals. Labour retains more of an interest in being tough on the causes of crime, not just its perpetrators. But this is now limited primarily to encouraging local interventions in the immediate contexts of crime, supply side interventions to reduce unemployment, and highly focused attacks on family poverty (Matthews and Young 2003; Newburn 2003; Stenson and Edwards 2004). Added to this are attacks on permissiveness, blamed on the '60s', that seem to be plagiarized from the *Daily Mail*. Completely absent are the old concerns of social democratic criminology, the structural sources of crime, such as inequality and unemployment (Downes 2004). The Tories primarily seem to be concerned to up the ante on toughness so as to regain the ground they lost in the 1990s, paradoxically combined with occasional attacks on some aspects of Labour policy from a civil libertarian direction, such as on identity cards. Thus law and order remains highly politicized, but in terms of a bidding war on effectiveness and toughness, not any fundamental differences of value or strategy.

Public discourse
The politicization of law and order is clearly related to broader changes in public discourse about crime and control. Opinion surveys broadly confirm the increasing salience of law and order concerns and generalized 'fear of crime' since the 1970s (Hope and Sparks 2000; Roberts and Stalans 2000; Roberts and Hough 2002; Nicholas and Walker 2004). There is also evidence of an increasing taste for 'cruelty' or 'punitiveness' in punishment (Simon 2001; Pratt *et al.* 2005).[10] This is bolstered by stereotypes of offending taken from media reports which, following a

---

[10] Matthews (2005) questions how far this has affected penal practice as distinct from rhetoric.

'law of opposites' (Surette 1998; Reiner 2002; Jewkes 2004), focus on the most atypical and grotesque crimes of violence. Although during the 1980s polls suggested a trend of declining police legitimacy, this has been reversed since the early 1990s, and the police remain a key security blanket in public imagery (Reiner 2000a: 11, 47; Loader and Mulcahy 2003).

Media discourse has moved increasingly to a law and order frame since the 1970s. In both fictional and news stories crime is represented as an ever greater threat. In the 1960s and 1970s there was a counter-trend, with an increasing minority of stories questioning the effectiveness and the legality of criminal justice agents (Reiner, Livingstone and Allen 2000, 2001). In the 1990s, however, this returned to overwhelming support of the police (Leishman and Mason 2003; Reiner 2003). Media stories increasingly dramatize the sufferings of individual victims as a means of demonizing offenders, orchestrating a vigilante discourse whereby cruelty inflicted on offenders is the only way of expressing sympathy for victims. This zero sum perspective was absent from media stories of the 1940s and 1950s, when concern to understand and rehabilitate offenders was presented as compatible with—if not a precondition of—helping victims (Reiner, Livingstone and Allen 2003).

Policy shifts
Criminal justice policy has shifted clearly, but not unambiguously, in a control-oriented direction in the past three decades. The style of policy-making has also altered. In the pre-1970s consensus era, criminal justice policy was characterized by calm, expert-led decision-making, exemplified by the Royal Commission. The post-Thatcher style is a combination of internal government inquiries, with input from business people and the police rather than lawyers, the judiciary or academics, and relatively little if any public consultation. However, there is also greater responsiveness to public opinion, as expressed in the popular media and populist campaigning (Ryan 2003, 2004).

During the Thatcher years the fierce rhetoric of statements on law and order was not matched by an unequivocal move towards tougher policing or punishment. Police expenditure did rise substantially in the first half of the 1980s as they performed their role in weakening the trade union movement and its resistance to de-industrialization, as well as keeping the lid on the resulting pressures in the inner cities. But once this job was done, the police became subject increasingly to the new regimes for ensuring economy, efficiency, and effectiveness in public services (Weatheritt 1993; McLaughlin and Murji 2000; Long 2003). The controversial Police and Criminal Evidence Act 1984 expanded police powers considerably, but was mitigated by accompanying safeguards (Reiner 2000a: ch. 6). In the late 1980s there was an attempt to move penal policy away from custodial sentencing, culminating in the Criminal Justice Act 1991 (Newburn 2003: 167–72).

During Michael Howard's period as Home Secretary policy shifted unequivocally in a tough law and order direction, as 'New' Labour attacked the record crime rises under the Tories, promising to be 'tough on crime, tough on the causes of crime'. 'Prison works' became Michael Howard's slogan to counter Labour's new toughness (Newburn 2003: 172–7). The police role was defined explicitly in narrow, crime-fighting terms, with managerial accountability to ensure 'businesslike' performance (Jones 2003).

Under the New Labour government since 1997 there has been a schizophrenic approach—pragmatic policies embodying the 'criminologies of everyday life', and demonstrative spasms of harsh control in response to moral panics about spectacularly shocking crimes (Garland 1996, 2001). The flagship Crime and Disorder Act 1998 embodied both elements (Newburn 2003: 92–4, 117–23, 206–23). On the one hand, it introduced a variety of measures reflecting a commitment to 'evidence-led', 'joined-up' policy. The Act required local authorities to form partnerships with the police and other agencies to develop strategies for reducing crime and disorder. It established a central Youth Justice Board and local Youth Offending Teams to co-ordinate, implement and monitor work with juveniles. It instituted a £400 million Crime Reduction Strategy to research, spread, and evaluate best practice, which has been eviscerated by short-term electoral pressures (Hough 2004; Maguire 2004). The Crime and Disorder Act 1998 also included tougher measures, such as new minimum mandatory sentences for various offences, curfews for juveniles, the ending of the presumption that a child between ten and thirteen is incapable of committing a crime (*doli incapax*), and the introduction of antisocial behaviour orders (ASBOs).

Since 1998 legislation and policies have shifted the balance towards the demonstratively tough, and away from the pragmatic and evidence-led (Downes 2004). This has been embodied in a stream of new police powers (without balancing safeguards), and tougher sentencing laws (Tonry 2003). There has also been flirtation with the 'zero tolerance' policing that has been credited with the achievement of huge reductions in serious violent crime in New York City by its celebrants (Dennis 1998), although the crime falls are most likely to be the result of wider social factors and smarter rather than tougher policing (Eck and Maguire 2000; Karmen 2001).

Socio-economic and cultural change

Developments in crime and criminal justice are intertwined with the profound socio-economic and cultural changes that have occurred in the past four decades (Taylor 1999; Young 1999; Garland 2001). The economic consequences of globalization, and the shift from Keynesian to neo-liberal strategies of economic management, have generated pressures that drive crime upwards. The proliferation of consumer goods creates tempting targets for crime whilst consumer culture heightens expectations (Hayward 2004). Labour market changes generate higher unemployment and a shift to low-paid part-time jobs, increasing poverty and inequality—which are exacerbated by the erosion of welfare state expenditure and less progressive taxation. The decline of deference, a more liberal culture, and changes in family life imply weaker informal social controls—conservatives' favourite explanation of rising crime.

Whilst criminogenic pressures have clearly increased in the past four decades, reflected in the large rise in recorded crime since the 1950s (paralleled in most Western countries although with some differences in timing), crime rates have been declining more recently. There is much debate about the relative parts played in the recent decline in crime rates by new modes of crime control ('smart' or 'tough'), and wider socio-economic change (Blumstein and Wallman 2000; Tonry 2004).

From criminology to contrology

Criminological paradigms have shifted in the past forty years, in interaction with these changes. Up to the mid-1960s criminology had for nearly a century consisted primarily of research on causes of crime, with sociological approaches increasingly predominant over individualistic biological or psychological explanations (Rock 1988, 2002). Although the political commitments of criminological researchers varied, most tacitly accepted a broadly social democratic perspective on crime, seeing it as shaped by social deprivation and inequality. Dealing with crime required a combination of immediate penal interventions, primarily aimed at rehabilitation, and the broader social and economic amelioration that Keynesianism and the Welfare State were expected to deliver.

The first chink in this consensus came from the left. In the mid-1960s a variety of radical critiques developed (S. Cohen 1988). The 'labelling' perspective turned a critical spotlight on criminal justice, which came to be seen as constructing crime in discriminatory and oppressive ways. Although not a monolithic movement, most labelling theorists were associated with the libertarian and radical counterculture of the 1960s, taking the standpoint of deviants against social control agencies (Becker 1967).

The 'rehabilitative ideal' came under increasing attack from liberals and radicals (Allen 1981), primarily because the indeterminate sentencing implied by a therapeutic rather than 'just desserts' rationale for penal intervention often meant longer incarceration and diminished prisoners' rights. This was joined with a growing body of research questioning the success of rehabilitative approaches in their own terms (Garland 2001: ch. 3). The positivist paradigm of research on causes of crime was criticized for being over-deterministic and taking the legitimacy of conventional definitions of deviance for granted, thus denying the meanings and autonomy of those labelled deviant.

These radical critiques did not for the most part question the political economy of crime suggested by social democratic criminology. They also saw crime as fundamentally rooted in the negative consequences of free market capitalism. The Marxist strand of critical criminology criticized social democrats for their lack of revolutionary zeal—*The New Criminology* castigated Merton as 'the cautious rebel' (Taylor, Walton and Young 1973)—but this was more a matter of attitude than analysis. *The New Criminology*'s concluding account of the ingredients of a 'fully social theory of deviance' is a sketch of what social democrats would also see as the categories for analysing crime and control. Social democrats would, however, question the prospects for a crime-free socialist society sketched in the last few pages as utopian and idealist—exactly as the authors themselves were to in the 1980s as they developed 'Left Realism' (Taylor 1981; Lea and Young 1984).

The fundamental assumptions of social democratic criminology were explicitly attacked with the advent of realism, in its initial right-wing guise, in the mid-1970s. The pivotal moment was James Q. Wilson's head-on assault on the idea of 'root causes' of crime (Wilson 1975). Of course what he meant was *social* causes of crime; after all ten years later he co-authored a 700-page tome on the causes of crime—individual biological and psychological causes (Wilson and Herrnstein 1985).[11] At the same time the resurgent rational choice theories, both in the guise of neo-classical economic theories (Becker 1968), and in the form of situational prevention (Cornish and Clarke 1986) and routine activities (Felson 2002) theories, explicitly rejected the notion of crime having any special causes at all. Crime was normal profit-maximizing behaviour. It resulted from the open windows of opportunity left by irresponsible citizens, and from life-patterns that reduced informal guardianship, which enterprising individuals could profit from by offending. As Felson and Clarke put it explicitly, 'opportunity makes the thief' (Felson and Clarke 1998).

Left realism in the 1980s incorporated a political economy of crime that was very close to the mainstream of social democratic criminology. In their seminal book *What Is To Be Done About Law and Order?* Lea and Young offer an account of trends in crime and disorder in terms of relative deprivation[12] (Lea and Young 1984) that is very similar to Merton's anomie analysis.

Nonetheless, Jock Young explicitly sought to distance left realism from older social democratic criminology. This was

---

[11] This represents a broader resurgence of individualist theories of crime, biological and psychological (Fishbein 1990; Rose 2000; Hollin 2002).

[12] The concept of relative deprivation figured prominently in Merton's work (Merton and Rossi 1957) but strangely was not related by him to his parallel analysis of anomie.

primarily by his account of a supposed 'aetiological crisis' in social democratic criminology. 'The central problem for social democratic or Fabian positivism was that a wholesale improvement in social conditions resulted, not in a drop in crime, but the reverse' (Young 1988: 159). This misrepresents social democratic criminology as positing that poor social conditions directly cause crime, a view that may be dubbed 'vulgar' social democracy. As argued earlier, social democrats like Mannheim or Merton did not suggest any simple link between poverty and crime. In so far as they had a theory of causal connections between deprivation and offending this was in terms of relative not absolute deprivation (precisely the left realist account of aetiology). They also saw the acquisitive and anomic culture produced by consumerism and materialism as demoralizing and criminogenic. Thus several social democratic commentators anticipated that the new mass affluence after the late 1950s would exacerbate delinquency (Labour Party 1964: 5; Downes 1966; 1988: 103–9).

Whatever Happened to Social Democratic Criminology?

From Right and Wrong to Risk

Clear shifts in crime control have thus developed in recent years, most apparently 'the new punitiveness' (Pratt *et al.* 2005), best interpreted as a form of 'acting out' (Garland 2001: 131–5). The key theme of practical crime control has become 'smartness': evidence and intelligence-led analysis of how to identify and neutralize risky places and people. Criminal justice is said to have become actuarial, concerned with calculating and minimizing risks through analysis of potential offenders and crime-prone situational contexts, rather than justice or reform (Feeley and Simon 1994; Ericson and Haggerty 1997; Rose 1999; Hope and Sparks 2000; Stenson and Sullivan 2000; Hudson 2003; O'Malley 2004).

This, of course, reflects a wider social and cultural turn identified by theorists of 'risk society' (Beck 1992). Whilst the terminology of 'risk' has become ubiquitous, it has been used in a variety of divergent ways. As Garland opens his comprehensive analysis of these: 'Risk is a calculation. Risk is a commodity. Risk is a capital. Risk is a technique of government. Risk is objective and scientifically knowable. Risk is subjective and socially constructed. Risk is a problem, a threat, a source of insecurity. Risk is a pleasure, a thrill, a source of profit and freedom. Risk is the means whereby we colonise and control the future. "Risk society" is our late modern world spinning out of control.' (Garland 2003: 49).

In relation to crime and control the rise of 'risk' seems to have two main dimensions: (a) increasing public and policy concern with risks of crime, problematically related to 'objective' patterns of risk of victimization; (b) new 'actuarial' ways of thinking about and responding to crime in terms of analysis of risky people, places, pursuits, etc. The essence of risk-based approaches is usually seen as their instrumentalism, replacing attribution of blame, rehabilitating offenders or meting out retributive justice with pragmatic, business-like calculations of what works in terms of cost-effective harm reduction.

Giddens has claimed that the ascendancy of abstract systems of risk calculation in general spells the 'evaporation of morality... moral principles run counter to the concept of risk and to the mobilising dynamics of control' (Giddens 1991: 145). Ericson and Doyle challenge these arguments, pointing out that identifying phenomena as dangerous or risky 'is based on judgements about "goodness" and "badness" and distinctions between right and wrong' (Ericson and Doyle 2003: 2). Indeed risk perspectives, they argue, extend moral responsibility in that people who might once have been seen as innocent victims (whether of crime or accidents, disease or other suffering) are now often seen as at least partly culpable (ibid: 4–9). This interpretation seems to make any evaluation, and any attribution of causal responsibility, a 'moral' judgement. However the term 'morality' is usually taken to be something much more specific, at the very least evaluation of behaviour with some degree of intentionality. I experience as 'bad' my window breaking in a storm. I also see it as 'bad' if someone smashes a brick through it. But it is only the latter that would normally be discussed in terms of *moral* badness.

Risk-based approaches differ fundamentally from older criminological perspectives in a number of other ways. Like the 'correctionalism' that was a prime target of 1960s and 1970s radical criminology, actuarialism takes for granted the legitimacy and purposes of crime control. However, unlike correctionalist approaches, it is not interested in the causes of offending other than as diagnostic indicators of risk (Metcalf and Stenson 2004).

Why has the social democratic criminology outlined earlier been displaced by the amoral and limited pragmatism of risk-based approaches? Most accounts of contemporary criminal justice assume that social democracy is dead, and security can only be found in smarter risk assessment and neutralization. But the explanations of why this perspective, all-pervasive until some three decades ago, has withered or died seem somewhat perfunctory, taken for granted as what everyone already knows. The 'social' has been buried without much of an inquest on why or how it died, or indeed whether it is really dead or just dormant. The death certificate for social democracy is hastily read, and then the analysis moves on to detailed accounts of the implications for crime and criminal justice, and the emerging contours of new modes of control and governance.

There can be little doubt that a fundamental shift in political economy, social relations, and culture has occurred during the last quarter of the twentieth century, with profound implications for crime and control. As outlined above, there has been a massive rise in crime rates (albeit with some attenuation recently). Concern about crime has become central in contemporary culture and politics. Responses have bifurcated between smart, fine-tuned, analytically based attempts to reduce risk, and cathartic emotional spasms of vindictiveness and cruelty against some identified offenders, in the name of justice to victims. In so far as causes of crime are considered at all they are seen in terms of individual or localized pathologies, or simply as radical evil. What has been eclipsed is the social democratic focus on analysing broader causes of crime and their amelioration through social reform.

Why has this happened, and what are its implications? There are at least three possible accounts.

Was the social democratic analysis of crime proven wrong?
The claim that the social democratic analysis of crime has been refuted is presented primarily in terms of what Jock Young referred to as the 'aetiological crisis'. As argued earlier, this attacked a straw person version of social democratic criminology—that crime is caused by absolute poverty. In its strongest forms

social democratic criminology did not postulate any mechanical relationship between economic conditions and crime. Whether economic circumstances were criminogenic depended on how they were experienced, and their consequences for morality and aspirations. Social democrats would expect crime to rise in a culture that is increasingly governed by economic success as the touchstone of all values, especially when this is coupled with an increasingly unequal social structure. Indeed Jock Young's analysis of the 'bulimia' of our contemporary culture itself shows this persuasively (Young 1999, 2003).

Such arguments can only be loosely tested by econometric studies of the relationship between economic variables and crime. Measures of poverty do not tap the meaning of it to those who are defined as poor. Indices of inequality cannot capture the concepts of anomie or relative deprivation, or a sense of injustice that could act as a 'technique of neutralisation' legitimating offending (Sykes and Matza 1957). Proportions of the population registering as unemployed cannot be translated straightforwardly into measures of deprivation, criminal opportunity, or the absence of the disciplining effects of work.

Nonetheless, on balance econometric studies *do* support the predictions of social democratic criminology about the crucial importance of the political economy for crime trends and patterns. Box's seminal 1987 review of the literature showed that even then a majority of studies found higher inequality and unemployment was related to more crime (Box 1987). Many of the studies he analysed were conducted during the post-war full employment decades when unemployment was primarily transitional and voluntary, without the criminogenic consequences of the growth of long-term exclusion of young people from the labour market since the 1970s.

The evidence of the significant links between political economy and crime is much clearer from later studies (Fielding, Clarke and Witt 2000; Marris 2003; Hale 2005a). Economic prosperity, as measured by levels of consumption or GDP for example, has a complex relationship to crime trends (Field 1990, 1999; Pyle and Deadman 1994; Hale 1998; Dhiri *et al.* 1999). In the long run it is positively related to overall recorded crime (which is predominantly property crime), probably above all because of the expansion of criminal opportunities. In the short run, however, the relationship is negative; that is, recorded crime increases with economic downturns—possibly because of an increase in relative deprivation as incomes suddenly fall. Violent crime is positively related to short-term cyclical fluctuations, increasing with economic up-turns, possibly because of increasing alcohol consumption and socializing (Field 1990, 1999). The labour market is related to crime levels in part because of evidence that crime increases when unemployment is higher (Farrington *et al.* 1986; Witt, Clarke, and Fielding 1999). The long-term shift to the predominance of part-time, insecure 'Mcjobs' in the service sector is also related to higher crime rates (Freeman 1995; Hale 1999; Grogger 2000). There also continues to be a plethora of evidence about the links between economic inequality and crime (Hale 2005a: 334–43). In short, there is plentiful evidence to confirm that the economic consequences of the neo-liberal economic policies pursued since the mid-1970s have had disastrous consequences for crime, exactly as social democratic criminology would predict (Davies 1998; Dorling 2004; Downes 2004; Garside 2004b; Hale 2005a).

Was social democratic criminology defeated by political campaigns?

During the heyday of the dominance of social democracy there was a relentless campaign against it mounted by business and free-market pressure groups (Fones-Wolf 1994; Frank 2001). They promoted a stream of publications and advertisements promoting the virtues of free markets (both in terms of efficiency and ethics) against the then dominant Keynesian, mixed economy, welfare state consensus.

In the crime control field too there were always powerful voices against the dominance of penal welfarism and social democratic criminology. These were found for example in the judiciary and the Conservative Party, most of whose members and backbenchers championed tougher punishments and greater social discipline (Ryan 1983; Morris 1989). During the late 1970s law and order became central to the Conservative Party's campaigning in the build-up to Margaret Thatcher's 1979 victory. They were aided in this by the emergence from the early 1970s of a vocal law and order lobby spearheaded by the Police Federation and some police chiefs (Reiner 1980; McLaughlin and Murji 1998; Loader and Mulcahy

2003). The mass media was also changing in its portrayal of crime, constructing law and order as a major issue with a growing focus on the (graphically represented) suffering of victims at the hands of demonized and feral offenders (Reiner, Livingstone, and Allen 2000, 2001, 2003). The shift in discourse and practice about crime and control cannot be attributed solely to political and media campaigning (Ryan 2004). Nonetheless the campaigning was successful, because it resonated with profound changes in culture and political economy with which law and order perspectives had an elective affinity.

Was social democratic criminology politically defeated by 'New Times'?
An interlocking and mutually reinforcing set of changes from the late 1960s made law and order approaches to crime and control more congruent with emerging social and cultural patterns. Some of these were deep structural transformations, others were contingent policy choices—but once these had been made they set in train processes that embedded them and made reversal hard, if not impossible.

The huge long-term rise in recorded crime described earlier was pivotal. In Jock Young's analysis it was 'the central motor of change' in post-war criminal justice and crime control (Young 1999: 35), and it is important in all accounts (Garland 2001: ch. 6; Loader and Sparks 2002: 85). However, this raises two more fundamental questions. What underlay the rise in recorded crime itself? Why did responses to rising crime rates take the law and order form? The answers to both questions lie in the package of wider social and cultural transformations.

The initial rise in recorded crime from the late 1950s is most plausibly explained by mass consumerism. This multiplied tempting targets for crime, and enhanced anomie throughout the social structure, fuelling motivations to acquire desired objects by whatever means were available. Consumerism also made it more likely that thefts would be reported, not least because of the spread of household insurance, increasing recorded crime rates much faster than crime itself. However the huge increases in recorded crime, and in political and industrial disorder, in the 1980s almost certainly reflect real increases in offending, as victimization studies confirm.

Rising crime and disorder was in large part explicable by the economic and social consequences of the adoption of neo-liberal economic policies after the mid-1970s. These hugely increased unemployment—largely in the shape of permanent never-employment for swathes of the young, especially amongst ethnic minorities in inner city areas. Many areas suffered economic and cultural devastation as they lost the industries that were the basis of their whole way of life (Davies 1998). Inequality rapidly increased, reversing nearly two centuries of slow progress towards greater social solidarity and inclusive citizenship. The result was literally murder. 'Behind the man with the knife is the man who sold him the knife, the man who did not give him a job, the man who decided that his school did not need funding, the man who closed down the branch plant where he could have worked, the man who decided to reduce benefit levels so that a black economy grew, all the way back to the woman who only noticed "those inner cities" some six years after the summer of 1981, and the people who voted to keep her in office... Those who perpetrated the social violence that was done to the lives of young men starting some 20 years ago are the prime suspects for most of the murders in Britain.' (Dorling 2004: 191).

There is of course another story. In July 2004 Tony Blair announced a new Home Office Strategic Plan which 'marks the end of the 1960s liberal, social consensus on law and order'. He explicitly blamed the '1960s revolution' for encouraging 'freedom without responsibility', when 'a society of different lifestyles spawned a group of young people who were brought up without parental discipline, without proper role models and without any sense of responsibility to or for others' (Blair 2004: 1). This embodies the quintessential conservative analysis of rising crime. In this view, the 'permissiveness' of the 1960s represented a dangerous democratization of the Enlightenment values of personal liberty, autonomy, and self-realization. As it spread to the masses it brought the destruction of family, responsibility, and self control—the bulwarks of civilization (Wilson and Herrnstein 1985; Dennis and Erdos 2005). This line of argument cannot explain why tolerant and liberal cultures like those of Holland and the Scandinavian countries are not racked by crime, violence, and law and order politics (Downes 1988; Tham 2001; Bondeson 2005)—though these are emerging with the impact of neo-liberalism and erosion of social democracy since the 1980s. This is not to suggest that crime is a direct reflection of economic factors. Cultural and moral issues are crucial to explaining or understanding crime trends. What the conservative analysis completely ignores is that neo-liberal economic policies undermine informal control institutions and morality, producing cultures in which there is no restraint on egoism. The formation and stability of families, for example, has been undermined not by liberal ethics but by the erosion of secure and adequately paid employment, especially for men lower in the social scale (Campbell 1993; Currie 1998; Hale 1999; Taylor 1999). Exactly as forecast by Tawney eight decades ago,[13] the acquisitive society encouraged by free market liberalism has washed away the ethical values of responsibility for others and for 'society' (Tawney 1921). The character of the corporation director enjoined by company law (which 'dedicates the corporation to the pursuit of its own self-interest' Bakan 2004: 34–9) precisely fits the psychiatric model of the psychopath (ibid: 56–7). The same is true of the 'responsibilized' citizen encouraged by neo-liberal strategies of governance—responsible, but only for oneself. In this culture of encouraged egoism the values of mutual concern and respect that animated social democracy seem to have no purchase, almost to have no meaning (as has been said of ethics more generally in the haunting opening of Macintyre 1981).

Conclusion: Barbarism or Social Democracy?

I have tried to show that social democratic criminology can provide an analysis of the changes in crime and control in the decades since it ceased to be the dominant paradigm, despite all the talk of its aetiological crisis. As represented by such figures as Merton, Mannheim or more recently David Downes (and outside criminology, Tawney), its primary emphasis was not a

---

[13] And indeed as Marx and Engels anticipated 150 years ago, when they famously declared: 'the bourgeois epoch...has torn away from the family its sentimental veil...All fixed, fast-frozen relations, with their train of ancient and venerable prejudices and opinions, are swept away...All that is solid melts into air, all that is holy is profaned' (Marx and Engels 1848: 38).

mechanical relation between absolute poverty and crime—although economic factors are in fact an important part of explaining crime. Social democracy's focus was on the moral forces emphasizing the importance of legitimate means above goal attainment at any price, and shaping the aspirations that underlie the experience of deprivation and unfairness. The acquisitiveness of the consumerist society that developed from the late 1950s would have been—and was—predicted to fan the flames of crime, especially when it was coupled with the increasing social injustice brought by neo-liberalism.

The problem is that neo-liberalism has not only exacerbated the pressures leading to crime, and undermined the legal and ethical constraints aimed at holding individuals and corporations to socially responsible practices. It has relinquished the tools available to social democratic states to try and remedy this. For example greater mobility of capital flows, partly because of technological and cultural changes associated with globalization, but crucially because of liberalization of controls over financial movements, has weakened the regulatory and taxation capacity of individual governments in relation to corporations. However the extent to which this has systematically and irretrievably weakened governments' abilities to tax for redistributive and welfare purposes is debatable, and the position still varies considerably between different countries (Held 2004: 22–33). In any event, to the extent that the regulative capacity of states to achieve social democratic ends has been undermined this could be seen as a challenge not a fatal conclusion. The social democratic deficit of states could lead to a search to develop 'collaborative mechanisms of governance at supranational and global levels' (ibid: 15).

If no attack on the fundamental causes of crime is mounted then recorded crime will be likely to resume its upward march, especially if economic conditions become more adverse. Beyond this, the morally if not legally 'criminal' activities of corporations and states, inflicting far greater harms and cruelties—as 'zemiologists' rightly argue (Hillyard *et al.* 2004)—will multiply. Amongst these are the crime control practices documented by many penal analysts: increasingly cruel punishment for apprehended offenders (Garland 2001; Simon 2001; Pratt *et al.* 2005). Coupled with this is the 'responsibilized' self-protection enjoined

Beyond Risk: A Lament for Social Democratic Criminology 39

on the majority of citizens, producing ever greater social division and exclusion (Davis 1990; Taylor 1999; Young 1999; Reiner 2000b: 86–9). Paraphrasing Rosa Luxemberg, on present trends the choice is social democracy or barbarism.

Optimists and Blairites may say this flies in the face of the recent trend for crime rates to fall. Most analysts accept that crime has indeed decreased—although it is possible to debate this (cf. Garside 2004a and Dennis and Erdos 2005 from very different perspectives). But crime reduction has certainly not yet taken us away from what are still 'high crime' societies. There is also considerable debate about the sources of the trend to falling crime rates (Blumstein and Wallman 2000; Tonry 2004). The evidence suggests that it is in *very* small part a product of greater toughness on crime (the huge increases in imprisonment above all, rather than the much vaunted 'zero tolerance' policing), and in greater measure increased smartness: more analytically based crime prevention and policing.

The more significant factors, however, have been nothing to do with criminal justice policy. Demographic trends have been important—declining proportions in the age-groups most prone to ordinary crime. The declines have also been to do with favourable economic trends: lower unemployment, and a partially successful attack on family poverty (Downes 2004)—a taste of social democracy by stealth. But because of its anxiety not to alienate *Daily Mail*-reading circles by seeming to return to old Labourism, the government has had to disclaim those aspects of its policies that probably have the greatest impact on crime.

There is, however, some potential for a more overt espousal of social democratic criminology. Despite decades of propagandizing against it, there is evidence of latent public support for elements of the social democratic analysis of crime, hidden behind the more overt punitiveness revealed in surveys (Hart Research 2002; Allen 2004). In one recent study 65 per cent of Americans saw tackling causes as the key to controlling crime, compared to only 32 per cent favouring greater toughness—a substantial increase since a 1994 study when the respective proportions were 48 per cent and 42 per cent (Hart Research ibid: 1–2). There is also growing, though of course still very tentative, discussion of social democracy in political and economic analysis

(Bakan 2004, Held 2004). This has been largely absent in criminology, but without it the future is bleak. Criminologists of the world unite—you have nothing to lose but your research grants.

Bibliography

Allen, F.A. (1981) *The Decline of the Rehabilitative Ideal* (Yale University Press: New Haven).

Allen, R. (2004) 'What Works in Changing Public Attitudes: Lessons From Rethinking Crime and Punishment' 1 *Journal for Crime, Conflict and the Media* 55–67.

Bakan, J. (2004) *The Corporation* (Constable: London).

Barclay, G. and Tavares, C. (1999) *Digest 4—Information on the Criminal Justice System in England and Wales* (Home Office: London).

Bauman, Z. (1995) *Life in Fragments* (Blackwell: Oxford).

Beck, U. (1992) *Risk Society* (Sage: London).

Becker, G. (1968) 'Crime and Punishment: An Economic Approach', 76 *Journal of Political Economy* 175–209.

Becker, H. (1967) 'Whose Side Are We On?', 14 *Social Problems* 239–47.

Beckett, K. (1997) *Making Crime Pay* (Oxford University Press: New York).

Bemmelen, J.M. (1960) 'Willem Adrian Bonger' in H. Mannheim (ed.), *Pioneers in Criminology* (Stevens: London).

Blair, T. (2004) 'A New Consensus on Law and Order', Speech launching Home Office Strategic Plan for Criminal Justice, 19 July 2004 <www.labour.org.uk/news/tbcrimespeech>.

Blumstein, A. and Wallman, J. (eds.) (2000) *The Crime Drop in America* (Cambridge University Press: Cambridge).

Bondeson, U. (2005) 'Levels of Punitiveness in Scandinavia: Description and Explanations', in J. Pratt, D. Brown, M. Brown, S. Hallsworth, and W. Morrison (eds.), *The New Punitiveness* (Willan: Cullompton).

Bonger, W. (1936) *An Introduction to Criminology* (Methuen: London)

Bottoms, A.E. and Stevenson, S. (1992) 'What Went Wrong? Criminal Justice Policy in England and Wales 1945–70' in D. Downes (ed.), *Unravelling Criminal Justice* (Macmillan: London).

Boutellier, H. (2000) *Crime and Morality* (Kluwer: Dordrecht).

Bowling, B. and Phillips, C. (2002) *Racism, Crime and Justice* (Longman: London).

Box, S. (1987) *Recession, Crime and Punishment* (Macmillan: London).

Campbell, B. (1993) *Goliath: Britain's Dangerous Places* (Methuen: London).

Clarke, P. (1978) *Liberals and Social Democrats* (Cambridge University Press: Cambridge).
Cohen, G. (2000) *If You're An Egalitarian, How Come You're So Rich?* (Harvard University Press: Cambridge, Mass.).
Cohen, S. (1988) *Against Criminology* (Transaction: New Brunswick).
—— (1998) 'Intellectual Scepticism and Political Commitment' in P. Walton and J. Young (eds.), *The New Criminology Revisited* (Macmillan: London).
Cornish, D. and Clarke, R. (eds.) (1986) *The Reasoning Criminal* (Springer-Verlag: New York).
Currie, E. (1998) *Crime and Punishment in America* (Holt: New York).
—— (2000) 'Reflections on Crime and Criminology at the Millennium', 2 *Western Criminology Review* 1–15.
Davies, N. (1998) *Dark Heart* (Verso: London).
Davis, M. (1990) *City of Quartz* (Vintage: London).
Dennis, N. (ed.) (1998) *Zero Tolerance* (IEA: London).
—— and Erdos, G. (2005) *Cultures and Crimes* (Civitas: London).
—— and Halsey, A.H. (1988) *English Ethical Socialism* (Oxford University Press: Oxford).
Dhiri, S., Brand, S. Harries, R. and Price, R. (1999) *Modelling and Predicting Property Crime Trends* (Home Office: London).
Ditton, J. (1979) *Controlology* (Macmillan: London).
Dodd, T., Nicholas, S., Povey, D. and Walker, A. (2004) *Crime in England and Wales 2003/4* (Home Office: London).
Dorling, D. (2004) 'Prime Suspect: Murder in Britain' in P. Hillyard, C. Pantazis, S. Tombs and D. Gordon (eds.), *Beyond Criminology* (Pluto: London).
Downes, D. (1966) *The Delinquent Solution* (Routledge: London).
—— (1983) *Law and Order—Theft of an Issue* (Fabian Society/Labour Campaign for Criminal Justice: London).
—— (1988) *Contrasts in Tolerance* (Oxford University Press: Oxford).
—— (2004) 'New Labour and the Lost Causes of Crime' 55 *Criminal Justice Matters* 4–5.
—— and Morgan, R. (2002) 'The Skeletons in the Cupboard: the Politics of Law and Order at the Turn of the Millennium' in M. Maguire, R. Morgan and R. Reiner (eds.), *The Oxford Handbook of Criminology* (3rd edn., Oxford University Press: Oxford).
Dworkin, R. (2000) *Sovereign Virtue* (Harvard University Press: Cambridge, Mass).
Eck, J. and Maguire, E. (2000) 'Have Changes in Policing Reduced Violent Crime? A Review of the Evidence' in A. Blumstein and

J. Wallman (eds.), *The Crime Drop in America* (Cambridge University Press: Cambridge).
Engels, F. (1880) *Socialism: Utopian and Scientific* in *Marx and Engels—Selected Works* (Lawrence and Wishart: London, 1968: 375–428).
Ericson, R. and Doyle, A. (eds.) (2003) *Risk and Morality* (University of Toronto Press: Toronto).
—— and Haggerty, K. (1997) *Policing Risk Society* (Oxford University Press: Oxford).
Farrington, D., Galagher, B. Morley, L. St. Ledger, R.J. and West, D.J. (1986) 'Unemployment, School Leaving and Crime' 26 *British Journal of Criminology* 335–56.
Feeley, M. and Simon, J. (1994) 'Actuarial Justice: The Emerging New Criminal Law' in D. Nelken (ed.), *The Futures of Criminology* (Sage: London).
Felson, M. (2002) *Crime and Everyday Life* (3rd edn., Pine Forge: London).
—— and Clarke, R. (1998) *Opportunity Makes the Thief: Practical Theory for Crime Prevention* (Home Office: London).
Field, S. (1990) *Trends in Crime and their Interpretation* (HMSO: London).
—— (1999) *Trends in Crime Revisited* (Home Office: London).
Fielding, N., Clarke, A. and Witt, R. (eds.) (2000) *The Economic Dimensions of Crime* (Macmillan: London).
Figes, O. (2005) 'The Fiddler's Children' 52 *New York Review of Books* no. 10, 8–12.
Fishbein, D.H. (1990) 'Biological Perspectives in Criminology' 28 *Criminology* 27–72.
Fitzgerald, M. (2004) 'Understanding Ethnic Differences in Crime Statistics' 55 *Criminal Justice Matters* 22–3.
Fones-Wolf, E. (1994) *Selling Free Enterprise: The Business Assault on Labour and Liberalism, 1945–1960* (University of Illinois Press: Urbana).
France, A. (1992) *Le Lys Rouge* (Flammarion: Paris).
Frank, T. (2001) *One Market Under God* (Secker and Warburg: London).
—— (2004) *What's the Matter With America?* (Secker and Warburg: London).
Freeman, R.B. (1995) 'Crime and the Labour Market' in J.Q. Wilson and J. Petersilia (eds.), *Crime* (ICS Press: San Francisco).
Garland, D. (1985) *Punishment and Welfare* (Gower: Aldershot).
—— (1996) 'The Limits of the Sovereign State: Strategies of Crime Control in Contemporary Societies' 36 *British Journal of Criminology* no. 4: 1–27.

—— (2001) *The Culture of Control* (Oxford University Press: Oxford).
—— (2003) 'The Rise of Risk' in R. Ericson and A. Doyle (eds.), *Risk and Morality* (University of Toronto Press: Toronto).
—— and Sparks, R. (2000) 'Criminology, Social Theory and the Challenge of Our Times' 40 *British Journal of Criminology* 189–204.
Garside, R. (2004a) *Crime, Persistent Offenders and the Justice Gap* (Crime and Society Foundation: London).
—— (2004b) 'Is It The Economy?' 55 *Criminal Justice Matters* 32–3.
Gatrell, V. (1980) 'The Decline of Theft and Violence in Victorian and Edwardian England' in V. Gatrell, B. Lenman and G. Parker (eds.), *Crime and the Law* (Europa: London).
Gelsthorpe, L. (2002) 'Feminism and Criminology' in M. Maguire, R. Morgan and R. Reiner (eds.), *The Oxford Handbook of Criminology* (3rd edn., Oxford University Press: Oxford).
Giddens, A. (1991) *Modernity and Self Identity* (Polity: Cambridge).
Grogger, J. (2000) 'An Economic Model of Recent Trends in Violence' in A. Blumstein and J. Wallman (eds.), *The Crime Drop in America* (Cambridge University Press: Cambridge).
Hale, C. (1998) 'Crime and the Business Cycle in Post-war Britain Revisited' 38 *British Journal of Criminology* 681–98.
—— (1999) 'The Labour Market and Post-war Crime Trends in England and Wales' in P. Carlen and R. Morgan (eds.), *Crime Unlimited* (Macmillan: Basingstoke).
—— (2005a) 'Economic Marginalisation and Social Exclusion' in C. Hale, K. Hayward, A. Wahidin and E. Wincup (eds.), *Criminology* (Oxford University Press: Oxford).
—— (2005b) 'The Politics of Law and Order' in C. Hale, K. Hayward, A. Wahidin and E. Wincup (eds.), *Criminology* (Oxford University Press: Oxford).
Hart Research (2002) *Changing Public Attitudes Toward the Criminal Justice System* (Peter D. Hart Research Associates: Washington).
Hayward, K. (2004) *City Limits* (Glasshouse: London).
Heidensohn, F. (2002) 'Gender and Crime' in M. Maguire, R. Morgan and R. Reiner (eds.), *The Oxford Handbook of Criminology* (3rd edn., Oxford University Press: Oxford).
Held, D. (2004) *Global Covenant* (Polity: Cambridge).
Henry, S. and Lanier, M. (eds.) (2001) *What is Crime?* (Rowman and Littlefield: Lanham, MD).
Hillyard, P., Pantazis, C., Tombs, S. and Gordon, D. (eds.) (2004) *Beyond Criminology* (Pluto: London).

Hollin, C. (2002) 'Criminological Psychology' in M. Maguire, R. Morgan and R. Reiner (eds.), *The Oxford Handbook of Criminology* (3rd edn., Oxford University Press: Oxford).
Hope, T. (2005) 'What Do Crime Statistics Tell Us?' in C. Hale, K. Hayward, A. Wahidin and E. Winup (eds.), *Criminology* (Oxford University Press: Oxford).
—— and Sparks, R. (eds.) (2000) *Crime, Risk and Insecurity* (Routledge: London).
Hough, M. (ed.) (2004) 'Evaluating the Crime Reduction Programme in England and Wales' 4 *Criminal Justice* no. 3 (Special Issue).
Hudson, B. (2003) *Justice in the Risk Society* (Sage: London).
Jackson, T. (2004) *Chasing Progress: Beyond Economic Growth* (New Economics Foundation: London).
Jefferson, T. (1990) *The Case Against Paramilitary Policing* (Open University Press: Milton Keynes).
Jenkins, P. (1989) *Mrs Thatcher's Revolution* (Pan: London).
Jewkes, Y. (2004) *Media and Crime* (Sage: London).
Johnston, L. and Shearing, C. (2003) *Governing Security* (Routledge: London).
Jones, T. (2003) 'The Governance and Accountability of Policing' in T. Newburn (ed.), *Handbook of Policing* (Willan: Cullompton).
—— and Newburn, T. (1998) *Private Security and Public Policing* (Oxford University Press: Oxford).
Kant, I. (1785) *Groundwork of the Metaphysics of Morals* (Cambridge University Press: Cambridge [1998]).
Karmen, A. (2001) *New York Murder Mystery: The Story Behind the Crime Crash of the 1990s* (New York University Press: New York).
Labour Party (1964) *Crime: A Challenge to Us All* (Labour Party: London).
Lacey, N., Wells, C. and Quick, O. (2003) *Understanding Criminal Law* (Butterworths: London).
Lea, J. (2002) *Crime and Modernity* (Sage: London).
—— and Young, J. (1984) *What is to be Done About Law and Order?* (Penguin: Harmondsworth).
Leishman, F. and Mason, P. (2003) *Policing and the Media* (Willan: Cullompton).
Levinas, E. (1969) *Totality and Infinity* (Duquesne University Press: Pittsburgh).
Loader, I. and Mulcahy, A. (2003) *Policing and the Condition of England* (Oxford University Press: Oxford).
—— and Sparks, R. (2002) 'Contemporary Landscapes of Crime, Disorder and Control: Governance, Risk, and Globalisation'

in M. Maguire, R. Morgan and R. Reiner (eds.), *The Oxford Handbook of Criminology* (3rd edn., Oxford University Press: Oxford).
Long, M. (2003) 'Leadership and Performance Management' in T. Newburn (ed.), *Handbook of Policing* (Willan: Cullompton).
Lukes, S. (1985) *Marxism and Morality* (Oxford University Press: Oxford).
Macintyre, A. (1981) *After Virtue* (Duckworth: London).
Maguire, M. (2002) 'Crime Statistics: The Data Explosion and its Implications' in M. Maguire, R. Morgan and R. Reiner (eds.), *The Oxford Handbook of Criminology* (3rd edn., Oxford University Press: Oxford).
—— (2004) 'The Crime Reduction Programme in England and Wales', 4 *Criminal Justice* 213–38.
Mannheim, H. (1946) *Criminal Justice and Social Reconstruction* (Routledge: London).
Marris, R. (2003) *Survey of the Research Literature on the Economic and Criminological Factors Influencing Crime Trends* (Home Office: London).
Marshall, T.H. (1950) *Citizenship and Social Class* (Cambridge University Press: Cambridge).
Marx, K. (1867) *Capital Vol.1* (Lawrence and Wishart: London [1970]).
—— and Engels, F. (1848) *The Communist Manifesto* (Verso: London [1998]).
Matthews, R. (2005) 'The Myth of Punitiveness' 9 *Theoretical Criminology* 175–202.
—— and Young, J. (eds.) (2003) *The New Politics of Crime and Punishment* (Willan: Cullompton).
McLaughlin, E. and Murji, K. (1998) 'Resistance Through Representation: "Storylines", Advertising and Police Federation Campaigns' 8 *Policing and Society* 367–400.
—— —— (2000) 'Lost Connections and New Directions: Neo-liberalism, New Public Managerialism and the "Modernisation" of the British Police' in K. Stenson and R. Sullivan (eds.), *Crime, Risk and Justice* (Willan: Cullompton).
Merton, R. (1938) 'Social Structure and Anomie' 3 *American Sociological Review* 672–82 (rev. R. Merton, *Social Theory and Social Structure* (Free Press: London [1957]).
—— (1995) 'Opportunity Structure: The Emergence, Diffusion and Differentiation of a Sociological Concept, 1930s–1950s' in F. Adler and W.S. Laufer (eds.), *The Legacy of Anomie Theory* (Transaction: New Brunswick).

Merton, R. and Rossi, A. (1957) 'Contributions to the Theory of Reference Group Behaviour' in R. Merton, *Social Theory and Social Structure* ch.8 [originally 1950].
Metcalf, C. and Stenson, K. (2004) 'Managing Risk and the Causes of Crime' *Criminal 55 Justice Matters* 8–9.
Morris, T. (1989) *Crime and Criminal Justice Since 1945* (Blackwell: Oxford).
Morrison, W. (2005) 'What is Crime? Contrasting Definitions and Perspectives' in C. Hale, K. Hayward, A. Wahidin and E. Wincup (eds.), *Criminology* (Oxford University Press: Oxford).
Nelken, D. (2002) 'White-collar Crime' in M. Maguire, R. Morgan and R. Reiner (eds.), *The Oxford Handbook of Criminology* (Oxford University Press: Oxford).
Newburn, T. (2003) *Crime and Criminal Justice Policy* (2nd edn., Longman: London).
Nicholas, S. and Walker, A. (2004) *Crime, Disorder and the Criminal Justice System: Public Attitudes and Perceptions* (Home Office: London).
Nietzche, F. (1885) *Beyond Good and Evil* (New York: Random House: New York, 2000).
O'Malley, P. (2004) *Risk, Uncertainty and Government* (Glasshouse: London).
Palast, G. (2004) *The Best Democracy Money Can Buy* (Plume: New York).
Pratt, J., Brown, D., Brown, M., Hallsworth, S. and Morrison, W. (eds.) (2005) *The New Punitiveness* (Willan: Cullompton).
Pyle, D. and Deadman, D. (1994) 'Crime and the Business Cycle in Post-war Britain' 34 *British Journal of Criminology* 339–57.
Radzinowicz, L. and Hood, R. (1985) *A History of English Criminal Law vol. 5: The Emergence of Penal Policy in Victorian and Edwardian England* (Stevens: London).
Rawls, J. (1971) *A Theory of Justice* (Harvard University Press: Cambridge, Mass).
Reiner, R. (1980) 'Fuzzy Thoughts: The Police and Law and Order Politics' 28 *Sociological Review* 377–413.
——(1984) 'Crime, Law and Deviance: The Durkheim Legacy' in S. Fenton *Durkheim and Modern Sociology* (Cambridge University Press: Cambridge).
——(2000a) *The Politics of the Police* (3rd edn., Oxford University Press: Oxford).
——(2000b) 'Crime and Control in Britain' 34 *Sociology* 71–94.
——(2002) 'Justice' in Penner, J., Schiff, D. and Nobles, R. (eds.), *Introduction to Jurisprudence and Legal Theory* (Oxford University Press: Oxford).

—— (2003) 'Policing and the Media' in T. Newburn (ed.), *Handbook of Policing* (Willan: Cullompton).
—— (2007) *Law and Order: An Honest Citizen's Guide to Crime and Control* (Polity: Cambridge).
—— and Cross, M. (eds.) (1991) *Beyond Law and Order* (Macmillan: London).
—— Livingstone, S. and Allen, J. (2000) 'No More Happy Endings? The Media and Popular Concern About Crime Since the Second World War' in T. Hope and R. Sparks (eds.), *Crime, Risk and Insecurity* (Routledge: London).
—— —— —— (2001) 'Casino Culture: The Media and Crime in a Winner–Loser Society' in K. Stenson and R. Sullivan (eds.), *Crime and Risk Society* (Willan: Cullompton).
—— —— —— (2003) 'From Law and Order to Lynch Mobs: Crime News Since the Second World War' in P. Mason (ed.), *Criminal Visions* (Willan: Cullompton).
Roberts, J. and Stalans, L. (2000) *Public Opinion, Crime and Criminal Justice* (Westview: Boulder).
—— and Hough, M. (eds.) (2002) *Changing Attitudes to Punishment* (Willan: Cullompton).
Rock, P. (ed.) (1988) *A History of British Criminology* (Oxford University Press: Oxford).
—— (2002) 'Sociological Theories of Crime' in M. Maguire, R. Morgan and R. Reiner (eds.), *The Oxford Handbook of Criminology* (3rd edn., Oxford University Press: Oxford).
Rorty, R. (1989) *Contingency, Irony and Solidarity* (Cambridge University Press: Cambridge).
—— (1999) *Philosophy and Social Hope* (Penguin: London).
Rose, N. (1999) *Powers of Freedom* (Cambridge University Press: Cambridge).
—— (2000) 'The Biology of Culpability: Pathological Identities in a Biological Culture' 4 *Theoretical Criminology* 5–34.
Ryan, M. (1983) *The Politics of Penal Reform* (Longman: London).
—— (2003) *Penal Policy and Political Culture in England and Wales* (Waterside: Winchester).
—— (2004) 'Red Tops, Populists and the Irresistible Rise of the Public Voice(s)' 1 *Journal for Crime, Conflict and the Media* 1–14.
Sartre, J-P. (1948) *Les Mains Sales* (Routledge: London [1985]).
Sassoon, D. (1996) *One Hundred Years of Socialism* (New Press: New York).
Simon, J. (2001) ' "Entitlement to Cruelty?": Neo-liberalism and the Punitive Mentality in the United States' in K. Stenson and R. Sullivan (eds.), *Crime, Risk and Justice* (Willan: Cullompton).

Stenson, K. and Edwards, A. (2004) 'Policy Transfer in Local Crime Control: Beyond Naïve Emulation' in T. Newburn and R. Sparks (eds.), *Criminal Justice and Political Cultures* (Willan: Cullompton).
Stenson, K. and Sullivan, R. (eds.) (2001), *Crime, Risk and Justice* (Willan: Cullompton).
Surette, R. (1998) *Media, Crime and Criminal Justice* (2nd edn., Wadsworth: Belmont).
Sutherland, E. (1983) *White-Collar Crime: The Uncut Version* (Yale University Press: New Haven).
Sykes, G. and Matza, D. (1957) 'Techniques of Neutralisation' 33 *American Sociological Review* 46–62.
Tawney, R.H. (1921) *The Acquisitive Society* (Bell: London).
Taylor, I. (1981) *Law and Order: Arguments for Socialism* (Macmillan: London).
—— (1999) *Crime in Context* (Polity: Cambridge).
—— Walton, P. and Young, J. (1973) *The New Criminology* (Routledge: London).
Tham, H. (2001) 'Law and Order As A Leftist Project. The Case of Sweden' 3 *Punishment and Society* 409–26.
Tonry, M. (ed.) (2003) *Confronting Crime: Crime Control Under New Labour* (Willan: Cullompton).
—— (2004) *Thinking About Crime* (Oxford University Press: New York).
Waddington, D. (1992) *Contemporary Issues in Public Disorder* (Routledge: London).
Waddington, P.A.J. (2003) 'Policing Public Order and Political Contention' in T. Newburn (ed.), *Handbook of Policing* (Willan: Cullompton).
Walzer, M. (2005) 'All God's Children Got Values' *Dissent* (Spring) 35–40.
Weatheritt, M. (1993) 'Measuring Police Performance: Accounting or Accountability?' in R. Reiner and S. Spencer (eds.), *Accountable Policing* (IPPR: London).
Weber, M. (1918) 'Science As A Vocation' and 'Politics As A Vocation', *The Vocation Lectures* (Hackett: Indianapolis [2004]).
Wilson, J.Q. (1975) *Thinking About Crime* (Vintage: New York).
—— and Herrnstein, R. (1985) *Crime and Human Nature* (Simon and Schuster: New York).
Witt, R., Clarke, A. and Fielding, N. (1999) 'Crime and Economic Activity: a Panel Data Approach' 39 *British Journal of Criminology* 391–400.
Young, J. (1986) 'The Failure of Criminology: The Need for a Radical Realism' in R. Matthews and J. Young (eds.), *Confronting Crime* (Sage: London).

—— (1988) 'Radical Criminology in Britain: The Emergence of a Competing Paradigm' 2 *Britsih Journal of Criminology* 289–313.
—— (1999) *The Exclusive Society* (Sage: London).
—— (2003) 'Merton With Energy, Katz With Structure: The Sociology of Vindictiveness and the Criminology of Transgression' 7 *Theoretical Criminology* 389–414.
—— (2005) 'Foreword' in C. Hale, K. Hayward, A. Wahidin and E. Wincup (eds.), *Criminology* (Oxford University Press: Oxford).
Zedner, L. (2004) *Criminal Justice* (Oxford University Press: Oxford).

3
Dangerous People: Beginnings of a New Labour Proposal
Andrew Rutherford

'I found myself trying to come to terms with those events, and that is where I hit upon the importance of beginnings, which, as opposed to origins, are something you fashion for yourself... it seemed to me more important in human life to be concerned about beginnings than about ends.'[1]

Introduction

At the start of the twentieth century the reformist enthusiasms of the New Liberals were largely constrained by an inherent watchful eye on the rule of law. A hundred years or so later when New Labour swept into power, brakes of this sort were to be applied with a lighter touch. The incoming government embraced a legal moralism that sought to blur distinctions between criminal and civil remedies and to side-step or neutralize traditional checks and balances. From this standpoint, when the criminal law is conceived as a mere instrument of social engineering, the significance of the offence condition may disappear almost to vanishing point.[2] In like manner, within the realm of mental health law, the offer of treatment as a condition

---

[1] Edward W. Said, *Power, Politics and Culture, Interviews with Edward W. Said*, London, Bloomsbury, 2004, 164.
[2] Auguste 't Hart, *Criminal Law, Enforcement and Legal Protection*, London, Howard League for Penal Reform, 1999, 12; see also Francis A. Allen, *The Habits of Legality, Criminal Justice and the Rule of Law*, New York and Oxford, Oxford University Press, 1996.

for detention becomes a bothersome legacy born of a rights-obsessed era. Within the immediate sights of the incoming government were two liberal reform measures, however unexpected, of the Thatcher years: the normative theme of 'just deserts' that reached fruition with the Criminal Justice Act 1991 and individual protections embraced by the Mental Health Act 1983.[3]

This chapter focuses upon one aspect of New Labour's tendency to think and act 'outside the box', by seeking to explore the early stages of policy-making with reference to persons who were to become labelled as 'dangerous, severely personality disordered' (more commonly 'DSPDs'). Interconnected and overlapping events are explored in terms of their confluence with a policy-making stance of government that switched between response, anticipation, orchestration, and prompting. The analysis that follows borrows rather less from the 'weak structuralist' and 'swarming circumstances' theses pursued by David Garland[4] than it does from the detailed identification and unravelling of events, personalities, and criminological schools pursued by David Downes in his exploration of the ideological and vested interests that underscored the reductionist stance to penal policy evident in The Netherlands over four decades following the Second World War.[5]

Within weeks of the Labour Party's election victory in May 1997 a small group of civil servants, drawn from the Home Office and the Department of Health, began work on proposals regarding persons with severe personality disorders and considered to pose a threat to others. These officials were encouraged

---

[3] Although Tony Blair has deplored the rights-obsessed 1960s his target may also have been the 1980s, which enjoyed a reputation for relatively liberal criminal policy-making. On this period, see Lord Windlesham, *Responses to Crime, Legislating with the Tide*, vol 3, Oxford, Oxford University Press, 1996; Andrew Rutherford, *Transforming Criminal Policy*, Winchester, Waterside Press, 1996, 85–123; and David Faulkner, *Crime, State and the Citizen*, Winchester, Waterside Press, 2001, 107–21.

[4] David Garland, *Punishment and Modern Society*, Oxford, Oxford University Press, 1990; and *The Culture of Control*, Oxford, Oxford University Press, 2001.

[5] David Downes, *Contrasts in Tolerance, Post-war Penal Policy in the Netherlands and England and Wales*, Oxford, Oxford University Press, 1988; see also, Paul Rock, 'The opening stages of criminal justice policy making', *British Journal of Criminology*, 35, 1995, 1–16.

to go beyond mere tinkering with existing powers.[6] Instead, from a radical reconsideration of the issues, the working party's mission was to develop a 'strategic direction' that pointed to 'robust solutions'. A year or so later, Jack Straw, the Home Secretary, in response to a parliamentary question about the high-profile murder conviction of Michael Stone, declared that changes in law and practice were required. This was followed four months later with a formal announcement that new measures were being developed to address 'a group of dangerous, severely personality disordered individuals' who were not effectively restrained by either the criminal or mental health law. Society could no longer rely on a 'lottery' in which, through no fault of the courts, such persons may for a limited period of time be sent to prison or hospital or remain in the community 'with no interventions whatever'.[7] Although on this occasion Michael Stone was not directly referred to by the Home Secretary,[8] he stressed that persons should not be regarded as untreatable by 'a particular group of psychiatrists' but rather 'be susceptible to treatment by clinical psychologists, psychoanalysts or psychotherapists, or just within a therapeutic community. We should not write anybody off. Above all, the root of our concern must be the risk that such people pose to the public.'[9] He was able to extract from the Fallon

---

[6] Two interdepartmental working groups, reporting in 1986 and 1992, were seen as having had unduly narrow terms of reference and that opportunities for bold initiatives had been missed. See Jill Peay, 'Offenders suffering from psychopathic disorder. The rise and fall of a consultation paper.' *British Journal of Criminology*, 28 (1) 1988, 67–81; and Dr John Reed, *Report on Working Group on Psychopathic Disorder*, Department of Health, 1994. Reed recommended a 'hybrid order' under which a person sentenced to imprisonment is in fact sent to hospital and thereby deemed to be treatable. A variation became the 'hospital and limitation direction' contained in the Crime (Sentences) Act 1997, enacted in the closing days of the Conservative government, but this provision turned out to be rarely used. A 'hybrid order' of this kind had been rejected in 1975 by the Butler Committee on the grounds that a clear choice needed to be made between punishment and treatment.

[7] Jack Straw, MP, Hansard, HC (series 5) vol. 325, col. 602 (15 February 1999).

[8] Mr Stone was, however, mentioned by the Shadow Home Secretary. 'It cannot be right to have dangerous people in the community, when there is a real belief that they may commit serious crimes, particularly when, as in the case of Michael Stone, the person himself seeks secure treatment.' Sir Norman Fowler MP, Hansard, HC (series 5) vol. 325 col., 603 (15 February 1999).

[9] ibid. col. 605.

Report on events at Ashworth Special Hospital[10] that there was a substantial debate among clinicians, and with the development of areas such as clinical psychology, 'a condition that we previously regarded as wholly untreatable may become treatable'.[11]

In the event, a further seven months elapsed before the proposals on 'DSPDs' were finally published on 19 July 1999.[12] The term, 'DSPD', it was stressed, was not intended to describe a psychiatric condition and Paul Boateng, the responsible minister, later explained: 'We have quite deliberately chosen this term, in order to avoid the confusion that would otherwise arise if we were to adopt a clinical or medical approach to this issue.'[13]

---

[10] *Report of the Committee of Inquiry into the Personality Unit, Ashworth Special Hospital*, vols. 1 and 2, Cm. 4194 (Chairman, Peter Fallon QC), January 1999 (hereinafter, 'Fallon').

[11] Hansard, HC (series 5) vol. 325, col. 608 (15 February 1999).

[12] *Managing Dangerous People with Severe Personality Disorders, Proposals for Policy Development* (Home Office and Department of Health, Consultation Paper, 19 July 1999) (hereinafter, '*The Proposals*') DSPD was said to refer to individuals showing a significant disorder of personality; present a significant risk of causing serious physical or psychological harm from which the victim would find it difficult or impossible to recover; and where the risk presented appears to be functionally linked to the personality disorder. It seems likely that publication was delayed until the government was able to take stock of the Fallon Report. In the event, as will be seen, there was little within Fallon that could be used in support of *The Proposals*. Four days prior to publication of *The Proposals* an Expert Committee (chaired by Professor Genevra Richardson), commissioned in October 1998 by the Secretary of State for Health, completed its Review of the Mental Health Act 1983. The Review was published in November 1999 and its conclusions on personality disordered persons were in some significant respects at odds with the government's proposals. Professor Richardson expressed irritation that her committee had not been given notice of the contents of the Consultation Paper (Q.292, *Minutes of Evidence*, Select Committee on Health, 6 April 2000).

[13] Paul Boateng, evidence to the House of Commons, Select Committee on Health, Question 710, 24 May 2000). Dr Mike Shooter (Registrar, Royal College of Psychiatrists) expressed alarm at 'the rate at which DSPD has become common currency, as though it existed as a valid diagnosis and it does not'. He further remarked that, 'we have some extraordinarily expensive proposals being looked at as though the research will prove—back to front if you like—a very tenuous philosophy which has been put forward' (oral evidence to the Select Committee on Health, 11 May 2000, Question 520). In similar vein, the Law Society warned: 'If people are to be deprived of their liberty, whether temporarily or indefinitely, because they are deemed to be in a particular category, that category must be clearly defined in the statute. It is insufficient to define it

Rather, as elaborated by the government, the definition would be refined 'as we develop a clearer picture of the nature and characteristics of this group'.[14]

Acting on their brief to be bold, the authors of *The Proposals* accepted that the status quo was unacceptable: 'At present individuals in this group may, broadly speaking, be detained in prison as punishment following conviction for an act they have committed, or in hospital to receive treatment designed to bring about an improvement in diagnosed mental disorder. The approach the Government has developed to managing severely personality disordered people involves the idea of detention based on the serious risk such people present to the public.'[15] *The Proposals* were primarily directed at persons due to be released from determinate sentences and at persons not before the courts for sentencing but regarded as untreatable under the Mental Health Act. The overriding objective was to enhance public safety, and legislation was required 'to provide authority for the detention of dangerous severely personality disordered people on the basis of the risk they present, and if necessary, for detention to be indefinite'.[16]

Estimates were presented that in England and Wales there were between 2,100 and 2,400 men falling within the DSPD category. This total comprised some 1,400 persons in prison, 400 in hospitals, and between 300 and 600 not in detention but 'who are generally well known to local police, health and social services because of their dangerous and demanding behaviour, and who might potentially fall into the DSPD group'.[17] Persons

---

by setting out a range of characteristics, many of which may be found amongst the general population. Without a clear statutory definition, people who have been diagnosed as having a personality disorder of some kind will be alarmed that the adjectives "severe" and "dangerous" may be applied to their diagnosis, through assessment procedures which are intrusive and demanding, resulting in their being subject to indeterminate detention...' *Response to the Home Office/Department of Health Consultation Paper*, The Law Society, December 1999.

[14] Cm 4480, Department of Health, 2000, para. 2.18.
[15] *The Proposals*, p. 6 (underlining in the original).
[16] *The Proposals*, para. 7.
[17] ibid., para. 9. These estimates had already been provided by Mr Straw in his statement to the House of Commons of February 1999. Of the 1,400 men in prison it was estimated that 1,000 were serving determinate sentences with

falling within this category, according to the Home Office, were 'at the very extreme of the spectrum of personality disorders, combining severe disorder and serious danger to the public. They will often come from a socially deprived background with a history of childhood abuse and cruelty. They will usually have demonstrated challenging behaviour during their childhood, graduating into petty offending in early adolescence and then into more serious offending as their teenage years progress, with a developing tendency towards violent or sexual offending. They will often have abused substances of different kinds. In the great majority of cases they will be very well known to the local police, probation, health and social services, and to the education and housing services.'[18]

Before further consideration is given to *The Proposals*, four aspects of the policy context within which this document was launched require some elaboration. First, while the cross-departmental authorship of the document should be underlined, the concerns of the two ministries were rather different. The focus of the Department of Health was largely upon the quality of care and therapeutic interventions offered to the offenders, while that of the Home Office was primarily directed at public safety. Although co-operation between these departments had often been poor, the arrival of a new government with a very considerable majority in the House of Commons promised an opportunity for a concerted move forward.

---

an average sentence length in the order of five years. The comment was made that had this situation pertained in 1990 'a fair proportion of this group would still be in detention' (Mike Boyle, evidence to Home Affairs Committee, 30 November 1999, Q 115). Dr Nigel Eastman (for the Royal College of Psychiatrists) told the committee that these numbers were expected to expand very substantially. In the wake of a draft mental health bill (2002) the government stated that the data did not permit an estimate of the numbers dealt with in the absence of criminal convictions (Lord Falconer, HL Written Answers, 22 July 2002).

[18] Home Office Memorandum to the Select Committee on Home Affairs, 1999, p. 7. A leading Australian forensic psychiatrist later commented that New Labour's proposals 'could also have other more subtle damaging effects. Anti-social personality disorder is heavily overrepresented among the poor and also among those with histories of childhood abuse and neglect...If enacted, the proposals could result in the further marginalisation of an already disadvantaged section of society.' Paul Moran, 'Dangerous Personality Disorder—Bad Tidings from the UK', *International Journal of Social Psychiatry*, 2002, 48 (1), 6–10.

Dangerous People: Beginnings of a New Labour Proposal 57

Second, for a generation the prevailing policy tone had been set by the Butler Report's endorsement of the general view amongst forensic psychiatrists that treatment (with or without drugs) was not generally effective with regards to personality disordered persons.[19] For Butler, the way forward resided within the criminal justice process as enhanced by an additional sentencing power, the reviewable sentence. Although in opposition, the Labour Party had broadly favoured this way forward, Butler was now recast as an obstruction to progress. This was because the Mental Health Act 1983, reflecting Butler's relatively narrow view of the role of the health services, had tightened the treatability test with respect to persons with personality disorders. As noted earlier, this aspect of the 1983 Act was now to be presented as an unfortunate departure from what had been traditionally a common-sense approach.[20]

Third, at the ministerial level the key players were Jack Straw, the Home Secretary, and Paul Boateng, who served as a junior minister for Health until the end of October 1998 when he was promoted to Minister of State at the Home Office. An aggressive champion of the DSPD *Proposals* from the beginning,

---

[19] *Report of the Committee on Mentally Abnormal Offenders* (Chairman, Lord Butler), Cmnd. 6244, 1975. Butler concluded that '...the great weight of evidence supports the conclusion that psychopaths are not, in general, treatable'. Butler's biographer comments that the report proved to be a thankless task that 'fell victim to inter-departmental and inter-professional rivalries and jealousies'. Anthony Howard, *R A B, The Life of R.A. Butler*, London, Jonathan Cape, 1987, 354.

[20] The Mental Health Act 1983, s. 1(2), defines mental disorder as 'mental illness, arrested or incomplete development of mind, psychopathic disorder and any other disorder or disability of mind'. The Act does not provide a definition of mental illness, leaving this to the professional judgment of clinicians. Under an important exclusions provision, s. 1(3) provides that a person may not be classified as mentally disordered 'by reason only of promiscuity or other immoral conduct, sexual deviancy or dependency on alcohol or drugs'. Psychopathic disorder is defined at s. 1(2) as being 'a persistent disorder or disability of mind (whether or not including significant impairment of intelligence) which results in abnormally aggressive or seriously irresponsible conduct on the part of the person concerned'. In dealing with psychopathic disorder and mental impairment, under ss. 37 and 47 of the Act respectively, in the imposition of a hospital order by the courts or taking an executive decision to transfer from prison to hospital, a 'treatability criterion' must be satisfied, namely as set forth at s. 3(2)(b) that 'such treatment is likely to alleviate or prevent a deterioration of

Mr Boateng readily embraced the mantle of moral entrepreneur.[21] From the start, the pace was set by the Home Office and, with Mr Boateng's arrival in that department three months after the *The Proposals* were published, any remaining clout slipped away from the Department of Health. As the chair of the Health Select Committee remarked to the Secretary of State for Health, 'the Home Office has taken over and is in the driving seat with a law and order message behind what is being put forward...in a sense you have been hijacked by the Home Office in this area of policy'.[22] Rejecting any such idea the Minister preferred to present the situation in terms of the government's *penchant* for joined-up policy-making. It is less clear what part the Prime Minister's office played with respect to this issue during the early stages of the first New Labour government. Given Tony Blair's decision to retain a special interest across the broad spectrum of matters relating to crime, it would be surprising if the various satellites of No. 10 Downing Street were far removed from an issue imbued with this degree of volatility. As noted below, the Prime Minister's spokesman became directly involved in a statement prepared for the press following the conviction of Michael Stone, and it seems highly likely that No. 10 remained closely in touch as the DSPD proposals were taken forward.[23]

his condition'. This is a tighter test than had been required under the Mental Health Act 1959. At the start of the century, the Mental Deficiency Act 1913 had allowed for the detention of personality disordered persons in terms of their mental state and the risk they presented. For historical overviews see Brenda Hoggett, *Mental Health Law*, London, Sweet and Maxwell, 1996 and Jill Peay, 'Mentally disordered offenders, mental health and crime', in Mike Maguire *et al.* (eds.) *The Oxford Handbook of Criminology*, 3rd edn., 2002, 746–91. More generally, see B. Dolan and J. Coid, *Psychopathic and Anti-social Personality Disorders: Treatment and Research Issues*, London, Gaskell, 1993. This study, undertaken following a recommendation in the Reed Report, concluded that there was no convincing evidence as to whether persons with severe personality disorders could be treated.

[21] Becker has suggested that rules which sought to define deviance are 'the products of someone's initiative and we think of the persons who exhibit such enterprise as moral entrepreneurs'. He maintained that as well as professional experts such as lawyers and psychiatrists, rule-creating of this kind requires a moral crusader. Howard Becker, *Outsiders, Studies in the Sociology of Deviance*, New York, The Free Press, 1963, 147.   [22] ibid., Q.715

[23] See generally, Seldon, *Blair*, London, Free Press, 2004; Paul Rock, *Constructing Victims' Rights, the Home Office, New Labour, and Victims*,

Fourth, the working group was chaired by Dilys Jones, a psychiatrist at the Department of Health, who played a key role in the events at Ashworth Special Hospital that were explored by the Fallon Inquiry. The lead Home Office member of the working group was Mike Boyle, head of the Home Office Mental Health Unit.[24] Mr Boyle was described by one observer as an 'evangelist' with regards to providing treatment for personality disordered patients, a flavour of which surfaced during his appearance before a House of Commons Select Committee in May 2000.

Q: The difference between the current legislation on mental health [and *The Proposals*] is that it is related to treatment. The idea is you are compulsorily admitting somebody for treatment. If we are talking about dangerous personality disorders, we are, by definition, saying these people are not amenable to treatment so you are then compulsorily detaining somebody not for the prospect of treatment because that is not available but purely for the prospect of locking somebody up. How will that fit in with human rights legislation?

A: I could not accept the statement that by definition these people are untreatable.

Q: If they were treatable they would come under the Mental Health Act as it currently stands.

A: What we are talking about is creating a specialist system. It may be if Ministers opt for Option A in the consultation document the people who would come in through this system would be in the NHS anyway.

Oxford, Oxford University Press, 2004, 496–501; David Downes, 'Toughing it Out: From Labour Opposition to Labour Government', Policy Studies 19 (4), 1998, 191–8; Andrew Rutherford, 'An Elephant on the Doorstep: Criminal Policy without Crime in New Labour's Britain' in Penny Green and Andrew Rutherford, *Criminal Policy in Transition*, Oxford, Hart Publishing, 2000, esp. 33–41.

[24] In addition to appearing before the Fallon Inquiry and the House of Commons Select Committees on Home Affairs and Health, Mr Boyle gave evidence in Edinburgh to the (MacLean) Committee on Serious Violent and Sexual Offenders. However, the MacLean Committee 'firmly rejected the proposition of pre-offence preventive detention'. *Report of the Committee on Serious Violent and Sexual Offenders*, the Scottish Parliament, SE/2000/68, June 2000, para. 10.36. This stance by the Scottish authorities was, to say the least, inconvenient for the development of DSPD policy south of the border.

Q: Michael Stone, a classic example, was turned down by the psychiatric service because he was untreatable. He then went and killed two people and that of course brought many of the issues to the fore. The fact is if somebody is treatable under the current system they do not need this new system at all, they simply detain them under the current legislation. So this new proposal is specifically designed, surely, to detain people who currently do not come under the Mental Health Act and by definition have not committed a crime so how do we justify their detention?

A: I will not be drawn into the Michael Stone issue because there are all sorts of separate issues on that, but I do take the general point. The issue of treatability, whether an individual is treatable or not, has become the key issue as to whether there is any means whereby the public can be protected from somebody who by common consent represents high degrees of risk to the public. I know that there is great concern amongst psychiatrists that they are already under pressure to take into secure hospitals individuals that they feel they can do nothing for in order to serve a different end of public policy—protecting the public. That is, I think, largely because for a whole host of reasons we have to some extent gone down a blind alley on the question of what treatment can be given for personality disorder. There has not been proper resourcing or proper research so fundamentally while there is—and clinical colleagues are better placed to comment on this than I am—still a considerable debate going on among not just psychiatry but within psychology as well as to how far individuals with personality disorders can or cannot be treated...

[A further question prompted Mr Boyle to remark that the government was looking at treatment inputs that went beyond medicine and psychiatry].

Q: Again, you are hiding behind this idea of treatability because you are now saying we can find new treatments for them. I am talking about people who have, by definition, been deemed untreatable otherwise they would not be subject to this new proposal. It will not do to say we will find some psychologist who says they have got something up their sleeve that might be able to help them. I am specifically talking about people who are not treatable otherwise they would not be in this position.

A: The bottom line has to be that we think we can do an awful lot better than we currently do in identifying new treatments and providing those treatments so that individuals who currently receive totally inadequate management across the system can be helped to make the changes in their behaviour, if not in their personalities, that will let them return to the community safely. We are reasonably confident and we certainly feel an obligation to put much greater effort into investigating that possibility but we do recognise there will be individuals who will be drawn into the system who will not be amenable to any kind of intervention of that kind and who may end up spending the rest of their lives in that system. The key point there is to recognise that those individuals currently are damaged individuals. They are suffering and they cause great suffering in the communities of which they are a part.[25]

The working group followed a well-trodden path, although, as already noted, a relatively lengthy period had elapsed before its report was published. Meetings were held with interested parties and in June 1998 health services and criminal justice practitioners were invited to a seminar at the Home Office. Additionally, two meetings were held with the Fallon committee, and members of the working group attended some of the Inquiry's public hearings that got underway in November 1997. Further insights were gained from observing selected overseas practice. Of particular interest was the TBS process in the Netherlands, and visits were made to the Pieter Baan Centre and the van der Hoeven Clinic.[26] Notably, these visits reaffirmed the working group's sense of optimism that, given a considerable investment of resources, decent treatment and management was possible. Also of significance to the working party's deliberations was Paul Boateng's visit to the Mendota Mental Health Institute in Madison, Wisconsin, and to the Moose Lake Psychopathic Offenders Treatment Center in Minnesota.[27]

---

[25] Select Committee on Health, *Provision of Mental Health Services, Evidence*, 18 May 2000, questions 630–4. The questions in this exchange were put to Mike Boyle by Dr Howard Stoate (Labour).

[26] For an historical account of TBS (Terbeschikkingstelling—a court disposal following a finding of guilt and a psychiatric assessment) and an insightful commentary on the work of Pieter Baan, as a member of the 'Utrecht School' see David Downes, see note 4 above esp. pp. 88–95. While Baan maintained that the psychiatrist should have an equal say with the judge on sentencing matters, it was other members of the School who more closely adhered to legal procedures and protections. For a recent account of TSB see H. J. C. van Marle, 'The Netherlands', Appendix 3, in Andrew Rutherford and Mark Telford (eds.), *Dealing with People with Severe Personality Disorders'*, ESRC, Future Governance Paper 7, December 2001.

[27] During the early 1990s both states enacted statutes allowing for civil commitment on completion of a prison sentence, e.g. the Minnesota Sexually

What Mr Boateng brought back from his American trip was that 'these people can be held in secure environments which, whilst they are not clinical environments and are not prison environments, are environments where you can ensure there is a range of interventions and activities which is far better than that which a number of them are presently ensconced in within existing prison and NHS services'.[28]

At the heart of *The Proposals* two policy options were set forth under the headings of Options A and B. There was little doubt that the government's preference was for the more radical course set forth as Option B. Under Option A, the existing statutory framework would be amended so as to facilitate a greater use of discretionary life sentences. The government expected that the use of discretionary life sentences by the courts would increase under section 2 of the Crime (Sentences) Act 1997, which provided for an automatic life sentence for persons convicted of a second specified violent or sexual offence and also by extending the availability of discretionary life sentences. In terms of civil powers relating to DSPD individuals, the 'treatability' criterion of the Mental Health Act 1983 would be replaced by a requirement of 'likely to benefit from hospital treatment'. Furthermore, where determinate sentences had been imposed there may be 'a significant demand for DSPD offenders to be considered for detention under civil proceedings' as they approach the end of their sentence. Special hospitals and prisons would retain their separate organizational status but might be drawn more closely together by new arrangements such as a shared commissioning of services for DSPD individuals.

Under the favoured Option B, a 'whole system' view pointed to the creation of a 'third way' service to be situated outside prison service and special hospital arrangements. New criminal and civil powers would allow for the indeterminate detention

---

Dangerous Persons Act 1994, under which 130 persons were detained out of 200 referrals between 1994 and 1998; in Wisconsin 107 persons out of 260 referrals were detained under similar legislation over the same period. See Leonard V. Kaplan, 'A summary report on Sexual Offender Civil Commitment Legislation and Practice in Wisconsin', unpublished paper, Madison, University of Wisconsin, 2001.

[28] HC, Home Affairs Committee, Memorandum submitted by Department of Health, 24 May 2000, para. 717.

(and supervision and recall) of DSPD individuals. Under criminal law, once the court was satisfied that it was dealing with an offender meeting the DSPD criteria a DSPD direction could be attached to any sentence passed by the higher courts. The effect would be that such persons would be detained in a specialist facility until such time as they were no longer considered to present a serious risk on the grounds of their disorder. As with Option A, sentenced prisoners could be subject to a DSPD order under civil powers involving transfer to specialist facilities. Also under civil proceedings the order would be available on the basis that the individual met the DSPD criteria and that person would be detained until it was deemed that he or she could safely be released. There would be a new legal framework for detention of all DSPD individuals based 'on the risk they present and their therapeutic needs, rather than whether they have been convicted of any offence'. They would be managed by the same service regardless of whether or not they had committed an offence.[29]

It was emphasized that policy decisions should not await research findings. 'To put in place the kind of system needed for the future will require changes in the law, significant organisational, attitudinal and cultural change among the services and professionals involved with dangerously severely personality disordered people, and investment. It will take time and will be an incremental process.'[30] As a first step, the working group squarely disposed of the *quid pro quo*, established by the Mental Health Act 1983, of the provision of treatment in exchange for the compulsory detention of persons with psychopathic disorders.[31] The problem, as articulated by the government, was recited in what was becoming a well worn *mantra*: '(t)he addition of the treatability criterion marked a fundamental shift away from the previously held view that the management and, where possible, treatment, of people with psychopathic disorder (or, in more modern terminology, dangerous severely

[29] *The Proposals*, paras. 26–7.   [30] *The Proposals*, 6.
[31] Larry Gostin regarded the Act as seeking to balance legalism (providing safeguards for patients) and welfarism (professional discretion to access treatment). Larry Gostin, *Mental Health Services—Law and Practice*, London, Shaw and Shaw, 1986; see also, Andrew Ashworth and Larry Gostin 'Mentally Disturbed Offenders and the Sentencing Process' in *Criminal Law Review*, 1984, 195–212.

personality disordered people) was a legitimate function of the health service'.[32] The arrangements envisaged in *The Proposals* represented 'in a more modern and up-to-date form the position as it stood earlier in [the twentieth century]'.[33] In other words, persons with personality disorders, whatever view might be taken as to their treatability, should be dealt with in a similar manner to people with mental illness and severe mental impairment.

Two sets of events, both of which have already been referred to, played a crucial role in the development and presentation of *The Proposals*. While these events gave shape and direction to the policy-making process they were, themselves, also shaped by it. This interactive theme between events and policy-making is pursued further after reviewing the spate of problems at Ashworth Special Hospital and the arrest and conviction, for the high-profile Chillenden murders, of Michael Stone, a man with a troubled history of criminality and mental health problems.

Ashworth Special Hospital

The sorely troubled life of Ashworth Special Hospital during the 1990s was the focus of inquiries at the start and close of that decade.[34] In 1992 an inquiry headed by Louis Blom-Cooper QC (hereinafter Blom-Cooper) reported on allegations, first raised in a television programme, that nursing staff at the Special Hospital had ill-treated patients.[35] Six years later the further inquiry, chaired by Peter Fallon QC, was highly critical of the treatment-oriented regime for personality disordered patients that had been rapidly launched on the back of the Blom-Cooper

---

[32] Written evidence from the Home Office, House of Commons Select Committee, *Managing Dangerous People with Severe Personality Disorder*, Session 1999–2000, HC 42, para. 7.   [33] ibid., para. 11.

[34] Ashworth is one of four Special Hospitals in England and Wales. In 1989 the Special Hospitals Service Authority (SHSA) was established and took over the management of Special Hospitals from the Department of Health. This administrative arrangement was still in place at the time of the Fallon Inquiry.

[35] Louis Blom-Cooper QC was chairman of the Mental Health Act Commission, 1987–94. Knighted in 1992, he has led several inquiries into a variety of public policy isues, including the deaths of children in local authority care.

recommendations.[36] In the first of these reports, Blom-Cooper concluded that 'the cultural attitudes at Ashworth appear not only to be condoned, but also shared by many medical staff'.[37] It added: 'The over-riding conclusion is of therapeutic pessimism, of lack of positive change, of a depressing acceptance that patients will stay in the institution for many years... We are not advocating that medical staff should adopt unreasonable optimism but a hopeful, enquiring and therapeutically optimistic approach is a necessary first step to achieving success.'[38] This optimistic theme resonated within the higher reaches of a Department of Health that was determined to bring about a climatic transformation in terms of the staffing and management of Special Hospitals.

Blom-Cooper provided an opportunity for treatment enthusiasts to stake out a much enhanced place within the policy-making arena. These standard bearers of the treatment ideal castigated the Hospital's management for failing to take on the Prison Officers' Association that represented many members of the nursing staff. It was their view, and this was accepted by Blom-Cooper, that instead of being identified with the conventions of a penal establishment, Ashworth should be a setting for therapeutic interventions. To a large extent, treatment proponents were forensic clinical psychologists and Blom-Cooper provided a spur for this professional group to redress what had traditionally been a relatively weak position in relation to medically qualified personnel.[39] Blom-Cooper acknowledged the difficult relationship that psychologists had with some psychiatrists and the consequential marginalization of their activities. This state of affairs arose from confusion as to the role that psychologists had in treating patients and that '[w]hatever may have been the theoretical division of the therapeutic input to patients between psychiatrists and psychologists, there seemed to be no consensus at Ashworth about the responsibility carried

---

[36] Fallon noted that his inquiry was the latest in a line that had drawn Special Hospitals in terms of being 'a picture of insular, closed institutions whose predominantly custodial and therapeurtic pessimistic culture had isolated them from the mainstream of forensic psychiatry'. (Fallon, vol.1, 1.19.7).

[37] Blom-Cooper, vol. 1, 156.   [38] Blom-Cooper, vol. 1, 158.

[39] Three of the 'Ashworth Five' (senior staff members who gave evidence to Blom-Cooper) were principal clinical psychologists.

by psychologists'. Statutory responsibility for a patient's care is placed on the Responsible Medical Officer (RMO) and the psychologist's involvement is subject to that doctor's discretion. There was little multi-disciplinary teamwork and the regime was so dominated by nursing staff that 'other professional groups, particularly psychologists... were marginalised to the point where they were perceived as "visitors"'. Blom-Cooper observed further that this lack of collaborative professional work had had the consequence of 'distracting from its credibility, not to say to discredit it—even sabotage—psychological input'.[40] Accepting, in part, that the problem arose from the RMO's statutory responsibility for his or her patients, Blom-Cooper concluded that 'psychologists can play a central role in the care and treatment of many patients... but this does not absolve doctors from their wider responsibilities'. Blom-Cooper's conclusions were championed by the Department of Health against the resistance of Ashworth's management. Furthermore, the Special Hospitals Service Authority (SHSA) was far from receptive to Blom-Cooper's recommendations and had to be pressurized into acting upon them.[41]

Following media coverage of allegations by a patient who had absconded from the Hospital, a Committee of Inquiry into events at the Hospital's Personality Disorder Unit (PDU), headed by Peter Fallon QC, was set up on 5 February 1997, during the closing months of the Conservative government.[42] Claims of misuse of drugs, financial irregularities, and the circulation of pornographic material were largely upheld by Fallon. That there

[40] Blom-Cooper, vol. I, 159.
[41] Evidence to Fallon from Professor Ronald Blackburn. Blom-Cooper later commented that the SHSA regarded his report as antipathetic to its mission. 'What is not generally known is that when the SHSA was given the final draft of the Report it was exceedingly displeased with its contents. So much so was its rejection of the general tenor and thrust of the Report about the future management of the Special Hospitals, that the SHSA desired to say publically [sic] that it did not accept any of the ninety recommendations. In the event, the SHSA was ordered by the Secretary of State to accept the Report and all the recommendations, save for the recommendation to phase out and ultimately end the practice of seclusion.' (Letter from Sir Louis Blom-Cooper to Peter Fallon QC, 20 August 1998, cited in Fallon at vol.1, 2.15.35).
[42] Peter Fallon QC had recently retired as a senior circuit judge. The allegations by this patient were first reported in the *Daily Express* on 22 January 1997.

had been episodes of child abuse on the PDU was not ruled out. Within a matter of months of the Unit being established its management and staff were not really in control and crisis had followed upon crisis. In the wake of Blom-Cooper, the SHSA established a task force that sought to implement the liberalizing recommendations irrespective of variations in security requirements across the Hospital's patient population. One of Fallon's central strictures was that the SHSA had made no policy distinctions between different types of mentally disordered persons and that, in particular, 'the radical changes brought about following the task force recommendations were fatally flawed because they failed to recognise the differential needs of the personality disordered patients'.[43] Noting that witnesses from the SHSA had stressed the degree of political pressure to which they had been subjected in carrying out the across-hospital implementation of the recommendations, Fallon concluded that this was 'a ministerially driven fundamental mistake'. One of the task force's key recommendations was that a PDU be established to provide a therapeutic environment for these patients.[44] However, Dr James Higgins (a forensic psychiatrist who was a non-executive director of the SHSA and leader of the task force) acknowledged that he and his colleagues had been largely unable to engage the various staff groups in developing ideas about the future and that concerns about the viability of such a unit were not raised very vigorously. Fallon concluded that the SHSA had lacked the boldness to insist that the PDU 'could not be administered properly, even with the best managerial system backed by wholly adequate professional services'.[45] In Fallon's scathing words: 'A radical new change had been made too fast, with

---

[43] Fallon, vol.1, 2.0.20.

[44] By the time of the Fallon Inquiry, Ashworth held a little under five hundred patients of whom about one-quarter were diagnosed as having a pschopathic disorder. The PDU, which was established in April 1994, held one hundred and twelve patients in six wards, eighty-six of whom were said to have a 'pure personality disorder classification'. Most of these persons had been transferred from the prison system under Sections 47 and 48 of the Mental Health Act 1983. Relatively little research has been conducted on such transfers although it appears that they became less frequent after the Mental Health Act 1983. For a study drawing on data from the two decades preceding the Act, see Adrian Grounds, 'Transfers of Sentenced Prisoners to Hospital' *Criminal Law Review*, 1990, 544–51. [45] Fallon, vol.1, 2.15.37.

inadequate preparation... Such an innovative venture required an in-depth consideration of the implications of putting one hundred and fifty personality disordered patients together... Nobody emerges from this with any credit. The risks involved in creating such a large PDU were recognised from the start, but were sharply increased by poor leadership and implementation... It was a high risk that was sharply increased by incompetence.'[46]

Following a site visit, conducted at Fallon's request, a group of clinicians from outside the Hospital reported that leadership did not appear to emanate from the RMOs. The group concluded: 'At the time of the visit very good work by nurses and psychologists was compensating for the lack of equivalently good medical input.'[47] Good quality nursing staff were in place and the contribution made to treatment by clinical psychologists was excellent, highly valued and ideally needed to be increased. The Inquiry also heard from John Reed (formerly Senior Principal Medical Officer at the Department of Health) about a 'self-reinforcing circle of unattractive posts leading to less able candidates being appointed, to the hospitals being even less attractive places to work'.[48] Fallon noted a minute, dated July 1992, written by Dilys Jones (then a Senior Medical Officer at the Department of Health and before that the medical director of the SHSA) in which she stated that medical leadership was 'really non-existent at the Ashworth site. Many consultants had negative and anti-therapeutic attitudes and a tendency to collude with the prevailing culture, probably as a means of survival.'[49]

As with Blom-Cooper, Fallon provided an opportunity for psychologists to champion the treatment possibilities for personality disordered patients. A particularly trenchant witness in this regard was Ronald Blackburn,[50] who accepted that, while a

---

[46] ibid., 2.13.1–2.13.26.   [47] ibid., 4.2.15.   [48] ibid., 4.4.3.

[49] While Fallon was to conclude that the failure by consultants to provide professional leadereship was a serious error by all concerned at Ashworth, he was not persuaded by the British Psychological Society that the Mental Health Act 1983 be amended so as to allow a psychologist to be in charge of the patient's treatment. Fallon did, however, recommend that the input of clinical psychology to the PDU be sharply increased.

[50] Professor of Clinical and Forensic Psychological Studies, University of Liverpool.

few studies suggested that clinical psychopaths did not respond very favourably to traditional therapeutic interventions, there was 'insufficient evidence to support the opinion of some clinicians that "nothing works" with this group'. Furthermore, there 'is at least preliminary evidence that some offenders with personality disorders, including most "legal psychopaths" in special hospitals, do change with psychological treatment'.[51] He stressed the importance of psychologists playing a lead role in the delivery of multi-disciplinary services and suggested that hospitals such as Ashworth should have a director of treatment services and that a psychologist might well be the most qualified person to hold such a position.[52] This would directly counter the 'tendency there has been in special hospitals to assume that a psychiatrist will be the leader of any kind of treatment service and nobody else gets a look in...'[53]

Ronald Blackburn told Fallon that in 1989 he had agreed to set up an experimental unit at Ashworth of fifteen to twenty patients for the treatment of personality disorders. While the RMO would have retained overall responsibility for the patients within this unit, treatment would effectively have been under the general direction of himself. However, the unit never materialized and his idea was overtaken by the ('not clinically wise') decision to establish the PDU.[54] Senior managers appeared to lack interest in the views held by psychologists, and in early 1996 Professor Blackburn resigned as the Ashworth's honorary director of research. 'I was a non-medical person in a relatively powerful role in relation to research and I think there was some objection to that from some psychiatrists.'[55] Asked to comment on the nature of this strained professional relationship he replied: 'After the Blom-Cooper report, which had criticized the lack of medical leadership, I think that there was a reaction in

---

[51] Written and oral evidence of Professor Ronald Blackburn, Fallon, vol. 2, Blackburn evidence, 6. [52] ibid., 38.
[53] ibid., 39.
[54] Professor Blackburn told Fallon that he 'did not think there was a very clear conception of what personality disorder was all about and what treatment needs there were'. But by that time he was not in a position of influence and he did not, for example, have the opportunity to discuss his concerns with Dr Higgins who was a member of the team that devised the PDU concept (ibid. 30).
[55] ibid., 12.

the opposite direction, that medics should be running everything...' By abolishing the Psychological Department and making psychologists (together with social workers) accountable to the Head of Nursing, they were 'pushed down the ladder as it were'.[56] More specifically, 'there was a feeling among psychologists after 1993 that they were getting their comeuppance for criticizing medical and nursing staff in the Blom-Cooper Inquiry'. Additionally, the RMO assumed leadership of the multi-disciplinary teams, although Professor Blackburn did not think that it was absolutely essential that this should be the case. While he was not pressing for a modification of the statutory responsibilities of the medical consultant, he believed that 'there are ways of operating within the system in which the power of the consultant is very much in the background'.[57]

This theme was closely connected to another of Ronald Blackburn's key points, namely the need to revisit the treatability test constructed by the Mental Health Act 1983. 'Forensic psychiatrists are the gatekeepers to services for PD [personality disordered] patients in special hospitals, for example through their responsibility for decisions about treatability that determine admission. It is desirable that those who deliver psychological treatments should play a more prominent role in treatability decisions.'[58] He was asked whether there ought to be a common way of looking at whether or not treatment is needed. Why should they all not get the same chance of treatment? He replied: 'I am not sure forensic psychiatry has reached the level of maturity where you would insist on one approach across a national system. You have to allow for idiosyncracies... the idiosyncracies do not relate so much to the treatment as to the views of some psychiatrists that personality disorders really should not be part of psychiatry.' Pressed further, he remarked that vagueness around the treatability criteria as set forth in the

---

[56] ibid., 13.
[57] ibid., 15. It might be noted that as of September 2005 the eighty-four-bed DSPD unit at HMP Whitemoor, the clinical director was a clinical psychologist and that the clinical staff included two full-time forensic psychiatrists. Although the Whitemoor unit opened in September 2000 the formal entry criteria were not in place until a year later. By 2005 discharge criteria still had to be operationalized. [58] ibid., 8.

Act contributed to 'a lottery', with psychiatrists not using the test in a consistent way.[59]

In March 2000, fifteen months after the publication of his report, Peter Fallon wrote to the Home Affairs Committee and attached a paper, 'Comments on Proposals for Policy Development' that he had sent to Dilys Jones, then chair of the interdepartmental working party on DSPDs. He recalled that prior to writing his report he and his colleagues on the Inquiry had been told by the working party 'that Option B was being seriously considered. Indeed we were left with the impression that it was the preferred option.' This impression seems likely to have been created in the summer or early autumn of 1998 and the Fallon committee 'debated at length' the merits of the two options before deciding that Option B was not the route to follow. For Fallon, three conditions had been persuasive, namely: first, the numbers involved were too small to justify a new third service; second, it would be even more difficult for an isolated service to recruit staff than was the case for Special Hospitals and prisons; and third and crucially, that treatment was not regarded as viable with this group of people. Instead, Fallon maintained that the prison system was the appropriate setting alongside the introduction of reviewable sentences, as had been first proposed in the Butler Report. This way forward, Fallon added, would better protect the public against violent offenders such as Michael Stone, who had been convicted five months before his report was published. Indeed, Fallon added that, at the time when he was last sentenced, prior to the Chillenden murders, Michael Stone 'would have been a classic candidate to be assessed for a reviewable sentence'.[60]

All of this must have been especially exasperating for ministers. After all, Michael Stone had been regarded, at least initially, as graphically illustrating the urgency of *The Proposals*. New Labour appears to have anticipated that Fallon would provide further reinforcement. Instead, Fallon concluded that *The Proposals* and, in particular, Option B was not the way to go and revived the notion of the reviewable sentence. Had Fallon fallen into line with the government's agenda, it seems likely that the

---

[59] As noted earlier, the Home Secretary, Jack Straw, used the term 'lottery' in his statement to the House of Commons on 15 February 1999.

[60] Fallon, vol.1, 7.9.12.

launch of *The Proposals* would have coincided with publication of the Fallon Report early in 1999. From New Labour's perspective, Fallon had become a wild card and the appearance of *The Proposals*, which in the event made only scant reference to Fallon, was delayed by a further six months.[61] However, in one respect Fallon had considerable significance for *The Proposals*. As noted earlier, the Inquiry process itself provided a catalyst for forensic psychologists to promote the notion that dangerous persons with severe personality disorders were treatable and that, as professionally qualified practitioners, they should be accepted as major players in the provision of assessment and treatment.[62] This revival of criminological positivism and its message of optimism in terms of persons regarded as untreatable by many psychiatrists was from the government's standpoint, at the very least, most welcome.

Michael Stone

If, from a presentational point of view, Fallon turned out to be a disappointment for New Labour, the Michael Stone case and the uses to which it might be put seemed to be especially promising.

On 9 July 1996 the wife and daughter of a university lecturer were savagely killed on a country lane in Chillenden, Kent. Another daughter, left for dead, survived the ordeal. At the time of the first anniversary of this murder, following a telephone call from a psychiatrist to a television programme, *CrimeWatch*, a thirty-eight-year-old man, Michael Stone, was arrested and charged with two cases of murder and one of attempted murder. Held in the segregation wing at Canterbury Prison, Mr Stone confessed his guilt through a heating pipe to a fellow prisoner.[63] He made further damaging statements to two other prisoners, and it was largely on the basis of this evidence that he was

---

[61] Highly selective inferences were drawn from Fallon by Jack Straw in his statement to the House of Commons on 15 February 1999.

[62] On the rise of 'psycho-fixers' see Aldous Huxley, *Brave New World*, London, Chatto and Windus, 1932; for another fictional and prescient exploration, see David Karp, *One*, New York, Vanguard Press, 1953.

[63] The other prisoner was a police informer as was Stone himself. Indeed, it was reported that Mr Stone had met with his police officer handler on 5 and 10 July 1996, *The Independent*, 24 October 1998.

convicted on 23 October 1998 and sentenced to three life terms.[64]

In the wake of Mr Stone's conviction, political activity was fast and furious. For the media, the immediate focal point was the West Kent Health Authority, which was responsible for the Trevor Gibbens Unit. The Authority's chief executive was quoted as saying that mistakes had not been made with Mr Stone's healthcare. She stated: 'This is not a case of someone released from a hospital when they should not have been or lost in the system.' Mr Stone had never been held in a Special Hospital, had not been diagnosed as a schizophrenic, but had an 'anti-social personality disorder' exacerbated by abuse of alcohol and a wide range of drugs. He had spent many years in care and in prison and was on probation throughout 1995 and early 1996. In April 1994 he was sectioned under the Mental Health Act for the first and only time. He had been taken to a hospital in Hull, but after a period of assessment it was decided that he was not mentally ill. Although he had been seen by various health and social workers shortly before and after the killings, he did not give them reason to suspect him. She described him as a psychopath who was incapable of feeling guilt and was resistant to treatment.[65] Furthermore, she was reported as saying that everything possible had been done to help him and that the health authority was powerless to detain him in spite of his frequent threats to kill. 'Was Michael Stone bad or was he mad? I have to say with some certainty today that Michael Stone was not mad.'[66] These press reports were based on a statement that 'was read by [the chief executive] on behalf of the agencies involved. A written statement was never produced or circulated to the media (or anyone else) at the time.'[67] Prior to the jury's verdict the press had assembled at a hotel in Maidstone. At this time officials from the Department of Health were in touch with the chair of the Health Authority on three occasions, making additions and deletions to the draft press

---

[64] Mr Stone appealed twice against conviction. On the first occasion he was granted a retrial and was reconvicted in October 2001. His second appeal was dismissed by the Court of Appeal in January 2005.

[65] BBC News, *On-line*, 24 October 1998.

[66] *The Times*, 24 October 1998.

[67] Communication to the author from the Briefings Manager, Kent and Medway Strategic Health Authority, 20 November 2003.

statement. Once the verdict became known a large section was taken out at the insistence of a very senior Home Office official. Five minutes later a further section was removed at the behest of the Prime Minister's official spokesperson. The excised passages appear to have spelled out the considerable level of support invested by local agencies in the care of Mr Stone. An implication that might be drawn from this curious episode is that attempts were made by persons acting for the government to encourage the Michael Stone case to be viewed as depicting a substantial shortfall of resource and response across the country.

The following day it was claimed that in evidence not put to the jury Michael Stone had frequently threatened to kill people and that, according to 'health sources', he suffered from 'a severe psychopathic or antisocial personality disorder widely regarded as untreatable'. The Department of Health was reported to be working with the Home Office to develop new policies on the 'management and containment of people who pose such a grave risk'. An investigation had been launched as to how 'the care in the community killer' was free to commit murder and that 'questions were being asked how the murderer, who had a long history of mental problems with violence, was refused a bed in a secure psychiatric hospital only days before the bloodshed. He had told staff of his fantasies of killing children.'[68] In a further article, published by *The Times* on the same day, under the heading 'Psychiatrist gave warning of Stone's killing fantasies', it was reported that a few days before the murders Mr Stone had visited the Trevor Gibbens Unit in Maidstone, where he was an

---

[68] *The Times*, 24 October 1998; the official inquiry, set up by the Department of Health in January 1999, was led by Robert Francis QC. The four-person panel included Dr James Higgins, formerly a non-executive director of the SHSA and chair of the task force established at Ashworth Hospital in the aftermath of Blom-Cooper. Robert Francis and his team completed their work expeditiously, but publication was delayed by Mr Stone's two appeals. During 2005 there were further delays in releasing the report and in December 2005 Mr Stone's legal team sought a judicial review of the decision to publish the report. A statement from the agencies involved (Kent Department of Social Services, the Kent and Medway Strategic Health Authority and the National Probation Service, Kent) stated that: 'Michael Stone says that while he welcomes the publication of the report's findings he objects to the publication of confidential and social care information contained in the full report.' BBC News, *On-line*, 18 December 2005.

Dangerous People: Beginnings of a New Labour Proposal 75

outpatient under the care of a forensic consultant psychiatrist. Mr Stone told this doctor he had been fantasizing about killing children. Furthermore, this article stated that, concerned that he might harm someone, Mr Stone had asked to be admitted to the Unit but was refused a bed. Five months later this story was retracted and, in apologizing, the newspaper stated: 'We now understand, and accept, that both statements were incorrect. In fact, Stone did not even see [the psychiatrist] at that particular time. We apologise unreservedly to [the psychiatrist] for any implication that he had failed in his duty to take the necessary steps to protect the public from the danger that Stone posed, and for any embarrassment which [the psychiatrist] has been caused.'[69]

On 26 October 1998, three days after Michael Stone's conviction, the Home Secretary was asked whether further measures were needed to deal with offenders deemed to be extremely violent because of mental illness or personality disorder, but whom psychiatrists diagnose as not likely to respond to treatment, and 'was he aware that this concern has arisen not simply following the conviction of Michael Stone for those two brutal and horrible murders, but because there has been a tendency in recent years for psychiatrists to diagnose a number of violent people as not likely to respond to treatment?'. Mr Straw replied that 'there must be changes in law and practice' and that the matter was receiving urgent consideration by the Home Office and the Department of Health. He went on to summarize comments made on the radio a day or so before by Sir Louis Blom-Cooper, to the effect that 'one of the problems that has arisen is a change in the practice of the psychiatric profession which, twenty years ago, adopted what I would call a commonsense approach to serious and dangerous persistent offenders, but these days goes for a much narrower interpretation of the law'. Furthermore 'ten, fifteen, twenty years ago... persons with personality disorder and exhibiting signs of dangerousness would have been ordinarily regarded as treatable and detained within the Mental Health Act. I think in more recent years there are many people in the psychiatric profession who have come to the conclusion that people with psychopathic disorder are not

[69] *The Times*, 16 March 1999.

treatable.'[70] Mr Straw added: 'Quite extraordinarily for a medical profession, the psychiatric profession has said that it will take on only patients whom it regards as treatable. If that philosophy applied elsewhere in medicine, no progress would be made in medicine. It is time that the psychiatric profession seriously examined its own practices and tried to modernize them in a way that it has so far failed to do.'[71]

The following day, Mr Straw was reported to be planning 'to close the loophole which allows potential killers such as Stone to walk the streets because people with personality disorders cannot be held against their will'. This press report, based upon Home Office briefings, added that a joint Department of Health/Home Office working party was expected to report by the end of 1998 and that this may lead to tougher powers for people with personality disorders to be monitored closely and, if necessary, detained. The crux of the dilemma, as seen by the Home Office, was starkly put: 'The problem arises because, if people are not being treated, they cannot be detained under the Mental Health Act and if they have not committed a crime they cannot be held under the criminal law.' A 'senior government official' briefed *The Times*: 'The Home Secretary feels strongly that this has to be sorted out. Psychiatrists should not be able to wash their hands of these cases and take on people only regarded as treatable.'[72] Mr Straw was by now in the midst of an extraordinary public spat with the Royal College of Psychiatrists and a few days later, responding to a letter to *The Times* from the President of the Royal College,[73] Mr Straw reiterated his view that 'psychiatrists are not making as much use as they could of the 1983 Mental Health Act to care for those people who do fall within the remit of the Act... it is the opinion of many experienced observers of the system that psychiatrists are all too often using the treatability test in the Act as a way of absolving themselves from their duty of providing health care'. He added: 'The Government

---

[70] Sir Louis Blom-Cooper was one of a small group of persons that took part in occasional meetings with Mr Straw after he became shadow Home Secretary in 1994.

[71] *Hansard*, HC (series 5) vol. 318, col. 9, 26 October 1998. The question was put to Mr Straw by Alan Beith, home affairs spokesperson for the Liberal Democrats. [72] *The Times*, 27 October 1998.

[73] *The Times*, 29 October 1998.

recognises that there is a need for special provision for people who are dangerous but should not be in prison and who, because they cannot effectively be treated, should not be in hospital either. We are determined to address this issue and both the Department of Health and the Home Office have been working together so that we can better manage and control those who present a risk to the public and who prove resistant to treatment.'[74] Mr Straw's urging that psychiatrists should not retreat into a defensive mode prompted two academic members of the profession to retort that they suspected the Home Secretary was asking health professionals to carry out preventive detention as there was no criminal legislation open to him for this purpose.[75]

From the day of his arrest in early July 1997, the presentational potential of the Michael Stone case was apparent. On the face of it, Michael Stone had stepped directly from central casting. The stage management itself, of course, had to await the jury's verdict delivered some sixteen months later. In the event, two obstacles constrained the extent to which the Stone case could be used to promote the DSPD proposals. First, Mr Stone continued to insist upon his innocence and a retrial and a further appeal meant that the case remained *subjudice* for a considerable time. Second, reports in the media that the local health authority had rebuffed Mr Stone's attempts to seek treatment were challenged (and, as noted earlier, in one case retracted by a leading national newspaper). Significant as these constraints were, the Stone case played a crucial role in the period from Mr Stone's conviction in October 1998 up to the immediate aftermath of *The Proposals* being published during the summer of 1999. Vivid accounts of the Chillenden murders and the portrayal of a psychopath left free by the psychiatric profession to

---

[74] *The Times*, 31 October 1998.
[75] *The Times*, 5 November 1998. Within a few years much of this furore had dissipated. Several of the key participants, including ministers, had moved on and a number of clinicians, including some psychiatrists, had become recipients of research grants through the DSPD programme. One of the leading academic critics of the DSPD programme retired and was replaced as Head of the Department of Forensic Mental Health Science at London University's Institute of Psychiatry by a Canadian clinical psychologist and a keen supporter of the DSPD programme.

wreak tragedy lingered on in the public imagination as a human narrative that carried profound policy implications.

Discussion

It is instructive to consider the beginnings of *The Proposals* with reference to a scheme developed by Edwin Sutherland in his exploration of the spate of 'sexual psychopath' statutes enacted in the United States during the late 1930s.[76] Each of thirteen jurisdictions legislated that persons defined as sexual psychopaths be confined for an indeterminate period in a state hospital for the insane. Such confinement was not intended to serve a punitive purpose but was available to civil courts for the protection of the public. In some, but not all, of these statutes conviction for a sexual offence was a prerequisite of a civil commitment order. Sutherland's essentially reactive scheme held that the sexual psychopath laws were associated with a number of conditions. These were, (i) a state of fear is aroused, usually prompted by one or more events, often involving the sex murder of children. This fear, however, was seldom related to statistical trends; (ii), agitated activity in the community focused on sex crimes, and 'people in the most varied situations envisage dangers and see the need of and possibility for their control'; (iii) appointment of a high-profile committee that continued to work towards a legislative outcome even though the general fear usually subsides after a few days. The committee is likely to take on board unsubstantiated propositions that are presented as 'science'. The bill, which is sometimes introduced in the legislature ahead of the committee's report, is presented as being enlightened and effective and also unlikely to attract much legislative discussion; and (iv) the support is required of professionals who can draw up the new rule in an appropriate form. For example, the 1938 Illinois legislation was drafted by a group of psychiatrists and neurologists. Sutherland observed that such professional groups were likely to bring their own distinct interests to the creation and implementation of the new policies.

---

[76] Edwin Sutherland, 'The Diffusion of Sexual Psychopath Laws', *American Journal of Sociology*, vol. 56, 1950, 142–8; significantly, none of these jurisdictions were in the South, a region of the United States where sexual offenders continued to be regarded as criminals rather than patients.

To what extent are the two events that are linked with the genesis of the DSPD proposals consistent with Sutherland's scheme? Without doubt, the Chillenden murders engendered a state of fear. Furthermore, the trial and conviction of Michael Stone encouraged the view that existing legislation fell short of protecting the public. While the interdepartmental working group of officials was by its nature a low-profile affair, the fit with the Sutherland analysis is strongest in terms of the progress made by a professional interest group. In the wake of the two reports on Ashworth Special Hospital the optimistic note struck regarding the treatment of personality disorders and calls to radically revise the Mental Health Act 1983 were largely prompted by forensic psychologists who were able substantially to strengthen their position at the expense of psychiatrists. Although psychologists were not directly represented on the interdepartmental working party their upbeat and 'can do' message found immediate resonance with its members and with ministers.

Overall, however, the gestation of the DSPD proposals represents a significant departure from Sutherland's approach. Instead it is suggested that *The Proposals* are more appropriately located within a proactive rather than a reactive scheme. The starting point is to accept, as the government itself has insisted, that work was underway prior to the arrest of Michael Stone. The working group therefore came into existence at some point between the General Election of 7 May 1997 and Mr Stone's arrest two months later.[77] In other words, a radical way forward was decided upon first, and specific events were then assembled to assist in the development of policy and in its public presentation.[78] While the latest scandal at Ashworth surfaced in the public domain in January 1997 the worsening situation within the Hospital's PDU had been known to officials in the Department of Health for some considerable time.[79] The setting up of

---

[77] Fallon commented that the working group was set up shortly after his Inquiry was established.

[78] This proactive approach to events perhaps requires a reconsideration of Harold MacMillan's famous dictum, 'Events, dear boy, events' and Donald Rumsfeld's succinct observation, 'Stuff happens'.

[79] Although Fallon details notable failures in alerting senior officials and ministers to several disturbing incidents.

Fallon occurred just at the point when New Labour was appreciating how close it was to almost certain victory whenever an election was called. The Inquiry's public proceedings and its eventual report promised an abundance of material that might be drawn upon. As to the timing of Michael Stone's arrest, this was regarded, at least in the early stages, as being highly fortuitous in terms of shaping the public reception to the emerging policy proposals. Viewed this way, the events explored here were of less importance in prompting the development of policy than they were in providing a narrative into which embryonic proposals might be located alongside the rationale and justification to carry them forward into the political arena.[80]

Concluding Thoughts

In suggesting a proactive analysis of *The Proposals* it might be supposed that the seeds of *The Proposals* were in place before New Labour assumed office in May 1997. Two aspects of the approaches to public policy within the New Labour project might be considered with regard to this supposition. These are the warm embrace of risk and a vigorous renaissance of positivism towards offenders underlying themes of New Labour's emerging criminal policy.

---

[80] This chapter does not extend to the incremental developments following publication of *The Proposals* but it might be noted that these were taken forward through the draft mental health bills of 2002 and 2004 and a further bill was in the wings at the start of the parliamentary session of 2005/06. In the second of these draft bills compulsory treatment depended upon whether or not such intervention was 'clinically appropriate'. Under this bill, the RMO was replaced by a clinical supervisor who may be a consultant in another mental health profession such as clinical psychology. In terms of more concrete achievement, extensive new powers for the courts were created under Chapter Five ('Dangerous Offenders') of the Criminal Justice Act 2003 with a broadened life sentence and new and innovative sentencing arrangements for 'public protection'. The public protection sentence promises a regular supply of candidates for the DSPD units, and overall the 2003 Act seems likely to shift the balance away from DSPD provision within Special Hospitals and towards the prison system. Additionally, under the auspices of a DSPD office, manned by the Home Office and the Department of Health, an ambitious research programme was launched alongside four thirty-bed units within two prisons and two Special Hospitals. It was envisaged that in due course the DSPD programme would consist of 300 high-security beds in addition to medium-security and community-based provision.

Dangerous People: Beginnings of a New Labour Proposal 81

New Labour's early thinking about risk reached across the broad terrain of public policy. A central figure setting this scene was Tony Giddens, widely acknowledged to be Tony Blair's guru on the Third Way.[81] Building on Beck's notion of a risk society, with risk as a pervasive feature of contemporary life, Giddens (as Jenny Steele nicely puts it) 'eulogized' the energizing properties of risk.[82] While risk may often carry negative connotations it can also be viewed in a positive light 'in terms of taking bold initiatives in the face of a problematic future'.[83] This reconsideration of risk was bound up with aspirations of controlling the future that opened up an expanded array of possibilities for positive political engagement. 'In a world where one can no longer simply rely on tradition to establish what to do in a given range of contexts, people have to take a more active and risk-infused orientation to their relationships and involvements.'[84] Risk therefore becomes associated with 'initiative and the exploration of new horizons'.[85]

Furthermore, the advent of the risk society forced a rethink of the political agenda of Britain and other countries. Giddens added: 'The emergence of risk society is highly relevant to Tony Blair's project for New Labour. Blair is often spoken of as a conservative, who is destroying the values and perspectives of the left. I think it could be said, on the contrary, that he is one of the few leading politicians who is actively trying to come to terms with the profound changes affecting local life and the global order.'[86] He added: 'The issues I have discussed demand to be brought directly into the political arena. A party able to

---

[81] See, for example, Anthony Giddens, *The Third Way and its Critics*, Cambridge, Polity Press, 2000. Giddens accompanied Tony Blair and Jack Straw to the second Third Way seminar held at Camp David, the US Presidential retreat in Maryland, in February 1998.

[82] Anthony Giddens, 'Risk and Responsibility', *The Modern Law Review*, 62 (1), January 1999, 1–10, and Jenny Steele, *Risks and Legal Theory*, Oxford, Hart Publishing, 2004, 44; see also, Giddens' Chorley Lecture, May 1988 and 'Risk Society: the Context of British Politics' in J. Franklin (ed.) *The Politics of Risk Society*, Polity Press, 1998, 23–34.

[83] Anthony Giddens, 'Risk and Responsibility', n. 82 above, 3–4.

[84] ibid., 4. [85] ibid., 10.

[86] Anthony Giddens, 'Risk Society: the Context of British Politics' n. 82 above, 30.

address them cogently would be in a prime position in the political encounters that will unfold over the coming years.'[87]

From a quite different perspective, Nikolas Rose has argued that these contemporary developments are best understood in terms of the emergence and routinization of a 'risk thinking' style of thought. The excluded are not merely cast out but become subject to strategies of control. For those for whom affiliation (i.e., social inclusion) is regarded as being impossible measures are required that seek to neutralize the dangers they pose. Consequently, new strategies of risk management are created along with new zones of exclusion. The role of custodial institutions is redefined within these 'exclusionary circuits' and for those who appear intractably risky 'a whole variety of paralegal forms of confinement are being devised' and that may require waiving the rule of law.[88] As David Downes has observed with reference to the United States, imprisonment is not in itself a utopian device as in earlier eras. 'Rather, utopia consists in the removal of criminals from American society by penal means. It rests on exclusion and banishment rather than inclusion and hopes of reform.'[89]

The centrality of risk to *The Proposals* was bluntly reinforced by the Home Office a few months after publication when it was put to a select committee that '...the idea that detention can only be justified as a response to the commission of an offence reflects the view that the purpose of detention can only be punitive...If it is agreed that detention based on risk is acceptable in principle, it is in logic irrelevant whether someone assessed as highly dangerous and needing to be detained should have committed any previous offence...The real question to ask becomes the essentially pragmatic one of whether sufficiently reliable indicators of future behaviour can be found to allow the risk an individual presents to be assessed and a decision taken on

---

[87] 'Risk and Responsibility', 7.

[88] Nikolas Rose, 'Government and Control' in David Garland and Richard Sparks, *Criminology and Social Theory*, Oxford, Oxford University Press, 2000, 199-200; see also Andrew Rutherford, 'Criminal Justice and the Eliminative Ideal', 31, *Social Policy and Administration*, 1997, 116-35.

[89] David Downes, 'The Macho Penal Economy' in David Garland (ed.), *Mass Imprisonment, Social Causes and Consequences*, London, Sage, 55.

whether they need to be detained.'[90] Six years later, in its *Risk Framework Document*, the Home Office presented risk assessment as a central tool in the management of crime, stressing that: 'Risk-based decision-making also involves making effective use of opportunities to maximise benefits to society.' A particular welcome was given to the position taken by the Audit Commission that it would not criticize government departments for taking what it considered to be well-judged risks. Furthermore, in putting forward as a lead example of this 'precautionary approach', the Home Office chose to highlight the management of DSPDs.[91]

Within the firmament of ideas and tactics under discussion within New Labour the meeting point for its enthused notions of risk and a rekindled positivism was social defence. After a brief flowering of neo-classicist ideas during the 1980s, culminating in the just deserts theme embedded in the Criminal Justice Act 1991, the renaissance of positivism at the turn of the millennium was largely inspired by practitioner forensic psychologists rather than resulting from publications by academic lawyers or criminologists. With New Labour in power, it was quickly evident that these psychologists with their optimistic treatment plans for a wide array of offenders found that they were pushing at an open door. Notions that prisons could be made to work, in treatment terms, have to a large extent crossed the Atlantic, not in this instance from the United States but from Canada. As two observers of the Canadian scene have commented: '[T]he correctional vision imagined by the network of psychologists central to CSC [the Correctional Service of Canada] is marketed throughout the world and some of their work has become canonised reading in criminal psychology.'[92] These authors go

---

[90] Home Office Memorandum to the House of Commons Select Committee on Home Affairs, November 1999, paras. 14–16.

[91] Home Office web page, accessed 16 May 2005, 2. Interestingly, this document also contains the comment that in the course of the consultation process following publication of *The Proposals*, Option B emerged as the prefered way forward 'with the emphasis on research'.

[92] Dawn Moore and Kelly Hannah-Moffat, 'The liberal veil: revisiting Canadian Penality' in John Pratt *et al.* (eds.), *The New Punitiveness, Trends, Theories and Perspectives*, Cullompton, Willan, 2005, 88. However, an early research paper acknowledges the limitations of the rehabilitative ideal within the DSPD Unit. 'While prisoners may hope that their chances of release on

on to conclude that the apparent liberalism of Canadian punishment has provided a veil that conceals an extremely punitive system. Be that as it may, ultimately an agenda of public protection places issues of risk to the fore of those of individual rights and the accent becomes pre-emptive rather than reactive. In this regard the interwar years in Italy serve as a timely reminder of the implications of what may follow the prioritizing of social defence as an objective of criminal policy. As Leon Radzinowicz noted, Enrico Ferri's 1921 model penal code project was no mere reshuffling of terminology. Central to this positivist structure was the offender's state of danger, to be determined by the gravity and nature of the criminal act, dominant motives and personality. With a characteristic flourish, Radzinowicz wrote: 'Untrammelled by the so-often tortuous process of harmonising the legal definition of responsibility with the mental state of a particular offender, disregarding the traditional concepts of moral guilt, expiation or retribution; rejecting the insistence upon proportionality between crime and punishment and determining the latter on the basis of predominantly utilitarian concerns of social defence, Ferri was enabled to give full rein to his resourcefulness and imagination in redesigning a system of unorthodox, variegated and elastic sanctions.'[93] Even before Mussolini came to power, Ferri and his associates maintained that individual rights had been unduly emphasized at the expense of the state. For Ferri, criminological positivism fitted perfectly 'the purposes of fascism and could be adapted with good results as its criminal policy'.[94] Ferri's penal

parole would be increased by the treatment, in fact the probability of DSPD prisoners on determinate sentences being released early is likely to be low irrespective of the treatments they have received; no single treatment is likely to have a crucial effect.' David P Farrington and Darrick Jolliffe, *A Feasibility Study into Using a Randomised Controlled Trial to Evaluate Treatment Pilots at HMP Whitemoor*. London, Home Office Online report, 14/02.

[93] Leon Radzinowicz, *Adventures in Criminology*, London, Routledge, 1999, 16; see also, Enrico Ferri, 'Reform of Penal Law in Italy', *Journal of Criminal Law and Criminology*, 12, (1921–2), 178–98.

[94] ibid., 22; In 1927 Ferri joined a commission set up by Mussolini's minister of justice, Alfredo Rocco, to formulate a new Criminal Code. The resulting Codice Rocco (1930), an adaptation of Ferri's draft Code was endorsed by him. The Codice Rocco 'will win the unstinting admiration of the civilised world' concluded one British contemporary observer. See W. T. S. Stallybrass,

code was the most radical legal interpretation of the Positivist School's ideas. A constellation of security measures of a very long duration, to be served after the original sentence, was introduced for certain categories of 'dangerous' offenders. In certain cases the police were given the power of administrative action before the commission of an offence through regular supervision or exile to an island.[95] Indeed, the Rocco Codice of 1930, which drew overwhelmingly on Ferri's work, 'promised to extend the reach of the criminal justice system over an ever larger proportion of the population as even non-criminals were subjected to security measures'.[96] In her astute assessment of these years, Mary Gibson has commented that, '...the [Mussolini] dictatorship found a useful tool in positivist criminology, with its emphasis on surveillance, classification and control'.[97] For good measure, she added: 'The ease with which positivist criminology adapted to fascism laid bare its authoritarian tendencies, as the supposedly "scientific" techniques of examination and classification easily developed into regimentation and repression.'[98]

The DSPD programme, along with a host of measures that address issues ranging from low-level antisocial behaviour to international terrorism, have reinforced the impression that a fundamental reconstruction of the criminal law and criminal justice arrangements may be under way.[99] *The Proposals* might

'A comparison of the general principles of criminal law in England with the "Progetto Definitivo di un Nuovo Codice Penale" of Alfredo Rocco' in Leon Radzinowicz and J. W. C. Turner (eds.), *The Modern Approach to Criminal Law*, Cambridge, Cambridge University Press, 1945, 390–466.

[95] Compare with guidance issued to police forces in England and Wales in 2005: 'Where concerns exist but it is ascertained that the alleged perpetrator has no convictions of either a violent or sexual nature the matter should be brought to the attention of the CAIU (Child Abuse Investigation Unit) supervisior with a view to determining what action is appropriate. Such people are referred to as potentially dangerous persons (PDPs). The statutory duties of the police and social services to prevent further serious harm and to protect children allow action to be taken to reduce the harm posed by PDOs.' *Guidance on Investigating Child Abuse and Safeguarding Children*, Centrex, 2005.

[96] Mary Gibson, *Born to Crime, Cesare Lombroso and the Origins of Biological Criminology*, Westport, Conn., and London, Praeger, 2002, 235.

[97] ibid., 130.   [98] ibid., 202.

[99] See, for example, Tony Blair's speech at the launch of the *Respect Action Plan*, 10 January 2006.

be viewed as a bellwether for a wide-ranging transformation of criminal justice. To borrow a metaphor applied by David Downes,[100] it is when the protective shields become buckled that conditions for the pursuit of utopian criminal policy become most favourable.

Bibliography

Allen, Francis A., *The Habits of Legality, Criminal Justice and the Rule of Law* (Oxford University Press: New York and Oxford, 1996).

Ashworth, Andrew and Larry Gostin, 'Mentally Disturbed Offenders in the Sentencing Process' [1984] *Criminal Law Review* 195–212.

Becker, Howard, *Outsiders, Studies in the Sociology of Deviance* (Free Press: New York, 1963).

Blom-Cooper, Louis QC (chairman) et al., *Report of the Committee of Inquiry into Complaints about Ashworth Hospital*, vols. 1 and 2 (Cmnd. 2028, 1992).

Butler, Lord (chairman), *Report of the Committee on Mentally Abnormal Offenders* (Cmnd. 6244, 1975).

Downes, David, 'The Buckling of the Shields: Dutch Penal Policy 1985–95' in R. Weiss and N. South (eds.), *Comparing Prison Systems* (Gordon and Breach: Amsterdam, 1998).

—— *Contrasts in Tolerance, Post-war Penal Policy in the Netherlands and England and Wales* (Oxford University Press: Oxford, 1998).

—— 'The Macho Penal Economy' in David Garland (ed.), *Mass Imprisonment, Social Causes and Consequences* (Sage: London, 2001) 55.

—— 'Toughing it Out: From Labour Opposition to Labour Government' (1998) 19 *Policy Studies* 191–8.

Dolan, Brigit and Jeremy Coid, *Psychopathic and Anti-social Personality Disorders: Treatment and Research Issues* (Gaskell: London, 1993).

Fallon, Peter QC (chairman) et al., *Report of the Committee of Inquiry into the Personality Unit, Ashworth Special Hospital*, vols. 1 and 2 (Cm. 4194, 1999).

Farrington, David P. and Derrick Jolliffee, *A Feasibility Study into Using a Randomised Controlled Trial to Evaluate Treatment Pilots at HMP Whitemoor* (Home Office London, Online Report, 14/02).

---

[100] David Downes, 'The Buckling of the Shields: Dutch Penal Policy 1985–1995' in R. Weiss and N. South (eds.), *Comparing Prison Systems*, Amsterdam, Gordon and Breach, 1998.

Faulkner, David, *Crime, State and Citizen* (Waterside Press: Winchester, 2001).
Ferri, Enrico, 'Reform of Penal Law in Italy' (1921-2) 12 *Journal of Criminal Law and Criminology* 178-98.
Garland, David, *Punishment and Modern Society* (Oxford University Press: Oxford, 1990)
—— *The Culture of Control* (Oxford University Press: Oxford, 2001).
Gibson, Mary, *Born to Crime, Cesare Lombroso and the Origins of Biological Criminology* (Praeger: Westport, Conn. and London, 2002).
Giddens, Anthony, 'Risk Society: the Context of British Politics' in J. Franklin (ed.), *The Politics of Risk Society* (Polity Press: Cambridge, 1998, 23-34).
—— 'Risk and Responsibility' (1999) 62 *The Modern Law Review*, (1) 1-10.
—— *The Third Way and its Critics* (Polity Press: Cambridge, 2000).
Gostin, Larry, *Mental Health Services—Law and Practice* (Shaw and Shaw: London, 1986).
Grounds, Adrian, 'Transfers of Sentenced Prisoners to Hospital' (1990) *Criminal Law Review*, 544-51.
't Hart, Auguste, *Criminal Law, Enforcement and Legal Protection* (Howard League for Penal Reform: London, 1999).
Hoggett, Brenda, *Mental Health Law* (Sweet and Maxwell: London 1996).
Home Office and Department of Health, *Managing Dangerous People with Severe Personality Disorders, Proposals for Policy Development* (19 July 1999).
Howard, Anthony, *RAB, Life of R. A. Butler* (Jonathan Cape: London, 1987).
Huxley, Aldous, *Brave New World* (Chatto and Windus: London, 1932).
Kaplan, Leonard V., 'A Summary Report on Sexual Offender Civil Commitment Legislation and Practice in Wisconsin' unpublished paper (Madison, University of Wisconsin, 2001).
Karp, David, *One* (Vanguard Press: New York, 1953).
MacLean, Lord (chairman), *Report of the Committee on Serious Violent and Sexual Offenders* (Edinburgh, SE/2000/68, June 2000).
Marle, H.J.C., van, 'The Netherlands' in Andrew Rutherford and Mark Telford (eds.), *Dealing with People with Severe Personality Disorders* (Future Governance Paper 7) (ESRC: London, 2001).
Moore, Dawn and Hannah-Moffat, Kelly, 'The Liberal Veil: Revisiting Canadian Penality' in John Pratt *et al.* (eds.), *The New Punitiveness, Trends, Theories and Perspectives* (Willan: Cullompton, 2005) 88.

Moran, Paul, 'Dangerous Personality—Bad Tidings from the UK' (2002) 24 *International Journal of Social Psychiatry* 6–10.

Peay, Jill, 'Offenders Suffering from Psychopathic Disorder: The Rise and Fall of a Consultation Document' (1998) 28 *British Journal of Criminology* 67–81.

—— 'Mentally Disordered Offenders, Mental Health and Crime' in Mike Maguire *et al.* (eds.), *The Oxford Handbook of Criminology* (3rd edn, Oxford University Press: Oxford, 2002), 746–91.

Radzinowicz, Leon, *Adventures in Criminology*, (Routledge: London, 1999).

Reed, Dr John (chairman), *Report of Working Group on Psychopathic Disorder* (Department of Health: London, 1994).

Richardson, Professor Genevra (chair), *Review of the Mental Health Act 1983, Report of the Expert Committee* (Department of Health: London, 1999).

Rock, Paul, 'The Opening Stages of Criminal Justice Policy Making' [1995] *British Journal of Criminology* 1–16.

—— *Constructing Victims' Rights, The Home Office, New Labour and Victims*, (Oxford University Press: Oxford, 2004).

Rose, Nikolas, 'Government and Control' in David Garland and Richard Sparks, *Criminology and Social Theory* (Oxford University Press: Oxford, 2000), 183–208.

Rutherford, Andrew, *Transforming Criminal Policy* (Waterside Press: Winchester, 1996).

—— 'Criminal Justice and the Eliminative Ideal' [1997] 31 *Social Policy and Administration* 116–35.

—— 'An Elephant on the Doorstep: Criminal Policy without Crime in New Labour's Britain' in Penny Green and Andrew Rutherford, *Criminal Policy in Transition* (Hart Publishing: Oxford, 2000), 33–61.

—— 'Criminal Policy Without Crime in New Labour's Britain' in Penny Green and Andrew Rutherford, *Criminal Policy in Transition* (Hart Publishing: Oxford, 2000).

Rutherford, Andrew and Mark Telford (eds.), *Dealing with People with Severe Personality Disorders* (Future Governance, Paper 7) London: ESRC, 2001.

Said, Edward W., *Power, Politics and Culture, Interviews with Edward W. Said* (Bloomsbury: London, 2004).

Seldon, Anthony, *Blair* (The Free Press: London, 2004).

Stallybrass, W.T.S., 'A Comparison of the General Principles of Criminal Law in England with the "Progetto Definitivo di un Nuovo Codice Penale" of Alfredo Rocco' in Leon Radzinowicz and

J.W.C. Turner (eds.), *The Modern Approach to Criminal Law* (Cambridge: Cambridge University Press, 1945), 390–466.

Steele, Jenny, *Risks and Legal Theory* (Hart Publishing: Oxford, 2004).

Sutherland, Edwin, 'The Diffusion of Sexual Psychopath Laws' (1950) 56 *American Journal of Sociology*, 142–8.

Windlesham, Lord, *Responses to Crime, Legislating with the Tide*, Vol. 3 (Oxford University Press: Oxford, 1996).

4

With Respect to Order, the Rules of the Game have Changed: New Labour's Dominance of the 'Law and Order' Agenda

Rod Morgan

Setting the Scene

In late July 2004 the Prime Minister, Tony Blair, delivered a carefully crafted speech, well publicized in advance, at a 'community' centre in North London. His text included a good many qualifications. But the phrase we must presume he and his No. 10 advisors thought would hit publicity pay dirt was 'the end of the 1960s liberal consensus on law and order' (Blair 2004a). The ploy worked brilliantly. On the same day the *Guardian* made it their lead, front page story below the banner headline, 'Liberal law and order days over, says Blair'. This theme subsequently framed the massive coverage given by every TV channel, radio station, and newspaper the following day for Home Secretary, David Blunkett's, House of Commons speech introducing a Home Office Five-Year Plan for policing and criminal justice policy. By the end of that week every BBC satirical comedy programme or talk show was joking about or debating: whether there had ever been a '60s liberal consensus'; whether, if there had been, what it comprised; whether it was the progenitor of any of the social ills in the new millennium; and whether the ills *possibly* attributable to the 1960s *were* indeed ills. With a single stroke the New Labour leadership achieved three things. The Prime Minister pre-emptively: set the stage for the Labour Party national policy forum due to take place at the end of July; fired the first Conservative-Party-out-manoeuvring shots in the General Election then predicted to take place in May 2005; and further distanced New Labour from its Old Labour roots.

My aim in this chapter is to extend the analysis in which David Downes and I engaged in our joint essay on 'law and order' politics over three editions of the *Oxford Handbook of Criminology* (Downes and Morgan 1994, 1997, 2002). In doing so I shall reflect on developments since the new millennium. I propose taking as my starting point Prime Minister Blair's pronouncement that the excesses to be laid at the door of the liberal 1960s are now to be tackled head on. This represents, I shall argue, the latest effort by New Labour finally to expel the Old Labour 'skeletons in the cupboard', as David and I termed it (Downes and Morgan 2002), thereby preventing the Tories from recovering their traditional stronghold to the 'law and order' right of Labour. The Tories have been made to appear weak in this regard and the Liberal Democrats fragile and unsafe in a country made nervous by world and domestic events. Labour subsequently won the General Election of June 2005, albeit with a much-reduced majority. Their victorious achievement of a 'third term' owed much to the fact that they continued to hold the populist high ground with regard to 'law and order' issues. I want also to argue that their 'tough' stance on law and order is thematically at one with their tough approach to foreign policy, and that with the threat of Islamic terrorism now on the home front, the two spheres have become enmeshed.

Old Labour's 'Demons' Banished, New Labour's 'New Consensus'

Blair's 2004 speech proclaiming the end of the '1960s liberal social consensus on law and order' announced 'a new consensus'. The '1960s revolution' had not, he said, been without benefits. It saw 'a huge breakthrough in terms of freedom of expression'. It signalled progress 'against discrimination' and 'for women's equality'. It involved a decline in 'deference' and a 'rejection of rigid class divisions'. But these freedoms had not always been developed with accompanying responsibilities (for a similar line of argument, see Blunkett 2003). 'A society of different lifestyles spawned a group of young people who were brought up without parental discipline.' People had 'had enough of this part of the 1960s consensus'. The public today, he asserted, do not 'want a return to old prejudices and ugly discrimination'. But they do want 'rules, order and proper behaviour'. They want a 'society of respect'. They want a 'community where the decent law-abiding majority are in charge; where those that play by the rules do well; and those that don't, get punished'. He recalled that he had campaigned on these issues when shadow Home Secretary and subsequently resolved that something had to be done on gaining office. In 1997 he had campaigned on these issues because 'anti-social behaviour was a menace, without restraint'. The new consensus involved 'putting the law abiding citizen at the centre of the criminal justice system'. Law-abiding citizens are, the Prime Minister said, 'our boss'. The public want 'a say in how they are policed. They want to be in charge. Our proposals... do that.' The public would therefore be given a say in how they are policed. Offenders rather than offences would be targeted. And local communities and police would be given additional powers 'to enforce respect on the street'. These powers would include 'summary justice through on-the-spot fines' and 'the naming and shaming of persistent anti-social behaviour offenders'.

These themes were recapitulated in the Home Office Five-Year Plan (Home Office 2004) which the Home Secretary launched in the House of Commons later that day. In the Home Office Plan, however, the themes were couched in the broader framework of policy spanning the whole of the Department's remit and included an array of policies many of which sounded rather less 'big stick'. The 'law-abiding citizen' was to be put first, but her interests would be served by the Government also working 'with offenders', making prisons more 'decent' and regimes more 'constructive'. Further, because 'studies have shown that for many offenders short-term prison sentences do not reduce reoffending. It is important that there is a range of custodial and community sentences to address the behaviour of different types of offender.' A new National Offender Management Service (NOMS) would bring together the Probation and Prison Services and better ensure the 'end-to-end management of offenders, and clearer accountability for reduced offending'. The Government's combination of reforms aimed to 'stabilise the prison population at 80,000 by 2008' (ibid, 2.8). The following year, however, a more selective, rhetorically tough approach was outlined in the Labour Party's 2005 Election manifesto. As in Blair's 2004 speech certain aspects of the Government's policies were played up, and others played down. In the chapter devoted to 'law and order' issues it was reiterated that the Government's 'progressive case' was the building 'of strong communities built on mutual respect and the rule of law'. A well-supported 'neighbourhood policing team' would be provided in every area, local communities would be able to set local police priorities and, armed with additional powers, 'local people will be able to take on "neighbours from hell" by triggering action by councils and the police'. Though commitments were made to making more use of intensive community programmes, including electronic tagging and tracking, for young offenders, and funding additional treatment programmes for drug users, the predominant emphasis was again on the big sticks. The Party boasted, in a manner that would have been almost unthinkable before the early 1990s, that: sentences had got tougher; 16,000 additional prison places had been provided since 1997; almost 4,000 Anti-social Behaviour Orders (ASBOs) and 66,000 fixed penalty notices had been issued. These boasts suggested continuity with, rather than rejection of, Michael Howard's famous 1993 statement that 'prison works'. There was no mention of the implied cap on the prison population and reference to the new NOMS was preceded by the assurance that 'by 2007 every offender will be supervised after release; we will increase the use of electronic tagging; and we will test the use of compulsory lie detector tests to monitor convicted sex offenders' (Labour Party 2005, Chapter 3).

Thus by 2005 New Labour was able confidently to proclaim itself as the party that delivered 'law and order'. The number of recorded crimes had fallen by more than one-third since the mid-1990s and the Party had banished what it readily acknowledged were the Old Labour 'demons' of the 1960s and 1970s: 'we showed we could run the economy well, cut crime and stand up for Britain abroad. We proved our competence.' (ibid, Preface).

Why, if punitively populist policies characterize fundamentally *insecure* administrations, did New Labour, with unprecedentedly large majorities in the House of Commons, having already introduced in the late 1990s a raft of legal innovations and able to claim, with some justification, to have achieved so much with regard to crime reduction, feel the need to emphasize 'We are ready to go further' on the 'law and order' front? Why did they need so firmly to monopolize the centre-right policy ground traditionally occupied by the Conservatives? They undertook, *inter alia*, to introduce a comprehensive ID card system about which there were substantial reservations in their own ranks, to appoint council wardens empowered to issue on-the-spot fines and make more vigorous use of ASBOs (ibid, 44).

The answer must incorporate a variety of factors. First, the evidence from successive sweeps of the British Crime Survey (BCS) indicates that the public doubts that crime has fallen to the extent that the BCS and police statistics suggest, that a high proportion of people remain concerned about crime and that confidence in the police and criminal justice systems, though marginally improved, remains relatively low by historical standards (Nicholas *et al.* 2005). One reason for the widespread disbelief in falling crime levels is probably that significant minorities of BCS respondents are concerned about what they perceive to be the high levels of disorder prevailing in their neighbourhood. Analysis of the various indices of social disorder—police-recorded complaints and offences, legal actions taken by landlords, complaints to departments of environmental health, BCS and English Housing Survey data—generates a confusing picture (see Armitage 2002; Whitehead *et al.* 2003, para. 4.1). But it is clear that several major groups of practitioners and sizeable sections of the public perceive various categories of social disorder to be a serious and growing problem. It follows that as far as a substantial proportion of the electorate is concerned the self-proclaimed competence of New Labour regarding 'law and order' remains unproven, that the Party has yet to deliver.

Second, these doubts are capable of being fostered—something the Conservative Party vigorously attempted during the 2005 Election campaign—by drawing attention to the fact that changes in recording rules have made it complex to interpret the most recent crime statistics, that the BCS does not survey youths under sixteen and effectively excludes certain categories of crime. Whereas volume property crime undoubtedly has fallen, the latest data indicate that violent crime almost certainly has not, and crimes of violence generally inspire more fear and concern than do property crimes. As a result Labour's 'law and order' achievements are less than secure. This message, particularly that regarding the prevalence of 'disorder', the Party acknowledges and both the Prime Minister and Home Office ministers have repeatedly testified that it is a frequent source of complaint at their constituency surgeries.

We can assume, therefore, that New Labour has an electoral need *visibly* to demonstrate that the Government is addressing disorder and taking practical steps effectively to combat it. Yet because New Labour, particularly Blair and other leading ministers, have devoted so much of their thinking, speaking, and writing to the restoration of order, civic renewal and balancing rights and freedom with duties and obligations (see, for example, Blunkett 2003), we must also assume that they have a personal mission to change the character of civic relations in Britain. The Prime Minister's ambition, recently articulated in relation to parenting, is 'to change the culture of our country' (Blair 1995). They have consistently given priority to this objective both whilst in opposition and since 1997. They are true believers. They believe they can engineer social relationships in the public realm, though not, note, through the traditional Labour Party, socialist, means of greater economic equality and redistribution of wealth, the language and means for which they eschew. They also espouse deregulation, marketization, and the promotion of choice, processes which have arguably promoted disorder (the current, burning issue being growth in the consumption of alcohol, the phenomenon of binge-drinking and the extension of licensing hours).

They are populists in the positive democratic sense—the law-abiding people are 'our boss'. They are also moral authoritarians: they recognize right conduct and believe that people can be persuaded to play by the rules if big sticks and a few carrots are wielded. They do not shrink from the language of punishment, nor are they chary about devising new sanctions which can be applied speedily with as many procedural impediments swept away. Indeed they laud their achievements in that regard. Following a summary of the various measures taken to deal with anti-social behaviour (ASB) between 1997 and 2005 the Prime

Minister has explained: 'All of these measures... have one thing in common: they by-pass the traditional way the criminal justice system used to work... the rules of the game have changed' (ibid). If one of New Labour's signal achievements is passage of the Human Rights Act it must equally be said that the Party seems content to waive or diminish the rights of those who allegedly threaten the tranquillity of the society New Labour aspires to create. In this sense, as we shall see from an examination of the development of the ASB agenda, New Labour's domestic policies have an essentially Manichean and procedurally pragmatic character.

Anti-Social Behaviour and the Restoration of Respect

It is of course normal for ministers to emphasize in political and high-profile public fora the core rhetoric of policy which they believe will meet public approval, relegating the detailed complexity of policy to civil service documents and operational managers. What is interesting about New Labour is the degree to which No. 10 has taken hands-on control of aspects of operational delivery, ensuring that its form is visibly seen to support the core political rhetoric.

Prior to their 1997 Election victory, in a series of consultation papers, New Labour developed radical proposals designed to combat ASB, ranging from 'excess noise from sound systems or dogs, to repeat burglaries, and actual vandalism and repeated violence' (Labour Party 1996, 4). Shadow Home Secretary, Jack Straw, gained much publicity by attacking the existence of public spaces inhabited by 'winos and addicts, beggars and squeegee merchants', 'where families are unable to use parks for fear of harassment; and where motorists, often women, feel initimidated into paying for having their windscreens cleaned' (Straw 1995). These pronouncements followed an initiative already taken by the Conservative Government by means of the Criminal Justice and Public Order Act 1994 which created a new offence of 'causing intentional harassment, alarm or distress by using threatening, abusive or insulting words or behaviour or disorderly behaviour, or displaying any writing, sign or other representation which is abusive or insulting'. The new 1994 offence was punishable by up to six months' imprisonment and supplemented an existing offence, introduced by the Public Order Act 1986, of 'using threatening, abusive or insulting words or behaviour likely to cause harassment, alarm or distress' which was punishable only by a fine.

New Labour's proposals while in opposition were grounded on the contention that the Government's enactments inadequately dealt with a social disorder and harassment problem from which, as 'left realist' criminologists repeatedly emphasized in the late 1980s (see Young 1994), the most deprived sections of the community disproportionately suffered. But New Labour's proposals nevertheless gave rise to considerable controversy on the grounds that they were illiberal. Critics pointed out that the examples of ASB cited in New Labour speeches and pamphlets included both serious crimes and unpleasant but not necessarily criminal behaviour. The Party maintained that ASB needed to be broadly defined because repetitive ASB capable of making neighbours' lives a misery was often accompanied by culprits intimidating victims, thereby making it difficult to collect sufficient evidence to bring criminal charges. It was proposed that professional witnesses—police or housing officers, for example—might testify to the existence of the ASB, thereby relieving the victims of any need to appear in court. This led critics to object to the proposed lower, civil, standard of proof required. The Party also proposed that the courts be empowered to issue civil ASBOs (initially termed community safety orders) requiring that the objectionable behaviour cease *and* imposing other directives or prohibitions. Breaches of an ASBO would be a criminal offence for which a severe criminal sanction could be imposed. These proposals the critics judged disproportionate, dangerous, and in breach of the European Convention on Human Rights, Article 6.2 of which has been interpreted as requiring proof beyond a reasonable doubt for criminal charges (see Von Hirsch *et al*. 1995; Gardner *et al*. 1998).

The objections raised by academic lawyers were widely shared by local government councillors and officials such that, following passage of the Crime and Disorder Act 1998, several of the new powers, which included child curfew and parenting orders as well as ASBOs, were little used. The Act provided that an ASBO could not be made for less than two years and that breach was punishable with imprisonment for up to five years, powers widely considered draconian. Yet with the Conservative Party snapping at its 'law and order' heels and the focus groups and government surveys indicating that incivilities and disorder were widely perceived to be a continuing problem, New Labour, terrier-like, kept relaunching its ASB policies so as to maintain a high profile. In 2003 the Government created a specific unit within the Home Office, the Anti-Social Behaviour Unit (ASBU), to deliver what was entitled the TOGETHER campaign ('a campaign across England and Wales that takes a stand against anti-social behaviour and puts the needs of the local community first' (www.together.gov.uk)), published a White Paper on the topic (Home Office 2003), and passed further legislation with additional powers, the Powers of Criminal Courts (Sentencing) Act 2001, the Criminal Justice and Court Services Act 2000, the Criminal Justice and Police Act 2001 and, in particular, the Anti-Social Behaviour Act 2003.

The 2003 Act added to ASBOs and the other provisions of the 1998 Act a whole raft of new powers including: closure notices and orders on premises believed to have been used for the unlawful use, production or supply of Class A drugs; extended use of fixed penalty notices; injunctions under housing legislation against persons causing nuisance or annoyance; provisions for terminating secure tenancies because of ASB; parenting contracts where a child or young person has been referred to a youth offending team (YOT) if a member of the team has reason to believe that the child or young person has engaged, or is likely to engage, in ASB; and police powers to disperse two or more persons in a public place whose behaviour is believed to have resulted, or is likely to result, in any member of the public being intimidated, harassed, alarmed, or distressed.

As important, however, was the high-profile campaign mounted by the Home Office ASBU headed by Louise Casey, who the *Observer* has described as a celebrity civil servant, with heavy backing from No. 10 and the Prime Minister personally. The work of ASBU has been judged by No. 10 to be so successful that in September 2005, in yet a further boost, Blair announced that Louise Casey would now head a Task Force to promote 'respect' and the use of parenting orders which, following further legislation, would be capable of being applied for by education and housing authorities in circumstances not previously available. 'The new powers will apply to children at a much earlier stage. Not just when they have committed a criminal offence or been excluded [from school], as is currently the case, but if they are about to get involved in anti-social behaviour. This is about prevention, not just punishment' (Blair 2005). Louise Casey, moreover, would be personally accountable to the Prime Minister, not the Home Secretary.

The ASBU campaign has been about 'taking action'. Noting that 'in many places anti-social behaviour is not tolerated' the campaign was designed to ensure that 'this happens everywhere'. ASBU established a website and appointed 'academy ambassadors', local authority enthusiasts for the programme who promulgated what was decided were 'good practices'. These ambassadors, together with members of the central ASBU team, held roadshows around the country and periodically put on high-profile national presentations during which an array of ministers were on stage to urge local decision-makers—crime and disorder co-ordinators, local government housing department officials, volunteers and police—to make greater use of the powers now in place from the 1998 Act onwards. In the same way that Blair tended to emphasize the tough messages from the Home Office Plan so, at these various events, Louise Casey and her team emphasized the use of ASBOs. It was 'enforcement' that was stressed rather than the community 'support' mechanisms outlined in the 2003 White Paper for those individuals and families responsible for ASB, many of whom, most practitioners argued, have a variety of welfare, mental health, drug abuse and other problems and needs. The operational reality was, to adapt the famous New Labour mantra, 'being tough on ASB rather more than being tough on the causes of ASB'. Whereas the White Paper talked at length about intensive family support, and cited restorative justice programmes and the National Drugs and Alcohol Harm Reduction Strategies (Home Office 2003), ASBU ambassadors single-mindedly promoted the use of ASBOs and implicitly criticized those many local authorities making little or no use of them. Failure to apply for ASBOs was equated with failure to take ASB seriously. The campaign employed what has been described as ' "no nonsense" rhetoric' (Millie et al. 2005) and took no prisoners.

The TOGETHER campaign was by any standards brilliantly successful from a publicity and action standpoint. Within a year of its launch, being made subject to an ASBO, like being 'red-carded', had become a colloquialism. ASBOs were even referred to on Radio 4's *The Archers* and it became commonplace for all newspapers, national and local, to run stories about young people, including juveniles named and photographed, subject to them. If the purpose was as much to demonstrate that action was being taken as to achieve the outcome of reduced ASB, then the campaign was possibly the most effective ever mounted from within the Home Office. And the pressure exerted from the centre worked. In 1993 Blair backed ASBU's activism by exhorting local authorities: 'We've given you the powers, and it's time to use them' (Blair 2003). At a booster speech in 2004 he said: 'The challenge I gave you last year was to make sure you used them [your legal powers]. You have risen to that challenge in a hugely impressive way. And I want to thank you all' (Blair 2004b).

The number of ASBOs sought and granted increased from 1,130 in the four years to the end of March 2003 to 3,136 in the following eighteen months to the end of September 2004 and 5,557 a year later. Or, to put the matter another way, whereas the number of orders imposed was running at around a hundred per quarter until the end of 2002 the rate by the end of 2004 was over five hundred per quarter (Home Office evidence to the Home Affairs Committee 2005, vol. II) rising to six hundred per quarter in 2005. Most police force plans now included targets for either the number of ASBOs to be sought or aimed generally to increase their number. The Inspectorate of Constabulary focused on actions taken by Basic Command Units (BCUs) to tackle ASB and on occasion noted, negatively, when one had made less use of ASBOs relative to neighbouring BCUs (see, for example, the inspection report on Stockton BCU compared to Middlesborough BCU, Cleveland Police, HMIC 2004, para. 1.52). At conferences police commanders and local government middle managers in areas that, for whatever reason, had hitherto made little use of ASBOs, reported that they were under pressure from above and from the centre now to do so. These expectations were difficult to resist. Certain local authorities, those in Greater Manchester and West Yorkshire,

Manchester City Council, and Leeds in particular, led the way and accounted for a disproportionately high proportion of the ASBOs granted. The North Wales Police introduced a yellow card scheme, handing out yellow cards, without reference to the youth justice service, to any youths they judged to be miscreants, after two of which an ASBO was to be applied for. In several of these local authorities every opportunity was used to 'name and shame' offenders, adult and juvenile, subject to ASBOs by distributing leaflets to households on the estates where they lived providing personal details, including a photograph, and inviting people to call the local ASB team if any of the many specified court-ordered prohibitions to which they were now subject was, according to the informant, being breached.

Evidence-based Policy

Given the lack of precision in the definition of ASB (see Whitehead *et al.* 2003; Harradine *et al.* 2004; Millie *et al.* 2005), assessing the degree to which the TOGETHER campaign, and use of the various legal powers made available by recent legislation, has successfully reduced ASB is inherently difficult. Promoting social intolerance of whatever the public deem to be ASB and empowering people to do something about it—the essence of the TOGETHER campaign—is likely greatly to increase the degree to which the public reports, and the police and other agencies record, complaints of incidents. It follows that changes in incident records or even self-defined concerns are as likely to reflect changes in public attitudes and the extent to which those attitudes are given voice, as changes in particular forms of ASB. Furthermore, what the public defines as ASB varies from one neighbourhood and part of the country to another. It is doubtful, therefore, whether further counts of the various agencies' reports of ASB of the sort undertaken by the Home Office in September 2003 (see Whitehead *et al.* 2003, para. 4.2) would demonstrate very much. Yet what is striking about the manner in which New Labour has pursued the ASB agenda is that little or no research has been commissioned to test any of these issues or, with one or two exceptions (at the time of writing pilots regarding the use of fixed penalty notices for juveniles aged ten to fifteen years are being conducted in six

New Labour's Dominance of the 'Law and Order' Agenda 103

areas), evaluate the impact of use of particular administrative or legal provisions. The 'evidence' deployed has been almost entirely anecdotal, voiced at presentations and in TOGETHER pamphlets by campaigning victim activists whose courage in tackling local 'yobs' has been celebrated with awards and stage-managed applause:

> The strategy launch in late 2003 used video footage to illustrate graphically how people's lives can be ruined by ASB—and how some people can find the resilience and real moral courage to fight back against the threat posed by this sort of behaviour. After the video had been screened, the audience was asked to give a standing ovation for the survivors of ASB in the video (Millie *et al.* 2005, 37).

These populist, evangelical, marketing techniques may be highly effective in promoting messages. Spreading by such means what local practitioners and campaigners *believe* to be good practice is a perfectly respectable way of galvanizing the energy of local activists and the commitment of decision-makers. Nevertheless the contrast between the manner in which the ASB policy has been rolled out and the rigorous evidential tests required by the Treasury for funding other Home Office policy initiatives is noteworthy. The character of the ASB initiative has been a good distance removed from the language and procedures earlier announced in *Modernising Government* (Cabinet Office 1999) and ostensibly required by comprehensive Treasury spending reviews (HM Treasury 2003). It is very different from, for example, the history of the Crime Reduction Programme (CRP), and its accompanying research strategy, launched in 1999. Indeed it is possibly because the CRP programme was so fatally flawed in execution and so unproductive in its results (see the August 2004 issue of *Criminal Justice*, in particular the articles by Maguire, Hough, and Hope) that the Government and Home Office appear to be adopting a dual-track approach to evidence, policy initiatives, research, cost—benefit assessments and expenditure. On the one hand is the rhetorical, high-profile, evangelical approach to ASB, pursued apparently without evidence that it will deliver cost-beneficial behavioural change, *because* it is popular with sections of the electorate who are 'our boss'. On the other hand are the methodologically rigorous evaluations (much more so than required for the CRP in 1999) required for crime prevention and penal policy initiatives that have little or no popular appeal to establish that 'they work'(see NOMS 2005).

It is precisely this contrast which has in part fuelled the suspicion that it is the highly publicized *appearance* of the interventions rather than the *reality* of their *effectiveness* which has prompted the growing body of criticism regarding the Government's ASB agenda. The doubts have been expressed by critics from both home and abroad. It was notable, given the generally diplomatic nature of such international documents, for example, that the Council of Europe Commissioner for Human Rights, following his visit to the UK in late 2004, observed with respect to ASBOs:

> The ease of obtaining such orders, the broad range of prohibited behaviour, the publicity surrounding their imposition and the serious consequences of breach all give rise to concerns... What is so striking... about the multiplication of civil orders in the United Kingdom, is the fact that the orders are intended to protect not just specific individuals, but entire communities. This inevitably results in a very broad, and occasionally, excessive range of behaviour falling within their scope as the determination of what constitutes anti-social behaviour becomes conditional on the subjective views of any given collective... such orders look rather like personalised penal codes, where non-criminal behaviour becomes criminal for individuals who have incurred the wrath of the community... I question the appropriateness of empowering local residents to take such matters into their own hands. This feature would, however, appear to be the main selling point of ASBOs in the eyes of the executive. One cannot help but wonder... whether their purpose is not more to reassure the public that something is being done—and, better still, by residents themselves—than the actual prevention of anti-social behaviour itself. (European Commissioner for Human Rights 2005, paras. 109–11)

This withering critique, which in several respects echoes that made when ASBOs were first mooted, is also being made by a growing number of domestic commentators. Academic lawyers are critically examining ASBO practice and pointing out that, by circumventing conventional criminal procedure, criminal reform (for example, the decriminalization of suicide) and fundamental principles (the defence of mental incapacity) are also being abrogated (see Simester and Von Hirsch 2006; Von Hirsch and Simester 2006). An evaluation of *Anti-social Behaviour*

Strategies commissioned by the Joseph Rowntree Foundation has concluded, on the basis of a survey of practitioner and public opinion in three case-study neighbourhoods, that respondents subscribed to one of three narratives, not mutually exclusive or discrete, regarding the nature and origins of ASB. The first two narratives, termed 'social and moral decline' and 'disengaged youth and families', assume that the problems of ASB are getting worse either because of a generalized process of decline or 'because of the increasing disengagement of a minority of British youth and/or their families. The third narrative does not assume that problems of ASB are necessarily getting worse in themselves, but suggests that the *context* of youthful misbehaviour is changing, and as a result people are more likely to perceive young people's behaviour as anti-social and to worry about it' (Millie *et al.* 2005, viii). The authors found that older generation respondents tended to endorse the first view and young generation respondents and ASB practitioners to favour the second and to a lesser extent the third.

The Rowntree study encountered 'deep cynicism about current efforts by central government and local agencies to tackle ASB'. The public was aware of several of the enforcement initiatives, particularly ASBOs, but was dismissive of their likely effectiveness. In their conclusions the authors stress the complexities of the ASB issue, complexities which they suggest are not fully acknowledged by the methods employed by the TOGETHER campaign which implicitly accepts, legitimates, and encourages the view that standards are falling: 'The TOGETHER campaign draws on the "declining standards" narrative to offer images of the struggle between ordinary decent folk and the tide of loutishness.' The authors accept that this approach recommends itself as a means of mobilizing action by a government impatient for action. It 'resonates with real public anxieties...cogently reshapes those worries into a sense of vulnerability...and presents the image of tough, resolute government action' (ibid, 38). It may, in the short term, lead to electoral gain. But what if the ostensibly tough actions prove ineffective in the long term? What if the 'declining standards' narrative promotes a deep social sense of pessimism that any solution will work? What if the language of threats, naming and shaming and enforced sanctions sets one neighbourhood group against another? What if the community at large does not agree about what constitutes ASB or fails to engage in a genuine partnership with the key local state agencies promoting interventions? What if the local agencies responsible for enforcing sanctions, or dealing with the welfare needs fall-out of their application (housing evictions, the separation of family members, the enforcement of proscriptions, and the supervision of orders, etc.) have resources insufficient to do the job effectively?

The rate of use of particular ASB sanctions is, self-evidently, not *necessarily* an indicator of either a commitment to address ASB or effectiveness in dealing with it. To say otherwise would be the equivalent of suggesting that the greater the number of people in prison or hospital the lower the rate of crime or ill-health. The reverse *might* just as plausibly be the case with regard to ASBOs and ASB; namely the lower the number of ASBOs being imposed, the more effective the policies being taken locally to deal with ASB.

Consider the case of the South Wales Police, where the Chief Constable has publicly expressed reservations about the use of ASBOs (resort to them being seen as a failure) and the evidence presented in the Inspectorate of Constabulary's report on the Bridgend BCU. The police in Bridgend have what Her Majesty's Inspectorate of Constabulary (HMIC) concludes are 'excellent examples of effective partnerships' termed 'Communities First'. These comprise dedicated teams of officers, operating in high-deprivation areas, whose priorities are set in consultation with the community. On one estate, Wildmill, an area with very little in the way of youth services and characterized by extensive ASB and youth nuisance, the police team has developed with the community what are termed 'distraction tactics'. These have included establishing a 'Youthworks' Project and Centre to engage young people. These specific 'problem solving' initiatives operate in the context of a four-stage approach to ASB. The first stage involves a database recording and a letter to the individual or his or her parent or guardian, as appropriate. Stage two involves a second letter and home visit from the police during the course of which the ASB and the change of behaviour required is fully discussed. Stage three brings into play a partnership meeting, a third letter and an acceptable behaviour contract (ABC) with the ASB perpetrator. Stage four precipitates an application to the court for an ASBO. The HMIC report records that in three months 330 ASB incidents had been recorded and 420 persons referred. The report concludes that 'there is tangible evidence that interventions at the lower levels are causing immediate improvements in behaviour... so far no case has proceeded beyond stage 2' (HMIC 2004b, paras. 16 and 47).

This tiered, graduated, or incremental approach to ASB, working simultaneously with the communal needs of neighbourhoods *and* the individuals and their families engaged in ASB, can, it appears, be effective without often resorting to ASBOs. Further, in the advice jointly offered to youth offending teams (YOTs) by the Youth Justice Board, ASBU and the Association of Chief Police Officers (ACPO), it is the strategy to which, despite the rhetoric deployed by ASBU-sponsored ambassadors in favour of ASBOs, the Home Office is officially signed up. The guidance to YOTs describes in detail what the 'incremental' approach comprises—use of non-statutory warnings and notifications to perpetrators, restorative justice proceedings, ABCs, and parenting contracts (Youth Justice Board/ Home Office 2005). And this approach is probably that favoured by most local authorities and local police commanders. For, despite the current upward trend, relatively few ASBOs have been sought and granted in most local authority areas. What is clear is that a high proportion of ASBOs, currently 42 per cent, are breached, that significant numbers of breaches result in custodial sentences, that the prison population stands at a record high—at the time of writing approximately 78,000— and, if the current trend continues, the Home Office Five-Year Plan, whether or no the Government remains committed to it, of capping the prison population at 80,000, looks precarious.

What is unclear, because no research has been commissioned and no in-depth monitoring is being carried out, is whether the Government's ASB policies as exemplified by ASBU's activism, is dragging into prison offenders who would not otherwise have got there. This issue is being explored by the YJB, which is responsible *inter alia* for commissioning and paying for the custody of juveniles. The limited data collected by the YJB so far suggest that most juveniles received into custody where the primary offence is breach of an ASBO have committed many previous and relatively serious offences such that they would probably have ended up in custody at some stage. Indeed, approaching one-third had received a custodial sentence previously. The most that can be said, therefore, is that the ASBO and ASBO-breach route is possibly being used by the police to fast-track young offenders into custody. The procedure, after all, means that since most ASBOs are typically made for three to four years (two years is the minimum) and typically incorporate multiple conditions (not doing certain things, not contacting specified persons, not entering certain areas, etc.) it is for the police a relatively simple matter to bring breach proceedings compared to proving a further criminal offence. The ASB powers provide the police with what is a very convenient, evidential short cut. Furthermore, if custody is the outcome, then the ASBO conditions will most likely remain in place on release, to be activated again, and again. The risk is that the price being paid for high-profile ASB activism, which may or may not impact the incidence of whatever local communities and the authorities perceive to be ASB, is possibly an exponentially growing prison population with all the long-term criminal career-generating characteristics and costs with which penal analysts are familiar.

The degree to which this is possibly happening deserves urgent and thorough data collection and analysis. The task would ideally have been undertaken with pilot exercises before we embarked on a national policy which now has momentum and may prove difficult to reverse. If alleged jokes reveal grim realities the answer as to why this was not done may be found in the unguarded but widely reported quip of Louise Casey, now appointed Head of the Prime Minister's 'Respect' Task Force, in an after-dinner speech to a senior police audience in August 2005: 'If No. 10 says bloody "evidence-based policy" to me one more time I'll deck them' (*Guardian Profile*, 9 September 2005). We must presume she was referring to No. 10 officials rather than the Prime Minister, and conclude that the twin-track policy division has real substance at the heart of Whitehall.

It is possible, of course, that the ASB operational policies will change gear and direction, that greater weight will in future be given to support and rather less emphasis placed on enforcement. There is now a consortium, which includes the National Association of Probation Officers and the Howard League for Penal Reform, for 'ASBO Concern' and this body has generated increasing publicity, calling into question the appropriateness of particular ASBO decisions or the conditions attaching to them. The YJB has also raised doubts (see Home Affairs Committee 2005, vol. III, 217–20). It is doubtful, however, that these criticisms and cautionary noises will be able to quell the public expectations that have been generated, phase out the local authority enforcement structures that have been put in place, or diminish the prosecutorial advantages with which the police have been provided. The ASBO train has been fired up and it will not easily be slowed down in favour of a different strategic way forward.

Conclusion

The rules of the game have indeed changed, and are radically changing. In autumn 2005 many observers appeared to be under the impression that the Prime Minister's phrase, and the operational reality it reflects, has, as its origin and focus, distant, exogenous events, largely beyond our control: the changing world of the new millennium to which, domestically, we have to adjust—the growth of Muslim fundamentalism and terrorism, al-Qaeda, 9/11 and, bringing it all back home, the London underground and bus suicide bombings, successful and unsuccessful, of 7 and 21 July 2005. In autumn 2005 the 'rules' argument was focused on the Government's failed attempt to increase to ninety days the period that suspected terrorists might be detained without charge—a proposition amounting to internment. Though the Government lost that particular argument, Parliament agreed to extend detention without charge to twenty-eight days, twice as long a period as provided in any other European jurisdiction. This change comes additional to tighter immigration procedures and looser extradition agreements with countries seeking suspects resident in Britain, changes giving rise to equally controversial human rights concerns.

The autumn 2005 'rules' debate has of course been superimposed on a much more bitter argument about whether the 2003 invasion and subsequent occupation of Iraq was and is justified, and whether those events have made the world and Britain a more dangerous place. It would be inappropriate to go into that debate here save to say that there is an almost perverse inversion of President George Bush's conflation, contrary to all the evidence, of the 9/11 attack with invasion of Iraq as a necessary and justified part of the 'war against terror', and Prime Minister Blair's elision, contrary to all expert opinion, of our continued occupation of Iraq and the likelihood of terrorist attacks at home. What is striking is the parallel between George Bush's characterization of events post-9/11 and surrounding the invasion of Iraq as a 'war against terror' and the 'axis of evil', a Manichean struggle in which other nations 'are either for us or against us', and Prime Minister Blair's unequivocal placing of Britain in the 'for' camp, and his use of similarly Manichean language with respect to domestic law and order issues ranging from anti-social behaviour to terrorism. Victimhood, as we have noted, has been substantially merged with membership of the 'decent law abiding citizenry', who are our 'boss'. It is clear, moreover, that Blair and his senior ministers were dividing our domestic world into 'yobs' and 'law-abiding citizens', undertaking to rebalance policy and the shape of the criminal justice system, in favour of the latter, well before 9/11 or 7 July. In repeated, keynote, domestic speeches few shades of 'law and order' grey were conceded. The world was painted in Manichean terms, a stark conflict between innocent victims and mindless, predatory, thugs. The odds were to be changed in favour of the victims, which apparently meant amending the rights accorded to offenders. Big sticks were to be applied and Old Labour demons exorcized. The appeal has been not to the silent but to the unquiet majority of Middle Britain.

This theme was most strikingly driven home in the Prime Minister's speech to the Labour Party Conference in September 2005. His *leitmotif* throughout was the constancy of Labour's values, but the need to reinterpret them for a changing world, for markets, trade, and employment, for the delivery of public services, for the environment, for law and order. He sought to make out the case afresh, in other words, for the New Labour project. And with regard to law and order, he made it clear that the criminal justice system was itself the problem: 'we are trying to fight twenty-first century crime—ASB, drug dealing, binge-drinking, organised crime—with nineteenth-century methods, as if we lived in the time of Dickens'. Then came the remarkable, giveaway statement: 'The whole of our system starts from the proposition that its duty is to protect the innocent from being wrongly convicted... But surely our *primary* duty should be to allow law-abiding people to live in safety' (emphasis added). Between the two clauses was the caveat that the first 'must be the duty of any criminal justice system', and following this passage he asserted that his approach did not mean 'abandoning human rights'. But this was not the Government's 'primary duty': the interests of law-abiding people came first. This, I suggest, was not reinterpreting values for changing times, but advancing a new hierarchy of values.

Two points about this line of reasoning are worth emphasizing. First, it cannot be said that the Government paints all conflicts in Manichean terms or that it fails generally to make out the case for negotiation and compromise between conflicting parties or apparently irreconcilable differences. The brokering approach to the conflict in Northern Ireland and, in stark contrast to the French Government's repressive language and actions following the urban riots in Paris and elsewhere in autumn 2005, the multicultural assurances offered to Britain's 1.6 million Muslims in the wake of the July 2005 bombings, are testimony to the contrary. Second, as I have attempted to argue throughout this essay, a distinction has to be drawn between the balanced text of Government policy (for example, other regenerative social policies such as SureStart as well as Home Office guidance regarding ASB) and national hustings rhetoric and activist practitioner evangelism in some localities. In this essay I have drawn attention to a *tendency* rather than a fundamental *characteristic* of New Labour—a tendency to engage in authoritarian, punitive populism (Bottoms 1995, Roberts and Hough 2002) where the evidence suggests short-term electoral gain rather than effectiveness in changing behaviour or creating a safer world. Which is to say that I believe Government policy could, without great difficulty, be purged of this tendency.

The purging is necessary, for the Manichean approach is flawed in theory and dangerous in practice. The British population, no less than the world of nation states, is not so fundamentally divided. Most persistent offenders, particularly the young who are the principal target of the current anti-social behaviour agenda, are drawn from the most socio-economically deprived neighbourhoods in Britain. They, typically, are also multiple victims, of crimes perpetrated by others, often their elders, and of social practices which exclude them from services and facilities, particularly in the educational sphere, which would serve to provide them with an entrée to fulfilled adulthood (Commission on Families and the Wellbeing of Children 2005; New Philanthropy Capital 2005; YJB 2005). Many victims *and* offenders inhabit terrains sapped of resources and hope and have a shared interest in communal reinvigoration. Moreover, the Manichean tendency denies the Government's and every citizen's responsibility for the gross social and economic inequalities, the rapacious commercialism and exploitation and the everyday degradations of the society of which we are all a part. Creating and sustaining hostile images of the 'other' is ultimately a dishonest technique for not critically analysing the 'self': it is the corallary of refusing to acknowledge complicity and error.

The relationship between victims and offenders is not a zero-sum game. Better serving the interests of victims is in the public interest, but it should not involve whittling away the carefully built up safeguards for suspects and offenders which all citizens have an interest in preserving. In the so-called war against terror, zero-sum or 'balancing' arguments threaten to dismantle the very freedoms and rights which are the essence of the civilized society allegedly being defended. Likewise 'changing the odds' in the domestic sphere is presented as if no particular weight or priority can be allocated to the underlying interests involved, as if victims and offenders were separate categories in permanent conflict. It is not so, either at home or abroad. As Ashworth (1994, 292–6) has argued, we should not be talking of utilitarian risks on one or another side of an equation that may be thought of as scales to be tipped. We should rather decide what rights and duties are relevant—the rights of innocent people not to be convicted, questions of consistency of treatment and proportionality of punishment, and so on (see also Faulkner 2006, Chapter 23).

In its ambition to retain power New Labour is going beyond the exorcism of Old Labour demons. It is on the verge of removing safeguards which have arguably held the polity together. There is a point when empowering silent majorities represents the abnegation of principled leadership. If the rules are too often changed, or are applied unequally in different places to different groups, it eventually becomes unclear whether there are any legitimate rules at all. Finally, we should be wary of the lure of big sticks—threats, sanctions and the use of force. We British, it appears, cannot rid ourselves of our punitive obsession. 'Respect', the New Labour buzzword, does not issue from the barrel of a gun or the heavy hand of the law. It has to be earned. Both rap-culture youths and some of our politicians seem to imagine that simply intoning 'respect', and applying sanctions when the outcomes are judged 'dis', is sufficient. That is not how genuine respect is built or how it works.

Bibliography

Armitage, R. (2002) *Tackling Anti-social Behaviour. What Really Works*, NACRO Community and Safety Practice Briefing (NACRO: London).
Ashworth A. (1994) *The Criminal Process: an Evaluative Study* (Clarendon Press: Oxford).
Blair, T. (2003) Speech on Anti-Social Behaviour (QEII Centre, London, 14 October).
—— (2004a) 'A New Consensus on Law and Order' (Speech to Launch the Home Office Five-Year Plan, 19 July).
—— (2004b) Speech to Anti-Social Co-ordinators (Mermaid Theatre, London, 28 October).
—— (2005) Speech to launch a Respect and Parenting Order Task Force (Hertfordshire, 2 September).
Blunkett D. (2003) *Civil Renewal: A New Agenda* (text of the CSV Edith Kahn Memorial Lecture, 11 June).
Bottoms A.E. (1995) 'The Philosophy and Politics of Punishment and Sentencing' in Clarkson C. and Morgan R. (eds.), *The Politics of Sentencing Reform*, (Clarendon Press: Oxford).
Cabinet Office (1999) *Modernising Government* (Cmnd 4310, HMSO: London).
Commission on Families and the Wellbeing of Children (2005) *Families and the State: Two-way Support and Responsibilities—An Inquiry into the Relationship between the State and the Family in the Upbringing of Children* (Policy Press: Bristol).
European Commissioner for Human Rights (2005) *Report by Mr Alvaro Gil-Robles, Commissioner for Human Rights, on his Visit to the United Kingdom 4–12 November 2004* (Strasbourg: Council of Europe).

Downes, D. and Morgan, R. (1994) ' "Hostages to Fortune"? The Politics of Law and Order in Post-War Britain', in Maguire, M., Morgan, R. and Reiner, R. (eds.), *The Oxford Handbook of Criminology* (Oxford University Press: Oxford).

—— (1997) 'Dumping the "Hostages to Fortune"? The Politics of Law and Order in Post-War Britain', in Maguire, M., Morgan, R. and Reiner, R. (eds.), *The Oxford Handbook of Criminology* (Oxford University Press: Oxford).

—— (2002) ' The Skeletons in the Cupboard: the Politics of Law and Order at the Turn of the Millennium' in Maguire, M., Morgan, R. and Reiner, R. (eds.), *The Oxford Handbook of Criminology* (Oxford: Oxford University, Press).

Faulkner, D. (2006) *Crime, State and Citizen: A Field Full of Folk* (2nd edn, Waterside Press: Winchester).

Gardner, J., von Hirsch, A., Smith, A.T.H. *et al.* (1998) 'Clause 1—The Hybrid Law from Hell?' 31 *Criminal Justice Matters*, 25–6.

Harradine, S., Kodz, Lernetti, F. and Jones, B. (2004) *Defining and Measuring Anti-social Behaviour*, Home Office Development and Practice Report 26 (Home Office: London).

Her Majesty's Inspectorate of Constabulary (2004a) *Inspection of Stockton BCU, Cleveland Police, May 2004* (HMIC: London).

—— (2004b) *Inspection of Bridgend BCU, South Wales Police, June 2004* (HMIC: London).

HM Treasury (2003) *The Green Book: Appriasal and Evaluation in Central Government: Treasury Guidance* (HMSO: London).

Home Affairs Committee, House of Commons (2005) *Anti-Social Behaviour* (Fifth Report of Session 2004–05, HC 80 I-III) (HM Stationery Office: London).

Home Office (2003) *Respect and Responsibility—Taking a Stand Against Anti-Social Behaviour*' Cm 5778 (Home Office: London).

—— (2004) *Confident Communities in a Secure Britain: The Home Office Strategic Plan 2004–8* (Home Office: London).

Hope, T. (2004) 'Pretend it Works: Evidence and Governance in the Evaluation of the Reducing Burglary Initiative' 4 *Criminal Justice*, 287–308.

Hough, M. (2004) 'Modernization, Scientific Rationalism and the Crime Reduction Programme', 4 *Criminal Justice*, 239–54.

Labour Party (1996) *Protecting Our Communities: Labour's Plans for Tackling Criminal, Anti-social Behaviour in Neighbourhoods* (Labour Party: London).

—— (2005) *Britain Forward not Back: The Labour Party Manifesto 2005* (Labour Party: London).

Maguire, M. (2004) 'The Crime Reduction Programme in England and Wales: Reflections on the Vision and the Reality' 4 *Criminal Justice* 213–38.

Millie, A., Jacobson J., McDonald, E. and Hough, M. (2005) *Antisocial Behaviour Strategies: Finding a Balance* (Policy Press and Joseph Rowntree Foundation: Bristol).

National Offender Management Service (NOMS) (2005) *'What Works' Briefing 3/05 Understanding Research Methods and Findings*, Briefing 3/05 (Home Office: London).

New Philanthropy Capital (2005) *School's Out: Truancy and Exclusion—a Guide for Donors and Funders* (New Philanthropy Capital: London).

Nicholas, S., Povey, D., Walker, A. and Kershaw, C. (2005) *Crime in England and Wales 2004/5*, Home Office Statistical Bulletin 11/05 (Home Office: London).

Roberts, J. and Hough, M. (eds.) (2002) *Changing Attitudes to Punishment* (Willan: Cullompton).

Simester, A.P and Von Hirsch, A. (2006) 'Regulating Offensive Conduct through Two-Step Prohibitions' in Von Hirsch, A. and Simester, A.P. (eds.), *Incivilities: Regulating Offensive Behaviour* (Hart Publishing: Oxford).

Straw, J. (1995) 'Straw and Order', *New Statesman*, 15 September, 18.

Von Hirsch, A., Ashworth, A., Wasik, *et al.* (1995) 'Overtaking on the Right' *New Law Journal*, 13 October, 1501–16.

Von Hirsch, A. and Simester, A.P. (eds.) (2006) *Incivilities: Regulating Offensive Behaviour* (Hart Publishing: Oxford).

Whitehead, C.M.E., Stockdale, J.E., and Razzu, G. (2003) *The Economic and Social Costs of Anti-Social Behaviour: A Review* (London School of Economics: London).

Young, J. (1994) 'Incessant Chatter: Recent Paradigms in Criminology' in Maguire, M., Morgan, R., and Reiner, R. (eds.), *The Oxford Handbook of Criminology* (Oxford University Press: Oxford).

Youth Justice Board (2005) *Risk and Protective Factors: Research Undertaken by Communities that Care on Behalf of the Youth Justice Board* (Youth Justice Board: London).

Youth Justice Board/Home Office (2005) *Anti-Social Behaviour: A Guide to the Role of Youth Offending Teams in Dealing with Anti-social Behaviour* (Youth Justice Board/Home Office: London).

5
East Ending: Dissociation, De-industrialization, and David Downes[1]

Dick Hobbs

'This is the problem of character in modern capitalism. There is history but no shared narrative of difficulty, and so no shared fate (Sennett, 1998: 147).'

'There is no consciousness in the colony of itself as such, no common sentiment, no common interest (Zorbaugh, 1929: 180).'

1966 was an important year for East Londoners. The post-war employment boom was still two years away from any sign of obvious demise, and the London docks pushed the inevitability of containerization aside as the pre-industrial practice of casualization entered its final years. The bizarre worlds of the Kray twins had leaked into the nation's collective consciousness, and the local football club provided three players for England's World Cup winning team.

While for me the publication in 1966 of David Downes' *Delinquent Solution* does not quite rank with the achievements of Moore, Hurst, and Peters, this seminal study of mundane delinquency presented a rich and rewarding picture of East London in the early 1960s, and created a platform for scholars to interpret the worlds of successive generations of British Youth. *This* paper reconsiders the socio-economic changes that have taken place in the East End during the past forty years. A few of Downes' old

---

[1] Many thanks to Graham Hurley, Kenny Monrose, Rob Hornsby, Tim Newburn, and Paul Rock for their help in producing this chapter.

haunts will be revisited and described in a contemporary context, and the validity of the concept of dissociation that emerged from his fieldwork will be interrogated along with the relevance of the subcultural canon.[2]

Influenced by the Chicagoan study of Morris (1955), *The Delinquent Solution* (1966) located socialization in school as the prime reason for working-class youth accepting low-level work. Most importantly, however, Downes denied the existence of the youth gangs so vividly described by American researchers. Rather he discovered the existence of 'street corner groups', loose-knit friendship groups linked to territoriality via which youths acknowledged the futility of work, and dissociated themselves from middle-class-oriented aims and practices by engaging in deviant action. Most importantly, however, Downes established subcultural action as an essentially expressive medium for working-class youths seeking some respite. The more debasing, boring or repetitive the job, the more dissociated the youth will become, and the more he will try to recoup in the sphere of leisure the freedom, achievement, autonomy, and excitement that is unavailable at work.

The *Delinquent Solution* is a complex and detailed study of deviant youth in East London, and contemporary academic wisdom tends to consider this study largely in terms of its

---

[2] Supervised by Terry Morris, the three ethnographies of deviance that emanated from doctoral theses written at the London School of Economics by David Downes, Jock Young, and Stan Cohen during the mid-1960s to early 1970s, have been hugely influential upon subsequent generations of sociologists. Young's study of illicit drug use (1971) neatly related deviancy amplification to a subculture of deviance based upon his own experiences in London during the 1960s. Young attacked the preconceptions of control agents, and questioned the authority and validity of dominant moralities, indicating their role in the construction of deviant stereotypes, before developing a set of propositions regarding the role of the police in the deviancy amplification process (169–97). Stanley Cohen's study of the 'moral panic' that emanated from the bank holiday battles between Mods and Rockers at British seaside towns in the 1960s, is based upon documentary analysis, interviews, and questionnaires, as well as observation (1973: 205–10). The resultant study brought to public attention the concept of moral panic, where the mass media are the principal agents of the dramatization of mundane youth deviancy. Cohen's Durkheimian take on the functions of deviance is melded with symbolic interactionism to produce a sensitive analysis of subcultural meaning and membership.

sophisticated reading of British delinquent collaborations in the light of dominant American gang theory. However, Downes also utilized official statistics in order to create highly localized area profiles that complement his interview data and observations. Consequently, detailed variations in area crime rates are highlighted decades before central government deemed such data vital to policy formulation (Tierney, 2001).

The study also featured, 'informal observation', involving six months' field work in youth clubs, pubs and a late night 'caff'. Downes wrote of a white working-class world of cafes and bomb sites, of a two-tiered state education system from which most kids exited at age fifteen. The elite of these school leavers entered into three-, five- and, for those with ambitions to be a Thames Lighterman, seven-year apprenticeships, while the bulk engaged in unskilled, low-paid manual work. The latter were those observed and interviewed by Downes, boys who congregated on street corners and committed acts of petty crime and nuisance as a way of generating excitement in the absence of either adequate dedicated municipal funded provision, or a fully formed youth consumer market.

These disorganized street-corner groups were a far cry from the ubiquitous gangs of New York and Chicago, whose hierarchical structure and rigidly assigned roles contributed much to the popular perception of the growing problem of delinquent youth. The 'symbolic geography' of America (Crang, 1998: 115) and American popular culture provided most of the bench marks and icons of post-war adolescent *angst* (Hoggart, 1957; Abrams 1959; Gillet 1983: 254–7; Hebdige, 1988: 54–6; Bradley, 1992: 12–14; Street, 1992: 304). While British teenagers did their best with this 'borrowed cultural imperialism' (S. Cohen,1980: 20), and attempted to adapt teenage culture that had originated in Memphis, Brooklyn, and California, to church hall dances, chip shops and damp back alleys, Sharks and Jets it clearly was not. While the Mertonian logic of American aspirations inspired *angst*-ridden collaborations of intelligent, educationally frustrated corner boys (A.K. Cohen, 1955), and role-specific subcultures as a result of alienation (Cloward and Ohlin, 1960), East End boys of the 1960s when asked à la *The Wild One* 'What are you rebelling against?', replied à la Cliff Richard, 'Nothing', managing little more by way of rebellion than 'drape suits, picture ties and an American slouch' (Hoggart, 1957: 203).

The American Dream, as criticized by Merton, was clearly very different from the British version. The subcultural theories of Cohen, and Cloward and Ohlin, based respectfully upon anomie and alienation, focused upon the delinquents' reaction to failure. According to these two influential studies, the reaction led to the creation of one of the twentieth century's most influential informal social formations, which in turn enabled the construction of a youth consumer market built upon age-specific images of rebellion and resistance.

Downes' response to this orthodoxy, which is thankfully based upon dedicated empirical investigation, as opposed to self-indulgent polemics, or bohemian imaginings (see S. Cohen, 1980, for his devastating critique of Hebdige (1979)), retains much of its power as a distinctively British contribution that focused our attention upon the interconnectedness between expressive and instrumental subcultural action. The theoretical nugget at the core of *The Delinquent Solution* is the concept of dissociation. Adapted from Carter (1962), dissociation describes the process by which all aspects of middle-class culture are rejected, and this includes the primary engine of aspirational culture, education. Particularly in the work of Albert Cohen, an acceptance of upward mobility, and of education as a vehicle for attainment, lies central to the American 'corner boy's' frustration at his status, a frustration that is channelled into subcultural-based delinquency. However, the kids messing around on East End street corners had experienced school in a very different way. School demanded nothing other than mediocre performance, which is what it got. As a consequence, by the time the world of work intervened, youths correctly surmised that manual work was the only option. Consequently, school, work, indeed life did not disappoint, and status frustration did not figure as a motivation for deviance. 'Dissatisfaction is a measure of the gap between aspiration and achievement. For many, no such gap exists—their expectations and aspirations are centred on the world outside the factory' (Downes, 1966: 237).[3] Fighting,

---

[3] This highlights one of the two major points, both of Downes' study, that is the very different significance afforded to social class in the two societies at the

vandalism and generally loitering with little intent was fun, youth clubs offered insufficient and haphazard provision (Downes, 1966: 228–9),[4] and commercial recreational devices aimed specifically at youth were relatively sparse in a consumer market that had barely emerged from post-war austerity (Clarke *et al.*, 1976: 9–74).

The Delinquent Solution had an enormous impact upon the study of British youth subcultures. In particular, James Patrick (1973), Howard Parker (1974), Phil Cohen (1972), Paul Corrigan (1979), all utilized dissociation as a means of rejecting the polemical outpourings of writers intent on valorizing delinquency as noble resistance to capitalism. The relationship between youth culture and the parent culture, and the fact that the basic structural inequalities of working-class communities were shared by father and son, and mother and daughter were crucial in establishing the historical continuities that run through working-class cultures like a thread.

Of course, these continuities were relatively easy to establish in industrial society, where communities were entrenched and stable. Further, the immediate post-war period offered an unparalleled respite from the poverty and unemployment that had forged the East End (Gavron *et al.*, 2006). The Second World War had placed a uniquely positive spotlight on the East End's resilience and communality, and the numerous bomb sites that littered the area through the 1950s, 60s, and 70s were everyday confirmation of the price East Enders had paid for the Blitz. In this post-war period, with near full employment for the first time in its history, this unprecedented stability could be savoured, and this was a confident, tightly knit community, whose ultimate decline commenced with the decade-long demise of the timber and furniture industries between 1961 and 1971, which resulted in the loss of over 26,000 jobs (Hall 1962: 72), and in the same decade the loss of 40,000 jobs in London's

time. In America, class is sometimes conflated with moral performance and moral assessment and, as a consequence, being middle class can be presented as more honourable than being working class (see Centers, 1949), whilst membership of the working class in the United Kingdom was often taken to be a matter of collective pride.

[4] Forty years on and contemporary chroniclers of youth are still bemoaning the lack of proper youth club provision (Hallsworth, 2005).

clothing and footwear industries, which were also centred on the East End (Hall, 1962: 44–5). Despite the huge scale of job losses, these particular manifestations of industrial decline took place surreptitiously, against a backdrop of non-unionized, relatively small-scale units of production. However, it was the slow death of the London Docks, that marked the end of this classic period of entrenched, pragmatic, working-class community. Throughout the 1960s containerization and new handling methods reduced the demand for manual labour in the docks (Hill, 1976), and massive capital investment in the modernization of Tilbury, where the River Thames was deep enough to accommodate the new container ships, and with adjacent land sufficiently cheap and plentiful for the storage of containers, clearly signalled the imminent demise of the old East End. By 1971 the Port of London's workforce had shrunk to 6,000. The five Dockland boroughs (Tower Hamlets, Newham, Southwark, Lewisham, and Greenwich) lost 150,000 jobs between 1966 and 1976, mainly in transport, distribution, and food/drink processing, all sectors closely associated with port activity. This represented 20 per cent of all jobs in the area, and was in contrast to a decline of only 13 per cent in Greater London and just 2 per cent in Great Britain. And so, after a very brief period of unparalleled labour autonomy, and spectacular industrial strife that accompanied the end of casualization (Hobbs, 1988: Ch. 6), the London docker, and the communities that nurtured him, were no more.

In 1955, with East London in its political economic prime, Young and Willmott established East London, and specifically Bethnal Green, as a stereotypical British working-class community (Young and Willmott, 1957). Half a century later this seems frankly bizarre. Young and Willmott's emphasis upon matriarchy, and their avoidance of any meaningful discussion of work and employment, stand in stark contrast to studies such as Dennis *et al.* (1956), writing about a homogeneous, single-industry community underpinned by the commonality of one form of work, placing an emphasis on the work in working class, and situating masculine employment at the very epicentre of family and community life. However, even though they ignore the very peculiar nature of East London's political economy, Young and Willmott did succeed in conveying a sense of continuity, even when family ties were stretched to the eastern extremes of the Central Line.[5]

A decade later, with the exception of the notorious Cable Street, it is clear that Downes' East London was still characterized by cultural continuity. Even with a black population of 10,000 ensconced in London's equivalent of the rooming house district (Downes, 1966) large, white, working-class, extended families dominated the terrain. The Jewish population of Spitalfields and Brick Lane were long established, but then in decline as second and third generation refugees from the Pale of settlement moved north to Stamford Hill and east to Gants Hill. Although a scattering of Black, Asian, and Cypriot families, along with a dwindling ageing Jewish population, also lived in the area, the white population dominated the 1960s' streets of this working-class city.

'Nogoodniks, Prostitutes, Old Bags and Drunks'[6]

Time and word limits make it impossible to carry out a full retrospective discussion of all ten of the neighbourhoods covered by Downes. However, Spitalfields as a part of the West Stepney study, makes an ideal area with which to chart the changes that have beset East London over the past forty years. At the western extremes of Downes' map (at 275), wedged hard against the bowler-hatted walls of the City of London, in the 1960s this was an area of poverty, alcoholism, and homelessness, set alongside both long-established working-class communities, and a long-standing citadel of elite proletarian employment. Many of the once elegant Huguenot residences such as those in Elder Street, Blossom Street, and Fleur de Lis Street, were run down and abandoned, periodically occupied by homeless men and plagued by rats. The crypt and churchyard of Hawksmoor's Christchurch (the original Itchy Park) in Commercial Street was given over to homeless alcoholics (Phillimore, 1979: 34), or what one of White's (1980) respondents called 'the methylated people'. The same men scavenged fruit and vegetables from the

---

[5] This sense of the denizens of East London enjoying, although modest, a significant and distinctly proletarian post-war idyll has been recently reinforced by Gavron *et al.* (2006).   [6] White, 1980: 128.

vast Spitalfields wholesale market, while the more able-bodied sought cash-in-hand work in Brick Lane and Wentworth Street markets, and occasionally, until the P45 from a 'previous employer' failed to arrive, enjoyed a few weeks' work as a labourer in the warehouse of the builders' merchant in Shoreditch High Street. At night Spitalfields was for the adventurous only, as wooden pallets from the market were broken up and used to fuel large bonfires as the overflow from the crypt turned to alcoholic shadows in the flames (see Don McClullin's photograph *Near Spitalfields Market*, in Ackroyd, 2000).

There was a real vibrancy in Spitalfields in the 1960s. Working-class neighbourhoods, social dereliction, upwardly mobile villainy, and elite manual labour were wedged tight against the pervading power of the City of London. Yet these two diametrically opposed silos of British class history seldom impinged upon each other and had persisted as distinct parallel universes for centuries. Jewish businesses were still a feature of the area in the 1960s in the form of furriers, leather, and clothing workshops. Some streets hung on to a semblance of proletarian respectability, as working-class families attempted to establish themselves in direct opposition, not only to the frightening chaos of Itchy Park and its flaming satellites, but also to the legal and illegal clubs and spielers that were long-established features of the area. For instance the *Pen Club* in Duvall Street, described by Downes as 'a drinking club frequented by crooks' (at 225), was rumoured to have been established with the proceeds of a robbery of the Parker Pen Company, and in 1960 was the site of a notorious killing (Davidson, 2003: 23–38). Indeed, neighbourhood-based organized crime was a distinct feature of East London during the 1960s, most notably in the form of the Kray twins (Pearson, 1973). Downes does not mention organized crime as a feature of the area, and at first sight this is a marked omission. Yet there is tacit, and with hindsight, prudent acknowledgement of the phenomena in the author's comment that the area had 'long since acquired a reputation for... vice, protection and receiving' (Downes, 1966: 137). Although his statement that 'professional offenders' were not features of the area clearly proved to be wrong, given Downes' explicit focus and the subsequent mode of inquiry, a very informal ethnography, and analysis of official statistics, unravelling the intricacies of organized crime 'accidentally' was as unlikely in the 1960s as it is now.

Despite an intrinsically deviant identity going back over several centuries, and encompassing Jack the Ripper, prostitution, poor housing, and disease (Fishman, 1988; Hobbs, 1988: 84–118), Spitalfields was above all a world of work. The fruit and vegetable market had been in existence since the thirteenth century, and provided a focal point for the area. In the 1960s lorries would line Commercial Street at midnight, and loading would go on through the early hours, tapering off in mid-morning (see plate 11 in White, 1980). Small, family-run cafes studded the area serving market workers and drivers, and the pavements and gutters were clogged with rotten or discarded produce and various types of wrapping and packaging. Market work was highly sought after, well paid and indicative of good family connections and a sharp entrepreneurial instinct.

Downes' utility of dissociation as a theoretical device to understand a very British working-class response, was firmly grounded in the context of both the local political economy, and in the local operationalization of middle-class institutions, in particular the education system. Dissociation refers to a rejection of middle-class culture and values, and the youths of 1960s' Stepney and Poplar existed in distinct universes to those of the middle classes who commuted to the East End to teach, for the East End was a working-class city populated by proletarians untainted by middle-class mores. However, the legal requirement for children to attend school at least up to the age of fifteen made class confrontation inevitable. As Willis (1977) showed a decade later, the realities of class conflict in schools served to reproduce key assimilating aspects of industrial or 'shop floor' culture in the classroom that served as ideal preparation for life in low-status factory work. However, unlike Willis, Downes did not consider resistance as a factor of classroom interaction. Acceptance and resignation to the realities of working life and a rejection of the rhetoric of upward mobility run through *The Delinquent Solution*, as youths focused upon leisure as a recompense for the drudgery of the working week. In the absence of any significant bourgeois influence other than education, dissociation was a relatively simple and, in comparison to Willis's work, distinctly unheroic process.

The expansion of British criminology, and its emergence as a field that is increasingly distinct from the parent discipline of sociology, has enabled the scholarly wheel to be re-invented many times over (see Rock, 2005), and has resulted in a distinct freemasonry of professionally interconnected, yet intellectually insular clubs (Katz and Jackson-Jacobs, 2003). Such insularity has led to a considerable amount of inbreeding and criminological Karaoke, as criminology has gradually relinquished much of the theoretical and methodological rigour of its sociological bloodlines. With this in mind, the *Delinquent Solution*'s disciplinary base and the sheer sociological craft that is evident are worthy of attention.

Let us be clear that the small numbers of interviews carried out by Downes are unlikely to be acceptable to many contemporary PhD supervisors, or their increasingly bureaucratic managers. However, by carefully melding subcultural analysis with critical policy dissection, Downes utilizes local statistics as well as interview and observational data, deftly exploring the relationship between structure and agency in an attempt to explain the negotiated order, how interaction shapes and is shaped by structure, and how deviance is created and enjoyed. Partly as a consequence of this innovative mixture of methods, the study stands as a classic piece of British sociology, and serves as a timely reminder of the role of rigorous sociological analysis in the study of crime, offering in particular a somewhat broader perspective on social control than that of studies restrained by criminological orthodoxy. While Downes on occasions uses a language that resonates of post-war Fabianism, in the light of the faith shown by the current political regime in imposing the tenets of commerce upon public institutions via such obscenities as the Public Finance Initiative, the language of the *Delinquent Solution* now seems positively revolutionary. Consequently, the study remains the pivotal British study of youth delinquency, and is ripe for an attempt at replication, albeit a replication as pockmarked with contemporary sociology as twenty-first-century Spitalfields is with gastro pubs.

However, what would such a study look like? Some of the more theoretically convincing considerations of contemporary youth culture have located youth on a desolate post-industrial terrain of hopelessness (Hall, 1997), and such studies, rooted in the wastelands of industrial society, must surely take precedence over art school-inspired fashionistas with their obsession with (hair)style over substance (see S. Cohen, 1980). However, the bizarre conglomeration of historical forces that have had an impact upon East London, an area with a begrudging relationship with industrialism and the cultures and dubious rewards of heavy industry (Hobbs, 1988), require a set of sociological inquiries that commence with the knowledge that the shadows of industrialism have been replaced not by a void, but by edifices of glass and concrete that mock the area's not inconsiderable history of radical politics, union activism and struggle, as well as racism, everyday entrepreneurship and impudent, at times cartoonish, resistance (Hobbs, 1988: ch. 5).

Into this mix we now have to consider that 36 per cent of the population of Tower Hamlets are Muslim, and that the long-standing existence of British South Asian communities across East London requires any research into dissociation in East London to place the experiences of Asian youth to the forefront. Asian youths now contribute considerably to the street life of Tower Hamlets, and as a cultural force and a vehicle for the construction of identity, Asian youths are no longer ignored by cultural commentators (Gardner and Shakur, 1994; Alexander, 2000). The involvement of members of British South Asian communities in crime has been recognized by a number of journalistic (Harris and Wazir, 2002), law enforcement (NCIS, 2003), community activist (Asian Youth Conference, 2003) and academic sources (Webster, 1997; Akhtar and South, 2000). Writers have also mentioned the phenomenon in passing as part of a consideration of, for instance the relationship between drug dealing and social exclusion (Lupton *et al.*, 2002), a designated phase or sector of the overall market (Pearson and Hobbs, 2001), in terms of drug use amongst Asian youth (Patel, 2000; Patel and Wibberley, 2002), or in relation to efforts to deal with drug use within the Asian community (Pearson and Patel, 1998).

Yet the key to understanding East End delinquency has always been its ever-fluctuating economic fortunes, and the impact that these changes have had on a population constantly forced to be adaptable and pragmatic. Just as the decline of Spitalfields' Huguenot community was the result of a shift in global trade (Hollingshead, 1861; Gwynn, 2001), so the working-class population of Spitalfields can be seen to have been consistently exposed to the vagaries of global capitalism (P.G. Hall, 1962) as the population was forced to adapt (Hobbs, 1988: 84–118). Deviant activity is an integral part of these local contextualities and their subsequent adaptations: thriving illegal gambling clubs fading with the introduction of the 1960 Gaming Act, and a booming local hijacking trade disappearing with the queues of lorries that no longer lined Commercial Street. Consequently an exploration of contemporaneous dissociation amongst South Asian youth in Spitalfields would also necessitate locating those aspects of global economies that have an impact upon both legal and illegal opportunity structures, and inevitably this would place the drug trade high on the list of influences (Pearson and Hobbs, 2001; Heal, 2002; Choudrey, 2003; NCIS, 2003). But we must beware, for the contemporary obsession with 'branded' forms of non-British (i.e. non-white) organized crime (Hobbs, 2005) stands in stark contrast to the infamous gangsters and organized crime groups of previous eras. For instance, one of the mysteries of East End crime mythology is why in the first half of the twentieth century the powerful Sabini family were not portrayed as being indicative of an Italian crime threat, or in the 1950s Jack 'Spot' Comer did not represent the rise of the Jewish gangster. Similarly the Kray families' exotic, but by East End standards, mundane ethnic mix, was not regarded as being demonstrative of a particular Romany/Jewish/Irish threat to the social equilibrium of 1960s Bethnal Green.

However, an over-emphasis upon structure, as opposed to agency, would be a mistake, and one commonly made by criminologists seeking to locate the superstructure of criminal enterprise (Williams and Savona, 1995). Exaggerating, usually through cultural ignorance and an over-reliance upon rigid, state-sponsored, and institutionally based research, the knowledge possessed by deviants of criminal networks and economies that exist beyond their immediate enacted environment is a common attribute of criminological inquiry. This is due to the fact that deviant knowledge remains for large swathes of the academic community, special knowledge, with characteristics that are, unlike the mundane, bourgeois, everyday existence of the lecture hall and Senior Common room, exotic, interesting, and born of a spectacular *demi-monde* structured upon a highly specialized epistemological base. And they miss the point. Just as in 1966 a street-corner kid who worked as a gofer in Spitalfields market would not be expected to understand the agricultural policies that enabled certain parts of East Anglia to emerge as dominant in turnips, so it would be a mistake forty years later to expect individuals working at the lower ends of the drug trade to be knowledgeable about global drug economies or their enabling commercial structures (Hobbs, 2005).

It is to David Downes' credit that, while acknowledging the pressures and tensions of the broader political economy, he managed sensitively to locate those areas of the boys' lives that they could make sense of and articulate via activity that at first sight could appear aimless. In this way they were able to interpret structural constraints, whilst never needing fully to understand the forces that create them. Indeed given the boys' institutionalized powerlessness, any attempt by them to acquire knowledge of institutional power beyond the immediately instrumental would have been, in the worst tabloid sense, purely academic.

With national unemployment amongst young male Bangladeshis standing at 40 per cent (National Statistics, February 2006), the relationship between hedonism, leisure, and deviance is likely to be as strong as ever. Further, in any follow-up study, the process of dissociation would have to take into account continued white dominance of middle-class institutions as well as class. Indeed, the class homogeneity of Spitalfields in the 1960s limited the influences of middle-class culture to that of school teachers, probation officers, and social workers whose ideological drive was provided not by the market, but by East London's powerful tradition of municipal socialism (Shepherd, 2002). But now the City has cast more than a casual glance eastwards (Hamnet, 2003), and gentrification has pushed up the price of property, opening the door to writers, artists, and city types with a taste for 'Retrochic' (Samuel, 1994: 83–118), and who now extol the area's gritty urban virtues. For example:

Spitalfields E1
Impressive two/three bedroomed, two bathroomed house in a gorgeous cobbled cul-de-sac with original wood spiral staircase, fireplaces, conservatory, a pretty garden and a secure off-street parking space. Freehold. £950,000.

In 2002 the average price of a terraced house in Spitalfields and Banglatown was £396,000, compared to £103,000 in the rest of England and Wales. Consequently local youth are exposed, not only to the extremes of the housing market in an area where 28 per cent either own or are in the process of buying their homes (compared to 68 per cent in the rest of the country), but also to the range of middle-class cultural mores that now wallow, with various degrees of elegance, in their midst. Combine these recent experiences of Spitalfields with the skeletal chrome and glass shadows of Canary Wharf that spread eastwards into the Royal Docks, along with Stratford's instantaneous property boom in the wake of London's successful bid for the 2012 Olympics (*Evening Standard*, 11 January 2006), and the whimsical notion of East London being a working-class city (Hobbs, 1988) is destroyed for ever.[7]

Paul has worked as a labourer in Spitalfields since the late 1960s: 'I couldn't afford a cardboard box (in Spitalfields). The fucking city people have bought it up. The pubs are shit and you can't get fuck all to eat that you can afford. How do these people get the money to buy flats that used to be council, but now go for fortunes? ... Lottery or fuck all for me.'

So will Asian boys from Spitalfields be disassociating themselves from white, middle-class institutions, the bankers who commute, and the artists who reside? Will they distance themselves from the culture of self-sufficient, family-based entrepreneurship that is still apparent in the leather wholesalers of Spitalfields and the cafes and restaurants of Banglatown, or from their Muslim elders (62 per cent of the population are Muslim)? And what of the 30 per cent white minority? Is the process of dissociation as relevant to the grandchildren of Downes' street-corner deviants?

Not the Only Fruit

Despite the deluge of wealth that has flooded the area, opportunities to engage with the local economy are probably more restricted now than they were forty years ago. Downes' notion

---

[7] Brodie (2004) makes the point that historically the homogenous class imagery associated with East London can be contested, or at least refined. See also Davies (1989).

of dissociation was reliant upon the existence of a local job market that related directly to local perceptions of legitimate forms of masculine work. In turn, this work was sufficiently alienating to drive youths to explore their prospective adult identities via engagement with the severely restricted consumer options on offer, and petty crime and nuisance. Downes' study relies heavily upon the existence of traditional, low-level manual work that was in distinct opposition to the aspirational rhetorics, but not the instrumental functions, of the school system. If anything Downes downplays the importance of traditional work and traditional workplaces, and the role of masculinity is a relatively new concern for sociologists, and is unlikely to have featured in the perspective of a PhD student in the early 1960s.

Old Spitalfields Market, in the heart of London's creative and fashionable E1 quarter near Liverpool Street Station, is currently undergoing a dynamic transformation. Building on their success with the Sunday market, Ballymore, leaseholders of the Grade II listed Horner Buildings which house the market, have laid new plans to expand the existing range of weekday markets to include an exciting mix of fashion, craft, furniture and food stalls. Plans for the future include a gourmet food day, a farmers' market day, an antiques day and a collectors' books and records day.

Part of the markets' attraction for celebrities is the feeling of anonymity in the crowds. Another reason why personalities such as Madonna, Johnny Depp, Cher, Uma Thurman and Kate Moss shop here is because of the markets' diversity. Where else in London can you find market stalls, retail outlets, restaurants and cafes, specialist events and shows, under one roof, with the added benefit of it being open all year round?

The weekday fashion market, held every Friday, is already a resounding success. Renee Pratt, a regular stallholder and twice winner of the Young Designer of the Year Award, said, 'I can't believe it. This place is really booming during the week. I sold out all my stock in one day the last time I was at the fashion market.'

The market has wheelchair access and is buggy friendly.

(<http://www.visitspitalfields.com/osm.html>)

So local kids can now lock into the same urban groove as Madonna. But how do they perceive the influx of bars, and the marketing of Banglatown's restaurants (Eade, 2002)? What sense do they make of the *bourgeois* delights of the craft and cuisine outlets of the indoor Spitalfields market, which closed down as a wholesale fruit and vegetable market in the 1980s, and where 20,000 shoppers now flock on Sundays? Wentworth Street[8] Market which, during the week services lunchtime white-collar workers, and Brick Lane Market, really come alive on Sundays when nostalgic suburbanites revisit their roots in search of a salt beef sandwich, and Japanese and American tourists tread wide-eyed and careful in pursuit of an authentic London experience. But the stall-holders are no cockney wide boys and girls resisting the bailiff by living on their wits. These descendants of Mayhew's costermongers no longer keep their donkeys in the outside privy, but, particularly those with stalls in and around Wentworth Street, arrive from Billericay and Ashford to set out their stalls in late edition 4 × 4s, and sun themselves during the dead month after Christmas in Dubai and Florida.

Ghosts and Phantoms

Dennis Severs' House
18 Folgate Street, Spitalfields, E1
Described as a 'still-life drama' this restored house takes visitors through a range of moods and times—one of the most imaginative and atmospheric buildings in London, a time capsule in which visitors are immersed in a unique form of theatre. Guests are escorted, in total silence, into the candlelit chambers from which, apparently, their 18th and 19th century inhabitants have only just withdrawn. Powerful historical sensations and a family saga add up to a magical journey through time. Unsuitable for children.
(<http://www. dennissevershouse.co.uk>)

We may be less than a decade from replicating rickets and other maladies of deprivation in order to enhance such poverty tourism. The quest for, and subsequent marketing of authenticity, in an area so resonant of Hogarthian and Dickensian London, has been enabled by high property prices and the establishment of Spitalfields as a heritage centre for vital urban experiences such as 'Jack the Ripper Tours' (see Walkowitz, 1992;

---

[8] More commonly known as Petticoat Lane, or as Zangwill romantically entitled it, 'The beloved Lane' (1892: 203).

Samuel, 1994: 114). Estate agents now invoke such edgy icons of British art and Spitalfields residents as Tracy Emin, Gilbert and George, and Jeanette Winterstone to lure property buyers, and the irony of marketing 'live and work' spaces as an innovative, chic, urban lifestyle choice, in an area where for centuries, silk weavers, seamstresses, cabinet makers, and others lived and worked with their families in fetid, cramped, disease-ridden rooms, appears to have escaped all but nostalgics and ghosts. The white, working-class residuum now join the revitalized Huguenot heritage housing of Fleur de Lys Street and Blossom Street as remnants of a once vibrant community, and apart from several museums, only a 'heritage centre', and the Mosque in Brick Lane, originally built as a Huguenot chapel, and later used as a Methodist chapel and Synagogue, before being converted to its current use in 1976, offer any real sense of the enactment of ethnic succession that defines the proletarian inheritance sweated into the cobblestones of now gentrified streets.

Mudlarks

Further east, long established Black, White and Asian communities that had matured literally in the shadows of huge ships, are now dwarfed by Canary Wharf (see Foster, 1999) one of capitalism's more Disneyesque developments (Hobbs, 1988: 217–23), an 86 million square feet site where 63,000 people now work, and property prices have tripled in a decade. The process of modernization so apparent throughout the East End has even stretched to renaming large chunks of Tower Hamlets as part of the marketing of the area. While Brick Lane has become *Banglatown*, those large chunks of Poplar, Limehouse, and Isle of Dogs who share the E14 postcode shrouded by Canary Wharf's shadow, and whose living rooms are lit at night by the aircraft warning light which flashes 40 times a minute at the top of the 800 foot *One Canada Square* (the tallest building in Britain), are increasingly referred to as *Canary Wharf*. This confection, whose gesture to the working river is little more than an estate agent's acknowledgement of the potential value of heritage chic, effectively eliminates the cultural histories of those who dug out the docks, and worked on and around the river and its companion industries, and this repackaging of labour's inheritance can be observed all over East London. The Bryant and May factory in Bow, where in 1888 women workers famously organized to oppose the deadly conditions in which they worked (Stafford, 1961; Fishman, 1988; Charlton, 1999), is now *Bow Quarter*, a chic housing development. Similarly, the entire East London riverside, the site of epic disputes such as the 1889 Dockers' tanner strike (Champion, 1890), culminating in the strikes of the 1960s that finally killed off the obscenity of casualization (Howie, 1986), now constitutes an especially grotesque Klondike for property developers (Pawley, 1986).

Dockers Tanner Rd, Isle of Dogs, E14 £240 pw
Modern two double bedroom apartment with superb views over Millwall Dock and sailing club. The accommodation boasts modern fitted kitchen with appliances, two bathrooms (1 en-suite), reception room with balcony and two double bedrooms.

(Estate agents's blurb)

Keep moving eastwards and the solidly proletarian traditions of the London Borough of Newham are being rapidly erased in preparation for the 2012 Olympics, proximity to the *Olympic Village* being a more marketable feature than high crime rates, poor education, high infant mortality, and a general sense of tension that even the most coked up *flaneur* or greed-deluded estate agent would have difficulty in mistaking for urban *joie de vivre*.[9]

While there has been a population shift eastwards for many years (Hobbs, 1988), the current rebranding of the East End has accelerated this process and created enormous pressures amongst locals which are apparent in everyday conversations. Spitalfield's Asian youths talked of escaping to Ilford, and white youths of moving further East, to Chigwell or Epping (Watt, 2004).

---

[9] In the three months immediately after the 6 July announcement that London had won their Olympic bid, property prices in Newham rose by 10 per cent (*Evening Standard*, 16 November 2005). To put this in context, however, readers will note that international courier company DHL, who were one of the first companies to set up in Baghdad after the fall of Saddam, and who deliver in Afghanistan, decided that it was unsafe to make deliveries to Canning Town and Custom House, which are neighbourhoods of Newham.

The older residents were waiting for the coaches to take them to day-care centres, and for ambulances to deliver them to outpatients' departments. I will be forever in the debt of my good friend of forty years, Graham Hurley, for uttering one night while driving eastwards on the A13, 'Thames Gateway my arse!'.

'Bravos, Bullies and River Vultures'[10]

Not only labour history, but the very bricks and mortar of local family and social life have been eliminated. This makes it problematic for East Enders trying to explain to sons and daughters what their grandmother did for a living, and why she suffers from arthritis, how strikes were conducted, and how great-grandad was chased by a mounted policeman at the Battle of Cable Street, or to show them where great-great-grandad was crushed and crippled between packing cases while working in the docks, and where uncle was chased by skinheads. It makes it difficult to point out the hospital where Mum worked, to explain why Dad got sick, why the neighbourhood died and so much more. The gentrification of white history,[11] the Disneyfication of Asian history (Eade, 1996), and the invisibility of Afro-Caribbean history (Gilroy, 1987: Ch. 1) have created the impression in the East End of London of a blank screen onto which contemporary capital can cast images of past and present as cartoon-like as those drawn of the area's future: a future of 'samosas, saris, and steel bands' (Younge, 2005), adjacent to a themed, gated community where the river Thames is no more than a very large water feature.

The boys of Downes' study knew their limitations. The parameters of their world were clearly defined, for family, work, and community were bound within long-established precedents. As Zorbaugh noted when writing of 'Little Hell', local control has always been negotiated in terms of personal relationships

---

[10] Bermant, 1975: 25.

[11] One of the really strange realities of white working-class heritage in East London is the carefully preserved remnants of dockland. Especially within those parts of the old docks that now sit within sniffing distance of tourist traps such as the Tower of London, seemingly random bits of wall, or a gate, stand as some kind of memorial to the past amongst warehouses and wharfs now celebrated as up-market 'loft living'.

(1929: 177). However, particularly in East London, where the formal institutional structures were built on casualization, self-employment and flexibility (P. Cohen, 1972; Hobbs, 1988), the relationships of the street and pub were mediated through a uniquely informal political economy. The utter destruction of so much of this political economy, coupled with the uncertainties surrounding the fragmented but exclusionary nature of its replacement, with its, 'lumps of labor, pieces of work...' (Sennett, 1998: 9), means that the sociological exploration of youth dissociation within the context of the destruction of so much of this iconic, ironic negotiated order, comprises a fascinating, and unpredictable prospect.

With the success of the Respect Party in the 2005 General Election sparking memories of the area's radical social democratic past embodied in individuals such as Phil Piratin, the Communist MP elected in 1945, and the area's continued association with the far right British National Party,[12] political conflict and dislocation appear inevitable, and the cosy imagery of a cultural melting pot (Bermant, 1975) should be dispensed with once and for all to be replaced by a recognition that this is an area '...racially and class demarcated into white spaces and Asian spaces, middle-class and working-class' (Sharma, 2005), a cauldron of vibrant discontent, constantly augmented by new arrivals.[13]

In Poplar, Bengali parents escort their children carefully to school past the windows of flats and pubs adorned by nylon flags of St George.[14] The previous night the half-full pub had paid scant attention to the football on Sky. The sign on the door says 'No Travellers', but everybody knows what that means. The white clientele use the pub as a bunker to shelter from the storm. One of the players featured in the televised game is a local boy

---

[12] Although Fascist groups are no longer as overt on the streets of Spitalfields as they were in the 1970s and 1980s, they have far from disappeared.

[13] In the early hours of an unusually warm October morning in Poplar, I observed a two-hour running fight between some Kosovan men and a younger coalition of white and Bengali youth. The Kosovan battle cries were in English with Jamaican accents (see Zorbaugh's quote from a newspaper report of a fight between Persians in Chicago (1929: 15)).

[14] These were given away free by a tabloid newspaper during 'Euro 2004'.

and a renowned racist, but nobody in the pub boos when he gets the ball, and nobody seems too bothered when the commentator stumbles, for the umpteenth time, over the pronunciation of an African player's name. Try telling the half-a-dozen Asian kids patrolling the damp streets on chopper bikes, or the young black man wearing a Nike rain jacket over his security guard uniform that they are 'taking over the area'.

As the Gold Coast pressurizes the slum, so the riverside communities are colonized and the City continues to creep into Spitalfields. Here the parasites of the 'cultural quarter' press the locals for space and resources, and the area's youth become alienated and ultimately ostracized by *bourgeois* colonists. Time spent in Spitalfields, especially at night, confirms that the area's youth have responded in not dissimilar fashion to their predecessors, and late night noise, vandalism, and criminal damage are common complaints by Spitalfields residents of all classes. However, the local night-time economy is now such a prominent feature, that differentiating between drunken artists or businessmen and dissociated working- class youth is problematic, although local youths are invariably better dressed. Indeed the area's historical connections with leisure and vice are also being periodically revitalized, as this notice from 2002 indicates:

THE CONCERNED RESIDENTS OF SPITALFIELDS(CROS)
SAY NO!
TO THE PROPOSED 2AM STRIP VENUE
ON COMMERCIAL STREET E1

NO! to increased night time noise disruption—especially after 11.00 pm

NO! to the encouragement of more prostitution in to the locality

NO! to the potential of more drug peddling

Big business requires venues for the vices of its stressed out workers, and while strip clubs and pole dancing have no place in the leafy suburbs, the East End has been used as a base for 'noxious industries' for centuries (Bermant, 1975: 11; Hobbs, 1988: 91).

Spitalfields is a twenty-first-century *flaneur*'s delight. The streets are alive, vibrant, a little dangerous and stink of both money and its lack. The rat runs and desperate poverty that blights the lives of so many of the area's residents have not evaporated as a result of its proximity to an overheated property market. Yet Spitalfields is no longer in the shadow of the City of London, but is instead joined by the hip to a square mile that fetishizes the area's history, trivializing the flesh, blood, and bones of the successive working-class communities that created it. Rose-tinted analysis is especially stomach churning when applied to locations long associated with vice, organized crime, poverty and deprivation, but it is clear from Downes' study that, certainly for the white, working-class majority, 1960s Britain was, by today's chaotic standards, settled, and relatively secure. Downes' detailed exploration of social order confirms that, despite East London's long-term demonization, white teenage boys in the mid-1960s were not only beneficiaries of post-war social improvements that were apparent in working-class communities all over Britain, but were also an integral part of a very distinct social order based upon the changing contexts of peer relationships, family, community, leisure, and economic prospects (Hood and Joyce, 1999).

The context of Downes' original analysis, was of an area of single-class residence, with an emphasis upon integration and conformity, immune to bourgeois influence, where the middle classes entered only if they were part of the administration of education, criminal justice, or welfare. Now, however, neither new groups seeking to settle in the East End, nor long-term inhabitants can continue to depend upon natural settlement where, 'each new increment is added to the population... it does not at random locate just anywhere, but it brings about a resifting of the whole mass of human beings, resulting finally in the anchoring of each to a milieu that, if not most desirable, is at any rate least undesirable' (Wirth, 1928: 283). *Bourgeois* colonists, callow youths dressed in black and toting messenger bags tightly across their chests, are finding a foothold on the housing market by snapping up ex-council flats. Corporate letting agencies join the queue along with empty nesters from the suburbs and city types reluctant to use the Tube. All these and more are contesting with the working classes for space in a place traditionally despised and feared (Hobbs, 1988: 84–118), now suddenly desired, and rendering problematic the applicability of the notion of a single-class zone of transition to such a complex post-industrial setting.

Concussion: From Banglatown to Olympus (via Canning Town)

The eternal recurrence of poverty, immigration, unemployment, and vice is a remarkably consistent feature of the East End, and such consistency begs questions that have yet to be adequately addressed by empirical investigation. What sense do black and Asian youths make of living in the graveyard of industries that excluded their mothers and fathers, and whose workers marched with Enoch Powell, a former Conservative Member of Parliament, for the repatriation of their families (Schoen, 1977: 37)? What sense do young men and women of East London make of the fierce seduction of contemporary capital, which promises little but more of the same (Heywood, 2004)? Does contemporary youth still merge periodically into street-corner groups concerned with low-level criminality and short-run hedonism, or are gangs, in the classical sense formulated by Thrasher (1927), finally with us in the United Kingdom (Sanders, 2002; Baker and Benjamin, 2003; Aldridge and Medina, 2005)?[15] More specifically, given the replacement of stable industrial cultures with the realities of a global consumer culture, what impact has this made upon Downes' contention that it is local delinquent responses that should occupy our attention? While insular Poplar boys of the mid-1960s cited malignant influences from as far away as nearby Plaistow, their contemporary equivalents are subjected to the full force of global capitalism and its nodes of marketized youth transgression with an immediacy that is stunning (Slater and Tonkiss, 2001: 167–8; K. D. Hall, 2002: 8). Further, de-industrialization has been accompanied by the dissolution of traditional, essentially informal forms of social control (P. Cohen, 1972; Hobbs, 1995; Winlow, 2001), as well as the subsequent increase in state surveillance of youth (Coleman, 2004), and these political and economic changes will be as influential upon contemporary, transgressive, youthful

---

[15] I suspect that in their determination to establish gangs as a British phenomenon, future researchers will discard Thrasher's original criteria and invent a new definition. If this should occur, the subsequent tone of media reporting of gangs is almost certain to further stigmatize ethnic communities and their youth (Alexander, 2000; Tovares, 2002).

street manifestations as were full employment and social restraint in the 1960s.

From what is apparent on the night-time streets of Tower Hamlets, East London youths remain adept at transforming entrepreneurial competence into cultural capital (Bourdieu 1977: 186). Certainly the pragmatic entrepreneurial knowledge that is a deeply embedded aspect of East London's working-class inheritance (Hobbs, 1988), indicates that, despite the continuous devastation that roars through and around the area, a shared feel for a 'particular, historically determined game—a feel which is acquired in childhood, by taking part in social activities... may offer an expressive yet instrumental solution' (Bourdieu, 1990: 2). Are East Enders still players?

If the answer is affirmative, and this analysis is right, then our notion of cultural inheritance is pretty resilient, surviving post-industrialism, post-colonialism, and displaying an almost mystical,'... permanent capacity for invention, indispensable if one is to be able to adapt to indefinitely varied and never completely identical situations' (ibid). At the core of *The Delinquent Solution* lies a fierce rejection of American theories of delinquency, particularly those stemming from Mertonian conceptions of blocked aspirations in the context of the American Dream. But is the dream now with us? With the breakdown of so many of the consensual frameworks that structured post-war Britain, and the emergence of a multiplicity of electronic jungles of consumption, are contemporary East End youth now status-frustrated, or are they sufficiently cynical of late capitalism to be alienated (Downes, 1966: 236–41)? Indeed with much youth-orientated consumption focused upon home-based objects of desire, such as *X Box* and *Playstation*, it is an intriguing prospect to consider how dissociation, which was largely a device with which Downes exposed an anomic reaction to leisure opportunities, might play out in an era defined by engagement with virtual, rather than street-corner society.

With Canary Wharf mimicking Manhattan, and new configurations of immigrant youth emerging, is there any possibility of retaining a notion of a distinctively 'British' youth response to capitalism?. Most importantly for a group who are no longer equipped with the contradictory tools of assimilation and resistance afforded to previous generations by organized labour and their associated agencies, how do they negotiate class society? *The Delinquent Solution* was a pivotal text in the sociology of youth culture, and in its careful unravelling of the realities of being young in the 1960s Downes succeeded in contradicting some of the crude stereotyping of working-class youth, and in its place created a complex picture of a rich culture that was both oppositional and subservient. Perhaps dissociation could be a tool of exploration for understanding twenty-first-century East End youth. If so we will be lucky if it is wielded by a researcher and writer of David Downes' sense, sensitivity, and commitment.

Bibliography

Abrams, M. (1959) *The Teenage Consumer*, London Press Exchange, Paper 5, (Routledge and Kegan Paul: London).
Ackroyd, P. (2000) *London: The Biography* (Vintage: London).
Akhtar, S. and South, N. (2000) ' "Hidden from Heroin's History": Heroin Use and Dealing within an English Asian Community—A Case Study' in M. Natarajan and M. Hough (eds.), *Illegal Drug Markets: From Research to Prevention Policy* (Crime Prevention Studies, vol. 11) (Criminal Justice Press, Monsey, NY).
Aldridge, J. and Medina, J. (2005) 'Youth Gangs in an English City: Social Exclusion, Drugs and Violence' (forthcoming) (Economic and Social Research Council: London).
Alexander, C. (2000) *The Asian Gang. Ethnicity, Identity and Masculinity* (Berg: Oxford).
Asian Youth Conference (2003) House of Commons, 20 September 2003.
Aust, R. and Smith, N. (2003) *Ethnicity and Drug Use: Key Findings from the British Crime Survey* (Home Office: London).
Baker, A. and Benjamin, L. (2003). *A Survey of Gangs in London*. Paper presented during the VI Annual Meeting of the Eurogang Network, Straubing, Germany.
Bermant, C. (1975) *Point of Arrival* (Eyre Methuen: London).
Bourdieu, P. (1977) *Outline of a Theory of Practice* (Cambridge University Press: Cambridge).
—— (1990) *In Other Words: Essays Towards a Reflexive Sociology* (Polity Press: Cambridge).
Bradley, D. (1992) *Understanding Rock 'n' Roll: Popular Music in Britain 1955–1964* (Open University Press: Buckingham).

Brodie, M. (2004) *The Politics of the Poor: The East End of London 1885–1914* (Oxford University Press: Oxford).
Carter, M.P. (1962) *Home, School and Work* (Pergamon Press: London).
Centers, R. (1949) *The Psychology of Social Classes: a Study of Class Consciousness* (Princeton University Press: Princeton, NJ).
Charlton, J. (1999) *It Just Went like Tinder; the Mass Movement and New Unionism in Britain 1889: a Socialist History* (Redwords: London).
Champion, H.H. (1890) *The Great Dock Strike* (Swan Sonnaschein: London).
Choudrey, B. (2003) 'Asian Gangs Targeting Heroin Trade', (<http://www.bbcnews.co.uk>).
Clarke, J., Hall, S., Jefferson, T. and Roberts, B. (1976) 'Subcultures, Cultures and Class' in Hall, S. and Jefferson, T. (eds.), *Resistance through Rituals* (Hutchinson: London), pp. 9–74.
Cloward, R. and Ohlin, L. (1960) *Delinquency and Opportunity: A Theory of Delinquent Gangs*, (Free Press: New York).
Cohen, A. K. (1955) *Delinquent Boys. The Culture of the Gang* (Free Press: New York).
Cohen, P. (1972) *Subcultural Conflict and Working Class Community, Working Papers in Cultural Studies*, No. 2 (University of Birmingham, Centre for contemporary Studies: Birmingham).
Cohen, S. (1973) *Folk Devils and Moral Panics* (Paladin: London).
—— (1980) Introduction to the 1980 edn. of S. Cohen, *Folk Devils and Moral Panics* (Paladin: London).
Coleman, R. (2004) *Reclaiming the Streets: Surveillance, Social Control and the City* (Willan: Cullompton).
Corrigan, P. (1979) *Schooling the Smash Street Kids* (Macmillan: London).
Crang, M. (1998) *Cultural Geography* (Routledge: London).
Davidson, E. (2003) *Joey Pyle: Notorious—The Changing Face of Organised Crime* (Virgin Books: London).
Davies, J. (1989) ' "Jennings" Buildings and the Royal Borough: The Construction of the Underclass in Mid-Victorian Britain', in Feldman, D. and Stedman-Jones, G. (eds.), *Metropolis: Images and Representations of London Since 1800* (Routledge: London).
Dennis, N. Henriques, F. and Slaughter, C. (1956) *Coal is our Life* (Eyre and Spottiswode: London).
Downes, D. (1966) *The Delinquent Solution: A Study in Subcultural Theory* (Routledge and Kegan Paul: London).

Eade, J. (1996) 'Ethnicity and the Politics of Cultural Difference' in T. Ranger. Y. Samad and O. Stuart (eds.), *Culture, Identity and Politics* (Avebury: Aldershot).

—— (2002) 'Adventure Tourists and Locals in a Global City: Resisting Tourist Performances in London's "East End"', S. Coleman and M. Crang (eds.), *Tourism: Between Place and Performance* (Berghahn Books: New York) pp. 128–39.

Fishman, W.J. (1988) *East End 1888: A Year in a London Borough Among the Labouring Poor* (Duckworth: London).

Foster, J. (1999) *Docklands: Cultures in Conflict, Worlds in Collision* (UCL Press: London).

Gardner, K. and Shakur, A. (1994) 'I'm Bengali, I'm Asian and I'm Living Here', in R. Ballard (ed.), *Desh Pardesh: The South Asian Experience in Britain* (C. Hurst and Co: London).

Gavron, K., Dench, G., and Young, M. (2006) *The New East End: Kinship, Race and Conflict* (Profile: London).

Gillet, C. (1983) *The Sound of the City: The Rise of Rock and Roll* (2nd edn, Souvenir Press: London).

Gilroy, P. (1987) *There Aint No Black in the Union Jack* (Hutchinson: London).

Gwynn, R. D. (2000) *Huguenot Heritage, The History and Contributions of the Huguenots in Britain* (Sussex Academic Press: Brighton).

Hall, K. D. (2002) *Lives in Translation: Sikh Youth as British Citizens* (Pennsylvania Press: Pennsylvania).

Hall, P.G. (1962) *The Industries of London since 1861* (Hutchinson: London).

Hall, S. (1997) 'Visceral Cultures and Criminal Practices' 1 *Theoretical Criminology*, 453–78.

Hallsworth, S. (2005) *Street Crime* (Willan: Cullompton).

Hamnett, C. (2003) *Unequal City; London in the Global Arena* (Routledge: London).

Harris, P. and Wazir, B. (2002) 'Deadly heroin gangs carve up lucrative new trade', *The Observer*, 14 July 2002.

Heal, A. (2002) 'A Strategic Assessment of Crack Cocaine Use and Supply in South Yorkshire' (South Yorkshire Police and Partnerships Drug Strategy Unit: Sheffield).

Hebdige, D. (1979) *Subculture: The Meaning of Style* (Methuen: London).

—— (1988) *Hiding in the Light: On Images and Things* (Routledge: London).

Hayward, K. (2004) *City Limits: Crime, Consumer Culture and the Urban Experience* (GlassHouse: London).

Hill, S. (1976) *The Dockers* (Heineman: London).

Hobbs, D. (1988) *Doing the Business: Entrepreneurship, Detectives and the Working Class in the East End of London* (Clarendon Press: Oxford).
—— (1995) *Bad Business* (Oxford University Press: Oxford).
—— (2005) 'Organised Crime in the UK', in C. Fijnaut and L. Paoli (eds.), *Organised Crime in Europe* (Springer: Netherlands) 413–34.
Hollingshead, J. (1861) *Ragged London in 1861* (Smith Elder and Co: London).
Hoggart, R. (1957) *The Uses of Literacy* (Chatto and Windus: London).
Hood, R. and Joyce, K. (1999) 'Three Generations: Oral Testimonies on Crime and Social Change in London's East End' 39 *British Journal of Criminology* 136–60.
Howie, Lord (1986) 'Dock Labour History' in R. J. M. Carr (ed.), *Dockland* (NELP/GLC: London).
Katz, J. and Jackson-Jacobs, C. (2003) 'The Criminologists Gang in Markham, I' *The Blackwell Companion to Criminology* (Blackwell: Oxford) 91–124.
Lupton, R., Wilson, A., May, T., Workburdon, H., Turnbull, P. (2002) 'A Rock and a Hard Place: Drug Markets in Deprived Neighborhoods', Home Office Research Study No. 240 (Home Office: London).
Morris, T. (1957) *The Criminal Area* (Routledge and Kegan Paul: London).
National Crime Intelligence Service (NCIS) (2003) *Organised Crime Threat Assessment* (National Crime Intelligence Service: London).
Parker, H. (1974) *View from the Boys, A Sociology of Down Town Adolescents* (David and Charles: Newton Abbott).
Patel, K. (2000) *Using Qualitative Research to Examine the Nature of Drug Use Amongst Minority Ethnic Communities in the UK* (European Monitoring Centre for Drugs and Drug Addiction: Lisbon).
—— and Wibberley, C. (2002) 'Young Asians and Drug Use', 6 *Journal of Child Health Care* 51–9, 1741–2889.
Patrick, J. (1973) *A Glasgow Gang Observed* (Eyre Methuen: London).
Pawley, M. (1986) 'Electric City of Our Dreams' *New Society*, 13 June.
Pearson, G. and Patel, K. (1998) 'Drugs, Deprivation and Ethnicity: Outreach among Asian Drug Users in a Northern English City' 28 *Journal of Drug Issues* 199–224.
—— and Hobbs, D. (2001) 'Middle Market Drug Distribution', Home Office Research Study No. 227 (Home Office: London).
Pearson, J. (1973) *The Profession of Violence* (Granada: London).
Phillimore, P. (1979) 'Dossers and Jake-drinkers: the View from One End of Skid Row' in T. Cook (ed.), *Vagrancy: Some New Perspectives* (Academic Press: London) pp. 29–48.

Rock, P. (2005) 'Chronocentrism and British Criminology' 56 *British Journal of Sociology* 473–91.
Samuel, R. (1994) *Theatres of Memory* (Verso: London).
Sanders, W. (2002) 'Breadren: Exploring the Group Context of Young Offenders in an Inner City English Borough'. 26 *The International Journal of Comparative and Applied Criminal Justice* 101–13.
Sennett, R. (1998) *The Corrosion of Character* (Norton: New York).
Schoen, D.E. (1977) *Powell and the Powellites* (MacMillan: London).
Sharma, A. (2005) 'Rich Mix in Brick Lane' *Rising East*, no. 2.
Shepherd, J. (2002) *George Lansbury: at the Heart of Old Labour* (Oxford University Press: Oxford).
Slater, D. and Tonkiss, F. (2001), *Market Society* (Polity Press: Cambridge).
Stafford, A (1961) *A Match to Fire the Thames* (Hodder and Stoughton: London)
Street, J. (1992) 'Shock Waves: The Authoritative Response to Popular Music' in D. Strinati and S. Wagg (eds.), *Come on Down? Popular Media Culture in Post-war Britain* (Routledge: London).
Thrasher, F. (1927) *The Gang* (University of Chicago Press: Chicago).
Tierney, J. (2001) 'Audits and Crime and Disorder: Some Lessons from Research' 3 *Crime Prevention and Community Safety: An International Journal*, no. 2.
Tovares, R.D. (2002) *Manufacturing the Gang* (Greenwood Press: Los Angeles).
Walkowitz, J.R. (1992) *City of Dreadful Delight: Narratives of Sexual Danger in Late-Victorian London* (University of Chicago Press: Chicago).
Watt, P. (2004) 'Narratives of Urban Decline and Ethnic Diversity: White Flight and the Racialisation of Space in London and South East England' (Countering Urban Segregation Conference, Free University of Amsterdam, 14–15 October 2004).
Webster, C. (1997) 'The Construction of British Asian Criminality' 25 *International Journal of the Sociology of Law* 65–86.
White, J. (1980) *Rothschild Buildings: Life in an East End Tenement Block, 1887–1920* (Routledge and Kegan Paul: London).
Williams, P. and Savona, E. (eds.) (1995) 'The United Nations and Transnational Organised Crime' 1 *Transnational Organised Crime*, no. 3.
Willis P. (1997) *Learning to Labour: How Working Class Kids Get Working Class Jobs* (Saxon House: London).
Winlow, S. (2001) *Badfellas: Crime, Tradition and New Masculinities* (Berg: Oxford).
Wirth, L. (1928) *The Ghetto*. (University of Chicago Press: Chicago).

Young, J. (1971) *The Drugtakers* (Paladin: London).
Young, M. and Wilmott, P. (1957) *Family and Kinship in East London* (Routledge and Kegan Paul: London).
Younge, G. (2005) 'Cricket Test to Citizenship: How the War on Terror is Wrecking Britain's Racial Landscape', Hobhouse Lecture Series, Wednesday 30 November 2005, LSE.
Zangwill, I (1892) *Children of the Ghetto* (Heinemann: London).
Zorbaugh, H. (1929) *The Gold Coast and the Slum* (University of Chicago Press: Chicago).

6

Opportunity Makes the Thief-Taker: The Influence of Economic Analysis on Crime Control

Lucia Zedner[1]

Introduction

Theoretical reflection, pure research, and the very attempt to understand the root causes of deviance have increasingly been replaced by anti-theoretical and avowedly pragmatic policy-oriented endeavours. Emblematic is *Opportunity Makes the Thief*, a 1998 position paper written for the Home Office by Marcus Felson and Ron Clarke. In it, the authors contend '[c]riminological theory has long seemed irrelevant to those who have to deal with offenders in the real world'. They charge criminology's focus on offenders with producing 'a lop-sided picture of the causes of crime'.[2] In its place they espouse a 'practical theory' for reducing crime, which, by contrast, is applauded as 'readily understandable', 'down to earth', and 'far more tangible and immediately relevant to everyday life'.[3] Felson and Clarke insist 'Criminologists no longer need be

---

[1] Thanks are due to Joshua Getzler, Benjamin Goold, and Carolyn Hoyle for their most helpful comments and criticisms. I also gratefully acknowledge the support of the British Academy for a two-year Research Readership, during which leave this chapter was written.
[2] Felson, M. and Clarke, R.V., *Opportunity Makes the Thief: Practical Theory for Crime Prevention*, Police Research Series No. 98 (London: Home Office, 1998) 1.   [3] Felson and Clarke (n. 2 above), 2 and 3.

confined to abstractions or discussion of class, or race or intelligence quotients. They can deal with the here-and-now of everyday life.'[4] The clear implication is that discussion of social, demographic, or economic factors is an academic indulgence of little consequence for those engaged in the hard reality of controlling crime. Dedicated to the silver bullet[5] of opportunity reduction, this literature declares itself singularly uninterested in why people turn to crime in the first place. Instead they argue that 'opportunity is a "root cause" of crime'; that opportunity plays a role in causing all crime (not just common property crime); that crime opportunities are highly specific (depending upon different constellations of opportunities for each type of offence); that crime opportunities are concentrated in time and space (creating dramatic differences between one address and another, one hour and another); and that they depend upon everyday movements or activity (by offenders and their targets).[6] They posit a central role for opportunity also in the observation that one crime produces opportunities for another (burglary, for example, creates opportunities for buying and selling stolen goods); that some products (particularly those of high value and low inertia) offer more tempting crime opportunities; and that social and technological changes produce new crime opportunities (particularly in the growth and marketing of new goods). These observations lead them to propose opportunity reduction as the primary tool of crime prevention. They further deny that reducing opportunities displaces crime and claim instead that reduced opportunity in one location can lead to a 'diffusion of benefits' to nearby times and places. Finally, opportunity theory is sold as a means 'to reduce crime immediately'[7] and promoted as a means of escaping criminological abstractions and interest in more remote causes of crime. This rejection of academic theorizing is similarly reflected in subsequent Home

---

[4] Felson and Clarke (n. 1 above), 33.
[5] To borrow from Marx, G. T., 'The Engineering of Social Control: The Search for the Silver Bullet' in Peterson (ed.), *Crime and Inequality* (Stanford, Calif.: Stanford University Press, 1995).
[6] Felson and Clarke (n. 2 above), v-vi.
[7] Felson and Clarke (n. 2 above), 33.

Office papers whose very titles, for example—*Not Rocket Science*—broadcast their antipathy to the scientific pretensions of criminological inquiry.[8] They too eschew interest in the larger underlying causes of crime in favour of 'problem-specification' and tactical 'problem-solving' mechanisms.

These texts pose a direct challenge to the sociology of deviance. Whereas sociologists have typically defined 'deviance' as behaviour that is undesirable in relation to social norms,[9] this breed of criminology engages in no such critical inquiry. It is little interested in the meaning of crime, still less does it consider who defines crime or according to what value structures. Crime is taken as a given, both as a classificatory device and in the literal sense of being an acknowledged, ineradicable facet of modern life.[10]

What factors explain this readiness to dismiss the sociological endeavour to understand deviance in favour of the short-termism of opportunity reduction? Is it possible that the sociology of deviance has written itself out of existence? Is it that, always critical and prone to conflict, 'the combatants over the years, in their enthusiasm for the fight, have completely demolished the terrain'?[11] Or is it that this terrain has been conquered by an administrative criminology less interested in addressing the big sociological questions than in satisfying the immediate demands of its paymasters for cheap and easy pragmatic solutions? The sociologically-minded scholar may dismiss the administratively-minded as 'a kind of specialist underlabourer, a technical specialist'[12] but the 'underlabourer' is equally quick

---

[8] For example, Dhiri, S. and Brand, S., *Analysis of Costs and Benefits: Guidance for Evaluators* (London: Home Office, 1999); Read, T. and Tilley, N., *Not Rocket Science? Problem-solving and Crime Reduction*, Crime Reduction Series Paper 6 (London: Home Office, 2000).

[9] Lermack, P., 'Review of Understanding Deviance' (1999) 9 *Law and Politics Book Review* 141–3: 141.

[10] A view articulated most fully in Felson, M., *Crime and Everyday Life* (3rd edn, London: Sage, 2002).

[11] Sumner, C., *The Sociology of Deviance: An Obituary* (Buckingham: Open University Press, 1994) ix.

[12] Garland, D. and Sparks, R. 'Criminology, Social Theory and the Challenge of Our Times' in Garland and Sparks (eds.), *Criminology and Social Theory* (Oxford: Oxford University Press, 2000) 18.

to dismiss his critic as a self-indulgent, abstract 'head-in-the-clouds' theoretician.

In this chapter, I shall argue that, despite its professed pragmatism, opportunity theory has deep theoretical underpinnings. Chief amongst them is the influence of economic analysis or, more precisely, rational choice theory.[13] Crudely put, rational choice theory models behaviour by assuming that humans act intentionally and rationally; that they are purposive and goal-orientated; that they have sets of hierarchically ordered preferences, or utilities; and that, in deciding how to behave, they seek to maximize utility.[14] Both its core assumptions and the tools with which rational choice theory analyses human behaviour have had a profound impact not only in criminology but also in neighbouring social science disciplines. It has, with justification, been described as 'nothing short of the invasion of economic man ... the ultimate imperialist assault of economics on sociology—the subordination of *homo sociologicus* to *homo economicus*'.[15] This characterization holds true also for opportunity theory. Rather than being vanquished by economics, however, it is arguably the opportunity theorists who borrow, even plunder, economic theory without necessarily adhering to the operating assumptions or integral constraints of the highly stylized, abstract models upon which it is based.[16] Given their willingness to play fast-and-loose with these assumptions, it is questionable whether economic analysis has gained such sway among criminal policy-makers on its intrinsic merits; because it furnishes persuasive explanations for the apparent failure of sociologies of deviancy to 'do anything' about crime; or because it is simply a convenient means of validating political

---

[13] Newman, G., Clarke, R.V. and Shoham, S. G. (eds.), *Rational Choice and Situational Crime Prevention: Theoretical Foundations* (Ashgate: Dartmouth, 1997).

[14] There are myriad versions of rational choice theory: this list simply enumerates the basic assumptions to which most adhere.

[15] Baert, P., *Social Theory in the Twentieth Century* (Cambridge: Polity Press, 1998) 154.

[16] Posner, R., 'An Economic Theory of the Criminal Law' (1985) 85 *Columbia Law Review* 1193–231.

preferences. Certainly the fundamental premise of individual responsibility and choice mirrors the larger political environment of neo-liberalism more closely than its sociological predecessors.

This chapter charts how the sociology of deviance's influence in policy-circles has declined as a simplified form of economic analysis has emerged as key driver of crime control policies. Concomitant to this shift is the displacement of larger inquiry into the causes of crime by a narrower, instrumental concern with crime reduction. It goes on to explain the present vogue for the quick fix of opportunity theory by reference to a convergence of intellectual fashion and political style. The intellectual dominance of economics coincides with the managerialist tendencies of modern political life to make thief-taking[17] an activity predicated upon opportunity theories and, itself, an opportunistic endeavour.

Tough on the Causes of Crime

In order to grasp the degree of rupture represented by the championing of economic analysis, it is worth saying a little about the sociological schools of deviance that have predominated until recently. The sociology of deviance is a broad church embracing multiple different interpretations, schools of thought, and diverse value systems bound only by their common interest in the substantive topic of crime and its causes. That attempts to understand deviance have been characterized by conflict and dispute more than coherence of approach is testimony to the rich theoretical underpinnings and strong political convictions of those engaged in the endeavour.[18] Its flourishing in Britain may be traced back to the first National Deviancy Conference (NDC) held in York in 1968. This was the first

---

[17] To revive an eighteenth-century forebear of modern crime reduction strategies, Zedner, L., 'Policing Before and After the Police: The Historical Antecedents of Contemporary Crime Control' (2006) 46 *British Journal of Criminology* 78–96.

[18] Downes, D., 'Promise and Performance in British Criminology' (1978) 29 *British Journal of Sociology* 483–502.

sizeable gathering of sociologists of deviance in Britain and represented a significant shift in the history of British criminology. A provocative and deliberate break with the 'positivist methods and functionalist orthodoxy of much British sociology', the NDC was described by one of its most notable participants as 'an off-shore laboratory for the distillation of ideas fermented in the U.S.A.'.[19] Arguably few in Britain did more to import, disseminate, and develop those ideas than David Downes. Over the course of his career, through his teaching, supervision of doctoral students, and, not least, his writing,[20] Downes introduced generations of budding criminologists to the vitality and excitement of theories that were simultaneously imaginative, critical, and in perpetual, often impassioned debate with one another.

One of the most valued attributes of the sociology of deviance is its breadth and depth of vision. No peddler of reductive explanations or simple solutions, Downes' own work invariably deals in the complexities of social problems and the equally multifaceted means of tackling them. Typical is his characterization of crime as 'a vast, complex and ill-charted array of activities, clumped together on the sole common denominator that they are infractions of the criminal law'.[21] For Downes, understanding deviance is inseparable from understanding the wider sources of misery in modern society. Crime is ineradicably linked with the big social and economic problems of poverty, inequality, poor education, housing, and health care. His appreciation of the relationship between these problems and crime springs from a profound sociological understanding of his subject. It springs also from a deeply held political belief in the pillars of the Welfare State—education, the National Health

---

[19] Downes, D., 'The Sociology of Crime and Social Control in Britain 1960–1987' in Rock (ed.), *A History of British Criminology* (Oxford: Oxford University Press, 1988) 46.

[20] From the seminal Downes, D., *The Delinquent Solution: A Study in Subcultural Theory* (London: Routledge & Kegan Paul, 1966), through numerous articles on the sociology of deviance to Downes, D. and Rock, P., *Understanding Deviance* (4th edn, Oxford: Oxford University Press, 2003).

[21] Downes, D., 'What the Next Government Should Do About Crime' (1997) 36 *Howard Journal* 1–13: 1.

Service, economic management, and public sector housing—as the means of reducing the inequalities, insecurities, and poverty that generate crime. In a clarion call to the incoming government in 1997, Downes insisted that tackling crime must entail addressing social problems that are not themselves crime-specific, key amongst which is unemployment. As he argued: 'It has been presumed for far too long that crime, unlike any other form of activity, is somehow unaffected by economic policies and their social consequences.'[22] The social, economic, and cultural sources of crime control thus extend deep into social policy and cannot be supplied by the criminal justice system alone.

Attention to the larger causes of crime has not been entirely absent from the political agenda of the present government. Tony Blair famously declared his early determination to be 'Tough on crime; tough on the causes of crime'. That said, the latter part of his pledge has since been conspicuously downplayed. Subsequent crime control policies arguably have more in common with the 'warfarist' stance of the preceding Conservative regime than this rhetorical pairing might have led one to expect.[23] Downes credits the Labour government with giving greater weight to tackling the social and economic causes of crime than its predecessors, but, with evident reluctance, is obliged to acknowledge that: 'it is the resemblances rather than the differences between the two main parties which have registered'.[24] Perhaps one of the most striking resemblances is Blair's decision to make crime control a central plank of his electoral platform in 1997 and his determination to keep it there in subsequent electoral campaigns. The decision reeks of political opportunism. In seizing the Tory high ground, Blair sought to make law and order his own and, in so doing, to secure electoral success for Labour.

[22] Downes (n. 21 above), 4.
[23] Hoyle, C. and Rose, D., 'Labour, Law and Order' (2001) 72 *Political Quarterly* 76–85: 81.
[24] Downes, D., 'Four Years Hard: New Labour and Crime Control' (2002) 46 *Criminal Justice Matters* 8–9: 8. See also Downes, D. and Morgan, R., 'The Skeletons in the Cupboard: the Politics of Law and Order at the Turn of the Millennium' in Maguire, Morgan and Reiner (eds.), *Oxford Handbook of Criminology* (3rd edn, Oxford: Oxford University Press, 2002) 291ff.

The history of criminologists' continuing attempts to wrest political attention to the causes of crime is also a vital facet of our story.[25] A central feature of Downes and Rock's inquiry in *Understanding Deviance* is the relationship between efforts to understand the causes of crime and their political consequences. The persuasiveness of one form of explanation over another has profound repercussions for public policy. Which theory dominates depends in part upon its inherent validity, in part on the influence of its academic protagonists and its attractiveness to policy-makers. The possibility that sociological theories could supply credibility for well-intentioned policy-making has always been tempered by the counter-risk that theories would be put to ends far from those envisaged by their authors. With dark sardonic wit, Downes elsewhere observes the fulfilment of this risk in respect of the Labour government's response to academic expertise:

New Labour might have based their control policies on an inversion of every criminological warning of the past fifty years. 'Net-widening'—great idea. 'Mesh-thinning'—no problem. 'Penetration' (of state into civil society)—why not? Dangers of increasing inequality?—get real! Doing something about the 'winner/loser culture'? come off it![26]

The uncontrollable potency of ideas or research findings once in the public domain leaves the criminologist, like the sorcerer's unfortunate apprentice, as the helpless onlooker having unleashed a chain of events it has little power to control.[27]

Still more worrisome is the strong possibility that, as academic criminologists become increasingly dependent upon government departments for research funding, the boot will be on the other foot. The exigencies of pleasing the paymasters will

---

[25] See Zedner, L. and Ashworth, A. (eds.), *The Criminological Foundations of Penal Policy: Essays in Honour of Roger Hood* (Oxford: Oxford University Press, 2003) particularly chs. 1, 2, and 4.

[26] Downes, D., 'Four Years Hard: New Labour and Crime Control' (2002) 46 *Criminal Justice Matters* 8–9: 8.

[27] Zedner, L., 'Useful Knowledge? Debating the Role of Criminology in Postwar Britain' in Zedner and Ashworth (eds.), *The Criminological Foundations of Penal Policy* (Oxford: Oxford University Press, 2003) 234.

determine the theoretical frameworks of academic researchers.[28] This chapter will go on to chart a shift from sociological interest in the causes of crime to economic analysis of the means to its efficient reduction. Whether this shift results from changing intellectual fashions or the changing structural arrangements within which criminologists work is debatable. Whilst the dominance of opportunity theory cannot be explained without reference to changes in the macro political landscape that have had a profound impact upon the policy framework,[29] it is arguable that British (though not American) criminologists have tended to underestimate the growing importance of economic analysis of crime control. This chapter will analyse the political environment in which economic analysis flourished, the basic features of the economic approach, and its implications for crime control policy.

Neo-liberalism and the Politics of Managerialism

The neo-liberal politics of the Thatcher era and beyond ushered in a period characterized by fiscal restraint, managerialism in government, consumer-driven policies, and the requirement of value for money. According to Garland, this style of reasoning: 'shaped how criminal justice practitioners make decisions, how they allocate resources and how they deploy their powers. It has changed how institutions control their staff and how they manage their internal actions. It has even affected how criminal justice authorities regard the conduct of offenders, probationers and prisoners.'[30] This paradigm shift manifested itself also in the types of criminological research for which the Home Office was

---

[28] Hillyard, P., Sim, J., Tombs, S. and Whyte, D., 'Leaving a "Stain upon the Silence": Contemporary Criminology and the Politics of Dissent' (2004) 44 *British Journal of Criminology* 369–90.

[29] Loader, I. and Sparks, R., 'Contemporary Landscapes of Crime, Order, and Control: Governance, Risk, and Globalization' in Maguire, Morgan and Reiner (eds.), *Oxford Handbook of Criminology* (3rd edn, Oxford: Oxford University Press, 2002).

[30] Garland, D., *The Culture of Control* (Oxford: Oxford University Press, 2001) 188. Garland labels this 'economic "style" reasoning' but, as he himself argues, it may have more to do with the financial economy than the academic discipline of economics.

prepared to pay. Criminology was co-opted as a collaborator in the managerialist task of pursuing the three 'E's—economy, efficiency, and effectiveness. This pursuit manifested itself most markedly in the increasingly short terms offered by government for research contracts and the concurrent shift away from pure or basic research towards hurried pilots of new measures and 'quick and dirty' evaluative studies of their implementation. Criminologists were steered away from the search for the underlying causes of crime in favour of hastily executed studies whose immediate benefits were readily demonstrable. As I have argued elsewhere: 'The impact of economic reasoning served not only to constrain the ambitions of official criminology but to inform its very thinking.'[31] Typical is this observation by John Croft, former head of the Home Office Research and Planning Unit: 'even if among some policy makers there is still an expectation, originally generated by social scientists some thirty years ago but now abandoned, that criminological research will solve the problems that beset the penal system, realists have adjusted their utilitarian perspective to new horizons'.[32] The 'realists', he went on, have discarded the search for social solutions to the problem of crime in favour of 'identifying options for the more economical and fruitful disposal of limited resources'.[33] This administrative conception of the discipline played down its sociological aspirations to propose a subservient position for criminology as handmaiden to government and obedient servant of the Treasury.

Clearly, this 'administrative criminology', as it became pejoratively known, continued to be distinguished from its academic counterpart. As Downes and Rock observe: '[i]t is constrained by rules of order which need not restrain a university lecturer. People working in official agencies are not expected primarily to be original. They are required to be reliable. To be

---

[31] Zedner (n. 27 above), 222.
[32] Croft, J., 'Criminological Research in Britain' in Tonry (ed.), *Crime and Justice: An Annual Review of Research* (Chicago, Ill: University of Chicago Press, 1983) 273. [33] Croft (n. 32 above), 274.

sure, agencies constantly hanker after new programmes and policies—there is a perennial hunt for the obviously efficient reform.'[34] Perhaps it is this search for efficiency which explains the enthusiastic take-up of rational choice theory within the Home Office when by comparison its influence within the British criminological academy was relatively weak. It may be that the pressures placed upon policy researchers within government circles to be 'efficient' and 'effective' created the conditions of receptivity to the ideas of economic analysis lacking in the freer environment of the universities.

From *Homo Sociologicus* to *Homo Economicus*

The sociology of deviance defines its subject matter by reference to norms from which the behaviour in question departs. As the following quote wryly observes: '[t]hus "deviant" is to a sociologist what "mutant" is to a biologist who studies genetics, or what "psychotic" is to a psychologist'.[35] Historically, sociological theories have attributed deviance to various root causes including degeneration, depravity, insanity, abnormality, and deprivation. This central concern with root causes is now starkly challenged by those who summarily dismiss the entire sociological enterprise. In one swift move Tilly and Laycock, for example, simultaneously acknowledge and write off the sociology of deviance:

[T]he meaning of 'root causes' is not clear. At one level if there were no laws there would be no crime, but this approach would not take us very far. Accepting that crime is a legal construct, research shows that the 'causes' of crime are many and varied—poor parenting, lack of education, poverty, greed, drug addiction, genetic predisposition, and so on. The most significant is, however, opportunity. If there were no opportunities there would be no crimes; the same cannot be said for any of the other contributory causes.[36]

---

[34] Downes, D. and Rock, P., *Understanding Deviance* (4th edn, Oxford: Oxford University Press, 2003) 16.
[35] Lermack (n. 9 above), 141.
[36] Tilley, N. and Laycock, G., *Working out What to Do: Evidence-based Crime Reduction*, Crime Reduction Series Paper 11 (London: Home Office, 2002) 30.

Personal life histories, influence of family, social class, race and gender on offenders' moral compass are excluded from consideration. Characteristic is Felson's claim that: 'it is a mistake to assume that crime is part of a larger set of social evils, such as unemployment, poverty, social injustice, or human suffering'.[37] Instead, crime is regarded as a normal feature of modern social life and its rise driven by increasing availability of opportunities (not least of readily portable, high-value goods) rather than any decline in moral standards. Opportunity theory is heavily influenced by environmental criminology, routine activity theory, and crime pattern theory.[38] Most influential, however, is rational choice theory, an offshoot of economic analysis that extends the ' "economic approach" to other areas of social life'.[39] By sharp contrast to the sociology of deviance, it assumes a rational actor making reasoned decisions within the parameters of choice available to her and within the constraints of her world-view.

A notable feature of decision-making according to rational choice theory is its lack of normativity. Hence obedience to the law is explained not by reference to norms, nor individual reflection upon norms, but according to opportunity costs. Explanations of criminality likewise proceed without reference to norms. Offenders are deemed to be rational utility maximizers and as such: 'are primarily not regarded as deviant individuals with atypical motivations, but rather as simple, normal persons like the rest of us'.[40] This thinking is consistent with the assumption of rational choice theory that all people have similar hierarchies of ordered preferences. Thus it is assumed not only that non-violent offending is commonplace but that it will be committed by most people where the opportunity costs are sufficiently low. Typical is Felson's observation that: 'It is good

---

[37] Felson (n. 10 above), 12.
[38] Felson and Clarke (n. 2 above), 4.
[39] Hindess, B., 'Rational Choice Theory' in Outhwaite and Bottomore (eds.), *Blackwell Dictionary of Twentieth-Century Social Thought* (Oxford: Blackwell Publishers, 1993) 542.
[40] Eide, E., 'Economics of Criminal Behaviour' in De Geest (ed.), *Encyclopedia of Law and Economics* (Ghent: Edward Elgar, 2000) 345.

to teach right from wrong, but you cannot really expect other people to do what you tell them when you aren't watching.'[41] Accordingly, the difficult question is not why people offend but why more do not: 'People are assumed to allocate time to criminal activity until marginal benefits equal marginal costs. For some people marginal benefits are probably always lower than marginal costs, and then we have a law-abiding person.'[42]

The application of the rational choice model to criminality can be traced back to the writings of Adam Smith, William Paley, and Jeremy Bentham[43] but was revived most influentially in a seminal article by Gary Becker entitled 'Crime and Punishment: An Economic Approach' in 1968.[44] His model assumed that an individual will commit an offence if the expected utility is positive and that she will not if it is negative. In lay terms, committing crime is a rational choice where the expected pay-off is higher than its legal alternative (working to earn the goods in question, for example) and higher than the anticipated costs of so doing (including the risk of detection, sanction, etc.). In its pure form, the model assumes that the offender has perfect knowledge of these costs and benefits. The rational offender is endowed with a set of preferences that, evidence to the contrary apart, are assumed to be constant and consistent. Hence recidivism results not from a lack of moral compass or self-control but is to be expected where preferences remain stable and there is no change in the offender's perception of opportunity costs. It follows that it is possible to manipulate preferences by changing opportunity structures. The greater the perceived opportunities for low-risk gain, the more valuable and readily obtainable the goods, and the less protection surrounding them, the more attractive is criminality.

Signalling plays an important role because it may be possible to communicate increased costs to the offender without altering the actual likelihood or severity of punishment. Thus by increasing

[41] Felson (n. 10 above), 15.
[42] Eide, (n. 40 above), 351.
[43] Ehrlich, I., 'Crime, Punishment and the Market for Crime' (1996) 10 *Journal of Economic Perspectives* 43–67: 43.
[44] Becker, G., 'Crime and Punishment: An Economic Approach' (1968) 76 *Journal of Political Economy* 169–217.

the *perceived* probability of detection or severity of punishment, the expected utility derived from crime might be shifted from positive to negative. This calculation assumes, of course, that offenders are risk averse. For the risk-averse offender greater certainty of detection or severity of punishment will tend to deter. Recognition that for some types of offender, and indeed some types of offence (joy-riding would be a good example), the thrill of risk-taking is part of the pleasure requires modification of the model. Yet even acknowledging that individual attitudes towards risk vary and that risk lovers will be less susceptible to increases in certainty of detection or severity of punishment, economic analysis assumes that, overall, increasing the marginal costs of criminality results in fewer crimes.

Economic analysis of crime is a massive industry in North America, yet has attracted relatively little academic interest amongst criminologists in Britain. There is a large American literature applying economic analysis to offending, policing, certainty of detection and arrest, the criminal process and, in particular, plea bargaining, jury deliberation, severity of punishment and deterrence, and victimhood and personal protection.[45] In Britain, by contrast, aside from some limited engagement in respect of studies on deterrence[46] and situational crime prevention,[47] there has been almost no interest by university criminologists in economic theory. Accordingly, it is hardly surprising that when Downes and Rock engage with 'situational' control theories they do so in the context of sociological control theories more generally. Though they acknowledge the growing centrality of rational choice, they attribute its rise to pragmatism. Take their observation that 'the presumption of rationality had a common-sense appeal: that is

---

[45] For an overview see Eide, E., 'Economics of Criminal Behaviour' in De Geest (ed.), *Encyclopedia of Law and Economics* (Ghent: Edward Elgar, 2000) and the twenty-page bibliography that accompanies this entry at <http://encyclo.findlaw.com/>.

[46] von Hirsch, A., Bottoms, A. E., Burney, E. and Wikstrom, P.-O., *Criminal Deterrence and Sentence Severity: An Analysis of Recent Research* (Oxford: Hart Publishing, 1999); Hood, R., *The Death Penalty: A World-Wide Perspective* (3rd edn, Oxford: Clarendon Press, 2002).

[47] von Hirsch, A., Garland, D. and Wakefield, A. (eds.), *Ethical and Social Perspectives on Situational Crime Prevention* (Oxford: Hart Publishing, 2000).

how most people, including politicians and officials, would care to explain their own and others' behaviour'.[48] Whilst they acknowledge the ascendancy in 'intellectual dominance and apparent success of economics',[49] their own analysis of its possibilities and limitations is thoroughly and unapologetically sociological.

It is true that the application of rational choice theory to crime has sociological antecedents. In *Delinquency and Opportunity*, for example, Cloward and Ohlin stressed the importance of the 'relative availability' of opportunities in 'accounting for the individual's readiness to employ illegal alternatives'.[50] And in *Delinquency and Drift*, Matza showed that offenders were less likely to be possessed of a deep motivational commitment to deviance than to drift into misconduct where opportunities presented themselves.[51] Offending was ascribed more to susceptibility to opportunity than innate disposition. Yet control theories more generally have failed to capture the sociological imagination. One possible explanation, proposed by Downes and Rock, is that their logicality and 'sheer obviousness' is inimical to the sociological mind.[52] Whereas earlier sociological studies saw opportunities as mediated through social learning, the 'reasoning criminal' posited by exponents of opportunity theory is a strikingly asocial character devoid of the personal and social characteristics that are the ordinary focus of sociological attention.[53] Thus Cohen observes:

We now have the criminal as consumer and market actor—someone who not only has more rationality than the determined creatures of sociological enquiry, but has *nothing* but choice and rationality. Disembodied from all social context—deprivation, racism, urban

---

[48] Downes and Rock (n. 34 above), 237.
[49] Downes and Rock (n. 34 above), 237.
[50] Cloward, R. A. and Ohlin L. E., *Delinquency and Opportunity: A Theory of Delinquent Gangs* (Glencoe, Ill.: Free Press, 1960) 145.
[51] Matza, D., *Delinquency and Drift* (New York: Wiley, 1964).
[52] Downes and Rock (n. 34 above), 226.
[53] Cornish, D. B. and Clarke, R. V. (eds.), *The Reasoning Criminal: Rational Choice Perspectives on Offending* (New York: Springer, 1986); Cook, P. J., 'The Demand and Supply of Criminal Opportunities' (1986) 7 *Crime and Justice: A Review of Research* 1–27: 3.

dislocation, unemployment are airily listed as—'background factors'—they take their risks, assess their opportunities, have their targets hardened and stay away from others' defensible spaces.[54]

For sociologists of deviance, particularly those working in a broadly Weberian tradition whose primary interest has been to understand the offenders' own sense of what they do and why, this presumption of rationality has seemed an anathema. The 'verstehen' in *Understanding Deviance* seems to be replaced by steadfast indifference to human actors' self-understanding and to operate instead with a universal account of human motivation. Its advocates counter that one of the most powerful attributes of rational choice theory is its ability to generate powerful explanations on the basis of a few relatively simple assumptions.[55] These assumptions also permit one successfully to predict human action in most cases and, to the extent that humans act in unpredictable ways, to provide the means of identifying non-rational elements in human action.

To the criticism that rational choice theory underestimates the irrationality of human action, some proponents have sought to incorporate greater attention to actual human behaviour. Modern behavioural economics acknowledges that individuals operate with bounded rationality, bounded self-interest, and bounded will-power.[56] In so doing it seeks to meet the common objection that classical economics is insufficiently alert to the limits of rationality and indifferent to the insights of psychology and other social science disciplines.[57] Behavioural economics

---

[54] Cohen, S., 'Crime and Politics: Spot the Difference' (1996) 47 *British Journal of Sociology* 1–21: 5.

[55] Posner, R., 'Rational Choice, Behavioural Economics, and the Law' (1998) 50 *Stanford Law Review* 1551–75; Hindess, B., 'Rational choice theory' in Outhwaite and Bottomore (eds.), *Blackwell Dictionary of Twentieth-Century Social Thought* (Oxford: Blackwell Publishers, 1993) 542.

[56] Jolls, C., Sunstein, C., and Thaler, R., 'A Behavioral Approach to Law and Economics' (1998) 50 *Stanford Law Review* 1471–550.

[57] Although it may be that this attempt to take full account of behaviour comes at a cost to the predictive power of the rational choice model. See Posner, R., 'Rational Choice, Behavioural Economics, and the Law' (1998) 50 *Stanford Law Review* 1551–75; Kelman, M., 'Behavioural Economics as Part of a Rhetorical Duet: A Response to Jolls, Sunstein and Thaler' (1998) 50 *Stanford Law Review* 1577–91.

offers the possibility of a more sophisticated understanding of how offenders make systematic errors in computing the costs and benefits of crime. The fact that young offenders, in particular, are radically present-orientated; that they may not be amenable to future rewards nor strongly deterred by any but the most immediate threats; that many lack self-control, are reckless and risk-loving rather than risk-averse; and that supposed deterrents may have currency as badges of honour in their circles can all be fed into economic models without difficulty. Particularly striking is the concept of 'hyperbolic discounting', or tendency of offenders radically to discount temporally distant costs in favour of immediate gains. Insights such as these take greater account of criminological research findings than criminologists acknowledge and have important implications for policy.

The Policy Implications of Economic Analysis

The elegance and simplicity of the rational choice model and its vaunted ability to predict has rendered it an appealing basis for policy-making. As, over the course of the 1980s and 1990s, crime crept up the national policy agenda, the need for an authoritative body of theory capable of ready translation into policy was acute. The combination of a decline of faith in the welfarist orientation of social control theories; the exigencies of managerialism; and the rise of neo-liberalism created a climate ripe for take-over. Economists were not slow to observe the market for their ideas nor reluctant to claim their superior ability to provide the intellectual resources for tackling the crime problem. The following is perhaps more than usually assertive but not untypical of the view that there was a:

> need for a body of policy-relevant knowledge about crime, for theoretical ideas and empirical findings that can be translated into popular discourse and carved into public laws... the professional criminologists, sociologists, political scientists, law professors, public management specialists and self-styled practitioners-scholars who have dominated the field are incapable of meeting this challenge... criminal justice is a field that needs to be conquered by economists.[58]

[58] Dilulio, J.J., 'Help Wanted: Economists, Crime and Public Policy' (1996) 10 *Journal of Economic Perspectives* 3–24: 3.

Setting on one side for the moment, the merits of this claim, let us examine the impact to date of economic analysis on the policy field.

First, to the extent that crimes are conceived not as deviations from moral order or culpable acts in need of punishment, they can be reduced to calculable costs. Understood this way, crime has little to do with the normative threat it poses or the responsibility of the offender and everything to do with the physical, psychological, and material losses it imposes. Thinking about crime in terms of loss reduction requires that victims minimize their exposure to risk.[59] It also requires policy-makers to pay attention to the costs of their own responses. This generally has the benign effect of calling into question expensive penalties whose burden on the Treasury might be reduced by cheaper alternatives. That this is not the invariable outcome of such analysis is evidenced by the following hard-nosed calculation of the costs of imprisonment: 'long-term imprisonment spells geriatric inmates and associated health costs. But many incarcerated persons enter prison with anemic work records, a history of welfare dependence and a fair probability of having to rely on government to pay for their health care whether or not they are incarcerated.'[60] Here the social and psychological costs of imprisonment are sidelined in favour of a ruthlessly monetized form of accounting.

The cost driven turn of economic analysis is mirrored also in the increasingly prudential orientation of crime policies concerned less with responding to crime as a moral wrong than with estimating, preventing, and minimizing losses and insuring against harm.[61] Emphasis on risk assessment has had the effect of promoting a form of 'actuarial justice' concerned primarily with identifying, classifying, and managing suspect populations according to the level of perceived risk they pose.[62] It also has

---

[59] Harel, A., 'Efficiency and Fairness in Criminal Law' (1994) 84 *California Law Review* 1181–229.

[60] Dilulio (n. 58 above), 19.

[61] O'Malley, P., 'Risk, Crime and Prudentialism Revisited' in Stenson and Sullivan (eds.), *Crime, Risk and Justice: The Politics of Crime Control in Liberal Democracies* (Cullompton, Devon: Willan Publishing, 2001).

[62] Feeley, M. and Simon, J., 'Actuarial Justice: The Emerging New Criminal Law' in Nelken (ed.), *The Futures of Criminology* (London: Sage, 1994).

interesting implications for crime control practices. Given the very small percentage of offenders actually subjected to the criminal justice process and the smaller percentage still who face cautioning or conviction, the capacity of penalties to affect the opportunity costs of crime is limited. The remote prospect of suffering a penalty, however harsh, acts as a poor disincentive upon the rational offender faced with the immediate, palpable rewards of offending. Rational choice theory requires greater attention therefore to analysing the situational conditions of offending. Yet empirical evidence that offenders are deterred more by certainty of detection than severity of punishment[63] has done little to counter increasingly punitive penal strategies. One possible explanation may be that susceptibility to the opportunity costs of crime prevention is limited for those whose capacity for rational calculation is dimmed by drugs, drink, or severe personality disorder. These groups tend to be demonized as distinct dangerous classes who must be managed and contained in the mass penal warehouses that are the hallmark of late modern penality.[64] Penal incapacitation denies such people the opportunity of choice of action and in so doing denies them also the opportunity to rejoin the moral consensus by desisting from crime.[65]

In general, however, the natural focus of rational choice theory is on situations rather than individuals, a fact recognized by Downes and Rock's early designation of this model as 'situational control theory'.[66] Situational crime prevention, as it has come to be known more generally, is characterized by a shift in attention away from the processes by which individuals become involved in crime. Typical is the argument by Felson and Clarke

---

[63] Though see Baker, T., Harel, A., and Kugler, T., 'The Virtues of Uncertainty in Law: An Experimental Approach' (2004) 89 *Iowa law Review* 443–94, the possibility that uncertainty is in fact a more potent deterrent than certainty of detection.

[64] Simon, J., 'From the Big House to the Warehouse: Rethinking State Government and Prisons' (1999) 3 *Punishment and Society* 213–34.

[65] Hudson, B., *Justice in the Risk Society* (London: Sage, 2003) 75–6.

[66] In the first edition of *Understanding Deviance* (1982) cited in Clarke, R.V., 'Situational Crime Prevention' in Tonry and Morris (eds.), *Crime and Justice: An Annual Review of Research* (Chicago: University of Chicago, 1995) 95.

that: 'social prevention implies improving people, which we regard as a goal almost sure to produce frustration'.[67] Instead, by targeting the situational aspects of crime, it focuses upon the immediate conditions under which offences occur. Informed by so-called 'routine activity approach', it identifies three minimal preconditions of crime: 'a likely offender, a suitable target, and the absence of a capable guardian'. This trio is said to have greater predictive and explanatory capacity than any 'speculation about the source of the offender's motivation'.[68] The opportunity structure of an offence is thus not a simple physical entity but the complex interplay between potential offenders, victims, and targets. Together these determine the scale and nature of opportunities for crime. Instead of attempting the expensive and difficult task of changing the welfare, education, social, and employment prospects of prospective offenders, advocates argue, situational crime prevention offers the possibility of making multiple small-scale, cost-efficient, and apparently effective changes. These changes include target hardening, access control, deflecting offenders, entry- and exit-screening, formal and informal (or 'natural') surveillance, target removal, and property marking.[69]

Situational crime prevention has become an important plank in government crime prevention policies but, consistent with the economic analysis that stands behind it, is by no means the exclusive preserve of government. The role of the public as potential providers of crime opportunities is central. The 'market for crime' assumes that potential victims, potential offenders, and potential buyers of illegal goods and services all behave in accordance with the rules of optimizing behaviour.[70] It follows that equilibrium in the crime market can be modified, for

---

[67] Felson, M. and Clarke, R.V., 'The Ethics of Situational Crime Prevention' in Newman and Clarke (eds.), *Rational Choice and Situational Crime Prevention* (Aldershot: Dartmouth, 1997) 205.

[68] Clarke, R. V., 'Situational Crime Prevention' in Tonry and Morris (eds.), *Crime and Justice: An Annual Review of Research* (Chicago: University of Chicago, 1995) 100.

[69] Clarke (n. 68 above).

[70] Ehrlich, I., 'Crime, Punishment and the Market for Crime' (1996) 10 *Journal of Economic Perspectives* 43–67: 44ff.

example, by encouraging potential victims to decrease the pay-off to crime by increasing their levels of self-protection.[71] The concomitant danger is that situational crime prevention becomes 'a fertile ground for the blossoming of market-driven projects in which the sponsors set the terms of the research agenda'.[72] The common result is a disproportionate focus on street crime and comparative neglect of hidden targets such as domestic and other violence, child abuse, crimes of the state, and corporate crime.[73] Calling upon victims to reduce opportunities is also open to the objection that it tends toward victim-blaming and the charge that victims were 'asking for trouble' by dressing in a particular way or frequenting a potentially hazardous environment.[74] Further ethical issues thrown up by situational crime prevention include loss of privacy rights, erosion of trust, problems of social exclusion and the transformation of safety into what economists term 'a club good' denied to those who stand outside its protection.[75] Addressing these ethical issues requires a keen appreciation of the assumptions that underlie opportunity theory.

Conclusion

Downes and Rock strenuously deny the demise of the sociology of deviance, citing Keynes to argue that 'No theory is ever dead.'[76] Instead they focus upon the metamorphosis of existing

---

[71] Cook, P.J., 'The Demand and Supply of Criminal Opportunities' (1986) 7 *Crime and Justice: A Review of Research* 1–27: 2.

[72] Hughes, G., *Understanding Crime Prevention: Social Control, Risk and Late Modernity* (Buckingham: Open University Press, 1998) 69.

[73] Hughes (n. 72 above), 68; Stanko, E., 'Where Precaution is Normal: A Feminist Critique of Crime Prevention' in Gelsthorpe and Morris (eds.), *Feminist Perspectives in Criminology* (Buckingham: Open University Press, 1990).

[74] Kleinig, J., 'The Burdens of Situational Crime Prevention' in von Hirsch, Garland and Wakefield (eds.), *Ethical and Social Perspectives on Situational Crime Prevention* (Oxford: Hart Publishing, 2000) 53–6. For a counterview see Harel, A., 'Efficiency and Fairness in Criminal Law' (1994) 84 *California Law Review* 1181–229.

[75] Hope, T., 'Inequality and the Clubbing of Private Security' in Hope and Sparks (eds.), *Crime, Risk and Insecurity* (London: Routledge, 2000) 86.

[76] Downes and Rock (n. 34 above), 356.

sociologies of deviance to accord with the changing social, economic, and political conditions of late modernity. Of all these theories, they suggest 'situational control theories, more than any other approach, have helped to fashion the character of late modernity'.[77] In this chapter, I have sought to show that situational control theories are better seen as deriving from the assumptions, insights, and conceptual tools of modern economic analysis than from sociology. In spite of its undoubted influence in policy circles, British criminologists remain sceptical about economic analysis principally because they see its approach as reductive and insufficiently concerned with the staple explanatory variables of the sociology of deviance. Chief among their criticisms is that economics reduces the biographical criminal to an abstract rationally calculating individual or 'situational man' devoid of character, social ties, or structural place. Arguably this is to miss the point: the abstract and purely hypothetical model of the rational actor does not purport to describe sociological reality. The rational actor should rather be understood as analogous to the hypothetical 'reasonable man' of legal invention: it is simply an error to assume that either model depicts a real person. Moreover, modern economics is not only analytically sophisticated, it is also increasingly willing to adapt its models to take account of the realities of its research subjects' lives and personalities. Recognition of the non-instrumental nature of much offending; of the limited rationality and self-control of offenders; of information costs, time discounting, and other elements of 'bounded' rationality, are all established features of modern rational choice theory.[78] It is also the case that economic analysis obliges one to specify basic assumptions, detail the limits of one's methods, and measure costs and benefits in a much more transparent way than has so far been the case in most criminological analysis.[79]

One of the great and enduring accomplishments of *Understanding Deviance* is that the political and policy implications of each theory are mapped out and distinguished from one another.

---

[77] Downes and Rock (n. 34 above), 365.
[78] Jolls, Sunstein and Thaler (n. 56 above), 1471–550.
[79] Dilulio (n. 58 above), 18.

As Downes' work has repeatedly shown, there are clear political consequences to preferring one theory over another. Intrinsic merits apart, academics ought, but rarely do, have one eye to the consequences of their ideas. If it is the case that economic analysis is driving modern opportunity theory, then criminologists concerned with its political, policy, and ethical ramifications might do well to tool up.

Bibliography

Baert, P. *Social Theory in the Twentieth Century* (Polity Press: Cambridge, 1998) 154.

Baker, T., Harel, A., and Kugler, T., 'The Virtues of Uncertainty in Law: An Experimental Approach' (2004) 89 *Iowa Law Review* 443–94.

Becker, G., 'Crime and Punishment: An Economic Approach' (1968) 76 *Journal of Political Economy* 169–217.

Clarke, R.V., 'Situational Crime Prevention' in Tonry, M. and Morris, N. (eds.), *Crime and Justice: An Annual Review of Research* (University of Chicago: Chicago, 1995).

Cloward, R.A. and Ohlin L.E., *Delinquency and Opportunity: A Theory of Delinquent Gangs* (Free Press: Glencoe, Ill., 1960).

Cohen, S., 'Crime and Politics: Spot the Difference' (1996) 47 *British Journal of Sociology* 1–21.

Cook, P.J., 'The Demand and Supply of Criminal Opportunities' (1986) 7 *Crime and Justice: A Review of Research* 1–27.

Cornish, D.B. and Clarke, R.V. (eds.), *The Reasoning Criminal: Rational Choice Perspectives on Offending* (Springer: New York, 1986).

Croft, J., 'Criminological Research in Britain' in Tonry, M. (ed.), *Crime and Justice: An Annual Review of Research* (University of Chicago Press: Chicago, Ill., 1983).

Dhiri, S. and Brand, S., *Analysis of Costs and Benefits: Guidance for Evaluators* (Home Office: London, 1999).

Dilulio, J.J., 'Help Wanted: Economists, Crime and Public Policy' (1996) 10 *Journal of Economic Perspectives* 3–24.

Downes, D., *The Delinquent Solution: A Study in Subcultural Theory* (Routledge & Kegan Paul: London, 1966).

—— 'Promise and Performance in British Criminology' (1978) 29 *British Journal of Sociology* 483–502.

—— 'The Sociology of Crime and Social Control in Britain 1960–1987' in Rock, P. (ed.), *A History of British Criminology* (Oxford University Press: Oxford, 1988).

Downes, D., 'What the Next Government Should Do About Crime' (1997) 36 *Howard Journal* 1–13.

—— 'Four Years Hard: New Labour and Crime Control' (2002) 46 *Criminal Justice Matters* 8–9.

—— and Morgan, R., 'The Skeletons in the Cupboard: the Politics of Law and Order at the Turn of the Millennium' in Maguire, M., Morgan, R., and Reiner, R. (eds.), *The Oxford Handbook of Criminology* (3rd edn, Oxford University Press: Oxford, 2002).

—— and Rock, P., *Understanding Deviance* (4th edn, Oxford University Press: Oxford, 2003).

Ehrlich, I., 'Crime, Punishment and the Market for Crime' (1996) 10 *Journal of Economic Perspectives* 43–67.

Eide, E., 'Economics of Criminal Behaviour' in De Geest, G. (ed.), *Encyclopedia of Law and Economics* (Edward Elgar: Ghent, 2000).

Feeley, M. and Simon, J., 'Actuarial Justice: The Emerging New Criminal Law' in Nelken, D. (ed.), *The Futures of Criminology* (Sage: London, 1994).

Felson, M., *Crime and Everyday Life* (3rd edn, Sage: London, 2002).

Felson, M. and Clarke, R.V., 'The Ethics of Situational Crime Prevention' in Newman, G. and Clarke, R. (eds.), *Rational Choice and Situational Crime Prevention* (Dartmouth: Aldershot, 1997).

—— and —— *Opportunity Makes the Thief: Practical Theory for Crime Prevention*, Police Research Series No. 98 (Home Office: London, 1998).

Garland, D., *The Culture of Control* (Oxford University Press: Oxford, 2001).

—— and Sparks, R. 'Criminology, Social Theory and the Challenge of Our Times' in Garland, D. and Sparks, T. (eds.), *Criminology and Social Theory* (Oxford University Press: Oxford, 2000) 18.

Harel, A., 'Efficiency and Fairness in Criminal Law' (1994) 84 *California Law Review* 1181–229.

Hillyard, P., Sim, J., Tombs, S. and Whyte, D., 'Leaving a "Stain upon the Silence": Contemporary Criminology and the Politics of Dissent' (2004) 44 *British Journal Of Criminology* 369–90.

Hindess, B., 'Rational Choice Theory' in Outhwaite, W. and Bottomore, T. (eds.), *Blackwell Dictionary of Twentieth-Century Social Thought* (Blackwell Publishers: Oxford, 1993).

Hood, R., *The Death Penalty: A World-Wide Perspective* (3rd edn, Clarendon Press: Oxford, 2002).

Hope, T., 'Inequality and the Clubbing of Private Security' in Hope, T. and Sparks, R. (eds.), *Crime, Risk and Insecurity* (Routledge: London, 2000).

Hoyle, C. and Rose, D., 'Labour, Law and Order' (2001) 72 *Political Quarterly* 76–85.
Hudson, B., *Justice in the Risk Society* (Sage: London, 2003).
Hughes, G., *Understanding Crime Prevention: Social Control, Risk and Late Modernity* (Open University Press: Buckingham, 1998).
Jolls, C., Sunstein, C., and Thaler, R., 'A Behavioral Approach to Law and Economics' (1998) 50 *Stanford Law Review* 1471–550.
Kelman, M., 'Behavioural Economics as Part of a Rhetorical Duet: A Response to Jolls, Sunstein and Thaler' (1998) 50 *Stanford Law Review* 1577–91.
Kleinig, J., 'The Burdens of Situational Crime Prevention' in von Hirsch, A., Garland, D., and Wakefield, A. (eds.), *Ethical and Social Perspectives on Situational Crime Prevention* (Hart Publishing: Oxford, 2000).
Lermack, P., 'Review of Understanding Deviance' (1999) 9 *Law and Politics Book Review* 141–3.
Loader, I. and Sparks, R., 'Contemporary Landscapes of Crime, Order, and Control: Governance, Risk, and Globalization' in Maguire, M., Morgan, R., and Reiner, R. (eds.), *Oxford Handbook of Criminology* (3rd edn, Oxford University Press: Oxford, 2002).
Marx, G.T., 'The Engineering of Social Control: The Search for the Silver Bullet' in Peterson, R. (ed.), *Crime and Inequality* (Stanford University Press: Stanford, CA, 1995).
Matza, D., *Delinquency and Drift* (Wiley: New York, 1964).
Newman, G., Clarke, R.V., and Shoham, S.G. (eds.), *Rational Choice and Situational Crime Prevention: Theoretical Foundations* (Dartmouth: Ashgate, 1997).
O'Malley, P., 'Risk, Crime and Prudentialism Revisited' in Stenson, K. and Sullivan, R.R. (eds.), *Crime, Risk and Justice: The Politics of Crime Control in Liberal Democracies* (Willan Publishing: Cullompton, Devon, 2001).
Posner, R., 'An Economic Theory of the Criminal Law' (1985) 85 *Columbia Law Review* 1193–231.
—— 'Rational Choice, Behavioural Economics, and the Law' (1998) 50 *Stanford Law Review* 1551–75.
Read, T. and Tilley, N., *Not Rocket Science? Problem-solving and Crime Reduction*, Crime Reduction Series Paper 6 (Home Office: London, 2000).
Simon, J., 'From the Big House to the Warehouse: Rethinking State Government and Prisons' (1999) 3 *Punishment and Society* 213–34.
Stanko, E., 'Where Precaution is Normal: A Feminist Critique of Crime Prevention' in Gelsthorpe, L. and Morris, A. (eds.), *Feminist Perspectives in Criminology* (Open University Press: Buckingham, 1990).

Sumner, C., *The Sociology of Deviance: An Obituary* (Open University Press: Buckingham, 1994).
Tilley, N. and Laycock, G., *Working Out What to Do: Evidence-based Crime Reduction*, Crime Reduction Series Paper 11 (Home Office: London, 2002).
von Hirsch, A., Garland, D. and Wakefield, A. (eds.), *Ethical and Social Perspectives on Situational Crime Prevention* (Hart Publishing: Oxford, 2000).
Zedner, L., 'Useful Knowledge? Debating the Role of Criminology in Post-war Britain' in Zedner, L. and Ashworth, A. (eds.), *The Criminological Foundations of Penal Policy* (Oxford University Press: Oxford, 2003).
—— 'Policing Before and After the Police: The Historical Antecedents of Contemporary Crime Control' (2006) 46 *British Journal of Criminology* 78–96.
—— and Ashworth, A. (eds.), *The Criminological Foundations of Penal Policy: Essays in Honour of Roger Hood* (Oxford University Press: Oxford, 2003).

7
Contrasts and Concepts: Considering the Development of Comparative Criminology
Frances Heidensohn

'Comparative criminology is nothing new' is the first line of David Downes' major contribution to the development of this area of the subject (Downes, 1988, p. 1). Yet, on the next page, he also observes that '[C]riminology has in general been strikingly incomparative'. These two comments sum up important aspects of this approach to the study of crime, that comparisons are both central to the enterprise and yet remained, at the time David Downes was writing 'an under-used resource' (Downes, 1988). *Contrasts in Tolerance* is widely regarded as a key contribution to comparative work and as one of the most important aspects of his long and distinguished career, and indeed one in which he is still engaged (Downes and Hansen, 2004) in retirement.

Since the publication of *Contrasts* there has been something of a boom in comparative criminological studies. Its appearance was quickly followed by the first modern texts which looked at Europe-wide crime and criminal justice: Cain, 1989; Hood, 1989; Heidensohn and Farrell, 1991. By 1993, Vagg was asserting that: 'comparative criminology has recently become a growth area, with the publication of several major texts' (Vagg, 1993, p. 541). *Contrasts* is the first of these which he lists. The early twenty-first century has seen many publications appearing which take comparative approaches (Garland, 2001; Edwards and Gill, 2003; Newburn and Sparks, 2004). There are other noteworthy milestones. The International Division of the

American Society of Criminology is the largest section of the organization; 2001 saw the founding of the European Society of Criminology, both of which have their own journals. The editors of one recent collection were able to find (and, as they delicately suggest, were very selective in their choice) fourteen contributors to reflect on their experiences of international comparative work (Winterdyk and Cao, 2004) which 'testify the rapid spread and development of international criminology' (op. cit., p. 3). Winterdyk and Cao put Mannheim in his 1965 *Comparative Criminology* as the originator of the comparative/international link and Downes' *Contrasts* appeared neatly at about half-way through the history of the field, thus placing it at a pivotal point.

My aim in this chapter is to explore David Downes' contribution, through both *Contrasts* and his earlier paper (Downes, 1982) to comparative criminology, especially in the context of the recent wave of studies. His own purposes, of course, were primarily directed at using a comparative study to answer questions about the *British* penal crises such as does: 'Some invariable law dictate(s) a rising recourse to custody in the context of rising crime?' and 'Would a falling prison population at a time of rising crime be politically feasible?' (Downes, 1988, pp. 4–5).

In the Netherlands in the 1980s he found very different answers from those that received wisdom in the United Kingdom then offered and his analysis of why these worked there, and at that time, forms the core of his book. One result of this was that it helped the Netherlands as a country:

to acquire beacon status...it came to see itself as an enlightening example to the rest of the world as to how to treat wrongdoers with a great deal of humanity and maintain a low level of crime at the same time, a position reinforced by foreign observers, *probably most notably by Downes*. (Pakes, 2004, p. 284, emphasis added).

As Pakes goes on to show, however, the situation in the twenty-first century is fundamentally different in the Netherlands with a crime and a penal crisis both fuelled by the politics of discontent (op. cit.). This is not to say that Downes' view of the contemporary Dutch system is wrong; Pakes credits Downes with prescience in acknowledging 'the fact that by the late 1980s the tide was already changing'. (Pakes, 2004, p. 293). Rather this historic shift can be better understood as a major change since Downes' work provides an important analysis which stands as a benchmark for later studies. This does, however, serve to highlight the importance of Downes' project in relation to comparative study.

Ironically, Pakes argues that the Netherlands now fits Garland's model (Garland, 2001) of a 'crime complex':

Garland's crime complex is usually discussed utilising both Britain and the United States as examples. In contrast, Garland (2001) himself mentioned the Netherlands as a country that experienced the social and economic disruptions of late modernity without resorting to these same strategies and levels of control.' (Pakes, 2004, p. 284).

In the twenty-first century, a series of domestic crises have formed a 'breeding ground for a reformulation of law and order policies towards that of a... Dutch-style Garlandian crime and security complex' (op. cit., p. 285).

Van Swaaningen (2005) charts the same developments and offers an alternative explanation of why the enlightened Dutch approach to penal policy changed so quickly to one that was intolerant and punitive, which also refers back to Downes. As I noted at the beginning of this paper, David Downes himself introduces *Contrasts* with a paradoxical observation: there is nothing new in comparative criminology, yet the subject has been 'strikingly incomparative'. This is not the only apparent contradiction surrounding the definitions, the history and even the naming of the area.

The editors of the collection cited above discuss the problems of the naming question (Winterdyk and Cao, 2004, pp. 1–2) and then sidestep the issue by giving their book the title *Lessons from International/Comparative Criminology/Criminal Justice*. Other authors use the term 'transnational' (e.g. Edwards and Gill, 2003) or 'global' (Raine and Cilluffo, 1994). These last two were specifically linked by title and object of interest to *organized* crime; 'cross-national' (Neuman and Berger, 1988) and 'cross-cultural' (Smandych *et al.*, 1993) have also been employed in this literature, sometimes all anthologized in a single volume (Beirne and Nelken, 1997). Almost without exception, every article or book with any of the above terms in its title begins with an account or discussion of their meaning, history and application.

Downes does this in the first pages of his book and is concerned to situate his project within an old established comparative framework which, he suggests, had not up to that time, had much resonance nor success, a failure he attributes to the fact that the: 'legendary insulation of criminology from mainstream sociology for most of its history meant that the significance which the comparative method held for the latter simply passed the former by' (Downes, 1988, p. 2). The very few preceding texts he quoted had been published many years earlier and so he did not have to address the first and most obvious question which arises when we look at later works: are all these studies with their many and varied titles engaged in the same enterprise? Have they filled the gap which Downes noted in the 1980s? Was he right to record such a deficit in the field, or does his project draw attention to a more complex and diverse history?

As Downes himself points out, instructive comparisons of criminal justice policies have a long history. The more humane and progressive Dutch system has 'in general been compared favourably with the rest of Europe on this score. John Howard was by no means the first to do so, though his accolade (1784) was based upon the most comprehensive survey of contrasting countries and carried the most weight' (Downes, 1988, p. 5). Karstedt (2004, p. 16) highlights Voltaire's role as the foremost intellectual and anglophile of his age in promoting the British model of governance and its rational legal and political systems.

Garland, to complicate this account still further, is rigorous in his history of the development of criminology in Britain (Garland, 2002, p. 19) in insisting on much narrower definitions of criminology and criminologists: 'Enlightenment writers such as Beccaria, Bentham and Howard wrote secular, materialist analyses...the writings...did not constitute a criminology' (op. cit.). Debates about the origins and diffusion of modern penal systems have flourished for decades. The American authors of a mid-twentieth-century text book ask: 'Who produced the first prison?' They concede 'we must admit Howard's influence', citing his descriptions of many European examples in his writings and that these 'were carefully studied by members of the [Pennsylvania] Prison Society' (Barnes and Teeters, 1951, pp. 397–8). They nevertheless conclude that, 'throughout the nineteenth century, all the important prisons of the world copied either the Pennsylvania or the Auburn types, or a combination of them' (op. cit., p. 398).

'Policy transfers' in criminal justice, as they would now be termed, have a long history in other areas too. Fosdick (1915) studied European and British policing systems before the First World War and Owings (1925) looked at the role of women in law enforcement internationally. Neither author was an academic; indeed, both were or had been serving officers. An even more striking early example of comparative study therefore is Beaujon's PhD. thesis, presented at the University of Utrecht in 1911. She undertook a systematic survey, commissioned by the National Women's Council of the Netherlands, sending a questionnaire to all the European cities where she knew policewomen were employed. She visited sixteen of these to collect more data and produced her findings in a tabulated, spreadsheet format, deriving 'general principles' from her research (Beaujon, 1911, p. 93). (This thesis was published in German, but it does not appear to have been translated into English.)

Despite this pedigree, as Downes notes, major examples of comparative work are few until the late twentieth century. Curiously, Mannheim's 793-page *opus* is entitled *Comparative Criminology* (1965) yet has no references in its index or contents list to the subject in its title, although it could be argued that the whole two volumes are a record of and a testament to a lifetime's international scholarship.

There are considerable differences even in the recording of the history and development of this subject. In an interesting essay which addresses these points, Barak puts the origin of the 'academic specialty, the study of comparative, cross-cultural crime and crime control' in the 1970s. He notes 'there are still alternative views, definitions, and theories of as well as approaches to comparative crime and crime control'. (Barak, 2000b, p. 1), but insists that 'as the number of comparative studies have grown, some clarity of purpose has been established in the field' (op. cit.).

Barak juxtaposes 'comparative criminology' with 'international and transnational criminology' and observes that the latter may soon overtake the former because of the rise of 'transnationalists' and the decline of the nation state. He sets out very specific definitions of what constitutes cross-national study: 'systematic and theoretically informed comparison of crime and crime control in two or more cultural states' (op. cit.). This is, as he notes, the approach taken in their selection by Beirne and Nelken (1997), although this of course results, as they acknowledge, in a somewhat arbitrary rejection of writings whose focus is a single culture, such as Downes' *Contrasts*. These editors also distinguish between comparative studies of *crime* and cross-cultural studies of 'the processes and institutions of criminal justice' (op. cit., 1997, xiii). Barak continues his essay with a summary of his major study of crime and control in fifteen nation states in which he and other contributors used a variety of methods and classifications to produce some interesting, if limited conclusions (Barak, 2000a).

Contrasts on the other hand, provides a model case study, despite the author's modesty about his achievement (Downes, 1988, p. 5). Downes conducted interviews with key policy makers, officials and academics in the Netherlands and also with prisoners in both countries as he sought answers to the question of why the Dutch 'solved' their crime and penal policy problems in a very different fashion and with quite opposite outcomes to those found in Britain at that time. In his analysis of the Dutch experience, he focuses on specific features of the criminal justice system such as the co-ordination of prosecution policies and sentencing and on the broader aspects of Dutch society, its 'pillarization' for instance (1988, Ch. 7 *passim*). That this situation was altering as he concluded his project is acknowledged in the final chapter and thus it is hardly surprising that the Dutch model was not adopted in Britain. On the contrary, as I recorded above, the Netherlands is now seen by commentators as a country which has discarded its past penal tolerance as a mistake and to have come to resemble a nation with a 'grand problem' (Pakes, 2004, p. 285) of crises in governance and criminal justice. What is not in doubt is the historic importance of this study as a signal for the growth of comparative work, especially looking at Europe as well as North America.

In the same year that *Contrasts* was published, the Institute for the Study and Treatment of Delinquency, the body which held the copyright of the *British Journal of Criminology*, of which David was then the editor, held the first major conference in the

United Kingdom on Crime in Europe at which David Downes was a keynote speaker. When a selection of the papers from this conference were published aş *Crime in Europe* (Heidensohn and Farrell, eds., 1991) I introduced them with a section on comparative criminology, since 'one purpose of this book (is) to illustrate the scope for the comparative study of crime across Europe'. Drawing on the experience gained from the 1988 conference and from other studies I was then engaged on (see Heidensohn, 2004, for an account), I suggested that:

In order to study crime comparatively three conditions need to be met. There must be sources of material and data with which to make comparisons: crime statistics, victim surveys, research studies. Second, translatable concepts have to be available to make possible the collecting, ordering and analysis of such data. Finally, *some kind of framework, part universe of discourse, part set of common concerns, must exist.* (Heidensohn, 1991, p. 10, emphasis added).

Although Nelken has criticized this approach as too positivistic (1994, p. 239), it still has some merit, I would argue, as one way of looking at the field. It is strikingly evident, for instance, that whereas Downes searched in vain for successful comparative texts in the 1980s, there has been such an enormous growth since then that the once-bare field is now thickly forested. Yet, is it possible to say that this is a coherent body of work, or that there are at least flourishing debates about its discourse and common concerns? The answer is contradictory both yes and no, as often in academic work, sudden abundance tends to create some confusion and turbulence. As I have illustrated above there is still much discussion about the history, terms, scope, and methods of this area. Yacoubian, for instance, crisply castigates those who use the terms 'comparative' and 'international' criminology interchangeably to reflect the study of crime outside of any one nation: 'this is a definitional *faux pas*'. In his view, *comparative* criminology involves the study of crime cross-culturally whereas, *international* criminology (my italics) is the study of violations of international law. Yacoubian, 2003, pp. 223–4). Interestingly, this note appears in the *International Journal of Comparative Criminology* [sic] which is published by de Sitter, who are also the publishers of the Winterdyk and Cao collection referred to above, whose title sidesteps these issues

(2004). In contrast, Zimring and Johnson see no such problem in their essay on the comparative study of corruption, where they state that their first ambition, 'is to show that a transnational comparative perspective can be of value in identifying topics worth studying in criminology and criminal Law' (2005, p. 793).

Another apparent disagreement is between those who find the 'very idea of a "comparative criminology" is a misnomer. All social scientific work requires comparison, whether across time, within different segments of a social system, or across societies' (Vagg, 1993, p. 541) and others, such as Pearson who, a decade later, could write that ' "comparative" criminology is massively under-developed' (Pearson, 2002, p. 235). Pearson was introducing a set of articles on crime and criminology in China and his views should properly be related to that region, except that we can also observe that Vagg was at the University of Hong Kong when he wrote the paper cited above and that the first main approach he distinguishes is that of linking 'crime trends or problems to common social, economic or political denominations...within for example, the *third world*' (op. cit., my italics).

Of course, it is hardly surprising that there are such basic disagreements about the naming of parts and the demarcation of territory here when these remain more widely contested within the discipline: 'globally, criminology does not have a single coherent, integrated body of knowledge or practice, nor should it' (Hardie-Bick *et al.*, 2005, p. 13). The same authors, having reviewed some of these 'difficult and worthy topics of enquiry' conclude, 'since there is no established paradigm for transnational and comparative criminology it is necessary to invent one' (op. cit., p. 3).

That is what I aim to do in the rest of this essay in order to contribute to some of the analyses which have tried to impose order on the confusions and contradictions which are pervasive in this area (see Nelken, 2002; Newburn and Sparks, 2004; Winterdyk and Cao, eds., 2004; Sheptycki and Wardak, 2005 Nelken, 2002;). In almost all of the many classifying schemes offered in the works listed above, the features considered are the *name* or *names* of the subject, its various *approaches* and its *methods*. My proposal is for a taxonomy of the various types or perspectives of different comparative researchers. This framework owes a little to Nelken's three possible strategies for comparative study 'virtually there, being there, researching there' (Nelken, 2002, p. 181) but not very much. David Downes' own invocation of Schutz's essay on 'the Stranger' is my main starting point: Downes argues that this, 'could be taken as a directive for sociological travel. The Stranger may be vouchsafed confidences withheld from fellow-members of the host community' (Downes 1988, p. 2).

Strangers who study criminal justice systems 'abroad' are, Downes suggests, mainly concerned with obtaining a message for 'home'. This proposition, however, ignores the particular example of refugees from the Third Reich who had such an immense impact on criminology in Britain. As Garland, ever the highly selective critic, puts it:

The transformation of British criminology from a minor scientific specialism into an established academic discipline...was by no means an inevitable or necessary development. Indeed, had it not been for the rise of Nazism in Germany and the appointment of three distinguished European emigrés, Hermann Mannheim, Max Grunhut and Leon Radzinowicz, to academic posts at elite British universities, British criminology might not have developed sufficient academic impetus to become an independent discipline. (Garland, 2002, p. 39).

Once again, Downes' thoughtful approach has raised interesting issues and indicated more paths to follow, even though, in this case, I shall argue that the idea of the 'stranger' in comparative research is far more complex and many-sided than many commentators allow (e.g. Melossi, 2004). It is, in consequence, an excellent first concept with which to start building this framework.

Towards a Taxonomy

In the preceding pages of this essay, I have used David Downes' *Contrasts* as a link to study and assess the burgeoning range of work on comparative criminology and criminal justice. This has proved a more complex and difficult task than I had expected. There is no established agreement on the relevant definitions, scope, history, or methods. While many writers acclaim the growth of comparative studies in criminology, others have deplored the continued ethnocentricity of the subject: Barbaret, writing as an American overseas, noted that only 7.4 per cent of articles published in *Criminology* (the major American journal) in the 1990s had 'any kind of international/comparative focus' (Barbaret, 2001). Zimring and Johnson, in an article strongly advocating the view: 'that a trans-national comparative perspective can be of value in identifying topics worth studying in criminology and criminal law, as well as an important method of conducting such studies' (Zimring and Johnson, 2005, p. 793) baldly assert that 'American criminology is provincial' (op. cit., p. 794). They then focus on the study of corruption, yet they make no reference to the extensive work of Nelken who has used comparative perspectives to explore corruption, its definition and its interpretation and has also reflected widely on comparative criminology (Nelken, 1994, 2003 a and b). This area can thus best be described as a land of perplexing contrasts and my own small contribution to sorting out and simplifying this will be to outline a classification of comparative scholars which will, I trust, aid future analysis.

I have indicated nine categories of comparative criminologists (see figure 1 below), but this is not meant to be a definitive list; rather it is an initial botanical guide to the many flourishing flora in the afforested field of comparative work; literally speaking it

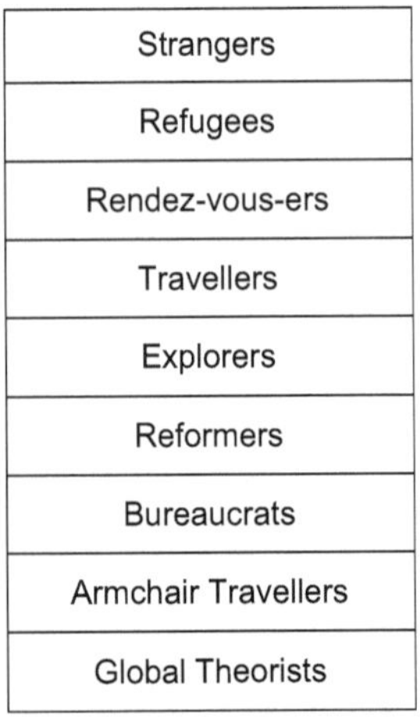

Strangers
Refugees
Rendez-vous-ers
Travellers
Explorers
Reformers
Bureaucrats
Armchair Travellers
Global Theorists

FIGURE 1. Comparative Criminology

Considering the Development of Comparative Criminology 183

is an identification manual for the planters who set the seeds which have bloomed so successfully.

It is intended to be applied alongside the other heuristic devices and classifications which have been offered so often to those who venture into, or settle in this area. By this I mean the specific listings of benefits or objectives which many commentators put forward as the aims or outcomes to be expected from comparative work. Using this framework it is possible to identify key features of various approaches to comparative work and to examine how well each fulfils the expectations which scholars have of them.

Nelken, one of the most interesting commentators on, and practitioners of, cross-cultural work on crime, has pointed out that most texts about comparative criminal justice 'contain relatively little about the actual process of doing cross-cultural research in criminal justice' (Nelken, 2002, p. 180). He argues that in order:

> to acquire sufficient knowledge of another culture for such purposes... either we can rely mainly on cooperation with foreign experts or we can go abroad to interview legal officials and others, or we can draw on our direct experience of living in the country concerned. These strategies I have... described as virtually there, researching there or living there' (Nelken, 2002, p. 181).

He both advocates, and practises, the last option as giving the fullest understanding of another culture, although he acknowledges the value of the fresh and naïve eye in viewing practices.

In constructing my taxonomy, I recognize Nelken's distinctions, but wish to put the emphasis on who the researchers are, or were, and what baggage as well as what investigative apparatus they brought to their studies. First, however, the importance of Schutz's essay on the role of stranger must be acknowledged as one of the best descriptions of the problems and the advantages of studying a society, group or culture different from one's own. To the stranger the new social world presents itself differently from the member of the in group who grasps its customs intuitively: 'his need (is) to acquire full knowledge of the elements of the approached cultural pattern and to examine what seems self-explanatory to the group' (Schutz, 1966, II, p. 104).

It is clear from this essay that in writing it Schutz had in mind his own position as a former exile from Austria after the Anschluss. While he maintained a career as a banker, as well as a part-time researcher at the New School of Social Research in New York, he and his family had had to flee from Nazism and start a new life in the United States (Embree, 2003). This is poignantly reflected in his observation that the stranger knows that, 'a man may lose his status, his rules even *his history*' (op. cit., emphasis added).

Strangers

In some senses, all comparative scholars are 'strangers' when they embark on the study of other cultures or systems and the themes associated with understanding, what Melossi calls: 'the problem of translation...conversation between different cultures is possible, but not translation from one to another' (Melossi, 2004, p. 80). Yet, those who caution *against* 'the conceptual and practical problems of translation' nevertheless argue *for* the importance of thinking '"oneself away" from the immediacy of local experience' and in favour of: 'an abiding place for comparative reflection at every level of theory and research' (Newburn and Sparks, 2004, p. 7).

What strangers can often do best is to ask questions which arise precisely from those attempts to translate, often ideas which they derive from their own backgrounds. In this sense, Downes himself acted as a stranger in his work on Dutch penal policy; as he makes clear, he was seeking answers to questions based on the British penal crisis of the day. In pursuing these inquiries, he found that the Dutch themselves had not developed their own full explanation of their system at that stage; as Pakes (2004, p. 284) notes, Downes' work contributed to the Netherlands' later status as a 'beacon' of enlightened treatment of wrongdoers. Nelken (2002, p. 183) cites two examples of the translation effect; one with approval, the other less so. Lacey and Zedner's work (1995, 1998) which showed that 'community' had a very different meaning in German discourse on crime prevention, he sees as helpful. He asserts however, that:

American research on...Japanese criminal justice...can be criticized for seeking to explain what is distinctive about Japanese legal culture in contrast to familiar American models without recognizing how much is derived from the civil law systems of Continental Europe from which Japan borrowed. (Nelken, 2002).

Curiously, considerable numbers of recent accounts of comparative projects or of whole careers, do not dwell on their 'stranger' experiences. Indeed few if any of the Winterdyk and Cao contributors do so, although van Dijk describes his distressing experiences when he transferred from one organizational culture in the Netherlands to another, the UN Office on Drugs and Crime in Vienna (van Dijk, 2004, pp. 78–9).

One of the most thoughtful twenty-first-century examples is Cain's account of her experiences of 'orientalism, occidentalism and the sociology of crime in the Caribbean'. She depicts the latter tendency as presuming the ' "sameness" of key cultural categories, practices and institutions. There is thus a *constant misdiagnosis* of problems' (Cain, 2000, p. 239). Significantly, hers is the only essay in this special edition of the *British Journal of Criminology* which addresses these issues.

Refugees

As I observed above, it is the contribution of a very small number of European refugees which provides one of the most striking historical examples of the role of strangers in comparative criminology. Leon Radzinowicz's major contribution to the establishment of criminology in Britain is very well known and has been fully recognized (Hood, 2002) not least by Radzinowicz himself (1999). While he was in England 'when the clouds of war gathered... he wisely decided not to return to his native Poland, where he would almost certainly have perished' he was here on Polish government business and he was a much younger and more dynamic man than his fellow Europeans (Hood, 2004, p. 469). He had already studied abroad, in Italy, and acquired the skills and resources, linguistic and cultural, to adjust and succeed. Grünhut and Mannheim, on the other hand, as Hood's moving account makes clear 'came to England virtually penniless and in a state of acute anxiety and depression' (op. cit., p. 470).

Hood describes their struggles to survive in pre-war and wartime Britain and the humiliations they endured as they learnt English and, as Mannheim put it, made 'himself familiar... with the crime situation and the penal system of this country'. (1940). He published extensively in English; Grünhut did so less, and his

Comparative Criminology was a major compilation for which 'he drew widely on literature from continental Europe in a way that only he, Grünhut and Radzinowicz could have done, in an effort to break the "American hegemony" on the subject' (Hood, 2004, p. 489). All three scholars coming from European backgrounds and bringing their accumulated knowledge to bear on Britain had immense impact. They were 'founders of what is of enduring worth in the English pragmatic and humanitarian approach to criminology and criminal policy' (Hood, 2004, p. 470).

Yet while their status as pioneers and founders of British criminology is known, it is only from the most recent tributes that one can appreciate that *all* their work in English was comparative and that, while all three gained post-war recognition in Europe, they could never send any messages 'home'. Home, in the sense of the countries and cultures they had matured in, no longer existed.

Rendez-vous-ers: Travellers and Explorers

David Downes himself invented this epithet for criminology in general to describe the way in which some scholars, such as Merton, for example, paid a single visit to the criminological world, produced one or two studies, but did not extend their work beyond this brief encounter. The term has special salience for comparative work since, inevitably, those who are forced into scholarly exile are fortunately few, as are voluntary exiles, such as Nelken; the majority of comparative scholars who go abroad to study their subjects are either travellers or explorers (but see below). Travellers I would describe as those who make foreign expeditions, rather than, say, longer sojourns. It is clear that this kind of approach has become both more feasible (travel is easier, money available) and that it is also seen as having value in solving problems. Carlen, for instance, has studied the penal treatment of women in a wide variety of settings and presented her own findings, and those of others, providing an important critique of UK policies and of wider trends. This work was funded by the Economic and Social Research Council (ESRC) and the award was titled *Women's Imprisonment: Models of Change and Cross-National Lessons* (Carlen, 2002, p. vii). Bayley has produced a series of studies which look at policing in many different settings which had as their goal 'worldwide description [as] an essential first step toward the long-term goal of learning about what may work better' (Bayley, 1999, p. 8). Mawby, in whose edited collection Bayley's paper appears, himself carried out comparative studies of policing (Mawby 1990, 1999) and also led a project on victims' 'perceptions of police services in east and west Europe' (Mawby, 1998) funded by the Central European University and by NATO and was published in a symposium funded itself by the ESRC. As Nelken notes, such visits are reliant upon local experts and translators for assistance, and lacking the background which locals may have, are vulnerable to misleading guidance or interpretation. Understandably, travellers are less concerned with translation and cultural issues and the reports and collections cited do not dwell on methodological or interpretive issues in comparative cross-national studies.

Explorers are a double category: there are many cross-national researchers who look at one or perhaps two societies, one of which is their own, and thus they can dig more deeply into their comparative example. Historically, Britain and the United States have provided the pair to compare, so much so that these views have been castigated as ethnocentric (see above). Other English-speaking countries are also often looked at, and the assumption clearly is that a common language, close historic and political ties and shared legal traditions assist such comparisons. In the late 1980s, I conducted one such inquiry myself, looking at the experiences and careers of female police officers in the United Kingdom and the United States (Heidensohn, 1991, 1994). Unlike Downes, I did carry out primary research in both nations and did, in some ways, find myself a stranger in both settings (Heidensohn, 1992, pp. 251–2) as I explored the culture of policing and the lives of female officers. An even lengthier such expedition is recounted in Paul Rock's *View from the Shadows* (Rock, 1986) his hugely detailed study of the development of the justice for victims of crime initiative in Canada. In a separate, later study (Rock, 1990) he charts the rise of victim support in England and Wales. Both these texts are based on lengthy participant observation and the use of documents and interviews and are imbued with constant comparative parallels.

Garland's much-discussed *Culture of Control* (2000) probably fits most easily into this category, although, as an emigré Scot working in New York, he could be classified as a stranger. In the *Culture of Control* he is broadly setting out to demonstrate that a fundamental shift has taken place in penal policy in the United States and the United Kingdom, with the decline of rehabilitation and the re-emergence of punitive justice (op. cit., pp. 8–9). This is both a history of the present and a theory about policy convergence. But his work has been criticized in particular because he exaggerates the *similarities* between the two nations and minimizes American exceptionalism in violent crime rates and levels of imprisonment. As Young tellingly commented: 'The use of the comparative method in ways which highlight similarities and repress differences fails to pick up on the very particular structural and criminogenic attributes of the United States when compared to the majority of advanced industrial countries.' (Young, 2003, p. 240). Explorers have clearly produced some of the most challenging and important cross-national studies and, increasingly, generate the most striking material (see Piacentini, 2004 on Russian prisons, for example).

Reformers

Unlike Garland, I consider that the early pioneer reformers in the sphere of criminal justice have some claims to be considered as criminologists, and certainly to have contributed to the subject's foundation. We therefore need a category of reformers for them, for John Howard, Elizabeth Fry, Raymond Fosdick and many others, who collected and disseminated material widely on criminal justice policies and practices. They earn their place in any list because of their impact and influence—for instance, Britain's main penal reform group is called the Howard League, and Canada has a network of Elizabeth Fry Associations. They set agendas and asked questions which still resonate, as Downes noted.

Bureaucrats

One of the most notable developments in criminology in the late twentieth century was the huge growth in the collection of crime and penal data, especially at the international level. The most prominent of these was the International Crime Victimization Survey (ICVS), which was one of the first examples of study which made use of a standardized questionnaire to elicit findings from respondents in a large number of countries. Five ICVSs have now taken place and other parallel surveys have been developed: at city level in countries in transition and in the developing world, mainly under the auspices of the UN

Interregional Criminal Justice Research Institute. There is thus now a vast data base held by the United Nations on crime and drugs problems (Smith, 2004), as well as many more such sources: in 1993 the Council of Europe began to collect figures from its member nations on police, prosecutions, offenders, and prisons and publishes these in its source books. Inevitably, the collection, collation, and production of data on international trends in crime and criminal justice require bureaucrats (known as administrative criminologists in Britain) to compile them. There are considerable limitations on the data sets generated, but they are used increasingly for cross-national comparisons, as are those from agencies such as Europol, or national centres, the British Home Office, for instance, which make their own comparisons. Mayhew and van Dijk give their own, separate accounts (2004) of two modern careers in international cross-cultural studies at this level.

For some criminologists, the rise of the European Union and especially the development of the Third Pillar of the Maastricht Treaty on justice and home affairs posed potentially sinister threats with regard to the collection of data and its uses. They feared that collecting material, co-ordinating policing and the growth of information technology would result in the loss of liberty (McLaughlin, 1992; Sheptycki, 1995; and see Heidensohn 1997 for a summary).

Some of these anxieties may remain, but integration and co-operation within and outside the European Union have proceded, given considerable impetus by the events of 11 September 2001 (Den Boer and Monar, 2002). There is now a much larger commissariat with the inevitable consequence of the collecting and storing of more data:

in the post-September 11 context... significant operational police and judicial engagement now exists between the EU and the USA... the relationship between EU and USA criminal police and judicial authorities is one thread in a web of global relationships that comprise a global strategy against transnational and organised crime. (Norman, 2005, p. 328).

Armchair Travellers

Since at least the time of Durkheim, armchair travellers have studied problems of crime and deviance cross-culturally without ever leaving their studies or their libraries. Durkheim famously used figures on suicide trends, religious affiliation, and marital status to produce his classic study of *Suicide* (1952), a project which did not include field trips.

Global Theorists

In more recent times, with easier and faster travel, such comparative empirical studies are less common, although, paradoxically, the availability of information on the worldwide web, and the diffusion of data outlined in the last section make it less necessary (Heidensohn, 2001). The great exception to this are those theorists who discuss worldwide trends towards penal punitiveness and the regulatory state without linking these to specific local examples. Some aspects of Garland's work have attracted this criticism (see above) as have Rose (2000) and even Braithwaite (2000). There is a strong counter-critique which argues that all cross-cultural studies need to be grounded in local, culturally and historically specific contexts (Young, 1999 and 2003; Newburn and Sparks, 2004).

If we seek now to establish which of these approaches fulfils my three requirements for achieving comparative criminology's goals best, we can find each question answered by a different type. Data can certainly be generated by *bureaucrats*, although explorers produce the deepest and richest material. Concepts come most fruitfully from *strangers*, whose insights into their new societies, and their old, will be the most telling. *Frameworks* are most productively produced by travellers of both types who gain overviews from their real or virtual journeys.

Comparative criminology, of the type David Downes pioneered twenty years ago is as vital an enterprise now as it was then, and much more vibrant today than when he wrote *Contrasts*, for the following reasons:

(1) We have a much greater penal crisis in the twenty-first century, with over 70,000 inmates in prison and forecasts of 100,000 or more.
(2) The size and complexity of 'Europe' has grown and gives us particular issues to deal with.
(3) Since 9/11 and 7/7 we face new problems at an international level which involve a great deal of cross-cultural and international understanding.
(4) Transnational crimes—trafficking, drugs, piracy—loom much more seriously than in the 1980s.

(5) Criminology itself is much more sophisticated, more 'grown up' as it were, and has to address global as well as local issues.
(6) Over-optimistic 'policy transfer' (Jones and Newburn, 2004) continues, despite vigorous critiques.

Perhaps the greatest contrast with Downes' book is that between the era in which it was published and the twenty-first century. Then, Downes allowed himself some optimism about the Dutch penal model and its scope for transfer; today that system is seemingly in ruins, but the scope for conducting comparative criminological studies has never been greater.

Bibliography

Barak, G. (ed.) (2000a) *Crime and Crime Control: A Global View* (Greenwood Press: London).
—— (ed.) (2000b) 'Comparative Criminology: A Global View' 10 *The Critical Criminologist* 2.
Barberet, R. (2001) 'Global Competence and American Criminology: An Expatriate's View' 26 *Criminologist* no. 21, 3–5.
Barnes, H.E. and Teeters, N.K. (1951) *New Horizons in Criminology* (2nd edn, Prentice-Hall: NewYork).
Bayley, D. (1999) 'Policing: the World Stage' in Mawby, R. (ed.), *Policing Across the World* (UCL Press: London).
Beaujon, C.M. (1911) *Die Mitarbeit der Frau bei der Polizei* (University of Utrecht: The Hague).
Beirne, P. and Nelken, D. (eds.) (1997) *Issues in Comparative Criminology* (Ashgate: Aldershot).
Braithwaite, J. (2000) 'The New Regulatory State and the Transformation of Criminology' 40 *British Journal of Criminology* 222–38.
Cain, M. (ed.) (1989) *Growing Up Good* (Sage: London).
—— (2000) 'Orientalism, Occidentalism and the Sociology of Crime' 40 *British Journal of Criminology* 239–60.
Carlen, P. (ed.) (2002) *Women and Punishment* (Willan: Devon).
den Boer, M. and Monur, J. (2002) '11 September and the Challenge of Global Terrorism to the EU as a Security Actor' 40 *Journal of Common Market Studies* 11–28.
Downes, D. (1982) 'The Origins and Consequences of Dutch Penal Policy Since 1945: A Preliminary Analysis' 22 *British Journal of Criminology* 325–62.
—— (1988) *Contrasts in Tolerance* (Clarendon Press: Oxford).

Downes, D. and Hansen, K. (2004) 'Welfare and Imprisonment in Comparative Perspective', paper delivered at the American Society of Criminology (Nashville, 17 November 2004).

Durkheim, E. (1952) *Suicide* (Routledge: London).

Edwards, A. and Gill, P. (eds.) (2003) *Transnational Organised Crime* (Routledge: London).

Embree, L. (2003) 'Reflective Analysis in and of Social Psychology' in Chenng, C. *et al.* (eds.), *Essays in Celebration of the Founding of the Organization of Phenomenological Organizations* (available at <http://at www.o-p-o.net>).

Fosdick, R. (1915) *European Police Systems* (reprint 1969, Patterson Smith: Montclair, NJ).

Garland, D. (2001) *The Culture of Control* (Oxford University Press: Oxford).

—— (2002) 'Of Crimes and Criminals: the Development of Criminology in Britain' in Maguire, M., Morgan, R. and Reiner, R. (eds.), *The Oxford Handbook of Criminology* (3rd edn. Oxford University Press: Oxford).

Hardie-Bick, J., Sheptycki, J. and Wardak, A. (2005) 'Transnational and Comparative Criminology in a Global Perspective' in Sheptycki, J. and Wardak, A. (eds.), *Transnational and Comparative Criminology* (Glass House: London).

Heidensohn, F.M. (1991) 'Introduction: Convergence, Diversity and Change' in Heidensohn, F. and Farrell, M. (eds.), *Crime in Europe* (Routledge: London).

—— (1992) *Women in Control? The Role of Women in Law Enforcement* (Clarendon: Oxford).

—— (1994) ' "We Can Handle it Out Here": Women Officers in Britain and the USA and the Policing of Public Order' 4 *Policing and Society* 293–303.

—— (1997) 'Crime and Policing' in Symes, V., Levy, C. and Littlewood, J. (eds.), *The Future of Europe* (Macmillan: Basingstoke).

—— (2001) 'Research on Women in the Criminal Justice System and Transnational Crime' in Ollus, N. and Nevala, S. (eds.), *Women in the Criminal Justice System* (European Institute for Crime Prevention and Control: Helsinki).

—— (2004) 'Finding New Frontiers to Cross in Criminology' in Winterdyke, J. and Cao, L. (eds.), *Lessons from International/ Comparative Criminology/Criminal Justice* (de Sitter: Toronto).

—— and Farrell, M. (eds.) (1991) *Crime in Europe* (Routledge: London).

Hood, R. (ed.) (1989) *Crime and Criminal Policy in Europe* (Centre for Criminology Research: Oxford).

—— (2002) 'Recollections of Sir Leon Radzinowicz' in Bottoms, A. and Tonry, M. (eds.), *Ideology, Crime and Criminal Justice* (Willan: Devon).

—— (2004) 'Hermann Mannheim and Max Grünhut: Criminological Pioneers in London and Oxford' 44 *British Journal of Criminology* 469–95.

Jones, T. and Newburn, T. (2004) 'The Convergence of US and UK Crime Control Policy: Exploring Substance and Process' in Newburn, T. and Sparks, R. (eds.), *Criminal Justice and Political Cultures* (Willan: Devon).

Karstedt, S. (2004) 'Durkheim, Tarde and Beyond: the Global Travel of Crime Policies' in Newburn, T. and Sparks, R. (eds.), *Criminal Justice and Political Cultures* (Willan: Devon).

Lacey, N. and Zedner, L. (1995) 'Discourses of Community in Criminal Justice' 22 *Journal of Law and Society* 301–20.

—— (1998) 'Community in German Criminology: A Significant Absence?' 7 *Social and Legal Studies* 7–25.

Maguire, M., Morgan, R. and Reiner, R. (eds.) (2002) *The Oxford Handbook of Criminology* (3rd edn, Oxford University Press: Oxford).

Mannheim, H. (1940) *Social Aspects of Crime Between the Wars* (Unwin: London).

—— (1965) *Comparative Criminology*, 2 vols. (Routledge: London).

Mawby, R. (1990) *Comparative Policing Issues: the British and American Experience in International Perspective* (Routledge: London).

—— (1998) 'Victims' Perceptions of Police Services in East and West Europe' in Ruggiero, V., South, N. and Taylor, I. (eds.), *The New European Criminology* (Routledge: London).

—— (ed.) (1999) *Policing Across the World* (UCL Press: London).

Mayhew, P. (2004) 'Comparative Research in a Government Environment' in Winterdyk, J. and Cao, L. (eds.) *Lesson from International/Comparative Criminology/Criminal Justice* (de Sitter: Toronto).

McLaughlin, E. (1992) 'The Democratic Deficit: European Union and the Accountability of the British Police' 32 *British Journal of Criminology* 473–87.

Melossi, D. (2004) 'The Cultural Embeddedness of Social Control' in Newburn T. and Sparks, R. (eds.) *Criminal Justice and Political Cultures* (Willan: Devon).

Nelken, D. (ed.) (1994) *The Futures of Criminology* (Sage: London).

—— (2002) 'Comparing Criminal Justice' in Maguire, M., Morgan, R. and Reiner, R. (eds.). *The Oxford Handbook of Criminology* (3rd edn, Oxford University Press: Oxford).

Nelken, D. (2003a) 'Corruption in the EU' in Bull, M. and Newell, J. (eds.) *Corruption and Scandal in Contemporary Politics* (Macmillan: London).
——(2003b) 'Legitimate Suspicion? Berlusconi and the Judges' in Segathi, P. and Bloudel, J. (eds.), *Politics in Italy 2003* (Berghahn: Oxford).
Neuman, W.L. and Berger, R. (1988) 'Competing Perspectives on Cross-National Crime: An Evaluation of Theory and Evidence' 29 *Sociological Quarterly* 281–313).
Newburn, T. and Sparks, R. (eds.) (2004) *Criminal Justice and Political Cultures* (Willan: Collumpton).
Norman, P. (2005) 'The Evolution of European Policing Strategies in Response to Transnational Crime' in Sheptycki, J. and Wardak, A. (eds.), *Transnational and Comparative Criminology* (Glass House: London).
Owings, C. (1925) *Women Police: A Study of the Development and status of the Women Police Movement* (Bureau of Social Hygiene: New York).
Pakes, I. (2004) 'The Politics of Discontent: The Emergency of a New Criminal Justice Discourse in the Netherlands' 43 *Howard Journal* 284–98.
Pearson, G. (2002) 'Introduction: Crime and Criminology in China' 42 *British Journal of Criminology* 235–9.
Piacentini, L. (2004) *Surviving Russian Prisons* (Willan: Cullompton).
Radzinowicz, L. (1999) *Adventures in Criminology* (Routledge: London).
Raine, L. and Cilluffo, F. (1994) *Global Organised Crime: The New Empire of Evil* (Washington DC Centre for Strategic and International Studies: Washington DC).
Rock, P.E. (1986) *A View from the Shadows: the Ministry of the Solicitor General of Canada and the Making of the Justice for Victims of Crime* (Clarendon: Oxford).
——(1990) *Helping Victims of Crime: the Home Office and the Use of Victim Support in England and Wales* (Clarendon: Oxford).
Rose, N. (2000) 'Government and Control' 40 *British Journal of Criminolog* 321–39.
Sheptycki, J. (1995) 'Transnational Policing and the Makings of a Postmodern State' 35 *British Journal of Criminology* 613–35.
——and Wardak, A. (eds.) (2005) *Transnational and Comparative Criminology* (Glass House: London).
Schutz, A. (1966) 'The Stranger' in Schutz, G. (ed.), *Alfred Schutz: Collected Papers*, vol. II, Problems of Social Theory (Nijhoff: The Hague).

Smandych, R., Lincoln, R. and Wilson, P. (1993) 'Toward a Cross Cultural Theory of Aboriginal Crime' 3 *International Criminal Justice Review* 1–24.

Smith, C. (2004) 'Slawomir Redo: the UN Criminologist' *Inter News Newsletter of the DIC of the ASC*, No. 19, pp. 2–6.

Vagg, J (1993) 'Contest and Linkage: Reflections on Comparative Research and Internationalism' 33 *British Journal of Criminology* 541–54.

Van Dijk, J, (2004) 'On the Victims' Side' in Winterdyk, J. and Cao, L. (eds.) *Lessons from International/Comparative Criminology/Criminal Justice* (de Sitter: Toronto).

Van Swaaningen, (2005) 'Public Safety and the Management of Fear' 9 *Theoretical Criminology* 289–305.

Winterdyk, J. and Cao, L. (eds.) (2004) *Lessons from International/Comparative Criminology/Criminal Justice* (de Sitter: Toronto).

Yacoubian, G.S. (2003) 'Disentangling the Definitional Confusion between Comparative and International Criminology' 3 *International Journal of Comparative Criminology* 223–6.

Young, J. (1999) *The Exclusive Society* (Sage: London).

—— (2003) 'Searching for a New Criminology of Everyday Life: A Review of Garland's Culture of Control' 42 *British Journal of Criminology* 228–61.

Zimring, F. and Johnson, D. (2005) 'On the Comparative Study of Corruption' 45 *British Journal of Criminology* 793–809.

8
Historicizing Contrasts in Tolerance

Nicola Lacey*

David Downes' *Contrasts in Tolerance*[1] is rightly regarded as a landmark in criminal justice scholarship. While its comparative analysis of post-war penal policy in England and Wales and The Netherlands set new standards for macro-level studies of the political economy in which criminal justice systems are embedded, its substantive theses about the conditions under which reductive policies can be politically feasible and practically effective had implications for penal policy well beyond the countries which it examined. Today, in the context of rapidly rising imprisonment rates and a depressing sense of their political inevitability, Downes' insights are yet more relevant—and his message more poignant—to British criminologists. The relevance becomes yet more apparent when we look across the Atlantic to the United States, an avowedly civilized society which nonetheless seems to be able to tolerate—indeed positively to demand—a penal system of staggering scale, cost, and inhumanity. Even in the Netherlands, the conditions which sustained the relatively tolerant penal culture which Downes, charted appear to have been eroded.

Urgent questions therefore occupy the agenda of contemporary comparative criminal justice scholarship. Are we

* My warm thanks go to Markus Dirk Dubber, Liora Lazarus, Jill Peay, Tim Newburn, James Q. Whitman, and Lucia Zedner for comments on an earlier version of this chapter, and to David Soskice for discussion of its argument.
 The arguments set out in this paper are developed more fully in Nicola Lacey, *The Prisoners' Dilemma: Political Economy and Punishment in Contemporary Democracies* (Cambridge University Press 2008).

[1] David Downes, *Contrasts in Tolerance* (Oxford: Clarendon Press, 1988).

witnessing, as Garland might be taken to suggest, a general move towards a 'culture of control',[2] in which a combination of repressive and managerial criminal justice strategies are becoming increasingly salient to governments' ability to present themselves as effective and, where relevant, electable? If so, can this be explained in terms of the globalization of the world economy, accompanying changes in demographic, employment, and family structure[3] and a consequent diminution in nation states' power to control their increasingly interdependent economies, leading to a greater resort to criminal justice policy as a tool of social governance? Additionally or alternatively, is globalization having an impact in terms of increased communication across national systems, with consequently greater co-ordination of policy and transfer of ideas across space? Or do national differences remain key to explaining the dynamics of criminal justice policy?[4] Such questions can only be approached in terms of comparative method. Yet, seventeen years on, *Contrasts in Tolerance* stands not only as a landmark but also as a somewhat lonely beacon in the terrain of comparative macro-level studies of criminal justice.[5] As Michael

---

[2] David Garland, *The Culture of Control*, (New York: Oxford University Press, 2001); see also David Garland (ed.), *Mass Imprisonment in the United States: Social Causes and Consequences* (London, Sage, 2001); Jock Young, *The Exclusive Society* (London: Sage, 1999).

[3] See in more detail Garland, *The Culture of Control* (n. 2 above), ch. 4.

[4] For thoughtful analysis of these questions, see Tim Newburn and Richard Sparks (eds.), *Criminal Justice and Political Cultures* (Cullompton: Willan Publishing, 2004). Many of the essays in this collection are trained on questions of policy transfer in relatively specific areas rather than on the macro-questions to which I am directing attention in this essay. Several, however, make important points about comparative methods more generally: see in particular Newburn and Sparks, 'Criminal justice and Political Cultures' pp. 1–13; Dario Melossi, 'The Cultural Embeddedness of Social Control', pp. 80–103; John Muncie, 'Globalisation and Multi-modal Governance' pp. 152–77. See also David Nelken, 'Comparing Criminal Justice', in Mike Maguire, Rod Morgan and Robert Reiner (eds.), *The Oxford Handbook of Criminology* (3rd edn, Oxford: Oxford University Press, 2002) p. 175.

[5] For other relatively lonely beacons, see Mirjan Damaska, *The Faces of Justice and State Authority* (New Haven: Yale University Press, 1986); Andrew Rutherford, *Prisons and the Process of Justice* (London: Heinemann 1984); Paul Chevigny, 'The Populism of Fear: Politics of Crime in the Americas' (2003) 5 *Punishment and Society* 77.

Tonry noted in 2001,[6] notwithstanding the existence of a great deal of empirical evidence and of a general acknowledgement of the need for sustained comparative research, the field remains patchily, even sparsely, populated. In the first chapter of his book, Downes offered a thoughtful analysis of the reasons underlying the dearth of comparative research. Some of them had to do with the relative isolation of criminology as a discipline and, in genres effecting a rapprochement with mainstream sociology, its association with methods such as interactionism which trained their focus on the details of local knowledge in particular spheres.[7] Others related to the dynamics of the contemporary academy and the costs of producing in-depth, large-scale comparative studies—particularly those with a qualitative as well as a quantitative dimension.[8] Unfortunately, both in Britain and elsewhere, these dynamics have become yet more powerful in the intervening years, with the pressure to publish on a regular basis acting as a serious disincentive to scholars wishing to undertake large-scale, long-term of projects of the kind necessary for serious comparative research.

In explaining the paucity of sustained comparative research, one might also cite the influence of a certain scepticism, in both postmodern scholarship and mainstream sociology, about the appropriateness of 'grand' theory in social research: a tendency to celebrate particularity and contingency and to castigate macro-theoretical perspectives, from Marxism through to methodologically individualistic rational choice theory, for producing obfuscating generalizations. In a classic instance of the baby being jettisoned along with the bathwater, these trends of theoretical scepticism have contributed to the relative dearth of just the sorts of mid-range, speculative comparative studies which might help us to explain the dynamics of contemporary criminal justice policy and to relocate criminal justice scholarship within the overall domain of political economy where, as Downes rightly argued in 1988, it belongs. Even Garland's

---

[6] Michael Tonry, 'Symbol, Substance and Severity in Western Penal Policies', 3 (2001) *Punishment and Society* 517–36 at 530–1.
[7] *Contrasts in Tolerance* (n. 1 above), pp. 4–5.
[8] The limits of linguistic competence, too, have an impact, not least in the bias towards British/American/Australian comparisons in the literature in English.

influential contribution,[9] though refreshingly free from any inhibition about launching large-scale hypotheses, shares in the prevailing non-comparative scholarly culture, and in doing so risks elevating an explanatory framework largely informed by the specificities of the US situation to the status of a general theory of penal dynamics in the modern world.[10] Properly understood, we must regard Garland's thesis as a provocation to comparative research—indeed as a powerful starting point for such research—rather than as a completed project in itself.

While speculative, macro-level comparative criminal justice scholarship remains relatively rare, there has, however, been an explosion of interest and publishing in another, related field: that of long-range historical studies of the development of criminal justice systems in a number of modern societies. At first sight, this is surprising: after all, one might have thought that, given its time-consuming nature, the institutional imperatives just discussed might have inhibited historical as much as comparative work. In fact, however, historical criminal justice studies are flourishing. This is perhaps to be explained by the somewhat more tractable nature of historical data as an object of research: working in archives is laborious but, particularly from the nineteenth century on, sources are predictably available and may not pose the sort of geographical and linguistic challenge that confronts the scholar keen to address two or more systems. Probably more important is the secure establishment of history as a discipline: indeed, the historical work on criminal justice has come as much from historians as from legal scholars and sociologists.[11] Another factor has almost certainly been the influence of Michel Foucault's work, and in particular of his

---

[9] *The Culture of Control* (n. 2 above); cf. Young's *The Exclusive Society* (n. 2 above), a book which is more sensitive to comparative dynamics.

[10] See Lucia Zedner, 'Dangers of Dystopia' (2002) *Oxford Journal of Legal Studies* 341–66; see also James Q. Whitman, *Harsh Justice* (Oxford: Oxford University Press, 2003) pp. 203–5.

[11] See for example John Beattie, *Crime and the Courts in England 1660–1800* (Princeton: Princeton University Press, 1986); *Policing and Punishment in London, 1660–1800* (Oxford: Oxford University Press, 2001); Martin Wiener, *Reconstructing the Criminal* (Cambridge: Cambridge University Press, 1991); *Men of Blood* (Oxford: Oxford University Press 2004); Peter King, *Crime, Justice and Discretion in England 1740–1820*

meditation on the emergence of the carceral system in *Discipline and Punish*.[12] This is somewhat ironic, given that Foucault was associated with poststructuralist theory, was himself a critic of 'grand' theories purporting to offer general 'Truths', and was, as Whitman has argued, curiously blind to the comparative dimensions of his thesis about a movement from punishment of the body to punishment of the soul.[13] Yet Foucault's blend of historical detail with bold, even sweeping hypotheses lent confidence, energy, and intellectual excitement to the project of analysing the history of social institutions, and arguably had its effect even on those most critical of his method and approach.[14] He produced a distinctive blend of history and social theory which has without doubt both invigorated the discipline and liberated it to some extent from the tendency to become embedded in detail to the point where it is difficult to discern the wood constituted by the trees: a tendency which it shares, of course, with some genres of comparative scholarship.[15]

In this essay, I want to examine two recent contributions to this flourishing debate about the history of criminal justice in modern societies so as to develop some ideas about how it can contribute to the structured, macro-level understanding which comparative studies also promise. Focusing on

(Oxford: Oxford University Press, 2000); though, as we shall see, legal scholars like John Langbein, *The Origins of Adversary Criminal Trial* (Oxford: Oxford University Press, 2003); Markus Dirk Dubber, *The Police Power* (New York: Columbia University Press, 2005); Lindsay Farmer, *Criminal Law, Tradition and Legal Order* (Cambridge: Cambridge University Press, 1997); and James Q. Whitman, *Harsh Justice* (Oxford: Oxford University Press, 2003), and sociologists such as David Garland, *Punishment and Welfare* (Aldershot: Gower, 1985) have also made a substantial contribution.

[12] Transl. A. Sheridan, (Harmondsworth: Penguin, 1977).

[13] *Harsh Justice* (n. 10 above), p. 5.

[14] See for example Whitman's swingeing critique: *Harsh Justice* (n. 10 above), p. 98ff. Whitman castigates Foucault both for his lack of comparative perspective and for his deployment of an obfuscatingly over-broad concept of 'modernity'.

[15] For a thoughtful discussion of the pitfalls of comparative research and a plea for an adequately theorized comparative law, see Pierre Legrand, 'How to compare now' (1996) 16 *Legal Studies* 232; 'Comparative Legal Studies and Commitment to Theory' (1995) 58 *Modern Law Review* 262; and Lucia Zedner, 'In Pursuit of the Vernacular: Comparing Law and Order Discourse in Britain and Germany' (1995) 4 *Social and Legal Studies* 517–35.

James Q. Whitman's *Harsh Justice* and Markus Dirk Dubber's *The Police Power*, I shall suggest that historical studies can usefully complement comparative research, can put questions on the agenda of comparative studies, and can fulfil some of the same explanatory and policy-relevant functions as comparative scholarship. When able to avoid getting too preoccupied by the fly's eye perspective invited by so much exotic detail, and when bold enough to work with large-scale hypotheses at the level of social theory, both comparativists and historians, I shall suggest, can provide an illuminating perspective—that of territorial or temporal distance—on the 'local knowledge' garnered by most criminal justice research, in just the way exemplified by Downes' classic study.

Harsh Justice: Socio-political Roots of Contrasts in Tolerance?

A work rich in scholarly detail and wide in analytical sweep, the main question and explanatory thesis of James Q. Whitman's *Harsh Justice* may nevertheless be simply stated. At the start of the twenty-first century, the United States stands not only as the world's one super-power but also as a country with a long democratic tradition, and one which prides itself on its robust constitutional culture and respect for civil rights. Yet its criminal justice system is of the sort which we should expect to find not in one of the world's great democracies but rather in one of the countries whose repressive regimes the United States so loudly decries (if unevenly acts against) in its foreign policy. In quantitative and in qualitative terms, punishment in the United States amounts to harsh justice indeed. Both the record and ever-rising prison population and the uneven distribution of the burdens of the system are striking, with the proportion of young black males now incarcerated inviting functional comparison with the institution of slavery.[16] Moreover, the conditions of life in many

---

[16] See Whitman, *Harsh Justice* (n. 10 above), p. 3, ch. 2; Garland, *The Culture of Control* (n. 2 above), chs. 5 and 6, pp. 208–9; Jerome Bruner, 'Do Not Pass Go' (review of Garland) (2003) 50 *New York Review of Books* 29 September; Marcellus Andrews, 'Punishment, Markets, and the American Model: an Essay on a New American Dilemma' in Seán McConville (ed.), *The Use of Punishment* (Collompton: Willan Publishing, 2003) pp. 116–48.

US prisons are staggeringly harsh: overcrowding is widespread, rape and other forms of violence endemic, and constructive prison regimes rare.[17] A glimpse of the usually closed world of prison life, and of the inhumanity with which the United States regards it as appropriate to treat even unconvicted carceral inmates, was recently to be had on the world's television screens with the transmission of images of detainees—shackled, bound, shuffling—at the Guantánamo Camp Delta in Cuba.

How, Whitman asks, has the United States, with its image of itself so strongly bound up with the notion of progress, civilization, and humanity, ended up with one of the world's harshest and most degrading criminal justice systems? The answer, he suggests, is to be found in social history, and in particular in a comparison between the long-range development of the criminal justice systems in European countries such as France and Germany and in the United States. To paint with very broad brush-strokes, his explanation is as follows: before the great movements of Enlightenment-inspired reform in the eighteenth and early nineteenth centuries, the criminal justice systems of the continent of Europe, like other social institutions, were inherently status-based. The bulk of punishment being carried out against those of low social status, and being orientated to their further degradation within an intensely hierarchical social structure, many punishments—think for example of the range of corporal punishments which formed the core of the penal repertoire—were vividly, and deliberately, humiliating. Moreover, there was a clear and elaborate set of distinctions between high- and low-status penalties. By today's standards, of course, punishments for those of higher social status were also brutal. The key point, however, is that there was a distinction, and that punishment was regarded as an essentially, and justifiably, degrading phenomenon.

But with the decisive turn against the bloody *ancien regime* associated with modernization, codification, and the political culture of the Rechtsstaat, there was a decisive turn away from these degrading forms of punishment, as there also was from

---

[17] For an eloquent—and horrifying—literary depiction of life in a US jail, see Tom Wolfe, *A Man in Full* (Jonathon Cape: London, 1998).

practices such as torture. Indeed, aiming for dignity in punishment and rejecting the old practices of degradation became one of the self-conscious marks of the new civilization. The trajectory, therefore, was a gradual levelling up: a generalization of the high-status, more respectful and humane forms of punishment. Through many twists and turns of history, the association of degradation in punishment with an older, uncivilized model of society now decisively rejected, gave birth to and sustained, in both France and Germany, a relatively mild penal system. As Liora Lazarus has shown in relation to Germany, it also generated a penal system which is regarded as strongly accountable to the courts for reaching constitutionally and otherwise appropriate standards of respect and treatment: the Rechsstaat implies that state coercion must have constitutional justification.[18]

In the United States, by contrast, there was never a revolutionary moment in which a key part of the self-conception of the new order was a rejection of an older, indigenous, status-based society with its implication of appropriate degradation in punishment. This was for the simple reason that no such historical experience existed to be rejected. There was, of course, the institution of slavery. But this lasted well into the late modern period, and indeed cast its own shadow on the development of US penal practice.[19] In the early context of a society of settlers distributed across a huge space, we might further suggest that the imperatives of social order favoured severity in punishment and, moreover, punishment orientated primarily to the exclusion of the deviant rather than to social reintegration. This is not, of course, to argue that this path is an inevitable one for newly founded societies located in a large and perhaps hostile terrain. As John Braithwaite has argued, the Australian experience was

---

[18] For an excellent description and analysis of these features of the contemporary German prison system, see Liora Lazarus, *Contrasting Prisoners' Rights* (Oxford: Oxford University Press, 2004). In what follows, I shall concentrate on Germany rather than France as a comparison point, both because of my greater familiarity with the German system, and because it seems arguable that the French system has developed along significantly different lines, having to do with the distinctive quality of the highly centralized French state.

[19] See Whitman, *Harsh Justice* (n. 10 above), pp. 11, 173–7, 198–9; for a further analysis of the cultural and historical roots of American punitiveness, see Dario Melossi, 'The Cultural Embeddedness of Social Control' (n. 4 above).

different, with the experience of mutual dependence fostering a culture of 'mateship' which, along with economic imperatives in a very sparsely populated country, favoured—at least for the settlers—inclusionary over exclusionary dynamics in mechanisms of social control.[20] In America, by contrast, the specific conditions—notably the existence of a substantial, formally excluded population of slaves, in stark contrast to the Australian trajectory of gradual socio-political inclusion of convicts from a relatively early stage—favoured the development of a harsh, exclusionary, and degrading penal system.

For Whitman, however, it is the absence of a rejected local history of pre-modern, status-based hierarchy which implies the absence of what in Europe was a crucial dynamic in shaping the move towards a humane and legally accountable penal system. Though defining itself in opposition to the hierarchical societies of Europe and strongly attached to status-egalitarianism, the new America opted gradually for a levelling down of punishment, generalizing low- rather than high-status penalties. The difference between the two families of systems is vividly symbolized in the generalization of beheading and of hanging as the modes of execution in the criminal justice systems of Europe and of Britain and the United States, respectively.

This is not the place for a full analysis or critique of Whitman's thesis. But certainly, if we add in the British case,[21] questions may be raised about the weight which he places on what we may call the 'degradation hypothesis'. In Britain, after all, there was if not a decisive revolutionary moment at least a substantial rejection, towards the end of the eighteenth century, of the harsher features of the 'bloody code', with the gradual reforms from then through the early nineteenth century oriented

---

[20] Braithwaite, 'Crime in a Convict Republic' (2001) 64 *Modern Law Review* 11.

[21] It should be made clear that Whitman does not purport to offer a general theory of penal harshness and in particular does not make any claim to explain the British case, which arguably lies outside the four corners of his explanatory hypothesis because, unlike France, Germany, and the United States, it did not experience any form of political revolution in the eighteenth or nineteenth centuries. It seems fair, however, to understand him as making a general argument that traditions of social hierarchy have an impact on practices of punishment, and to this extent to evaluate his thesis in relation to other systems.

to goals not dissimilar from those of the French or German systems. While formal codification of criminal law was never achieved (except in relation to Britain's colonies...), the overt violence of corporal penalties and, eventually, of public hanging was gradually rejected, while the large and unaccountable discretion inherent in the *ancien regime*, along with the harshness of its penalties and the wide scope for royal prerogatives of pardon and mercy, were gradually rationalized in a system orientated more firmly to predictability, certainty, formal justice, and the rule of law. Though certainly not motivated primarily by an ideal of respect for persons, even the austere prison systems of the early Victorian era were informed by an essentially humane view of prisoners as capable of reshaping their characters within a penal environment appropriately calibrated towards repentance and reform.[22] Doubtless this had to do both with the political movement towards a more democratic governmental structure, and with broad cultural changes in mentality and sensibility which, in Britain as in the rest of Europe, decisively affected factors such as the attitude to violence.[23]

Yet, despite these analogies between British and continental political history, Britain's criminal justice system today appears to be far less sensitive than, say, that of Germany to the need to ensure humanity in punishment. Indeed, in terms of indices like imprisonment rates, conditions of imprisonment, legal redress available to prisoners, and salience of criminal justice policy to politics, one might say that the British system looks more like its American than its German cousin, or at least constitutes a hybrid case. This implies that the degradation hypothesis is not the only explanatory factor which is needed to produce an adequate

---

[22] See Martin Wiener, *Reconstructing the Criminal* (Cambridge: Cambridge University Press, 1991). Such humanitarian instincts also shaped reform debates in early nineteenth-century America, with the British prison regimes themselves influenced by the American example: see Michael Ignatieff, *A Just Measure of Pain* (Harmondsworth: Penguin, 1989); Norval Morris and David J. Rothman, *The Oxford History of the Prison* (New York: Oxford University Press, 1998).

[23] See Norbert Elias, *The Civilising Process*, vols. I and II (Oxford: Blackwell Publishing 1978, 1982; first published 1939); V. A. C. Gatrell, *The Hanging Tree* (Oxford: Oxford University Press, 1994); Martin Wiener, *Men of Blood* (Cambridge: Cambridge University Press, 2004).

account of contrasts in penal severity across modern systems at relatively similar levels of economic development.

The degradation thesis is not, however, the only explanatory factor in Whitman's account. Alongside it sits an argument about the distinction between 'weak' and 'strong' states. As Whitman notes, Durkheim's prediction that the development of modernity and in particular the contractualization of social relations towards a 'horizontal' social culture would lead to mildness in punishment is decisively disproved by the American case.[24] Rather, curiously, Americans' attachment to status egalitarianism and their general suspicion of state power appear to have conduced to harshness in punishment. The German recognition of the strong state's legitimate right to proscribe a wide range of forms of conduct is balanced by an accompanying recognition of the state's right to exercise its prerogative of mercy. In the United States, by contrast, any generalized prerogative of clemency *de haut en bas* would be unthinkable: it is entirely inconsistent with the status egalitarian and minimal state mentality. It is significant for this aspect of Whitman's argument that the nineteenth century reforms in Britain and America, but not in Europe, involved a rejection of the prerogative of mercy other than in exceptional cases.[25] The rationale for criminal punishment, therefore, resides not in any sovereign power of the state, but rather in the inherent evil of crime—an attitude which itself conduces to a levelling up of harshness.

Whitman's dual thesis can, I would argue, shed light on some of the contrasts between England and the Netherlands identified and analysed by Downes. For he gives us an insight of the first importance. This is that contemporary differences between the penal systems of relatively similar societies may have long historical roots: roots which, in the light of institutional path-dependence, help to explain the persistence of contrasts even amid an increasingly globalized and intensely economically interdependent world. There is no particular reason to think,

---

[24] *Harsh Justice* (n. 10 above), pp. 194–9.
[25] In the United States, as in the United Kingdom, certain powers of clemency have survived, but they tend to be regarded with suspicion. A recent example would be Bill Clinton's use of the presidential pardon on leaving office, which attracted a great deal of criticism.

pace many criminal justice scholars,[26] that globalization, communication or interdepence imply policy convergence. I do, however, want to suggest that Whitman's argument requires some supplementation. Specifically, I want to suggest that the degradation thesis and a modified version of the strong/weak state thesis are most illuminating when located within a more differentiated comparison rooted in an analysis of political economy—a field in which comparative studies are flourishing.

In *Contrasts in Tolerance*, Downes was rightly cautious about making sweeping claims for the power of an intangible 'culture of tolerance' in the Netherlands, while acknowledging that a tolerant and inclusionary attitude to the treatment of crime among powerful elites had been an important factor in sustaining moderation in penal policy.[27] The Dutch political elite's support for moderation and humanity was, in Downes' view, itself sustained by the complex socio-economic structure of 'pillarization', in which complementary 'columns' 'of denominationalism...guaranteed social order to a high degree on the basis of informal social controls'.[28] The Netherlands' structurally pillarized society exhibited a high degree of group-based stratification: yet it was premised on a generalized norm of incorporation and mutual respect which implied the tolerant, parsimonious and civilized penal system, as well as the tight degree of multi-agency co-ordination and state steering through the prosecution process, which Downes charted. With the gradual breakdown of pillarization, the dynamics which sustained parsimony in the scale and scope of punishment began to be eroded: as the power of informal social controls fell, so the demand for formal controls rose. But, crucially, Downes saw no sign that the demand for an increase in formal social controls was accompanied by any erosion of the other dimension of tolerance: that is, the belief that the quality of punishment

---

[26] See, for example, Michael Tonry, 'Symbol, Substance and Severity in Western Penal Policies' (n. 6 above), pp. 527–31; Tim Newburn and Richard Sparks, 'Criminal Justice and Political Cultures' (n. 4 above).

[27] On the dangers of confounding variables and explanatory concepts in invoking ideas such as 'culture' see David Nelken, 'Disclosing/Invoking Legal Culture' (1995) 4 *Social and Legal Studies* 435–52; see also Nelken (ed.), *Comparing Legal Cultures* (Aldershot: Dartmouth, 1997).

[28] *Contrasts in Tolerance* (n. 1 above), p. 192.

should be humane, respectful and consistent with its subjects' status as members of the polity. While in Britain, the analogous pressures to expand the scale of punishment had led inexorably to an increase in inhumanity via overcrowded prisons which became dumping grounds for the socially excluded, in Downes' analysis, the Dutch demand for expansion in punishment had issued in a number of well-co-ordinated attempts to pre-empt any such outcome through decisive policy measures.[29]

What explains the difference? Here a blend of Whitman's degradation hypothesis and of Downes' interpretation may usefully be combined with the insights of recent political-economic analysis of comparative institutional advantage. In the Netherlands, the political economy depended on the stable integration of all social groups, albeit via a pillarized social structure: it amounted, in short, to what has been termed by Hall and Soskice a 'co-ordinated market economy'.[30] Such an economy, which functions in terms primarily of long-term relationships and stable structures of investment, not least in education and training, and which incorporates a wide range of social groups and institutions into a highly co-ordinated governmental structure, has strong reason to opt for a relatively inclusionary criminal justice system. It is a system which is premised on incorporation, and hence on the need to reintegrate offenders into society and economy.[31] Such a system is structurally less likely to opt for degradation in punishment. Britain, by contrast, falls into Hall and Soskice's model of a 'liberal market economy'. Such economies—of which the purest form, significantly for any argument about criminal justice, is the United States—are typically more individualistic in structure, less interventionist in regulatory stance and depend far less strongly on the sorts of co-ordinating institutions which are needed to sustain long-term economic and social relations. In these economies, flexibility and innovation,

[29] ibid, pp. 201–6.
[30] Peter A. Hall and David Soskice 'An Introduction to the Varieties of Capitalism' in Hall and Soskice (eds.), *Varieties of Capitalism* (Oxford: Oxford University Press, 2003) pp. 1–68.
[31] For an analysis of the impact of these dynamics on German criminal justice, see Nicola Lacey and Lucia Zedner, 'Discourses of Community in Criminal Justice' (1995) 22 *Journal of Law and Society* 93–113.

rather than stability and investment, form the backbone of comparative institutional advantage. It follows that, particularly under conditions of surplus unskilled labour, the costs of a harsh, exclusionary, criminal justice system are less than they would be in a co-ordinated market economy.

My suggestion is that the liberal/co-ordinated market economy distinction may be a more powerful analytical tool than the (undoubtedly overlapping) weak/strong state distinction. This is for two reasons. First, the strong/weak dichotomy may be misleading if applied beyond the rather specific context within which Whitman deploys it. For example, in terms of one of Whitman's key criteria of 'strength'—relative autonomy in policy-making and implementation—both the United Kingdom and, though to a lesser extent the United States,[32] are in some respects strong states. This is because, under certain electoral contingencies (and particularly in the simpler parliamentary structure of the United Kingdom with its strong form of party discipline), the dominance of the executive is such as to allow it to push through its policies in the face of both popular and other-party opposition. Second, the liberal/co-ordinated market economy distinction has an analytic reach into a wider range of interrelated political and economic institutions which characterize particular national systems and which have their impact on criminal justice policy.

Putting these two points together, we could take just one hypothesis which would be susceptible of—and worthwhile—testing within this model. There is an association between co-ordinated market economies and proportionally representative electoral systems and between liberal market economies and first-past-the-post, winner-takes-all systems—a difference which may itself feed into the relative 'strength' of different kinds of political economy under varying external conditions.[33] To put it crudely, the 'strength' (in the sense of policy-making autonomy) of co-ordinated market economies is rather regularly constrained by the need to negotiate with groups incorporated in the governmental process. But this consensus-building dynamic

---

[32] Its particular structure makes the United States a 'strong' state in relation to foreign but not domestic policy.
[33] See Arend Lijphart, *Patterns of Democracy: Government Forms and Performance in 36 Countries* (New Haven: Yale University Press, 1999).

may make them 'stronger' in the sense of less heteronymous in the light of swings of popular opinion. While clear winners of first-past-the-post elections in liberal market economies may feel relatively unconstrained by popular opinion early on in their terms, their unmediated accountability at the ballot box will make them highly sensitive to public opinion as elections loom. What is more, their increasing dependence on the approval of a large number of 'floating' median voters, sufficiently affluent to regard crime as a threat to their wellbeing, may feed into the political salience of criminal justice.[34] Under the sorts of economic and cultural conditions charted by Garland, therefore, it may be that there is a further association between the politicization of criminal justice and the impact of penal populism in liberal market economies such as the United States, with decisive implications for the harshness of punishment.

In Britain, notwithstanding a political history that might lead us to expect Whitman's degradation hypothesis to have some explanatory power, the dynamics of a liberal market economy have progressively eroded the anti-degradation sensibility. We can see, one might argue, the force of the anti-degradation sensibility at work in the early nineteenth century penal reform movements, as in the penal welfare movement of the late nineteenth and early twentieth centuries; in the borstal system, in the development of probation, and in much else besides.[35] (It is significant—and unsettling to Whitman's degradation thesis— that we can also identify American analogues to these instances of humanitarian penal reformism.) But the influence of the dynamics of a liberal market economy have increased markedly over the past twenty-five years, as many of the attitudes and

[34] Cf, Chevigny, 'The Populism of Fear' (n. 5 above); Bert Useem, Raymond V. Liedka and Anne Morrison Piehl, 'Popular Support for the Prison Build-up' (2003) 5 *Punishment and Society* 5; Mick Ryan, *Penal Policy and Political Culture in England and Wales* (Winchester: Waterside Press, 2003); J. Pratt, D. Brown, M. Brown, S. Hallsworth and W. Morrison (eds.), *The New Punitiveness* (Cullompton: Willan, 2005).

[35] See David Garland, *Punishment and Welfare* (n. 11 above); Michael Ignatieff, *A Just Measure of Pain* (New York: Pantheon Books, 1978). As Whitman also acknowledges, the differences between the United States and the French and German systems have become much starker since the collapse of the welfarist rehabilitative consensus in the early 1970s: see *Harsh Justice* (n. 10 above), p. 193.

values which sustained the post-war welfare state settlement have come to be eroded by a more aggressively market-orientated culture.[36] This political culture is itself premised in part on the imperative of high performance amid increasing global economic competition, with the collapse of Fordist production regimes and the availability of cheap manufactured goods from countries like Singapore, South Korea and, more recently, China and India. The inevitable upshot is structural economic insecurity for low-skilled workers in advanced liberal market economies.[37] In a short-term economic culture, the bottom third of the work force risks become a socially as well as economically excluded group.[38]

It is therefore no surprise that during this period we have seen not only a large increase in the absolute and relative size of the harsher end of the British and American criminal justice systems, but also a weakening of political sensibilities in favour of human rights and decent conditions for prisoners. There comes a point, we might suggest, at which both the absolute situation of the disadvantaged and disparities of wealth between rich and poor—disparities which are markedly greater in liberal than in co-ordinated market economies—become so acute as to amount in themselves to a form of status distinction.[39] And this in turn dissolves Whitman's apparent paradox about the co-existence of degrading punishment with (formal) status egalitarianism in the contemporary United States. In the face of political-economic imperatives, the anti-degradation mentality is relatively weak. Whitman's degradation and strong state hypotheses, in short, need to be articulated with a theory of the structure of political economy: the power of anti-degradation sentiments is itself a function of their resonance and consistency with broader dynamics of socio-economic organization.

[36] See Robert Reiner, 'Beyond Risk: A Lament for Social Democratic Criminology', ch. 2 above.
[37] On the sociological implications of this economic transformation, see Richard Sennett, *The Corrosion of Character* (New York: Norton, 1998).
[38] See C. Hale, 'Economic Marginalisation and Social Exclusion', in C. Hale, K. Hayward, A Wahidin and E. Wincup (eds.), *Criminology* (Oxford: Oxford University Press, 2005).
[39] On the criminological significance of relative deprivation, see Robert Reiner, 'Beyond Risk', ch. 2 above.

The Police Power: Tracing Patriarchal Power in Modern Penal Mechanisms

In Downes' characterization of the relatively tolerant nature of Dutch penality, as in Lazarus' analysis of the relatively humane contemporary German prison system, one important explanatory factor is the way in which penal practices sit within a broader legal framework which ensures the accountability of penal power to public and even constitutional standards. On the face of it, the existence of such a framework in a modern liberal democracy is hardly surprising. In such societies, with the exception of wartime or other emergency situations, penal power is the most coercive state apparatus, and it is taken as given that it calls for justification. Against a backcloth of respect for civil rights and formally equal membership of the polity, the infliction of criminal punishment has to be justified, one would assume, in terms of arguments which respect the interests of all.

Two main families of justification have dominated the field since the late eighteenth century. First there are deontological theories which emphasize the justice of punishment in terms of factors such as desert, often fleshed out in terms of the capacity of punishment to restore a moral equilibrium which has been upset by criminal conduct.[40] On the basis of some form of social contract generating reciprocal obligations of forbearance and respect, an offender may be seen as having taken an unfair advantage *vis-à-vis* fellow citizens: proportionate punishment is called for to wipe out the unfair advantage and to restore the normal relations of justice between citizens. On the basis of a robust requirement that offenders be proven to be truly responsible for their offences, such a theory claims to respect their autonomy and individual rights: indeed, on some versions of this theory, the offender is seen as having in some sense willed his or her own punishment.[41]

The second family of penal justifications is consequentialist.[42]

---

[40] Michael S. Moore, *Placing Blame* (Oxford: Clarendon Press, 1997).
[41] For a thoughtful critique of this genre of theory, see Stephen Paul Brown, 'Punishment and the Restoration of Rights' (2001) 3 *Punishment and Society* 485–500.
[42] Jeremy Bentham, *An Introduction to the Principles of Morals and Legislation* (1789), ed. H. L. A. Hart and J. H. Burns (London: Methuen, 1982).

These theories argue that punishment, though *prima facie* an evil, may be justified by its contribution to the good of all in society through effects such as deterrence, incapacitation, rehabilitation, reparation, satisfaction of victims' grievances, prevention of resort to private vengeance, and even moral education. Consequentialist theories, too, claim to respect the autonomy of individuals in that each person's welfare is taken equally seriously. As is well known, however, the distributive implications of pure consequentialist theories are problematic from the point of view of a moral position strongly committed to the independent importance of justice, rights, or individual autonomy. They would justify, for example, the framing of an innocent person or a grossly disproportionate punishment wherever this would maximize overall social benefits. For this reason, pure consequentialism is relatively rarely defended today, and most penal philosophers—like designers of penal policy—seek to draw on the insights of both families of justification, blending an appreciation of the importance of framing punishment so as to pursue social benefits while constraining its distribution in terms of individual rights and autonomy through a general requirement of responsibility and/or in terms of an overarching political theory such as republicanism.[43]

The recognition that punishment must be justified might therefore be thought to lie at the heart of the self-conception of a liberal-democratic modern society. Yet, as the contrasts unearthed by Downes suggest, the urgency with which this need for justification is felt varies markedly across systems. The tolerance of and, indeed, positive public support for 'harsh justice' in the United States undoubtedly discloses a weaker popular disposition to question the state's exercise of its power to punish than is suggested by the nature of the Dutch public debate in the

---

[43] See for example H. L. A. Hart, *Punishment and Responsibility* (Oxford: Clarendon Press, 1968); John Braithwaite and Philip Pettit, *Not Just Deserts: A Republican Theory of Criminal Justice* (Oxford: Oxford University Press, 1990); R. A. Duff, *Punishment, Communication and Community* (Oxford: Oxford University Press, 2001); Nicola Lacey, *State Punishment* (London: Routledge, 1988); Andrew von Hirsch, *Censure and Sanctions* (Oxford: Clarendon Press, 1993).

mid-1980s about how to reform the criminal justice system in the light of newly emerging crime problems associated with drugs,[44] or by the elaborate system of German prisoners' rights described by Lazarus.[45] Yet, as Whitman acknowledges, this is on the face of it paradoxical, given the American disposition to be suspicious of state power. Nonetheless, given the increasing salience of criminal justice to electoral politics, and the force of electoral discipline on democratic governments,[46] it seems obvious that these contrasts in popular attitudes to punishment constitute an important explanatory variable in any attempt to understand the differences between contemporary penal systems in relatively similar societies.

In *The Police Power*, Markus Dubber advances an historical thesis which may be of relevance to our understanding of these differences. Like Whitman's, Dubber's argument plays out over a very large historical and spatial canvass, but has an essentially simple structure. Looking back even as far as the city states of classical Greece, Dubber argues, we can discern two markedly different forms of public power: political power and police power. Political power is that through which a society of equals governs itself. It is, in effect, a form of self-government; it takes place through law and is constrained by the demands of justice, formal equality, and so on. Police power, by contrast, derives from the power of the head of a family to govern the resources—animate and inanimate—within his household. It is hierarchical and essentially patriarchal power, discretionary and vaguely defined in its essence, a power of management over persons and things themselves not invested with rights or autonomy. Instrumental and preventative in temper, the police power is orientated to goals such as peace, welfare, efficient use of resources, and security.[47] This is not to say that police power is unconstrained: the patriarch is under an obligation to govern his household so as to maximize its welfare; hence feckless or malicious exercises of police power will be regarded as

---

[44] See *Contrasts in Tolerance* (n. 1 above), chs. 5 and 7.
[45] *Contrasting Prisoners' Rights* (n. 18 above).
[46] As I argued in the previous section, this discipline may be more stringent in the winner-takes-all electoral systems typical of liberal market economies.
[47] *The Police Power* (n. 11 above), ch. 5.

illegitimate.[48] But the nature of these constraints of fitness and prudence are markedly different from the criteria of legitimacy governing the exercise of genuinely political power.

Dubber traces the distinction between political and police power through the centuries and through a wide range of influential legal and philosophical tracts from Aristotle through to Locke, Rousseau, Blackstone, and Smith.[49] In England, the emergence of an increasingly powerful monarch, and the expanding reach of the King's Peace, gradually overlaid the police power of landowners with the overarching police power of the monarch. Within this emerging structure, the monarch constituted, as it were, the macro-householder in relation to whom all subjects, including the landowning micro-householders, were regarded as resources to be managed efficiently (and as beneficiaries of the monarch's paternalist obligations). The police power of the monarch lay alongside the political and legal structures which treat persons as formally equal—notably jury trials. Looking far back into the history of early modern England, provisions such as the Statute of Labourers, anti-vagrancy and gaming laws were, Dubber suggests, quintessentially manifestations of the police power rather than of self-government through law. While exquisite status distinctions marked the system at every level, even the main law of serious crimes—the law of felony—found its origins in outlawry, was rooted in the notion of a breach of the feudal nexus, existed primarily to protect the Lords (just as Treason existed to protect the monarch) and was trained primarily on those of low status—the non-householders.[50] Where restitutive or reparative measures were ineffective, the primary resort of the criminal process was explicitly degrading, typically physical, punishment. Such punishments were designed to enact on the subject's body the degradation which, notwithstanding trial by jury, his or her offence implied, without thereby permanently unfitting him for productive labour (hence the prevalence of whipping). Criminal justice and punishment were, on this view, primarily a

---

[48] *The Police Power* (n. 11 above), p. 42 ff and ch. 8.
[49] *The Police Power* (n. 11 above), Part I.
[50] *The Police Power* (n. 11 above), pp. 14–16, 19.

hierarchical means of managing a population and not an expression of self-governance within a community of equals.

There was always, therefore, an ambiguity about the status of criminal justice, which lay on the muddy border between political/legal and police power. With the gradual emergence of modern sensibilities and a vestigially democratic structure of government, the place of the police power, and its relationship with legal/constitutional/political power, became yet harder to rationalize within an overarching political theory. Imported—ironically but enthusiastically—to America by the Founding Fathers, the police power, Dubber argues, flourishes to this day in the United States. Yet it has never been settled within a constitutional or other legal framework which could generate the sorts of accountability consistent with the overall attitude to public power in a liberal-democratic polity. It would generally be taken as obvious that criminal justice power is legal power: the subjects of modern criminal law have in most systems a panoply of procedural rights, and criminal justice systems are increasingly subject to the overarching regulation of bills of rights enshrined in national constitutions or supra-national legal instruments such as the European Convention on Human Rights. But, Dubber argues, if we look at the substance of criminal law—what may be criminalized and how—we see, even in a country with as robust a constitutional culture as the United States, something approaching a vacuum in terms of accepted constraints. While the power to punish may be weakly constrained by standards such as the prohibition on cruel and unusual punishments, the power to criminalize remains all but unconstrained. This, he suggests, discloses strong traces of the police mentality which characterized much of the early, premodern criminal justice system, particularly that trained on the governance of the lower status members of society.

Despite some discussion of the origins of the concept of police in French thought and of the continental development of a 'police science' in the eighteenth century,[51] Dubber unfortunately does not pursue any sustained comparative analysis. But his argument may certainly be put to comparative use. For the purposes of explaining contemporary differences in attitudes to

[51] *The Police Power* (n. 11 above), ch. 4.

the proper constraints on penal power, the key point in his story comes with the emergence of modern democratic sentiments and political structures. This is a point at which, as we have seen, the tension between law and police becomes much harder to manage than within the older, comfortably status-based societies which preceded the modern era. My suggestion is that there may be an important difference here between modern societies. On the one hand we have societies such as those of continental Europe, whose modern constitutional settlement made explicit the distinction between police and law. These settlements aimed to domesticate the police power within a new political framework, while explicitly differentiating it from legal power. On the other hand, we have societies such as Britain and the United States, which absorbed the police power, unacknowledged, within the new legal power. In these societies, as Dubber suggests has been the case in the United States, the police power infuses the self-governing, autonomy-respecting aspects of criminal law with a managerial mentality in which the ends always justify the means. It is worth examining this distinction in some detail.

As Dubber notes, in many countries—including both Germany and the United States—the debate about whether the police power is an aspect of legal power or whether it is a separate branch of government continued right up to the twentieth century, with marked differences of opinion as to the implications of locating the police power within the criminal justice system.[52] In the United States, for example, Roscoe Pound was inclined to regard the police power's consequentialist orientation as appropriate to the tasks of rational modern governance. By contrast, jurists like Sayre regarded it as having a dangerous capacity to subvert the procedural safeguards and autonomy-respecting constraints of a truly legal order. In effect, Dubber suggests, the views of Pound have won the day: the police power flourishes at both state and federal levels, albeit rationalized in different ways.[53] At the federal level, it is disguised as an exercise of the right to regulate commerce; at the state level, the constitutional appropriateness of police power is acknowledged, yet the state courts have been slow to develop the sort of theory of

---

[52] *The Police Power* (n. 11 above), ch. 7.
[53] *The Police Power* (n. 11 above), ch. 6.

substantive due process which might effectively constrain its definition and exercise.[54]

In both Britain and the America, probably the most obvious manifestation of the police power is the existence of widespread regulatory offences in areas such as driving, health and safety, licensing, low-grade public disorder. These *mala prohibita*—many of them attracting strict liability[55]—are often regarded by criminal law scholars as an embarrassing exception to the normal principles governing the law of *mala in se* or 'real crime'. They exist to promote the social welfare, and since their conviction does not imply the sort of stigma or the severe penalties attached to 'real crimes' such as murder or theft, the absence of a robust responsibility requirement and suspension of the procedural safeguards which purportedly characterize the criminal justice system are tolerated. Examine any treatise on criminal law, however, and you will find little about these numerous regulatory offences. Nor will a standard treatise give much space to troubling 'exceptions' to the 'normal' principles of criminal procedure such as anti-social behaviour orders,[56] which deploy a formally civil process to invoke a substantively criminalizing power. These absences reflect the difficulty of reconciling regulatory mechanisms with the predominant conception of criminal law as a quasi-moral normative system concerned with wrong-doing and culpability.[57] British and American criminal law therefore encompasses two markedly different sorts of

---

[54] Dubber himself begins to develop such a theory: see *The Police Power* (n. 11 above), ch. 9.

[55] i.e. liability without proof of fault in the sense of responsibility conditions such as intention, recklessness, negligence or knowledge.

[56] Crime and Disorder Act 1998; www.crimereduction.gov.uk/asbos5.htm; see Tim Newburn, 'Young People, Crime and Youth Justice', in Mike Maguire, Rod Morgan and Robert Reiner (eds.), *The Oxford Handbook of Criminology* (Oxford: Oxford University Press) pp. 531–78 at pp. 563–4; and Ken Pease, 'Crime Reduction', in Maguire *et al.* pp. 947–79 at pp. 969–70.

[57] For further analysis and discussion, see Nicola Lacey, Celia Wells and Oliver Quick, *Reconstructing Criminal Law* (3rd edn, Cambridge: Cambridge University Press, 2003) and Nicola Lacey, 'In Search of the Responsible Subject: History, Philosophy and Criminal Law Theory' (2001) 64 *Modern Law Review* 350–71. And for a recent, explicit, example of the marginalization of regulatory offences, see Victor Tadros, *Criminal Responsibility* (Oxford: Oxford University Press, 2005) p. 16.

regulatory systems. But because this is rarely acknowledged, there has been little effort either to rationalize the quasi-moral and the morally neutral, instrumental forms of social regulation or—more importantly—to develop a proper account of the limits of the state's regulatory power.

On the continent of Europe, however, this location of regulatory offences within the framework of criminal law 'proper' would be regarded as most unsatisfactory. Rather than sweeping the old police power within the modern framework of criminal justice, the modern governmental settlements of European codification of the early nineteenth century were inclined to separate out this form of social regulation within a discrete framework, leaving regulatory offences as a more visible and autonomous manifestation of state power. As Whitman puts it:

The strength of the bureaucratised European state also helps explain another crucial aspect of mildness in French and German punishment: the capacity of French and German law to define some forbidden acts as something less awful than 'crimes'—as mere *contraventions* or *Ordnungswidrigkeiten*. When European jurists define these species of forbidden conduct, they are able to make use of terms which would trouble Americans. The justification for punishing *Ordnungswidrigkeiten*, according to standard texts, lies in the pure sovereign prerogative of the state....

This, Whitman argues, has decisive implications for the severity of punishment:

[I]t is important to recognize what Europeans gain by pursuing this form of analysis. Because they are able to defer to state power, they are able to treat some offenses as merely forbidden, rather than as evil:—as *mala prohibita* rather than *mala in se*. The contrast with the United States is strong: our liberal, anti-statist tradition leads us to conclude that nothing may be forbidden by the state unless it is *evil*...[58]

And it is this association of crime with evil which has come to feed so intractably into other, political-economic dynamics favouring penal severity.

Doubtless we should not exaggerate the significance of this difference between the European and the British and American

---

[58] *Harsh Justice* (n. 10 above), p. 201 (both quotations).

systems. After all, explicitly administrative or regulatory power may be abused just as readily as criminal justice power. But there is nonetheless something important about the way in which the continental systems declined to sweep the old police power under the carpet of the modern criminal justice system: a recognition of the need for regulation in the name of social welfare, but equally a recognition that this is a different project from criminal justice and state punishment, calling for separate scrutiny and a different kind of justification. My suggestion is that this recognition of the distinctiveness of criminal justice and penal power may also be associated with a more robust attitude to the need for the state to justify its penal power, and for that penal power to be held to legal account, in countries like Germany and the Netherlands as compared with Britain and the United States. When combined with the political economy analysis sketched in the last section, this comparative legal framework may help us to understand the persisting differences between the German or Dutch and the British or American systems—as well as illuminating the dynamics which may be putting those long-standing differences under pressure.[59]

Conclusion

Further contributions to the genre of comparative scholarship exemplified by David Downes' *Contrasts in Tolerance*,

[59] In this context it is interesting to note the outcome of the German elections (September 2005), in which the Christian Democrats were widely predicted to gain a substantial victory. In the event, their neo-liberal agenda of economic reform—which would, had it been thoroughly pursued, have attempted to move Germany away from the co-ordinated towards the liberal market economy structure—appears to have deprived them of decisive electoral success, with the German electorate resisting transition to flexible labour markets and the dismantling of social protections characteristic of the postwar political settlement. (Some of the same dynamics appear to have influenced the French electorate's negative assessment of the European Constitution.) If my analysis in this paper is correct, this electoral outcome has been a positive thing from the point of view of the survival of a relatively tolerant German criminal justice policy—at least in relation to those successfully incorporated into the economy.

How much success a Christian Democratic majority government would have had in dismantling the institutional features which sustain Germany's

I have argued, are urgently required. In purely intellectual terms, the challenge of understanding the relationship between criminalization and broader features of the cultural, political, and economic environment remains one of the most fascinating—and incompletely met—in the social sciences. More pragmatically, in an increasingly interdependent world, and one in which both technologies of communication and supra-state political structures militate to the transmission of policy initiatives across space, the task of understanding the conditions under which particular policies are likely to be effective is compelling indeed. Only comparative research located within a broader understanding of how particular political economies function has any hope of generating a robust answer to this question. I have further argued, however, that comparative research may need an historical dimension; and that recent research on the development of criminal justice systems over long periods of time may produce important insights for the comparativist.

It follows that the legitimacy of criminology or criminal justice studies as autonomous disciplines must be questioned. Since criminal justice systems—the articulation of offences, their interpretation, and application through a range of social practices, and the imposition of punishment—are embedded in broader cultural, political, and economic institutional structures, it makes little sense to study them in isolation. A future of dialogue and co-operation between criminologists, historians, political scientists, sociologists, psychologists, and others therefore promises more illumination than a future of splendid isolation for the criminal justice scholar. This may be obvious, but it is perhaps worth stating in a context in which public funding is rather readily available for short-term research into pressing 'crime problems', but less readily available for

---

co-ordinated market economy is debatable. What seems clear, however, is that it is easier to dismantle such institutions than to construct them. To this extent, I would suggest that 'globalization'—primarily in the sense of economic exchange and interdependence—is likely to favour liberal over co-ordinated market economic structures. I therefore—regretfully—share Robert Reiner's pessimistic prognosis for the future of social-democratic criminal justice policy ('Beyond Risk', ch. 2, above).

long-term, collaborative projects exploring broader and less immediately policy-relevant hypotheses.[60]

In this essay, I have simply pointed to a small number of hypotheses, generated by historical research, which would be susceptible of careful comparative investigation. The broad hypotheses of theoretically inclined contemporary criminologists provide a further provocation to, and starting point for, comparative and historical research. But without such research, their hypotheses cannot be tested in a meaningful way. This insight, as much as his substantive account of the differences between Dutch and English post-war penal policy, is a lasting, and significant, contribution of David Downes' *Contrasts in Tolerance* to criminal justice scholarship.

Bibliography

Andrews, M. (2003) 'Punishment, Markets, and the American Model: an Essay on a New American Dilemma' in McConville, S. (ed.), *The Use of Punishment* (Willan Publishing: Collompton).

Beattie, J. (1986) *Crime and the Courts in England 1660–1800* (Princeton University Press: Princeton).

—— (2001) *Policing and Punishment in London, 1660–1800* (Oxford University Press: Oxford).

Bentham, J. (1982) ed. Hart, H.L.A. and Burns, J.H., *An Introduction to the Principles of Morals and Legislation* ed. Hart, H.L.A. and Burns, J.H., first published 1789 (Methuen: London).

Braithwaite, J. (2001) 'Crime in a Convict Republic' 64 *Modern Law Review* 11.

—— and Pettit, P. (1990) *Not Just Deserts: A Republican Theory of Criminal Justice* (Oxford University Press: Oxford).

Brown, S.P. (2001) 'Punishment and the Restoration of Rights' 3 *Punishment and Society* 485–500.

Bruner, J. (2003) 'Do Not Pass Go' (review of Garland) 50 *New York Review of Books*, 29 September.

Chevigny, P. (2003) 'The Populism of Fear: Politics of Crime in the Americas' 5 *Punishment and Society* 77.

---

[60] See Lucia Zedner, 'Useful Knowledge? Debating the Role of Criminology in Post-War Britain', in Lucia Zedner and Andrew Ashworth (eds.), *The Criminological Foundations of Penal Policy: Essays in Honour of Roger Hood* (Oxford: Clarendon Press, 2003).

Damaska, M. (1986) *The Faces of Justice and State Authority* (Yale University Press: New Haven).
Downes, D. (1988) *Contrasts in Tolerance* (Clarendon Press: Oxford).
Dubber, D.M. (2005) *The Police Power* (Columbia University Press: New York).
Duff, R.A. (2001) *Punishment, Communication and Community* (Oxford University Press: Oxford).
Elias, N. (1978/1982) *The Civilising Process*, vols. I and II (Blackwell Publishing: Oxford, first published 1939).
Farmer, L. (1997) *Criminal Law, Tradition and Legal Order* (Cambridge University Press: Cambridge).
Foucault, M. (1977) *Discipline and Punish* (transl. A. Sheridan) (Penguin: Harmondsworth).
Garland, D. (1985) *Punishment and Welfare* (Gower: Aldershot).
―― (2001) *The Culture of Control* (Oxford University Press: New York).
―― (ed.) (2001) *Mass Imprisonment in the United States: Social Causes and Consequences* (Sage: London).
Gatrell, V.A.C. (1984) *The Hanging Tree* (Oxford University Press: Oxford).
Hale, C. (2005) 'Economic Marginalisation and Social Exclusion' in Hale, C., Hayward, K., Wahidin, A. and Wincup, E. (eds.), *Criminology* (Oxford University Press: Oxford).
Hall, P.A. and Soskice, D. (2003) 'An Introduction to the Varieties of Capitalism', in Hall, P.A. and Soskice, D. (eds.), *Varieties of Capitalism* (Oxford University Press: Oxford), pp. 1–68.
Hart, H.L.A. (1968) *Punishment and Responsibility* (Clarendon Press: Oxford).
Ignatieff, M. (1989) *A Just Measure of Pain* (Penguin: Harmondsworth).
King, M. (2000) *Crime, Justice and Discretion in England 1740–1820* (Oxford University Press: Oxford).
Lacey, N. (1988) *State Punishment* (Routledge: London).
―― (2001) 'In Search of the Responsible Subject: History, Philosophy and Criminal Law Theory' 64 *Modern Law Review* 350–71.
―― and Zedner, L. (1995) 'Discourses of Community in Criminal Justice' 22 *Journal of Law and Society* 93–113.
―― Wells, C. and Quick, O. (2003) *Reconstructing Criminal Law* (3rd edn, Cambridge University Press: Cambridge).
Langbein, J. (2003) *The Origins of Adversary Criminal Trial* (Oxford University Press: Oxford).
Lazarus, L. (2004) *Contrasting Prisoners' Rights* (Oxford University Press: Oxford).

Legrand, P. (1995) 'Comparative Legal Studies and Commitment to Theory' 58 *Modern Law Review* 262.
—— (1996) 'How to Compare Now' 16 *Legal Studies* 232–42.
Lijphart, A. (1999) *Patterns of Democracy: Government Forms and Performance in 36 Countries* (Yale University Press: New Haven).
Melossi, D. (2004) 'The Cultural Embeddedness of Social Control' in Newburn, T. and Sparks, R. (eds.), *Criminal Justice and Political Cultures* (Willan Publishing: Cullompton).
Moore, M.S. (1997) *Placing Blame* (Clarendon Press: Oxford).
Morris, N. and Rothman, D.J. (1998) *The Oxford History of the Prison* (Oxford University Press: New York).
Muncie, J. (2004) 'Globalisation and Multi-modal Governance' in Newburn, T. and Sparks, R. (eds.), *Criminal Justice and Political Cultures* (Willan Publishing: Cullompton).
Nelken, D. (1995) 'Disclosing/Invoking Legal Culture' 4 *Social and Legal Studies* 435–52.
—— (ed.), (1997) *Comparing Legal Cultures* (Dartmouth: Aldershot).
—— (2002) 'Comparing Criminal Justice' in Maguire, M., Morgan, R. and Reiner, R., (eds.), *The Oxford Handbook of Criminology* (3rd edn, Oxford University Press: Oxford).
Newburn, T. (2002) 'Young People, Crime and Youth Justice', in Maguire, M., Morgan, R. and Reiner, R. (eds.), *The Oxford Handbook of Criminology* (Oxford University Press: Oxford).
—— and Sparks, R. (eds.) (2004) *Criminal Justice and Political Cultures* (Willan Publishing: Cullompton).
Pratt, J., Brown, D., Brown, M., Hallsworth, S., and Morrison, W. (eds.) (2005) *The New Punitiveness* (Willan Publishing: Cullompton).
Rutherford, A. (1984) *Prisons and the Process of Justice* (Heinemann: London).
Ryan, M. (2003) *Penal Policy and Political Culture in England and Wales* (Waterside Press: Winchester).
Sennett, R. (1998) *The Corrosion of Character* (Norton: New York).
Tadros, V. (2005) *Criminal Responsibility* (Oxford University Press: Oxford).
Tonry, M. (2001) 'Symbol, Substance and Severity in Western Penal Policies', 3 *Punishment and Society* 517–36.
Useem, B., Liedka, R.V., and Piehl, A.M. (2003) 'Popular Support for the Prison Build-up' 5 *Punishment and Society* 5–32.
von Hirsch, A. (1993) *Censure and Sanctions* (Clarendon Press: Oxford).
Wiener, M. (1991) *Reconstructing the Criminal* (Cambridge University Press: Cambridge).

Wiener, M. (2004) *Men of Blood* (Oxford University Press: Oxford).
Whitman, J.Q. (2003) *Harsh Justice* (Oxford University Press: Oxford).
Young, J. (1999) *The Exclusive Society* (Sage: London).
Zedner, L. (1995) 'In Pursuit of the Vernacular: Comparing Law and Order Discourse in Britain and Germany' 4 *Social and Legal Studies* 517–35.
—— (2002) 'Dangers of Dystopia' 22 *Oxford Journal of Legal Studies* 341–66.
—— (2003) 'Useful Knowledge? Debating the Role of Criminology in Post-war Britain', in Zedner, L. and Ashworth, A. (eds.), *The Criminological Foundations of Penal Policy: Essays in Honour of Roger Hood* (Clarendon Press: Oxford).

9

Contrasts in Intolerance: Cultures of Control in the United States and Britain

Tim Newburn[1]

Introduction

'Criminology has in general been strikingly uncomparative', David Downes (1988: 2) wrote in his introduction to his pathbreaking comparative study of penal policy in England and the Netherlands: *Contrasts in Tolerance*. Were David writing the preface to a new edition today there would be little need to revise the sentence. Despite something of a renaissance of interest in comparative criminology (see, for example, the chapters by Heidensohn and Lacey in this volume) such work still remains the exception. What has changed markedly, however, since the publication of *Contrasts* is the character of penal policy in both England and the Netherlands. Penal policy in England, as is well rehearsed (Garland, 2001a; Downes and Morgan, 2002), has taken a strongly punitive turn. However, far from this increasing the contrast between the two jurisdictions, recent developments in The Netherlands have, if anything, served to bring them closer together. The past decade-and-a-half have seen a substantial rise

---

[1] This paper draws on work in which Trevor Jones and I have been involved, in the interstices between other projects, for the past five or six years. Anything of value in this chapter therefore owes a huge amount to him. Any shortcomings are my responsibility alone. I am grateful to Iman Heflin for research assistance in the preparation of this paper and to Vanessa Barker, Mercedes Hinton, Hans N. Huggler, Trevor Jones, Paul Rock, Mike Shiner, Anna Souhami and Michael Tonry for hugely helpful comments on an earlier draft.

in the Dutch prison population which has grown threefold since 1992. From an all-time low of 25 per 100,000 in the mid-1970s, the incarceration rate in the Netherlands reached 127 by early 2006. This was only slightly lower than the incarceration rate (141) in England and Wales at the same point. In addition to the increasing frequency with which incarceration is used in the Netherlands, there has also been what David Downes and René van Swaaningen (2006) describe as a shift in the 'depth of imprisonment', with the Dutch penal system increasing its emphasis on security and efficiency and increasing penal austerity generally. The extent of these changes mark the end, they suggest, of 'Dutch exceptionalism' as a relative penal utopia and bring it closer into line with what is happening in jurisdictions like the United Kingdom and the United States.

To the extent that the Netherlands and Britain are becoming increasingly similar in the ways that crime is talked about, understood and responded to, such developments fit fairly neatly with one of the dominant criminological discourses of the age: the view that the economic and socio-cultural changes associated with late modernity, or late modern capitalism, are bringing about convergence among the criminal justice systems of the developed economies. Such arguments, which have been deployed at their most comprehensive, and subtle, by David Garland (2001a), are now exerting an enormous influence on criminological thinking. Considerable scholarship is focused upon understanding and unravelling elements of the 'new punitiveness' (Pratt *et al.*, 2005) and there seems little doubt that on a broad level the contemporary penal cultures of both England and the Netherlands share some important characteristics with those of the United States, not least in the rise of what appears to be an increasingly intolerant penal climate.

None of this reduces the opportunity for, or the importance of, comparative study, however, and a number of criminologists have begun to pay particular attention to continuing differences and divergences in the ways that late modern societies deal with crime and to the ways in which their policies, practices, and rhetorics may be distinguished from those in operation elsewhere—notably in the United States. Michael Tonry (2004a; 2004b), for example, has explored and sought to identify some of the distinguishing features of British penal policy, albeit within the context of a set of recent historical changes that have increasingly emulated American practices. His aim in such work, in parallel with others such as Whitman (2003), Melossi (2004), Cavadino and Dignan (2006) and others, is to explore how long-term historical conditions and particular cultural and political circumstances, shape and mould penal policies and practices in different jurisdictions in ways that limit the extent of convergence. Others, working within a shorter historical frame, have also explored the nature and limits of the global spread of Americanized penal policies (see Dixon and Maher, 2004; Muncie, 2004; Newburn and Sparks, 2004; Jones and Newburn, 2006a), pointing to the importance of *local* political cultures in the maintenance of important national and sub-national differences in systems of punishment. Characterized crudely, there are two somewhat contrasting—but far from incompatible—approaches emerging to the study of contemporary penal policy. First is that body of work, taking its lead from David Garland, that seeks to identify and analyse the characteristics and the aetiology of what appears to be a broadly similar *culture of control* sweeping across modern democratic societies. Second, is a generally smaller and less well developed literature that argues that it is equally possible to identify important and continuing differences in the penal landscapes and political economies of these democratic societies; that is to say, it is possible to identify *contrasts* within the emerging culture of control or, even, *contrasting cultures of control*.

My concern in this chapter is with the nature of the penal landscape of the United States and, to a lesser extent, the United Kingdom. My focus is therefore something of a contrast with much recent criminological work in this area in that it focuses on some of the continuing divergences that are visible between America and Britain. More particularly the aim is to focus on some of the divergences, distinctions, and differences within the American 'culture of control' itself. As a number of authors (Tonry, 2001; Garland, 2005) have noted, there are considerable dangers in treating the American system of crime control as monolithic. In practice there are some very significant variations in the ways in which criminal justice and penal policy is organized across the fifty states of the United States and yet this remains largely unstudied. In what follows my aim is to begin to explore penal variation in the United States. I begin by painting a very general picture of the current position regarding crime and its control in America. Following this I will explore some of the more important regional variations in America's contemporary culture of control before, in the fourth section, exploring some of the contrasts between the United States and the United Kingdom. I conclude with some general observations about convergence and divergence and about the contrasts in intolerance that continue to exist. These, I will argue, can only be understood if political cultures, institutions, and agency are placed at the heart of any comparative explanation of penal policies and practices.

Contemporary Crime Control in the United States and the United Kingdom

At the heart of David Garland's argument in *The Culture of Control* is the observation that the style and substance of penal policy in the United Kingdom and United States have become increasingly similar in recent years. In explaining this development he points to the fundamental shifts of social structures and cultural configurations associated with the coming of 'late modernity'. Garland argues that on both sides of the Atlantic two contrasting policy strategies have been introduced, first and more vigorously in the United States but subsequently in the United Kingdom. The first concerns the introduction of pragmatic or 'adaptive' approaches to the crime problem, such as the introduction of private sector management techniques to the criminal justice systems, the promotion of management reforms and privatization, rigorous systems of performance measurement, and the active 'responsibilization' of a range of private, voluntary, and community agents in the field of crime control. The second involves the simultaneous (and paradoxical) adoption of policies of 'denial', in which governments have adopted primarily expressive law enforcement and sentencing policies, the object of which is 'to denounce the crime and reassure the public' (2001a: 133). This new 'expressive justice' is simultaneously symbolic and instrumental, is populist and politicized and, Garland argues, at its heart there is a projected, politicized *victim* used as justification for increasingly harsh treatment of offenders.[2]

Garland's thesis raises important questions about pace of change in the American system of punishment. For most of the twentieth century the incarceration rate in the United States, though on the high side internationally, remained relatively stable at around 100 to 120 per 100,000 population. It started to rise steadily in the 1970s, however, and by 1995 had reached 600 per 100,000. By comparison, in 1995 the rate was 37 per 100,000 in Japan, 85 in Germany and Italy, and around 100 in England and Wales. The incarceration rate in the United States is now over 700 per 100,000. Where in 1972 there were under two hundred thousand Americans in federal and state prisons, this figure has now risen to over one and a half million. Add the 700,000 prisoners incarcerated in local jails and well over two million Americans are now imprisoned. The sheer scale of imprisonment in the United States now means that commentators routinely refer to this aspect of penal policy in the United States as 'mass incarceration' (see Garland, 2001b). Though the rise is by no means as spectacular as in America, nevertheless the consequence of the emergence in Britain in the early to mid-1990s of a punitive bipartisan consensus on crime has been a rapid and substantial increase in the prison population. In 1994 the prison population in England and Wales stood at a little over 44,000. A decade later it had reached 75,000 with the Labour government looking to institute measures to cap the population at 80,000. The bulk of this prison expansion took place during a period of declining crime.

Although obviously important, prison numbers only convey part of what has happened in the United States. The reach of the criminal justice system extends well beyond the incarcerated population. If one includes in the calculations those also under criminal justice supervision via probation or parole then the numbers are even more startling. As figure 1 illustrates, the numbers subject to parole and probation have also increased

---

[2] Though see Rock (2005), who argues that Garland's argument about the role of victims is overstated, certainly so far as the United Kingdom is concerned.

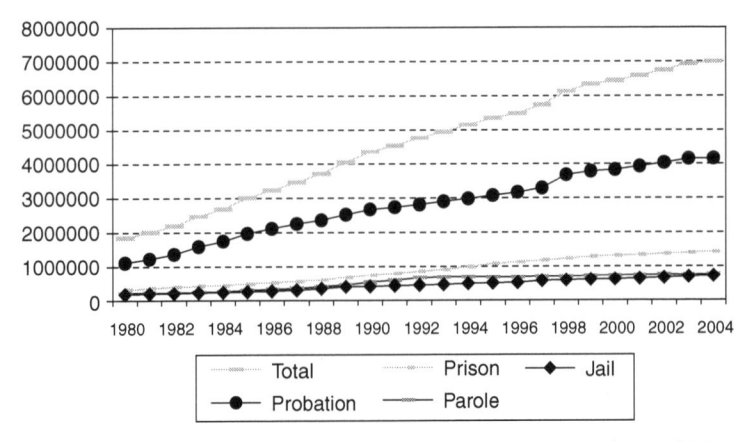

Figure 1. Adult Correctional Population, United States, 1980–2004

Source: Data from Bureau of Justice Statistics (<http://www.ojp.usdoj.gov/bjs/glance/tables/corr2tab.htm>)

markedly and the total under correctional supervision reached almost seven million by 2003.

What makes for such unprecedented growth in the correctional population generally and the prison population more particularly? In part the war on crime and, more particularly, the war on drugs have had a dramatic impact on the supply side—providing 'an almost limitless supply of arrestable and imprisonable offenders' (Simon, 2001). Second, there are features of what David Downes (2001) labelled the 'macho penal economy' itself, not least the expanding private corrections sector, which tend toward expansionism (Christie, 2000). The third, and possibly most important, factor is the general transformation of political culture that has occurred in America and elsewhere.

Crime is now a staple of political discourse and of electoral politics. Crucially, as numerous commentators have noted (Beckett, 1997; Gest, 2001; Downes and Morgan, 2002), recent decades have seen a progressively intensifying battle by the major political parties to be seen as the party with the toughest message on law and order. Initially in the Unites States, and subsequently in the United Kingdom and other jurisdictions, a 'tough on crime' stance has come to be associated with electoral success and its opposite, being 'soft on crime', with electoral failure. In the

United States, the spectacular defeat of Michael Dukakis in the 1988 Presidential election led the Democratic Party to rethink many of its public policy positions, not least that around crime and justice. Paralleling the remodelling of the Democratic Party after 1988, the Labour Party in the United Kingdom also sought to dump its various 'hostages to fortune' (Downes and Morgan, 1997), not least in the area of crime control. This meant attempting to modify the old-fashioned liberal penal-welfarism that the party had largely clung to throughout the 1980s and into the 1990s by adding into the mix what was by now considered the *sine qua non* of successful electoral politics: a healthy dose of punitive rhetoric—much of which was drawn from the Clinton administration (Newburn and Jones, 2005) and the promise of similarly punitive policies in response to what up until that point had been steadily rising crime rates. The amalgam has never been more successfully captured than in Tony Blair's 1993 soundbite, 'tough on crime and tough on the causes of crime'. Here, in only ten words, the relegation of traditional liberal concerns with poverty and social inequality as the generators of criminality was successfully conveyed whilst also using the new symbolic keywords (Fairclough, 2000) 'tough' and 'crime' twice each.

The 'culture of control' in America and Britain that Garland so vividly describes is by no means confined to those nations. Elements of this new configuration are visible elsewhere. Prison populations are rising sharply in many jurisdictions—including as previously mentioned even in hitherto quintessentially liberal societies such as the Netherlands—and the rhetoric of intolerance, often originating in the United States, has spread through much of northern and southern Europe and beyond (Wacquant, 1999). Just as there are global pressures transforming and seemingly homogenizing many aspects of national political cultures, the structural changes accompanying the shift to late modernity appear to be creating the conditions across the developed economies in which a newly punitive culture of control can flourish. These developments are so pervasive that they frequently appear irresistible. And, yet, despite this it is also possible to acknowledge the continued existence of considerable variations in penal practices both within and between jurisdictions. As an illustration of this I want briefly to explore contrasts in the penal practices visible in the different regions of the United States.

Contrasts within the United States

Whilst much of the literature on contemporary penal policy treats the United States as if it were to all intents and purposes a single, unified jurisdiction this is, of course, some distance from the reality. In practice, the United States' federalized criminal justice and penal system is highly fragmented and far from uniform. A contrast in the policing systems of the United Kingdom and United States illustrates this point well. There are currently forty-three police forces in England and Wales (quite likely soon to be reduced to perhaps a dozen) operating within a system that is so heavily centralized that our leading policing commentator has argued that we in fact have a *de facto* national police service (Reiner, 1989). By contrast, though it is difficult to know precisely, there are something in the region of 21,000 police agencies in the United States, of which 49 are state agencies, nearly 15,000 are local, over 3,000 are Sheriff-headed, and a further 3,000 are special agencies (Manning, 2006). The federalized system of government in the United States makes for a complicated and varied system of criminal justice. State and local government are administratively dominant: over 85 per cent of police jobs are state and local and over 95 per cent of prison and jail inmates are housed in state and local, rather than federal, institutions (Zimring, 2003). Crucially, the federal political system means that the bulk of criminal justice legislation is local in nature rather than national.[3] State legislatures, just as much as Congress, are crucial to understanding the nature and shape of the penal landscape in the US. Studies of local criminal justice policy-making in the United States are relatively rare but do provide clear illustrations of the considerable variation in both the symbolic and substantive nature of penal policy across the United States (Cummins, 2000; Zimring *et al.*, 2001; Zimring, 2003; Barker 2004, 2005).

At the very least, therefore, considerable caution is required when discussing *American* penal policy. Arguably, there is much

---

[3] That said, a strong case has been made by Gest (2001) among others that the reach of federal law has been progressively extended since the 1980s and, moreover, that federal government has increasingly sought to influence state policy and practice. The 'truth in sentencing' provisions introduced in the mid-1990s are a clear illustration of the latter development (Ditton and Wilson, 1999).

to be said for studying the contrasts in what might be thought of as the 'local' cultures of control within the United States. In what follows it is certainly not my intention to attempt even the beginnings of a project that might consider variations state by state within the United States. Rather, my much more modest objective is to point to some of the differences that exist between the main regions of the United States and in so doing to raise the possibility that these represent quite contrasting cultures of control in America—cultures that are worthy of further study.

Before we turn to penal policy a quick word about the main regions of the United States. Though there is no hard and fast categorization, the United States is generally described as having four main regions: the South; the Midwest; the Western states and the Northeastern states (figure 2). This division reflects elements of both the geography and the political and cultural history of the United States.

The northeast 'has long been associated with core American values of religious freedom, cultural diversity, liberty, capitalism, democracy, work and education' (Duncan and Goddard, 2005: 58). Politically, the Atlantic northeastern states are more obviously liberal than those of any other region of the United States and, although Presidential elections are by no means always a reliable guide, these states voted 56–39 in favour of Al Gore in the 2000 Presidential election and 56–44 in favour of John Kerry four years later. There are contrasting portrayals of the American Midwest. Centred on the western Great Lakes, the Midwest was the birthplace of the Republican Party, established in part to resist the spread of slavery, and has been predominantly Republican since, though states such as Illinois and Minnesota are generally more liberal. It is for many the heartland of the United States, a repository of American virtue, though often stereotyped as unsophisticated and insular. As Putnam's (2000) study of social capital in the United States illustrates, it is these states—the ones that are among the least tainted by the history of slavery—that tend to have the highest levels of social capital. Politically, the region is less easy to characterize than some. In the 2000 Presidential election votes for Bush and Gore were almost equal in the Midwest, with Bush picking up an extra percentage point. The 2004 election was even closer, with just over one half a percent separating the two

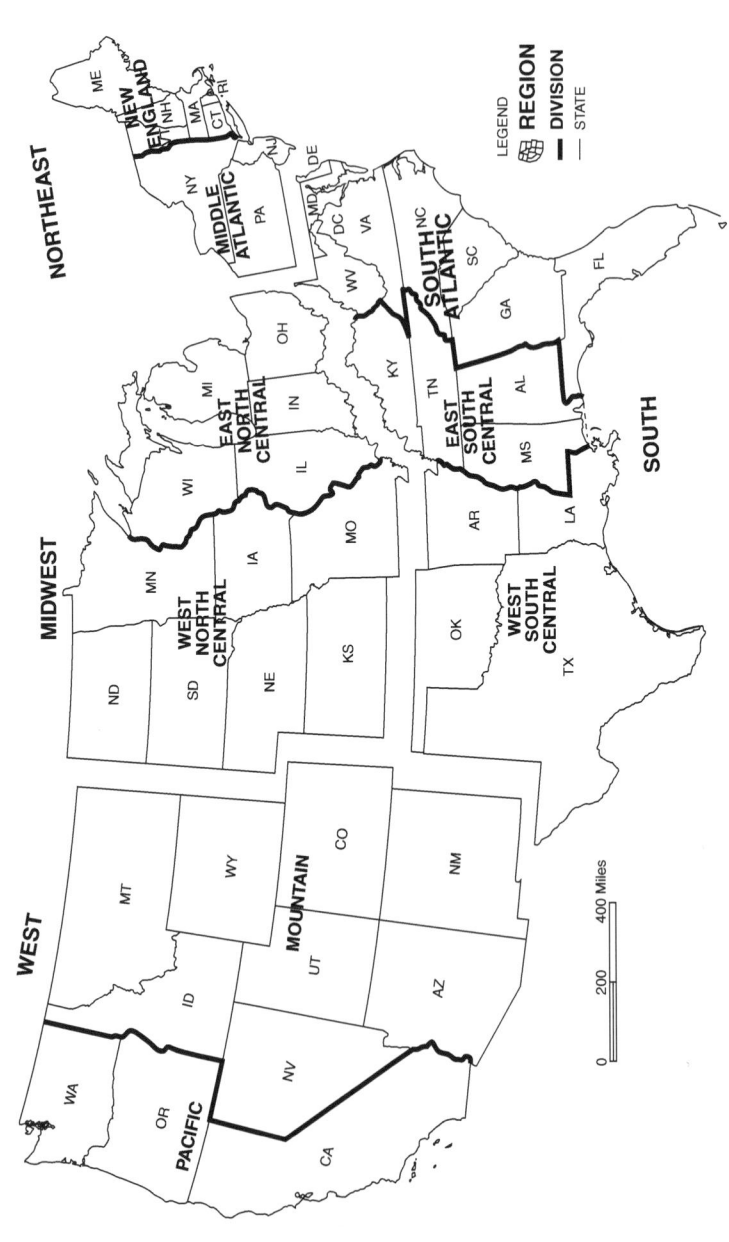

Source: US Department of Commerce Economics and Statistics Administration US Census Bureau. Available at: <http://www.census.gov/geo/www/us_regdiv.pdf>.

FIGURE 2. The Main Regions of the United States

main candidates even though Kerry won only three of the eleven Midwestern states. In the West, recent Presidential election results have also been very close, with Gore winning by two percentage points in 2000 and Kerry by one point in 2004. However, many of the Western states tend to be politically Republican and culturally conservative. In 2004, though Kerry won the popular vote overall in the region, Bush won nine of the thirteen states. The exceptions politically and culturally, generally speaking, tend to be the Pacific Rim states of California, Oregon, Washington, and Hawaii.

Of all the regions, however, it is the South that is historically the most distinctive region, having been shaped very fundamentally by the two great upheavals of the civil war and the civil rights movement. Initially, of course the South was both economically and culturally separate from the rest of what is now the United States. The development of some form of national identity in the United States during the nineteenth century was ended by the civil war, after which the South's close association with slavery and its continuing widespread poverty continued to distinguish it from much of the rest of the United States well into the twentieth century. Following the end of the Second World War much of the South was transformed by rapid economic growth and urbanization. Politically, the region had always been conservative in character, being predominantly old-style Democrat for much of the first half of the twentieth century—there were no Republican senators and only two Republic congressmen from the Southern states in 1950 (Micklethwait and Wooldridge, 2004)—then moving increasingly towards the Grand Old Party in the aftermath of the civil rights movement in the 1960s as the political parties themselves changed. In both 2000 and 2004 George W. Bush won all the Southern states.

To what extent then are regional variations evident in the American penal landscape? Are differences between the fifty states consistent in any form and, if so, do these differences follow a clear geographical pattern? In what follows I will point to the existence of precisely such regional variation. In particular, and perhaps not surprisingly given the political complexion described above, it seems clear that the Southern states are consistently more punitive than those of the Midwest and

Northeast. The Western states also tend to be less consistently punitive than those in the South, though they appear closer to the South in this regard than they are to states in the other two regions.

Before moving on, let me insert a word of caution. In discussing the possibility of identifying regional variations, I am neither seeking to mount an argument against the existence of a distinctive *national* culture of control nor am I advancing the idea that regional variations are more important than, say, differences at state level. Rather, I am simply using regional variation as one means of illustrating the value of *comparative* study of penal cultures—even when the comparisons are made within the boundaries of a single nation state. In what follows I will examine aspects of regional variation within the United States, focusing on incarceration rates, capital punishment, private prisons, mandatory sentencing, and felon disenfranchisement laws as my primary illustrations.

Regional Variation in the United States

Of all the characteristics of the American penal landscape, the one that draws the most comment is its use of imprisonment (Barker, 2006). The United States is routinely and correctly described as the highest incarcerator among all democracies. And, yet, it is all too easy to overlook the considerable variations that are evident state by state. As Zimring and Hawkins noted in relation to incarceration across the fifty states in 1980 'the most striking message...is that of diversity' (1991: 148). At that time North Carolina topped the list with an incarceration rate of 281 per 100,000, whereas New Hampshire's was only 28. Over two decades later, in 2003, another Northeastern state, Maine, had an incarceration rate of 149 but was by some distance the lowest incarcerator in the nation.[4] By contrast, the rate in Louisiana in the same year was almost 550 per cent higher at 814 per 100,000. As Barker (2006) points out, such differences are very important and not well understood. Not only is there very

---

[4] These figures are based primarily on data that exclude local imprisonment numbers and therefore potentially underestimate the overall numbers incarcerated state by state. The likelihood is that the inclusion of local figures would only serve to increase some of the contrasts highlighted.

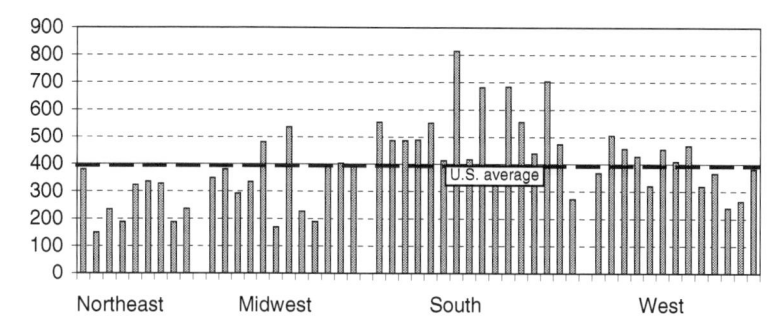

[Figure: bar chart showing incarceration rates by state, grouped into Northeast, Midwest, South, West, with a dashed line labeled "U.S. average" around 400]

Source: Data from Harrison, P.M. and Beck, A.J. (2005) *Prisoners in 2004*, Bureau of Justice Statistics Bulletin (Washington DC: US Department of Justice).

FIGURE 3. Incarceration Rates in the United States by State/Region, 2004

significant variation across the United States but such differences as exist exhibit considerable regional consistency. Thus, state incarceration rates are generally higher in the South than they are in the rest of America, and those in the west also tend to be higher than in either the Midwest or the Northeast (see figure 3). In this vein, Zimring and Hawkins (1991) noted that seven of the top ten incarcerating states in 1980 were in the South, while four of the bottom five states were to be found in New England. A similar pattern held in 2003 where eight of the top ten incarcerators were in the South and three of the lowest five incarcerators were in the Northeast. Of course, it is also true to say that crime rates, especially rates of violent crime, are generally higher in the South than they are in the other regions and this must undoubtedly form an important element of any explanation of variations in penal policy. However, studies of changing incarceration rates, for example, clearly show that although growth in prison numbers tends to be greater in states with higher levels of violent crime, this only provides a partial explanation for the trends observed (Greenberg and West, 2001).

Another feature which distinguishes the United States from almost all other liberal democracies is in its retention and use of capital punishment. In 1977, against the general trend toward abolition, the United States lifted the moratorium on the death penalty that had existed since 1967, and began executing people once again. Sixty people were executed in the United States in 2005 and a total of 1,004 people have been executed since the reintroduction of the death penalty. And, yet, the idea that capital punishment is an *American* phenomenon is potentially misleading. As Zimring (2003: 72) observes, 'the notion most foreign critics have of a national policy toward the death penalty in the United States is false. State policy toward the death penalty varies widely in both theory and practice.' Thus, a significant number of states (twelve) do not have the death penalty on their statute books. Michigan has not done so for 160 years and Minnesota and Wisconsin have not for approximately a century. Of the states that do have the death penalty, moreover, many do not conduct executions and seven states that retain statutes have not conducted any executions since the re-emergence of the death penalty in the late 1970s. What is particularly striking about the US death penalty statistics is that they are dominated by a handful of states and, as figure 4 shows, the vast majority of these are in the South—the main exceptions being Arizona in the West and Missouri in the Midwest. It is equally striking that 'no Southern state lacks either a death penalty or some history of recent execution' (Zimring, 2003: 73). Indeed, Zimring has calculated the regional execution rate and suggests that in the

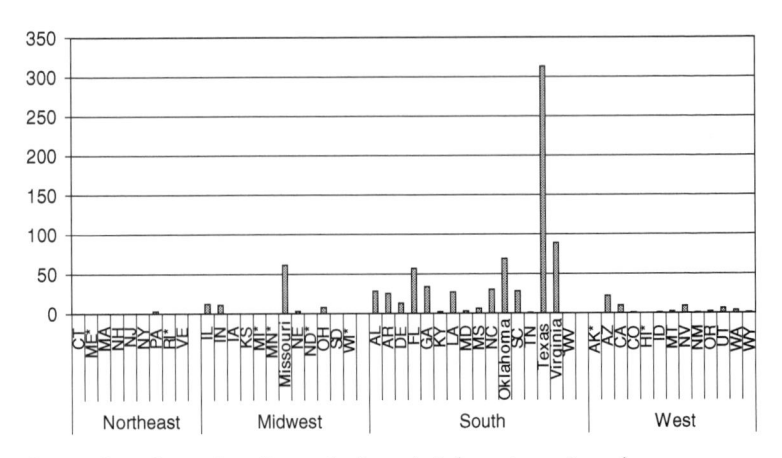

Source: Data from <http://www.deathpenaltyinfo.org/executions.php>.

FIGURE 4. Number of Persons Executed in the United States by State, by Region, 1977–2003

period 1977–2000 the rate in the Southern states was more than one hundred times the rate in the Northeastern states. One state that is among the most frequent users of the death penalty is in the Midwest (Missouri, with sixty-six executions since 1976) but both the Midwest and the West are generally much less frequent users of the death penalty than the states in the South. In the Northeast states the death penalty has all but disappeared; four of the nine Northeastern states do not have the death penalty and a fifth, New York, had its death penalty statutes declared unconstitutional in 2004. Of the 1,004 executions that have taken place in the United States since 1976, 821 (82 per cent) have been in the South, 116 (11 per cent) in the Midwest, 63 (6 per cent) in the West and only 4 in the Northeast.[5] Within this general regional pattern there is one state, Texas, that stands alone in the frequency with which it executes people. Even by the standards of the South, Texas is exceptional. Over one-third (356) of all executions in the United States since 1977 have occurred in this one state. In addition, therefore, to focusing on regional variations in penal policy there is also much to be learned from the study of the political economies of particular states and how these affect public policy choices such as the decision to retain and use the death penalty.

From the use of the death penalty let me turn to two other facets of the US penal system, each in their different ways characteristic of the new culture of control: the spread of privatized prisons and the removal of the franchise from those convicted of serious crimes. The rebirth of private corrections in the United States, which began during the 1960s, has been linked by numerous commentators to the punitive shift in contemporary penal policy, often as a result of the concern that the introduction of the profit motive into incarceration would in all likelihood lead to significant expansionism (Schlosser, 1998; Christie, 2000). The re-emergence of private prisons in the United States began when the Federal Bureau of Prisons (FBP) contracted with private firms to operate community treatment centres, youth facilities, and 'halfway houses' in the shallow end of the criminal justice system (Ryan and Ward, 1989). During

---

[5] Details of all executions since 1976 can be found at: <http://www.death penaltyinfo.org/executions.php>.

the late 1970s, the US Immigration and Naturalization Service (INS) contracted with private firms to detain illegal immigrants (McDonald, 1994). The first mainstream prison to be run on private lines opened in 1984 and during the mid- to late-1980s a number other private corrections corporations also emerged as significant competitors in the growing market at state and the local county level. The early- to mid-1990s saw continued growth in the private corrections sector (Mattera and Khan, 2001). Despite fears expressed by those concerned with the spread of privatized corrections (Ryan and Ward, 1989), private imprisonment remains very much a minority element of the overall prison system across the United States and in each of its regions (see figure 5) and by the late 1990s the private prison sector remained concentrated in twenty-three Western and Southern states. High-use states included Texas, Oklahoma, Florida, Louisiana, Tennessee, California, Colorado, Mississippi, and Washington DC (McDonald et al., 1998). More recent figures show that sixteen states in total have no prisoners held in private facilities (Harrison and Beck, 2004).

In no state is a majority of prisoners held in private facilities. New Mexico is the greatest user of private incarceration, with 42 per cent of its inmates housed in private prisons. Next come Alaska (31 per cent), Montana (30 per cent), Wyoming and Hawaii (28 per cent), and Oklahoma (25 per cent). In all, only six states had one quarter or more of their prison population in private prisons, all six being Western or Southern states. The biggest overall users of private prisons—absolutely rather than

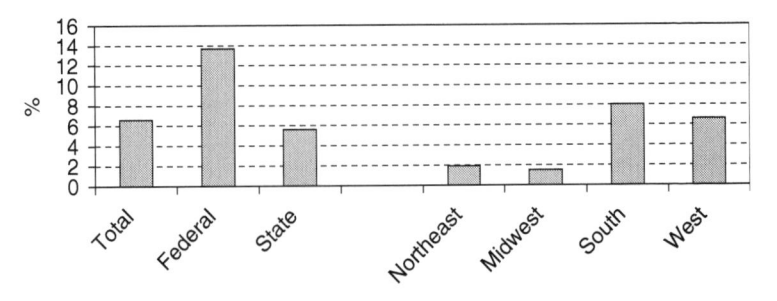

Source: Data from http://www.ojp.usdoj.gov/bjs/pub/pdf/pjim04.pdf.

FIGURE 5. Prisoners Held in Private Facilities (%) by region, 2004

proportionately—were Texas (with 16,668 state inmates in private facilities) and Oklahoma (with 5,905). By contrast, of the sixteen states without any private facilities, ten were in the Northeast and Midwest (Harrison and Beck, 2005). There is a long-term history to the regional patterning of prison management in the United States, some commentators linking developments in the late twentieth century to various forms of private correctional enterprise in the nineteenth century (Shichor, 1995). Such enterprises varied from the production of saleable items within the prison to the leasing of convicts to external organizations. This system of hiring out, mainly black, inmates to private contractors was particularly common in the Southern states—the Texas legislature in the late nineteenth century, for example, instructed its state correctional administrators to contract out all inmate labour to the private sector (Austin and Coventry, 2001). In many respects the recent development of private prisons has followed a predictable pattern. One of the most important factors behind the growth of private prisons in the United States was the threat of litigation in response to the problem of overcrowding (Jones and Newburn, 2004). Given this, it is of little surprise that it is generally those states with sizeable prison populations or rapidly expanding populations that should have been among the earliest (the first was Texas) and most extensive users of private correctional facilities. These states have also tended to be those that are more broadly committed to the 'rolling back of the state' and hence are sympathetic to private provision of services. By contrast, in states outside the South where public service employees' unions, such as the American Federation of State, County and Municipal Employees (AFSCME) are stronger, and pressure groups such as the Western Prison Project are operating, there have been significant and successful campaigns against the spread of private correctional facilities (see, for example, Sarabi and Bender, 2000).

Restrictions on voting rights have long been a feature of the American criminal justice system. Only two states, both Northeastern—Maine and Vermont—permit inmates to vote. All other forty-eight states and the District of Columbia prohibit inmates from voting whilst incarcerated for a felony offence. Within this general picture of prohibition some differences exist in relation to offenders on parole and probation—again with

244 Tim Newburn

distinctive regional variation. Thirty-five states prohibit felons from voting while they are on parole, and thirty-one exclude felony probationers as well. The most restrictive practices are in the Western and, more particularly, in the Southern states—where every state denies voting rights to felony parolees and probationers as well as those in prison. Three states deny the right to vote to all ex-offenders after the completion of their sentence: Florida, Kentucky, and Virginia. A further nine states, mostly in the South—Alabama, Arizona, Delaware, Maryland, Mississippi, Nebraska, Nevada, Tennessee, and Wyoming—either disenfranchize particular categories of ex-offender and/or allow the restoration of voting rights only after a specified waiting period. Recent research in this area suggests that the regional variation illustrated by figure 6 is heavily racialized. In their historical study of the emergence and reform of felony disenfranchizement laws Behrens *et al.* (2003: 585) conclude that:

[T]he racial composition of state prisons is firmly associated with the adoption of state felon disenfranchisement laws. States with greater non-white prison populations have been more likely to ban convicted felons from voting than states with proportionally fewer nonwhites in the criminal justice system.

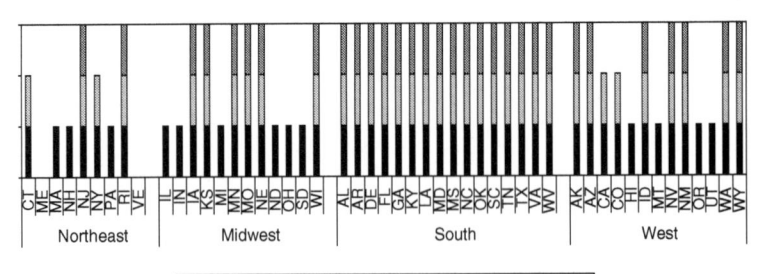

Source: Data from The Sentencing Project (2005).

FIGURE 6. Categories of Felon Disenfranchised under US State Law, by State

This finding holds even when controlling for timing, region, economic competition, partisan political power, state population composition, and state incarceration rate. I want to end this section by considering briefly the spread of mandatory minimum sentences—often cited as a key illustration of the increasingly punitive and intolerant nature of contemporary penal policy. Given that all fifty states and the District of Columbia now have some form of mandatory minimum sentence (Kennedy, 2000), superficially the spread of such provisions may appear to run counter to the argument developed here about variation in penal policy and practice across the United States. However, as Reitz (2001: 223) points out, 'there really is no such thing as "US sentencing practice"... primary responsibility for criminal justice resides at the state level—and that states have varied greatly in their individual experiences of crime and their governmental responses to it'. Sentencing reforms that broadly conformed to the 'three strikes' rubric spread rapidly in the United States during the mid-1990s. However, in practice approximately only half of all states passed such legislation. Where states passed three strikes laws the statutes varied significantly both in the precise nature of the legislation—the nature of a 'strike', the number of strikes needed, and the nature of the mandatory sentence that resulted (Clark *et al.*, 1997)—and in terms of the practical impact they have had. Table 1 provides data on the geographical coverage of two and three strikes legislation and, more particularly, on the numbers incarcerated in each state as a result of such statutes.

What stands out most obviously is the disproportionate impact of California's two and three strikes legislation. Four-fifths of all prisoners incarcerated in the United States under such legislation have been imprisoned in California and it is consequently difficult to exaggerate the extent to which this state has been out of step with the other three strikes states and with the federal legislation.[6] California, Georgia, and Florida account for over 97 per cent of custodial sentences under two and three strikes statutes and on this basis it might be argued that the impact of the three strikes movement has been relatively minor outside a handful of states (though these states account for one-fifth of the total US population). Indeed a US Department of

---

[6] The idea of 'three strikes' mandatory sentencing was endorsed by President Clinton in his 1994 State of the Union Address and eventually incorporated into federal legislation in the Violent Crime Control and Law Enforcement Act 1994 (Windelsham, 1998). The federal legislation generated fewer than forty sentences in its first five years of operation (Zimring *et al.*, 2001).

TABLE 1 Three Strikes Legislation in the USA, 2005

Region	State	2/3 Strikes legislation?	Numbers in prison under 3 strikes
NORTHEAST	Connecticut	Yes	1
	Maine	No	–
	Massachusetts	No	–
	New Hampshire	No	–
	New Jersey	Yes	10
	New York	No	–
	Pennsylvania	Yes	50
	Rhode Island	No	–
	Vermont	Yes	16
TOTAL			77
MIDWEST	Illinois	No	–
	Indiana	Yes	38
	Iowa	No	–
	Kansas	No	–
	Michigan	No	–
	Minnesota	No	–
	Missouri	No	–
	Nebraska	No	–
	North Dakota	Yes	10
	Ohio	No	–
	South Dakota	No	–
	Wisconsin	Yes	9
TOTAL			57
SOUTH	Alabama	No	–
	Arkansas	Yes	5
	Delaware	No	–
	Florida	Yes	1,628
	Georgia	Yes	7,631
	Kentucky	No	–
	Louisiana	Yes	N/A
	Maryland	Yes	330
	Mississippi	No	–
	North Carolina	Yes	22
	Oklahoma	No	–
	South Carolina	Yes	14
	Tennessee	Yes	14
	Texas	No	–
	Virginia	Yes	328
	West Virginia	No	–
TOTAL			9,972
WEST	Alaska	No	–
	Arizona	No	–
	California	Yes	42,322
	Colorado	Yes	4
	Hawaii	No	–
	Idaho	No	–

(*cont.*)

TABLE 1 (Continued.)

Region	State	2/3 Strikes legislation?	Numbers in prison under 3 strikes
	Montana	No	–
	Nevada	Yes	304
	New Mexico	No	–
	Oregon	No	–
	Utah	Yes	N/A
	Washington	Yes	209
	Wyoming	No	–
TOTAL			42,839

Source: Data from Schiraldi et al., 2004.

Justice review observed that 'from a national perspective the "three strikes and you're out" movement was largely symbolic' (Austin et al., 2000). There are, however, at least two reasons why even primarily symbolic initiatives remain important to this discussion. First, the symbolic intent behind two and three strikes legislation was to signal toughness, to indicate intolerance of certain forms of offending. As such this legislation was very much in line with many other changes that were occurring in the penal policies of the states concerned. That is to say, even those states that passed largely symbolic statutes might nevertheless be argued to have been sending an important message about the general nature and tenor of penal policy locally. Crudely, it might reasonably be hypothesized that those states where penal policy is generally less punitive would be less likely to pass three strikes legislation, even if the legislation were largely symbolic in intent. A second, and related, reason why the three strikes movement is important is that even if such initiatives were designed as primarily symbolic gestures, this is not to say that they might not have substantive consequences. As Garland (2001a: 22) observes in this regard, 'sometimes "talk" is "action" '. There is now some research evidence which suggests, for example, that sentencers are influenced by the zeitgeist of the moment (Hough et al., 2003). If this is so, then even largely symbolic legislative change, particularly if accompanied by noisy political rhetoric as was the case with many of the three strikes initiatives, might have significant substantive consequences elsewhere in the justice system. On this basis it seems reasonable to consider all three strikes statutes—whatever their form—as potentially significant indicators of the nature of local cultures of control. Looking, then, at which states enacted such statutes during the 1990s there is, once again, considerable variation between regions. Symbolic, substantive or both, it appears that with the exception of California it was in the Southern states that three strikes legislation was most commonly enacted. Despite the impression in the early 1990s of the three strikes movement having 'swept the United States' (Tonry, 2001: 529), few such statutes were passed in the Midwest, and they were also less frequently enacted in both the West and the Northeast. Indeed, it appears that under 150 people in total have been imprisoned as a result of three strikes laws in the Midwest and the Northeast.

There does then appear to be some fairly consistent regional variation in American penal policy. Incarceration rates are generally higher in the South than elsewhere and it is this region in which capital punishment is largely confined, where private prisons are most common and felon disenfranchisement laws most extensive. The picture is slightly more complex in relation to mandatory minimum sentences, however, as two Western states—Washington and California—are, respectively, the original source of the three strikes movement and far and away the most extreme example of the impact of such legislation. Once again, however, such initiatives were more common in the South than elsewhere though, as with all the other areas considered, the Western states tend to be more punitive in orientation than either those in the Midwest or the Northeast.

Understanding Regional Variation

Given the existence of consistent regional variation—and by implication significant local variation—in penal systems, then the interesting question becomes how might such patterns be explained? There are a number of helpful studies which provide important pointers to at least some of the areas where one might look for explanations of such variation. Again, the place to start is with variations in incarceration. In this connection Greenberg and West (2001) review previous studies of US imprisonment rates, including those that show them to be related to poverty and violent crime. They are critical of extant work in this area for its mechanistic portrayal of the way in which differing structural conditions are held to produce, 'automatically', particular penal responses. Such work, they rightly observe, 'slights the policy choices that structure a state's response to its circumstances' (2001: 616). Similarly, Zimring and Hawkins (1991: 220) found that not only did levels of imprisonment vary significantly over time and from state to state but that 'these variations are largely independent of variations in either crime rates or the provisions of penal codes'.

In looking to explain state variation Greenberg and West focus on four major variables that might constrain states' responses to local crime levels: fiscal constraints; cultural factors; state politics; and the presence of other 'threats'. In short, they found that states with more generous welfare payments tended to be the lower incarcerators and that states which generally had more politically and religiously conservative populations also had higher prison populations. Interestingly, and perhaps reinforcing the sense that tough penal policy has become a bipartisan matter in recent times, they found that party control of state government had no impact on state policy. Perhaps crucially, they found that states with higher unemployment levels and with a higher proportion of African Americans had a higher imprisonment rate (controlling for crime rates). Although many of the demographic, cultural, and political characteristics they identify as important in explaining geographical variation in imprisonment levels are characteristic of the Southern states, where incarceration rates are indeed generally higher, they point out that these characteristics do not explain prison population growth during the period 1971–1991. Intriguingly, it appears that growth rates were slower in the South during this period than elsewhere, leading Greenberg and West to conclude that 'in recent years regions outside the South have been catching up to the South in imprisonment' (2001: 637).

Greenberg and West's argument finds further support in the work of Beckett and Western (2001). Analysing variations in imprisonment between US states, the authors argue that there is a clear relationship between the welfare orientation of individual states and their incarceration rates. Crudely, those states with the weakest welfare systems were those with the largest penal systems. This leads Beckett and Western to argue that recent decades have witnessed the emergence of a new form of penal-welfare regime in which 'declining support for social welfare is part of a punitive policy development in which the state has a substantial and active role' (2001: 43). Moreover, they argue that states with larger poor and African-American populations, and with Republican-dominated legislatures, have been more inclined to 'adopt this approach to social marginality' (2001: 55).

Although there appear to be strong regional patterns in the use of imprisonment, this is by no means to suggest that such variation holds hard and fast for all states, and Zimring and Hawkins (1991) have, for example, cautioned against placing too great an emphasis on regional characteristics as a sole explanation for the growth in imprisonment. They argue, rightly, that 'unexplained variations in the pattern among the states should be regarded as an invitation to do policy research at the individual state level'. In this regard, interesting work on state-level political cultures and decision-making has recently been undertaken by Vanessa Barker. In comparing the recent histories of the use of incarceration in New York, California, and Washington, she seeks to build on Joachim Savelsberg's (1994) examination of the political organization of state power and differences in the exercise of criminal punishment. Barker (2006) argues that the nature of political participation is crucial in understanding why states differ in their use of incarceration. Noting that states with high levels of political participation appear to have been the ones that have had lower rates of incarceration—a position that echoes earlier arguments by Elazar (1966) and Putnam (2000)—she suggests (2006: 6) that 'when citizens participate in public life they may be more likely to keep a check on the repressive powers of the state. And conversely, when citizens withdraw from public life, we are more likely to see increased imprisonment; a crude policy response to high crime.'

Barker distinguishes between two dimensions of state power: variations in political authority (measured by the degree of centralization) and variations in political practices (measured by the degree of state activism and the degree of civic engagement). This leads her to identify four ideal types of state governance, populism, participatory democracy, pragmatism, and patronage, the first three of which are discussed in her case studies. In brief, she argues that California comes closest to the populism ideal type, Washington State to that of participatory democracy and New York to pragmatism. These differing orientations had clear outcomes in terms of the use of imprisonment with Washington State's participatory governance leading to a 'relatively parsimonious'[7] use of imprisonment', New York State's managerialist and strategic pragmatism leading to higher incarceration rates but ones that were significantly lower than the 'indulgent' populism of California in which citizens 'not only fail to keep a check on state repression, they often demand it' (2006: 15). The strength of Barker's work is precisely that it focuses attention on what we might refer to as 'local cultures of control' within the broader punitive context of the United States.

In understanding the impact of local forms of governance—or local political cultures—it is useful to think about and, where necessary, distinguish between, *intention* and *outcome* in penal policy (Jones and Newburn, 2006a). The spread of three strikes legislation provides a useful illustration of this. Using the distinction between intention and outcome it is possible to identify the development of three distinct forms of policy during the 1990s. First, was the largely symbolic. As Austin *et al.* (1999: 158) observed, 'with the noted exception of California, all of the states followed the initial lead of the state of Washington by carefully wording their legislative reforms to ensure that few offenders would be impacted [sic] by the law'. A prime example would be at the Federal level where the Clinton administration felt three strikes legislation to be irresistible, and yet wished to, and did, place significant limits on its reach. The second form emerged where the intentions of the framers of the legislation appeared to go beyond the symbolic but where their intentions were frustrated or mitigated by local political pressures. Calls were made for fairly punitive three strikes policies in a number of US states but, as we have seen, the harsher versions of the legislation were rarely enacted even in states such as Washington, where the original three strikes campaign emerged. The third and the most unusual form in the United States applies to jurisdictions where the legislation was deliberately framed to

---

[7] Readers from outside the United States might baulk at the application of the adjective 'parsimonious' to a state that had an incarceration rate of 264 per 100,000 in 2003 (i.e. over twice that of England and Wales).

have a practical effect equal to or greater than the symbolic message. Here, of course, California is the prime example. The explanation of Californian exceptionalism is to be found in part in the distinctive nature of that state's political system, not least its history of voter initiatives. Crucial, however, were a set of contingent political and social circumstances—a vicious gubernatorial election following hard on the heels of two high-profile violent crimes against young women—Kimber Reynolds and Polly Klaas—which coalesced to produce circumstances quite different from those that operated in most other states as subsequent three strikes statutes were passed (Abramsky, 2001; Gest, 2001). The Californian three strikes case appears, in part, to be another illustration of the fact that democratic decision-making systems that are not well insulated from partisan politics tend to have higher imprisonment rates (or in this case, harsher sentencing legislation) than those jurisdictions in which such decision-making is better protected (Greenberg, 2002).

The three strikes discussion, and the Californian case more particularly, highlights an important aspect of comparative penal policy analysis. As David Downes elaborates in *Contrasts*, an understanding of significant differences in the penal policies of different jurisdictions—or by extension different parts of the same jurisdiction—requires not only a careful unpicking of the nature and aetiology of penal policy but an analysis of the comparative political economies within which such policies emerge and become established. Recent scholarship of the American death penalty provides an example of both the importance of this approach, and of the differing interpretations that can arise from such analysis depending on the relative weight accorded to more immediate and contingent socio-political developments on the one hand and longer-term historico-cultural traits on the other.

An interesting facet of the history of the death penalty in the United States is that variations between states have been fairly stable historically. Those states that do not retain death penalty laws have generally been in that position for decades while those that are frequent executors have generally always been so. This leads Zimring to argue that the explanation for differences between states is not to be found in contemporary events or local history. Such is the degree of continuity, he says, that it 'warns us against attributing the revival of the death penalty in the United States to shifting values or changed social conditions in the 1960s and 1970s' (Zimring, 2003: 85). Rather, he suggests, we must look to longer-standing cultural traits and, in particular, the story and legacy of lynching in the United States as a means of making sense of the nature and persistence of such variation. In short, and at the risk of oversimplifying Zimring's detailed and subtle argument, lynching patterns in the United States are considered unusual because of the volume of such extrajudicial killings, their persistence historically, and their link with racial repression. According to Zimring the persistence of such a tradition of vigilantism has had a profound effect on capital punishment in the United States. Almost nine-tenths of lynchings took place in the South, 7 per cent in the Midwest, 5 per cent in the West and less than one-half of one per cent in the Northeast. Moreover, this appears to be closely linked to the pattern of contemporary executions:

When the regional patterns of both executions and lynchings of a century ago are compared with geography of recent executions, it is the lynching pattern rather than the earlier distribution of legal executions that best approximates the extremes found in the 695 executions recorded from 1977 to 2000. (Zimring, 2003: 93)

What links the two periods, according to Zimring, is that cultural factor he identifies as 'vigilante values'. His thesis has not passed without criticism. A recent response by Garland (2005) challenges the central explanatory idea of 'vigilante values' and what he takes to be Zimring's implicit advocacy of an argument based on a notion of 'American exceptionalism'. In fact, Garland argues, there is nothing especially exceptional about the United States and if one takes a long-term historical view then the place of the death penalty in American culture looks very like other western nations. That is to say, it has declined significantly, both in terms of its use and its legitimacy—all that remains is for it to be abolished.[8] Its existence currently is simply a 'residual continuation' of something that used to be standard in all western nations. What is particularly interesting about Garland's critique

---

[8] Garland is quite explicit about this. He states boldly that 'The USA is the last western nation to complete the abolition process.' (2005: 362).

is that it gives greater weight to political choices, particular circumstances and contingent decisions than his other recent work on the contemporary culture of control in America and Britain (Garland, 2001), which appears to place greater emphasis on deeper structural and cultural features. The persistence of the death penalty is not, he argues, a reflection of some long-standing cultural tradition but 'because the political mechanisms for nation-wide abolition do not exist there in the form that they exist in other nations' (2005: 362).

Irrespective of whether one sides with Zimring or Garland in this debate,[9] it remains the case, at least for the time being, that unlike other western nations the death penalty continues to be used in America and, importantly, its use is highly variable across the fifty states. As Zimring (2005: 382) observes:

In the first 25 years after [the reintroduction of the death penalty] for every 1 execution in the Northeastern states, there were 160 executions in the South... For 160 to 1 differences in execution to exist and to replicate long-standing state and regional differences without some elements of cultural difference to explain them seems more than improbable. The interesting question is not whether culture influences executions but what elements of culture are involved.

What seems clear is that there are important and continuing regional differences in penal practices, and arguably *penal cultures*, within the broader culture of control in the United States. Put differently, any attempt to explore the nature of the fairly consistent regional differences that appear to exist in the systems of punishment across the United States must inevitably consider the political economies within which these punishment systems are embedded.

Such a task lies well beyond the scope of this chapter. But, before moving on I would like to flesh out one or two thoughts

---

[9] Rather than being significantly at odds with each other, it is quite possible to read Zimring and Garland's accounts as being (potentially) in many respects mutually reinforcing. The identification of long-standing cultural patterns does not necessarily exclude the importance of more immediate and contingent political factors in explaining the continued existence of the death penalty—just as highlighting the importance of contemporary political mechanisms and decisions in its retention does not preclude the existence of more deeply embedded socio-cultural factors also.

about the political economies of the American regions that might plausibly form part of an explanation. I will limit my comments to three aspects: political culture; race; and political structures and agency. In each case the discussion will need to be brief. First, a potentially helpful discussion of variations in political culture can be found in Daniel Elazar's (1966) study of American federalism. Elazar argues that the United States shares a general political culture, one rooted in two contrasting views of the American political order. In the first, the political order is viewed as a *marketplace* in which bargaining between individuals and groups acting out of self-interest is the basis of primary public relationships. In the second the political order is conceived as a *commonwealth* in which there exists an undivided public interest and where citizens tend to act co-operatively to produce and maintain government and order. However, within the general political culture, Elazar identifies three distinctive political cultures: the 'traditionalistic' culture of the South; the 'individualistic' culture in the western and mid-Atlantic states; and, a 'moralistic' culture found in the Northeast, upper Midwest and Pacific northwest. Elazar argues that these three political cultures arose from the socio-political differences among the varying peoples that came and settled in America. The concentration of particular cultural groups is what ties otherwise very different states together within a particular regional identity and character. They have been modified as successive waves of migration have occurred from East to West and, later, South to North, producing a particular 'geology' of political culture.

The *individualistic* culture is based on a largely utilitarian view of government, formed to serve local people in whichever way them deem, rather than being driven by any broader conception of the good society. This culture, found primarily in the Western states, tends to view the democratic order as a marketplace in which politics is just one means by which individuals realize their goals. Regions displaying such a culture are much more likely to be characterized by populism. By contrast, the *moralistic* political culture places much greater emphasis on what Elazar calls the 'commonwealth conception' of democratic governance. In this ideal type the search for the good society is never far from the core of government. Government is viewed as having an overriding commitment to the general good and to general welfare, which may be thought to provide barriers to elements of popular punitiveness. Finally, the *traditionalistic* political culture combines 'an ambivalent attitude toward the marketplace coupled with a paternalistic and elitist conception of the commonwealth' (1966: 92–3). This ambivalent attitude allows for the greater involvement of government in the private lives of citizens than would be the case in the moralistic culture, but seeks to limit and regulate its extent. In some ways, Elazar argues, it is something of a throwback to earlier traditional and elitist times. This culture, found predominantly in the South, tends to be characterized by elitist politics and by resistance to innovation and change.

Now, it is not my intention to suggest that Elazar's typology can be easily and straightforwardly mapped onto the US regions as already described. Rather, it seems to me that it is plausible at least that the broad contours of the political cultures that Elazar identifies might be used to explain elements of what, in different ways, make the Southern and Northeastern states distinctive. It is one thing to identify the possible existence of distinctive regional cultural identities; it is quite another, of course, to relate these to patterns in penal policy and practice. However, an indication of the potential viability and application of Elazar's models can be found in Robert Putnam's work on American civic life. Intriguingly, several decades after Elazar's work, Putnam (2000) found the local and regional patterning of social capital in the United States to be remarkably similar to the distribution of the 'traditional', 'moralistic', and 'individualistic' political cultures identified by Elazar. In short, 'moralistic' states or areas tended to have relatively high levels of social capital, whereas 'traditionalistic' states or areas such as the South tend to be lowest in social capital. Unsurprisingly perhaps, but nonetheless intriguingly, Putnam also found the differing distribution of social capital in the late twentieth century to be closely linked to the pattern of slavery in the early part of the nineteenth century. In summary, he says, the 'more virulent the system of slavery then, the less civic the state today' (2000: 294). Putnam leaves hanging the question of the extent to which patterns of slavery and immigration provide an explanation for the twentieth-century patterning of social capital in the United States.

However, the clear implication of the data he presents is that there is some form of relationship. Related to this, of course, there has been a considerable amount of American criminological scholarship in recent years (Tonry, 1995; Wacquant, 2001) that has noted the important links between the politics of race and the pattern of punishment and control in the United States. The apparently close relationship between the history of slavery and the politics of race and the ideal typical pictures of general political cultures that Elazar lends further support to the argument that the analysis of political cultures has much to offer the investigation of regional differences in penality in America. Some of the deeper-rooted characteristics of such local and regional variation may also illustrate the residual power of what Hartz (1979) refers to as 'fragment cultures'—such fragments describing social formations arising from the movement of European and other populations and their settlement in contexts that lack the checks and balances of the original context.

Whilst understanding local or regional political cultures, together with the associated history and politics of race, appears to be central to any attempt to unpicking variation across the United States, there is a further, more particular, factor that it is important to consider: this is the impact of the more immediately contingent matters of political structures and agency. The history of the three strikes movement, for example, cannot be explained solely by reference to regional, or even local, cultures, or simply to the politics of race. Within different states three strikes policies were also shaped by their distinctive legal and political contexts and, crucially, by the agency of key political actors. The important and exceptional case of California, therefore, must also be related to the political structures and machinery of that state. In particular, as we observed earlier, the tradition of policy-making via voter initiative was absolutely central to what occurred in California (Zimring *et al.*, 2001; Jones and Newburn, 2006b) and this brings us back to Barker's (2006: 6) argument that 'differences in the ways in which states exercise, organize and institutionalize power will have differential effects on state reliance on confinement' and, by implication, on state penal policy more generally. Examining the political contexts—notably the nature of local political structures and practices—is crucial to understanding how particular social forces such as crime rates and racial politics have different effects in different political contexts. The spread and development of private prisons provides a good illustration of this point. As Trevor Jones and I have argued previously (Jones and Newburn, 2005: 76) the particular pattern of American private imprisonment:

almost certainly reflects a combination of 'structural' factors, including the political traditions and cultures of the states concerned, the differing legal systems, the degree of penal expansion etc. But it also reflects the importance of political *agency* in terms of the various strategies adopted by key actors, responding to these broader constraints and opportunities. Further research is needed here into such questions as to why private corrections corporations targeted some states rather than others for expansion, why coalitions of opposition arose in some states and not in others, and under what circumstances did private contractors and their opponents fail or succeed in their aims?

Similar questions can be asked of the spread of three strikes and truth in sentencing legislation in the 1990s, variations in the speed and extent of the growth of imprisonment since the 1970s (Zimring, 2001) and, of course, the continued use of the death penalty. All of these aspects of the contemporary American culture of control exhibit considerable regional and local variation. Moreover, there are good reasons to believe that such variations in criminal punishment reflect divergences in social and political values and, as such, are deserving of further attention and research. A further and more traditional illustration of this point is provided by returning to the more usual terrain of comparative criminology—the comparison of penal policies of different countries. In the penultimate section of this chapter I want to return to the two jurisdictions that have been the primary focus of recent discussions of the new punitiveness and outline very briefly some of the contrasts in intolerance that exist between the United States and the United Kingdom.

America and Britain: Contrasts in Intolerance?

As Lacey (2003: 90) has noted, 'even taking Garland's two principal examples, Britain and the USA, we can perceive significant variations in the political salience and tractability of criminal justice'. The example Lacey highlights in this regard is that of capital punishment. There is evidence that public opinion still favours the death penalty, in all European countries including the United Kingdom (Roberts and Hough, 2005) and yet such populism is not translated into political pressure for reform. By contrast, in the United States not only do many states maintain the death penalty and a number continue to execute prisoners but politicians are generally reluctant to be found campaigning for an end to executions. As Ignatieff (2005: 15) puts it, 'capital punishment has been abolished in most European societies not because electoral majorities support abolition...but because political elites... do not want the moral burden of ordering executions. These moral scruples are in direct contradiction to the expressed preferences of their own citizens.' In parts of the United States, exhibiting such independence from popular sentiment would be considered politically unthinkable.

Contrasts between the United States and the United Kingdom can also be made in relation to imprisonment though such contrasts fly in the face of much contemporary criminological commentary in this area. In a recent, and fascinating, comparative analysis Cavadino and Dignan (2006) identify four general models of political economy, which they relate to important differences in penal policy and practice. More specifically, Cavadino and Dignan argue that 'social democracies' such as Sweden and Finland tend to have the lowest rates of incarceration along with the one 'oriental corporatist' state—Japan—that they study; 'conservative corporatist' countries, such as Germany and The Netherlands, have somewhat higher incarceration rates, but the heaviest users of imprisonment are the 'neoliberal' countries. In this category they include the United States (with an incarceration rate of 701 in 2003), South Africa (402), New Zealand (155), England and Wales (141) and Australia (115). For broad purposes of comparison this analysis of political economies is both useful and persuasive. However, the argument that American and British trends in incarceration are indicative of broadly similar penal policies is, at best, I think debatable. Without wishing to underestimate the recent increases in the prison population in England and Wales, they are clearly dwarfed by those that have been evident in the United States (figure 7).

Indeed, there is far greater variation across American states in the use of imprisonment than there is across Western Europe

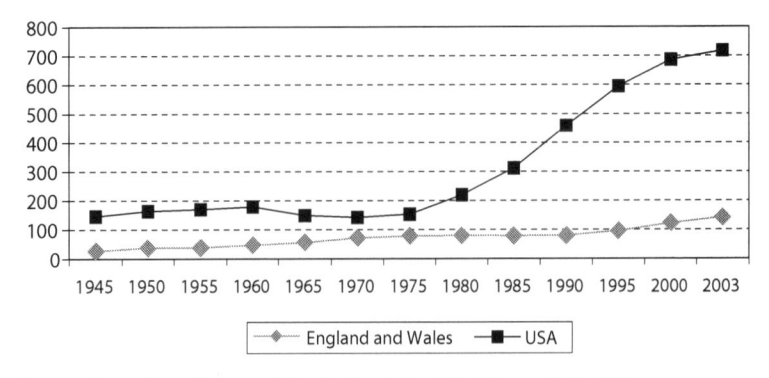

[Chart: Incarceration rates for England and Wales (roughly flat, ~150–200 per 100,000) and USA (rising sharply from ~100 in 1945 to over 700 by 2003), years 1945–2003]

Source: Data from Bureau of Justice Statistics, Washington DC: US Department of Justice and Criminal Statistics England and Wales (London: HM Stationery Office).

FIGURE 7. Incarceration Rates—United Kingdom and United States 1945–2003

(Zimring and Hawkins, 2001). Moreover, despite the very great variation that exists within the United States it remains the case that *every* state has an incarceration rate higher than that in England and Wales (see figure 8). Arguably, therefore, the starting point for an exploration of the similarities in penal policy on the two sides of the Atlantic ought to be to dispense with studies of the United States, and focus attention more on states such as Maine, Minnesota, Rhode Island, New Hampshire, and North Dakota (all with incarceration rates below 200). One further illustration of the scale of the differences we are discussing here can be seen if one calculates what would happen to the numbers in prison if the United Kingdom were truly to emulate US incarceration rates. If the incarceration rate in England and Wales rose to match that, say, of North Dakota (at 189), the prison population would increase from its current level of approximately 75,000 to nearer 100,000. If the incarceration rate reached that of the United States overall, the total number in prison in England and Wales would reach well over 300,000, and possibly approach 400,000.

Though the scale of imprisonment is certainly the most obvious difference between the outcomes of UK and US penal policy, there are other contrasts in the nature and extent to which

Contrasts in Intolerance 261

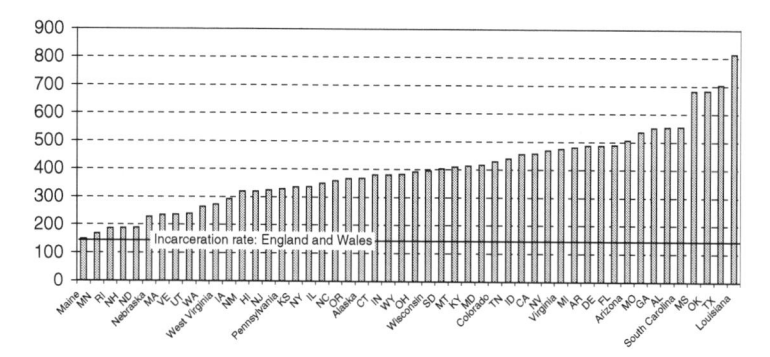

Source: Data from Bureau of Justice Statistics, Washington DC: US Department of Justice and Criminal Statistics England and Wales (London: HM Stationery Office).

FIGURE 8. Incarceration Rates in the United States, by State, 2004, compared with England and Wales

intolerance is evident on both sides of the Atlantic.[10] I will briefly mention two; first, sentencing policy and, more particularly, mandatory minimums. This is an interesting area for it is one in which there appears to be have been a degree of emulation by British politicians of the three strikes movement in the United States (indeed, in an unlikely move the baseball metaphor found its way into debates about reform of English sentencing law during the passage of the Crime (Sentences) Act 1997). In contrast with the United States, with its considerable history of habitual offender legislation there has been a long-standing resistance to moves to limit judicial discretion in this way in the United Kingdom (Morgan and Clarkson, 1995). Consequently, and notwithstanding the then Home Secretary's desire to introduce mandatory minimums that would have a substantive impact, it was a much more muted form of the three strikes policy that emerged in the United Kingdom. One of the reasons for this concerns the greater degree to which criminal justice policy remains buffered from the

---

[10] It is important to note, of course, that discussions of penal policy in *Britain* also run the risk of oversimplifying the reality. As one example, there remain some very significant differences between the juvenile justice system in England and Wales and that operating in Scotland. Political devolution in Scotland and Wales, and the potential return to at least an element of self-government in Northern Ireland may increase the contrasts in penal policy and practice within the United Kingdom.

direct impact of popular sentiment in the United Kingdom when compared with the United States. The outcome was in part an illustration of continuing differences in the political and legal cultures in which the legislation was passed, and also of the nature of the political and parliamentary conditions that existed at the time. Political processes in Britain continue to enjoy greater protection from direct voter involvement, and from politicized victim lobbying (Rock, 2005), as well as enjoying a stronger tradition of judicial independence. As David Downes (1988: 201) noted in *Contrasts* 'Criminal justice policy is seen almost as a contradiction in terms by the judiciary, since it is defined as encroaching on their own preserve.'

The second contrast concerns prisoner disenfranchisement. As Behrens *et al.* (2003: 562) point out, 'no other contemporary democracy disenfranchises felons to the same extent, or in the same manner, as the United States'. That said, the United Kingdom is in some respects closer to the United States in this regard than it is to many of its continental European neighbours. Under the Representation of the People Act 1983, amended by the Representation of the People Acts 1985 and 2000, all sentenced prisoners are prohibited from voting. A small number of prisoners subject to intermittent custody have been exempted from this rule and may vote if they are not in prison on the day of an election. In fact, the United Kingdom is one of only eight European countries with such automatic disenfranchisement (the others being Armenia, Bulgaria, the Czech Republic, Estonia, Hungary, Luxembourg, and Romania) (Unlock and Prison Reform Trust, 2004). By contrast, approximately eighteen European countries have no ban at all on voting by prisoners (including Denmark, Ireland, the Netherlands, Spain, Sweden, and Ireland). France and Germany have powers to impose loss of voting rights as a form of additional punishment. However, it remains the case that approximately two-thirds of American states have disenfranchisement statutes that go significantly further than British legislation by limiting the rights of convicted offenders on parole and probation. Indeed, as Uggen and Manza (2002: 778) note, the United States 'is unique in restricting the rights of nonincarcerated felons (who...make up approximately three quarters of the disenfranchised population)... The United States stands alone in the democratic world in imposing restrictions on the voting rights of a very large group of non-incarcerated felons.' At the very least, therefore, this and the other examples illustrate some of the important and continuing differences between the United States and the United Kingdom; indeed, arguably, between the United States and all other liberal democracies. In a number of important respects it appears that the United States stands alone (see also Melossi, 2003).

Conclusion: American Exceptionalism and Its Limits

On the surface there are some aspects of the contemporary US penal landscape that appear exceptional and, indeed, the language of exceptionalism regularly finds its way into discussions of comparative penal policy. Not least, of course, it is the US prison population that seems to set it apart. The number in prison now stands at well over two million and the United States has an incarceration rate that is five times that of England and Wales, six times that of Canada, seven times that of Germany and Italy and eleven times that of Sweden. Only Russia among the developed economies comes close to incarcerating a similar proportion of its population, and even it falls some way short (its incarceration rate of 577 per 100,000 in early 2006 was still considerably lower than America's at 724). The United States is currently responsible for approximately one-quarter of the entire globe's imprisoned population. It is not just the scale of imprisonment, but the harshness of its system of punishment which separates the United States from continental Europe (Whitman, 2003). Examples of this include the extent and nature of determinate sentencing in the United States, the spread of what Braithwaite (1989) has characterized as 'disintegrative shaming' rituals involving isolation and humiliation, the increased willingness within US criminal law to try juveniles as adults (Simon, 1995), the use of life without parole sentences for juveniles[11] and even, until declared unconstitutional by the

---

[11] The Untied States is the only industrialized democracy besides Israel to have juveniles serving sentences of life imprisonment without parole. As with other aspects of penal policy described in this chapter there is significant local and regional variation in the rate at which such sentences are used. Louisiana has the highest proportion of juveniles subjected to such sentences (per 100,000 population aged 14–17). Interestingly, and as a corrective to any crude

Supreme Court in March 2005, the execution of offenders who were under eighteen when their crimes were committed. In addition, and notably, the United States remains exceptional among democracies in its continuing use of the death penalty for adult offenders. According to Amnesty International over half of all the countries in the world have now abolished the death penalty and the pace of change internationally towards abolition has been exceedingly swift (Hood, 1998). Nevertheless, in the face of a worldwide human rights movement that has sought to restrict the death penalty, only twelve of the fifty US states and the District of Columbia have remained abolitionist.

And yet, of course, there are numerous ways in which the shape and direction of US penal policy is either similar to developments elsewhere or appears to provide a sign of what is likely to occur elsewhere in the future. It is clearly possible to identify a number of commonalities and differences in the trajectories of recent penal policy in the United States and the United Kingdom, as it is between the United States and other societies. As David Garland (2001a: 7) has argued in relation to the United States and the United Kingdom, it is possible to discern 'the strong similarities that appear in the recent policies and practices of these two societies—with patterns repeated across the fifty states and the federal system of the USA, and across the three legal systems of the UK' whilst acknowledging also that 'there are important national differences that distinguish the specific trajectory of these policy environments from one another and from those of other societies'. Consequently, despite the fact that there are a number of aspects of the US penal landscape that appear to be quite different from those evident in most if not all other liberal democracies, perhaps the idea of *American exceptionalism* has limited utility (Whitman, 2005). In practice it is almost always possible to identify similarities as well as differences. In a similar vein, although David Downes' study was called *Contrasts in Tolerance* he was careful to note that it was important 'not to overdraw the comparison between Britain and the Netherlands. The two have more in common than divides them' (1988: 205). Nevertheless, there remains

---

assumptions about regional variation, the states with the next highest rates are Michigan, Pennsylvania, and Iowa (Human Rights Watch, 2005).

something of a tendency to frame discussion of national and international trends in penal policy in terms of expectations of *either* convergence or divergence, and to view these as being mutually exclusive rather than exploring how processes of convergence and divergence may occur simultaneously. Downes' careful analysis of the Netherlands and England and Wales stands out as one of the few fully realized studies of 'convergent divergence' (Levi-Faur and Jordana, 2005) in post-war penal policy. In the period since the publication of *Contrasts* there has been a significant shift in most liberal democracies toward penal expansionism, and there is a pervasive sense of inevitability in much contemporary criminological scholarship about the likelihood that the coming period will see a further shift in the direction of mass incarceration and growing authoritarianism. Such assumptions should be challenged. As Downes (1988: 4) argues, the important question ' "Does it have to be so?" entails comparative study'. In this regard, further comparative exploration of penal policy in the United States and the United Kingdom and, more particularly, of the variety of practices that exist across the American regions and between American states, is arguably one important way in which we might extend our understanding of contemporary contrasts in intolerance.

Bibliography

Abramksy, S. (2001) *Hard Time Blues: How Politics Built a Prison Nation* (Thomas Dunne Books: New York).

Austin, J. and Coventry, G. (2001) *Emerging Issues on Privatized Prisons*, National Council on Crime and Delinquency, US Department of Justice Monograph (Washington DC: US Department of Justice, or available at <http://www.ncjrs.org/pdffiles1/bja/181249.pdf>).

Austin, J., Clark, J., Hardyman, P., and Henry, D. A. (1999). 'The Impact of "Three Strikes and You're Out"', *Punishment and Society*, 1(2), 131–62.

—— (2000) *Three Strikes and You're Out: Implementation and Impact of Strike Laws* (US Department of Justice: Washington DC).

Barker, V. (2004) *The Politics of Punishing: A Comparative Historical Analysis of American Democracy and Imprisonment Variation, 1965–Present*, unpublished PhD thesis, New York University.

Barker, V. (2006) 'The Politics of Punishing: Building a State Governance Theory of American Imprisonment Variation', 8 *Punishment and Society* 5–32.

Beckett, K. (1997) *Making Crime Pay: Law and Order in Contemporary American Politics* (Oxford University Press: New York).

—— and Western, B. (2001) 'Governing Social Marginality: Welfare, Incarceration and the Transformation of State Policy' 3 *Punishment and Society* 43–59.

Behrens, A., Uggen, C. and Manza, J. (2003) 'Ballot Manipulation and the "Menace of Negro Domination": Racial Threat and Felon Disenfranchisement in the United States, 1850–2002' 109 *American Journal of Sociology* 559–605.

Braithwaite, J. (1989) *Crime, Shame and Reintegration* (Cambridge University Press: Cambridge).

Cavadino, M. and Dignan, J. (2006) *Penal Systems: A Comparative Approach* (Sage: London).

Christie, N. (2000). *Crime Control as Industry* (3rd edn, Routledge: London).

Clark, J., Austin, J. and Henry, D. A. (1997) *'Three Strikes and You're Out': A Review of State Legislation* (National Institute of Justice: Washington DC).

Cummins, C. E. (2000) *Private Prisons in Texas, 1987–2000: The Legal, Economic and Political Influences on Policy Implementation*, unpublished PhD thesis, the American University, Washington DC.

Ditton, P. M. and Wilson, D. J. (1999) *Truth in Sentencing in State Prisons*, Bureau of Justice Statistics Special Report (Bureau of Justice: Washington DC).

Dixon, D. and Maher, L. (2004) in Newburn, T. and Sparks, R. (eds.), *Criminal Justice and Political Cultures* (Willan: Cullompton).

Downes, D. M. (1988) *Contrasts in Tolerance: Post-war Penal Policy in the Netherlands and England and Wales* (Clarendon: Oxford).

—— (2001) 'The Macho Penal Economy: Mass Incarceration in the U.S, A European Perspective' 3 *Punishment and Society* 61–80.

—— and Morgan, R. (2002) 'The Politics of Law and Order' in Maguire, M., Morgan, R., and Reiner, R. (eds.), *The Oxford Handbook of Criminology* (3rd edn, Clarendon Press: Oxford).

—— and van Swaaningen, R. (2006) 'The Road to Dystopia: Changes in the Penal Climate of the Netherlands', in Tonry, M. and Bijeveld, C., *Crime and Punishment in the Netherlands* (University of Chicago Press: Chicago).

Duncan, R. and Goddard, J. (2005) *Contemporary America* (2nd edn, Palgrave: Basingstoke).

Elazar, D.J. (1966) *American Federalism: A View from the States* (Thomas Y. Crowell Co: New York).
Fairclough, N. (2000) *New Labour, New Language?* (Routledge: New York).
Garland, D. (2001a) *The Culture of Control: Crime and Social Order in Contemporary Society* (Clarendon: Oxford).
—— (2001b) *Mass Imprisonment: Social Causes and Consequences* (Sage: London).
—— (2005) 'Capital Punishment and American Culture' 7 *Punishment and Society* 347–76.
Gest, T. (2001) *Crime and Politics: Big Government's Erratic Campaign for Law and Order* (Oxford University Press: New York).
Greenberg, D. F. (2002) 'Striking out in Democracy' 4 *Punishment and Society* 237–52.
—— and West, V. (2001) 'State Prison Populations and their Growth, 1971–1991' 39 *Criminology* 615–53.
Harrison, P. M. and Beck, A. J. (2004) *Prisoners in 2003*, Bureau of Justice Statistics Bulletin, November 2005 (US Department of Justice: Washington DC).
—— (2005) *Prisoners in 2004*, Bureau of Justice Statistics Bulletin (US Department of Justice: Washington DC).
Hartz, L. (1979) 'A Comparative Study of Fragment Cultures' in Graham, H. D. and Gurr, T. R. (eds.), *Violence in America: Historical and Comparative Perspectives* (Sage: Thousand Oaks, CA).
Hood, R. (1998) 'Capital Punishment' in Tonry, M. (ed.), *The Handbook of Crime and Punishment* (Oxford University Press: New York).
Hough, M., Jacobson, J. and Millie, A. (2003) *The Decision to Imprison: Sentencing and the Prison Population* (Prison Reform Trust: London).
Human Rights Watch (2005) *The Rest of their Lives: Life Without Parole for Child Offenders in the United States* (Human Rights Watch: New York or available at: <http://www.hrw.org/reports/2005/us1005/>).
Ignatieff, M. (2005) *American Exceptionalism and Human Rights* (Princeton University Press: Princeton, NJ).
Jones, T. and Newburn, T. (2004) 'The Convergence of US and UK Crime Control Policy: Exploring Substance and Process' in Newburn, T. and Sparks, R. (eds.), *Criminal Justice and Political Cultures* (Willan: Cullompton).
—— (2005) 'Comparative Criminal Justice Policy-making in the US and UK: the Case of Private Prisons' 45 *British Journal of Criminology* 58–80.

Jones, T. and Newburn, T. (2006a) *Policy Transfer and Criminal Justice* (Open University Press: Bukingham).

Jones, T. and Newburn, T. (2006b) 'Three Strikes and You're out: Exploring Symbol and Substance in American and British Crime Control Policy' *British Journal of Criminology*, forthcoming.

Kennedy, J. (2000) 'Monstrous Offenders and the Search for Solidarity Through Modern Punishment' 51 *Hastings Law Journal* 829–980.

Lacey, N. (2003) 'Principles, Politics and Criminal Justice' in Zedner, L. and Ashworth, A. (eds.), *The Criminological Foundations of Penal Policy: Essays in Honour of Roger Hood* (Clarendon Press: Oxford).

Levi-Faur, D. and Jordana, J. (2005) Regulatory Capitalism: Policy Irritants and Convergent Divergence 598 *The Annals* 191–7.

Manning, P.K. (2006) 'United States of America' in Jones, T. and Newburn, T. (eds.), *Plural Policing: A Comparative Perspective* (Routledge: London).

Mattera, P. and Khan, M. (2001) *Jail Breaks: Economic Development Subsidies Given to Private Prisons* (Good Jobs First: Washington DC).

McDonald, D. (1994) 'Public Imprisonment by Private Means' 34 *British Journal of Criminology* (Special Issue) 29–48.

——, Fournier, E., Russell-Einhorn, M., and Crawford, S. (1998) *Private Prisons in the United States: An Assessment of Current Practice* (Abt Associates Inc.: Massachussets).

Melossi, D. (2004) 'Theories of Social Control and the State Between American and European Shores' in Sumner, C. (ed.), *The Blackwell Companion to Criminology* (Blackwell: Oxford).

Micklethwait, J. and Wooldridge, A. (2004) *The Right Nation: Why America is Different* (Penguin: London).

Morgan, R. and Clarkson, C. (1995) 'The Politics of Sentencing Reform' in Clarkson, C. and Morgan, R. (eds.), *The Politics of Sentencing Reform* (Clarendon Press: Oxford).

Muncie, J. (2004) 'Youth Justice: Globalisation and Multi-modal Governance' in Newburn, T. and Sparks, R. (eds.), *Criminal Justice and Political Cultures* (Willan: Cullompton).

Newburn, T. and Jones, T. (2005) 'Symbolic Politics and Penal Policy: The Long Shadow of Willie Horton' 1 *Crime, Media, Culture* 72–87.

—— and Sparks, R. (2004) 'Criminal Justice and Political Cultures' in Newburn, T. and Sparks, R. (eds.), *Criminal Justice and Political Cultures* (Willan: Cullompton).

Pratt, J., Brown, D., Brown, M., Hallsworth, S. and Morrison, W. (eds.) (2005) *The New Punitiveness: Trends, Theories, Perspectives* (Willan: Cullompton).

Putnam, R. (2000) *Bowling Alone: The Collapse and Revival of American Community* (Simon and Schuster: New York).

Reiner, R. (1989) 'Where the Buck Stops: Chief Constables' Views on Police Accountability' in Morgan, R. and Smith, D. J. (eds.), *Coming to Terms with Policing* (Routledge: London).

Reitz, K. (2001) 'The Disassembly and Reassembly of US Sentencing Practices' in Tonry, M. and Frase, R. (eds.), *Sentencing and Sanctions in Western Countries* (Oxford University Press: Oxford) 222–58.

Roberts, J. and Hough, M. (2005) *Understanding Public Attitudes to Criminal Justice* (Open University Press: Maidenhead).

Rock, P. (2005) 'Victims' Policies as Contingent Accomplishments' in Vetere, E. and Pedro, D. (eds.), *Victims of Crime and Abuse of Power: Festschrift in Honour of Irene Melup* (United Nations: Bangkok).

Ryan, M. and Ward, T. (1989) *Privatization and the Penal System: The American Experience and the Debate in Britain* (Open University Press: Milton Keynes).

Sarabi, B. and Bender, E. (2000) *The Prison Payoff: The Role of Politics and Private Prisons in the Incarceration Boom* (Western Prison Project: Western States Center).

Savelsberg, J. (1994) 'Knowledge, Domination and Criminal Punishment' 97 *American Journal of Sociology* 1346–81.

Schiraldi, V., Colburn, J. and Lotke, E. (2004) *Three Strikes and You're Out* (available at http://www.justicepolicy.org/downloads/JPIOUTOFSTEPREPORTFNL.doc)

Schlosser, E. (1998) 'The Prison Industrial Complex' *Atlantic Monthly* (December) 51–77.

Sentencing Project (2005) *Felony Disenfranchisement Laws in the United States* (available at <http://www.sentencingproject.org/pdfs/1046.pdf>).

Shichor, D. (1995) *Punishment for Profit: Private Prisons/Public Concerns* (Sage: London).

Simon, J. (1995) 'Power Without Parents: Juvenile Justice in a Postmodern Society' 16 *Cardozo Law Review* 1363–426.

—— (2001) 'Fear and Loathing in Late Modernity: Reflections on the Cultural Sources of Mass Imprisonment in the United States' 3 *Punishment and Society* 21–33.

Tonry, M. (1995) *Malign Neglect: Race, Crime and Punishment in America* (Oxford University Press: New York).

—— (2001) Symbol, Substance and Severity in Western Penal Policies' 3 *Punishment and Society* 517–36.

—— (2004a) *Thinking About Crime: Sense and Sensibility in American Penal Culture* (Oxford University Press: New York).

—— (2004b) *Punishment and Politics* (Willan: Cullompton).

Uggen, C. and Manza, J. (2002) 'Democratic Contraction? Political Consequences of Felon Disenfranchisement in the United States' 67 *American Sociological Review* 777–803.

Unlock & Prison Reform Trust (2004) *Barred from Voting: The Right to Vote for Sentenced Prisoners* (Unlock & Prison Reform Trust: London, or available at <http://www.unlockprison.org.uk/campaigns/vfpbriefing.pdf>).

Wacquant, L. (1999) 'How Penal Common Sense Comes to Europeans: Notes on the Transatlantic Diffusion of the Neoliberal Doxa' 1 *European Societies* 319–52.

—— (2001) 'Deadly Symbiosis: When Ghetto and Prison Meet and Mesh' 3 *Punishment and Society* 95–134.

Walker, S. (1998) *Popular Justice: A History of American Criminal Justice* (Oxford University Press: New York).

Whitman, J.Q. (2003) *Harsh Justice: Criminal Punishment and the Widening Divide between America and Europe* (Oxford University Press: New York).

—— (2005) 'Response to Garland' 7 *Punishment and Society* 389–96.

Windlesham, Lord (1998) *Politics, Punishment and Populism* (Oxford University Press: New York).

Zimring, F. (2001) 'Imprisonment Rates and the New Politics of Criminal Punishment' 3 *Punishment and Society* 161–6.

—— (2003) *The Contradictions of American Capital Punishment* (Oxford University Press: New York).

—— (2005) 'Path Dependence, Culture and State-level Execution Policy: a Response to David Garland' 7 *Punishment and Society* 377–84.

—— and Hawkins, G. (1991) *The Scale of Imprisonment* (Chicago University Press: Chicago).

—— and —— (1997) *Crime is Not the Problem: Lethal Violence in America* (Oxford University Press: New York).

—— —— and Kamin, S. (2001) *Punishment and Democracy: Three Strikes and You're Out in California* (Oxford University Press: Oxford).

10
Governance and Restorative Justice in Cali, Colombia

Declan Roche[1]

A group of women in Aguablanca, a district of Cali, Colombia, run a community programme that attempts to spread peace and justice in one of the country's poorest and most violent urban areas. Using skills and information acquired in weekly meetings, the women assist local residents both by providing a range of essential services—from mediation to adult education—and by referring residents to other service providers and resources in the community. Addressing both the symptoms and causes of their community's problems, this group has been touted as a model for other poor communities in Colombia, and it is arguable that communities, policy-makers, and restorative justice advocates—both in Colombia and elsewhere—can learn much from the group's approach to restorative justice and, more broadly, from its network-based approach. Much of the debate about the conflict in Colombia focuses on national events and neglects the efforts of local communities to nurture peace and justice in their immediate environment, but the Aguablanca programme demonstrates that local initiatives can make an

---

[1] Declan Roche works for the Australian Government Solicitor but the views expressed do not reflect those of the Australian Government Solicitor. He thanks the Alvar Alice Foundation for hosting his trips to Colombia, to USAID and the International Organization for Migration for funding the research on which this chapter is based, to Carmen San Miguel and LSE colleagues Conor Gearty, Tim Newburn, and Paul Rock for helpful comments on earlier drafts of this chapter, and above all, to Hermana Alba Stella and her consejeras for all their assistance.

important difference in the lives of ordinary Colombians. To replicate the success of this programme in communities elsewhere, however, it will be necessary to identify local citizens who can provide the same leadership and commitment as the remarkable women of Aguablanca.

Introduction

The district of Aguablanca, in the city of Cali, is one of the poorest and most violent urban areas in Colombia. It also serves as base for one of the country's most dedicated and disciplined private armies, formed in 1998 after local residents, feeling that others had failed them, decided to take matters into their own hands. But this is no ordinary company of recruits: its leader is a Catholic nun, the troops are all women, and their weapons are not guns and grenades, but parenting classes, mediation skills, soup kitchens, violence prevention strategies, and economic development programmes. Together, however, they lead the fight against crime and conflict in Aguablanca, employing a strategy that combines swift responses to individual crimes with a large, almost astonishing, collection of programmes designed to address the underlying social problems.

Aguablanca is home to approximately 500,000 of Cali's two million residents. Many of them are Colombians displaced from their homes by armed groups, and the population continues to swell as new '*desplazados*' (displaced people) arrive on an almost weekly basis. Cali residents who do not live there refer to Aguablanca as 'the other Cali'. Life is hot, dusty, crowded, and uncomfortable. The better homes are built from brick, but in the poorer streets, residences are ramshackle buildings constructed from nothing more than planks of scrap wood, flour sacks and any other discarded materials that can be found. Despite people having lived there since the 1970s, it was not until 1988 that the Cali city administration began to recognize Aguablanca officially as a city district, and so provide basic government services, such as electricity and sewerage. Even today most of the roads remain unlit and unpaved, many houses rely on makeshift sewer systems and illegal electricity connections, and the shoulder of the main road in and out of Aguablanca serves as the local rubbish tip. (For a vivid description of life in Aguablanca see Amis (2005).)

Aguablanca's population is young and diverse: the district's residents, almost half of whom are under the age of eighteen, are a mix of African, indigenous American, European, and *Mestizo* (or mixed) descent. The population is beset by chronic unemployment, poor health, and high levels of illiteracy. But as severe as these social problems are, however, they are not the source of Aguablanca's notorious reputation; that comes from the district's crime problems. Crime in Aguablanca, like most places in Colombia, is a multifaceted phenomenon. Mention of crime in Colombia conjures up images of armed groups engaged in drug-trafficking and kidnapping, and certainly these groups are visible in Aguablanca: periodically paramilitaries round up and kill local street kids in actions called '*limpiezas*' (cleanings), while guerilla soldiers visit from their camps in the mountainous jungles surrounding Cali, to attempt to recruit young residents. But these are not the only, or even the most significant, perpetrators in Aguablanca. Youth gangs, who have balkanized the streets of Aguablanca, deal drugs, hide weapons for armed groups, and battle rival gangs. There are also many perpetrats of street crimes who are not attached to any group or gang that commit street crime. However, according to Helmer José Montana, one of the district's two criminal prosecutors, these types of violence are all less of a problem than the extraordinarily high levels of family abuse and sexual assault within families.

Crime in Aguablanca is compounded by victims' reluctance to seek the help of the local police. Residents appear as afraid of the police as they are of the criminals. In 2004, two police officers were convicted of murder after kidnapping and torturing three local residents, and then tossing their corpses into the river. Police are also suspected of turning a blind eye to crimes committed by local paramilitary groups, as well as of committing their own abuses. But whereas residents do not trust the police, they do trust the district's two state prosecutors, Henry Alberto and Helmer José. Through their long tenure as prosecutors in Aguablanca and their personal reputations for trustworthiness and integrity, Díaz and Montana have won over the suspicious local community, so much so that residents who want to press charges go straight to them and bypass the police altogether. As a result, on any day of the week, the waiting room outside the Prosecutors' offices is invariably full of local residents waiting to make allegations and seeking the Prosecutors' assistance.

Against this troubled and complicated background, one group of Aguablanca women is beginning to make some headway. Calling themselves *consejeras de familia*, or family advisers (hereafter 'consejeras'), the group consists of 125 women from Aguablanca, ranging in age from their early twenties to their late sixties. Since 1998, these women have set about tackling the crime in their communities, using a two-pronged approach that both addresses the aftermath of crime and attempts to alleviate the underlying causes of conflict in Aguablanca. The result is an army that is trained as mediators and counsellors, and which runs a suite of interlocking programmes that includes a crèche, a home for pregnant girls, youth centres, microfinance and other economic development initiatives, and classes in sewing, organic gardening, and cooking. As the slogan on their t-shirts puts it, '*Consejeras de familia*. The community organization at the service of the family'.

The heart of the organization is a group of twelve women who meet every Monday afternoon. At these weekly meetings the women discuss each other's work, support each other, and receive training and education, provided either by Hermana Alba Stella, who helped to start the programme, or by any one of a series of invited guests, who have included community nurses and medical doctors, academics, prosecutors, and agronomists from a local university. The twelve members of this group each represent their own similar-sized group of consejeras from their local neighbourhood, and they report back to these groups on a weekly basis to disseminate their newly acquired information and knowledge, so that the consejeras can use this information to help local families, whether by helping mediate disputes, giving suggestions and advice, or by referring them to relevant government services and private charities.

A number of the senior consejeras also co-ordinate programmes delivering a wide range of specific services. Nelly Ortega, a middle-aged *Mestizo* (mixed race) woman who has lived in Aguablanca for twenty years, is one of the founding members of the consejeras. She is also the co-ordinator of the gardening programme. Each week approximately eighty women learn how to grow a fruit and vegetable garden in their own small yards without using chemicals. They swap seeds, compare propagating and composting techniques, and learn about plants and their different uses. Ortega or one of the local women lead many of these sessions, while others are led by a local agronomist. Other consejeras co-ordinate programmes that teach parenting skills, stress management, and cooking to local residents, run a second-hand clothes shop, a number of youth centres, and help newly arrived *desplezados* settle into their new homes. For this work as co-ordinators they receive a small fee, funded by a private foundation, but all their other work as consejeras is done on a voluntary basis.

The Aguablanca Approach to Governance

The experience of the consejeras in Aguablanca is set against a national backdrop of continuing violence and instability. Colombia holds a number of dubious distinctions. It has often been described as the kidnapping capital of the world (see, for example, BBC, 2001) (although, increasingly, press reports attribute that unwelcome distinction to Iraq and Mexico). It is the world's biggest supplier of cocaine (supplying somewhere between 80 and 90 per cent of the world's cocaine) and it is also a growing source of heroin (Interpol, 2005). Colombia has one of the highest homicide rates in the world, and the highest reported rate among youth (WHO Report, 2002). It also has the most unequal distribution of wealth (including land ownership) in Latin America (Bannon, 2004). Furthermore, the 2004 UNHCR report on Global Refugee Trends reveals that there are more internally displaced people in Colombia than in any other country in the world, and that Colombia is also the seventh largest generator of refugees (UNHCR, 2004).

The term 'ungoverned spaces' has been used by the US military in the Bush administration to describe geographical areas, whether in rural areas or crowded cities, where governments do not exercise effective control. According to Donald Rumsfeld, the US Secretary of Defense, ungoverned spaces have become one of the key threats to peace and security, as they provide terrorists and other criminal groups bases from which they can— relatively free from interference—train, plan, and organize criminal operations. General Hill, the Commander of SOUTHCOM, the US military division responsible for all of Latin America to the south of Mexico, has expressed particular concern about the presence of ungoverned spaces in Colombia. Under Plan Colombia vast sums of Colombian and US money have been spent on long-term, large-scale military operations designed to provide governance to these areas (Hill, 2004).

Hill and other military figures have used the expression 'ungoverned spaces' to refer to rural areas in Colombia, especially in the jungles of the Amazon basin in the south, but it could also be argued that it is also an apt description of Aguablanca itself. Although the state has attempted to provide governance, it has struggled to provide effective, legitimate governance to Aguablanca's residents. As a result, residents are vulnerable to violence, extreme poverty, and illness. The government's response to the problem of ungoverned spaces has been characterized by an increased reliance on police and military presence, but the consejeras' work illustrates a different approach to extending governance. Although consejeras do not pretend to have all the answers to the multifaceted problems facing Colombia, they are nevertheless confident that their approach could be used beyond Aguablanca, in other areas of Colombia. In the following sections I consider six features of the consejeras' brand of governance.

Before doing that, however, it may be appropriate to explain briefly my own involvement. In May 2004 one of the programme's funders, Alvar Alice, a private Colombian philanthropic foundation, invited me to speak at a restorative justice conference in Cali. There I met Hermana Alba Stella and some of her colleagues who spoke about the work they were doing in the outskirts of the city. At the invitation of Hermana Alba Stella, and with sponsorship from USAID, and the International Organisation for Migration (IOM), I spent two weeks in Aguablanca in August 2004 conducting the research on which this chapter is based.[2] In February 2005, I returned to Cali to present an earlier version of this paper at a National Symposium on Restorative Justice and Peace, hosted by Javeriana University in Cali, and attended by Colombian President, Alvaro Uribe, the

---

[2] Unless otherwise indicated, quotations come from interviews conducted during this research trip.

South African Archbishop, Desmond Tutu, as well as human rights officials, indigenous leaders, academics, politicians, and community representatives from around the country.

Community-based Governance

The consejeras programme is run by local residents, for local residents. As Hermana Alba Stella says, 'First it allows local women to teach. It places faith in the abilities of local women to do things for themselves. Women are empowered.' A Franciscan priest who works in the community, and who assists the consejeras programme, pithily summarizes the programme's philosophy: 'We believe in the old saying that nobody is so ignorant that they have nothing to teach, and nobody so wise that they have nothing to learn.'

Self-reliance is an old tradition in Aguablanca. Before it became a residential area, Aguablanca was an agricultural zone on the eastern edge of the city of Cali. When civil war broke out in 1948, thousands of Colombians fled their rural homes for cities in a bid to escape the violence that would claim 200,000 lives over the next five years. During this period, known as *la Violencia*, many Colombians headed for Cali, the capital of the Cauca Valley, in the south-west of Colombia. The city administration, already battling problems of corruption and inefficiency, buckled under the increased demand for housing and services. Many new arrivals, unable to find housing in the city, moved to Aguablanca, where they either settled illegally on agricultural land, or purchased small plots that developers bribed the local councils to rezone for residential purposes.

The spirit of self-reliance lives on in the work of the consejeras, but with a new twist, as the consejeras embrace, rather than resent, their autonomy. By tapping into the knowledge and abilities of ordinary people, the program can be seen as an example of the popular education movement that has been embraced by poor communities across Latin America. Influenced by the writings of Brazilian educator, Paolo Freire (1972), its advocates reject conceptions of education in which the teacher is presumed to know everything, and his or her students nothing, and instead advocate education in which the teacher and the student learn from each other. Moreover, they argue, this learning should take place not in the classroom but in the real world, where ideas can be immediately applied, and then tested, reconsidered, and reapplied in an iterative process (Kane, 2001). This philosophy is strikingly apparent in the consejeras' weekly meetings in which there is a constant dialectal encounter between ideas (such as restorative justice, and human rights) and the human environment.

The philosophy of self-help pervades most aspects of the consejeras' work. For example, consejeras barter among themselves, swapping seeds for fruit and vegetables, or clothes for labour, and encourage other community members to do the same. Hermana Alba Stella says that she encourages this practice because it encourages families to appreciate all the things they can do without money. By advocating barter, however, they are not advocating the abandonment of capitalism. On the contrary, the consejeras are currently working to establish a micro-credit scheme that would help local community members start their own businesses. Hermana Alba Stella says that the consejeras are attempting to develop a more humane model of capitalism, in which social capital plays an important role. The concept of social capital is central to Robert Putnam's work on communal life in Italy (Putnam, 1993), and more recently in the United States (Putnam, 2000). Putnam highlights the importance of community associations to healthy, prosperous communities. These associations—whether savings societies or soccer clubs—nurture bonds of trust and reciprocity that provide a basis for economic and political co-operation. In some places these networks have always been an integral part of social life, but in others, such as Aguablanca, where they are much more fragile, they need careful, conscious nurturing.

The consejeras appear to have won the trust of the community. This is evident from the large numbers that make use of their services, but it is perhaps most strikingly illustrated in the way the women are able to move freely around Aguablanca, whereas most residents are highly fearful about crossing the streets that mark the borders between the territories of the two main rival gangs in the area. As one resident described the consejeras to me, 'they're the popular professionals'. Their independence is critical to maintaining the trust of the community. Consejeras are able to walk freely because they are seen as independent and honest. However, to maintain this status, it is essential that the consejeras are not perceived as being linked with the guerillas, the paramilitaries, or for that matter, the police. In practical terms, this means the consejeras are very wary about having contact with members of any of these groups.

The Role of Networks

Consejeras attempt to govern ungoverned spaces by nurturing organic informal networks. These informal networks are a feature of many communities, especially in poor communities, not only throughout Latin America, but in Northern Ireland, Bangladesh, and elsewhere. The consejeras network provides a simple, yet effective and accountable mechanism for disseminating knowledge and information to a large number of people. In this network knowledge flows in both directions, from the main committee outwards in a radial pattern to the local committees, and from the local committees back to the centre. Techniques and information flow outwards to the local committees, where they are used by members to reflect on how consejeras have handled individual cases; problems that cannot be resolved by them or that raise matters of general importance are then taken by the representatives of these meetings back to the Monday afternoon meeting, where they are considered by Hermana Alba Stella and the representatives of the other local committees. The learning cycle is completed when representatives then filter back decisions and advice to the local committees.

Although the consejeras emphasize their independence, they are in fact part of larger local and international networks that allow the consejeras to access expertise, finance, and support from a range of private and public sources. For example, in their restorative justice work the women have benefited from links to funding (banks, private foundations, and now, USAID, and the United Nations), to expertise (from restorative justice experts in Colombian universities, and international researchers), as well as from the support of the state (through the support of the local prosecutors' and welfare offices). This network is not permanent or unchanging. Instead, its configuration at any moment is determined by the needs of the programme at that particular point in time and by what is available. Previous links may be reactivated, or new links added.

This approach is characteristic of many modern social movements (Castells, 1997). It allows a group of poor women to access more resources than they would otherwise, without establishing a large bureaucracy. However, this decentred network approach does raise questions. The programme works with a number of private and government services, albeit on a very selective basis, and it avoids others. The underlying problem is that the state has a legitimacy problem in these communities. Such relationships that do exist between the state and the community owe more to the community's perception of the personal integrity of the office holders than to any underlying institutional legitimacy. This makes for fragile relationships, and prompts some longer-term questions about the future of the programme in Aguablanca as well as the possibility of expanding it to other places: is it feasible or advisable to have programmes that are truly independent of the state, or should programmes be encouraged to develop closer institutional links?

The Role of Leadership

The programme depends as much on strong leadership as it does on its links to a network of services. Hermana Alba Stella describes herself as 'just an old lady', but those who live and work in the community refer to her as 'their mother', 'their guide', and even 'their warrior'. Alba Stella, a Fransiscan missionary, was born in Bucuramanga, in the north of Colombia, a region renowned among Colombians for its strong women, and has lived in Aguablanca for eighteen years, where she is the director of *Paz y Bien* (Peace and Wellbeing), a private charitable foundation.

Without the leadership of Hermana Alba Stella, it is unlikely that the consejeras network would exist. As Elodia Nieves explained it, 'The consejeras have formalized an organic process. We women used to meet on street corners and in each other's homes. People used to say we were just gossiping', she said, laughing. 'But women would confess to each other—I'm having problems with my husband, or I'm having problems with my kids, and we'd give each other advice. But we realized we didn't really know what we were doing. We'd just say things like "Don't allow him (your husband) to hit you—hit him back." We realized that we needed to learn how to give advice. It was around this time when Hermana Alba Stella started to run her classes.'

Hermana Alba Stella explains that having witnessed the way in which women were neglected in the community, she decided to start a programme designed around helping women to care for themselves, beginning with a series of workshops designed to help women improve their self-esteem. However, when she advertised the workshops, as she explains, 'women came up to me and told me: "we don't want programmes for ourselves, we don't want self-esteem workshops, what we really need is help to deal with our husbands, and our children. If you want to help us, this is what we need."' So Alba Stella changed tack, and began to run a series of classes on parenting skills. It was in these classes that she and the local women 'began to see the full potential of what was happening, how the skills they were learning could be passed on to others. So together we devised the idea of a network of trained women. We decided to call ourselves "*consejeras de familia*".'

Her leadership has been crucial to the programme ever since. She is a constant source of ideas, encouragement, and advice. She provides all manner of practical assistance, from accompanying local boys to their medical exams to join the military, to providing shelter to women who have been beaten by their husbands. She combines physical stamina, and mental strength, with a warm smile, and a lively sense of humour. One woman explained that likening Alba Stella to their mother, as many women did, was especially apt, because like a mother, she helped them grow, and then set them free, with the knowledge they could return for more assistance as and when they needed it.

The crucial role played by a single person raises questions about the sustainability of the programme in Aguablanca, as well as about its replicability outside Aguablanca. In relation to the former, Hermana Alba Stella says: 'We are planning for the day when I will not be around to help. We are making sure that there are women around who will take over—and we've begun to assign responsibilities to these women.' Going away for trial periods has convinced her that the programme can function well without her. 'I've been away for periods of up to two or three months, and everything worked perfectly.'

There are many ingredients that go into making a successful community justice programme, but leadership is crucial. The most successful programmes are those where there is a person whose determination and leadership carries the programme, especially at key moments when obstacles appear and other people are not as committed. If this is true, when does this leave the communities that do not have the benefit of an Hermana Alba Stella to organize and inspire? This is a real problem, but the experience of the women of Aguablanca also provides a valuable reminder that even the most marginalized members of the most marginalized communities have the capacity to change their own lives, and to help others change theirs.

Alba Stella's religion is important to her work, less the institution than her faith: Hermana Alba Stella says that it is her daily meditation and prayer that gives her the strength to do her difficult and tiring work. There is a long tradition of the church's involvement in social activism in poor communities in Latin America. It is a history associated with a good degree of controversy, well illustrated by the life of its main spiritual leader, the Brazilian Bishop Helder Camara, who died in 1999. Early in his career he was feted for his work with poor communities in Brazil, but then he fell foul of the Catholic Church, which silenced him, and the Brazilian government, which imprisoned him. Camara famously explained his treatment in these terms: 'When I feed the poor, I am called a saint; but when I ask why the poor are hungry, I'm labelled a Communist.'

Perhaps mindful of this controversial history, Hermana Alba Stella is careful to ensure that the consejeras do not use their positions in the community to proselytize. Similarly, she is careful to ensure that the consejeras, the majority of whom are Catholics, base their work on training, personal experience, and solidarity with fellow consejeras. 'At first, it was frequently the case that the consejeras would pester people with their beliefs, moralizing about their problems, and trying to get them to attend church,' says Hermana Alba Stella. 'However, we drew attention to this, and after we'd discussed it, the women realized that it was inappropriate and they stopped doing it.'

The Role of Women

All of the 125 consejeras are women. Within Latin America there is a long, vibrant, tradition of women's groups, the most famous of which is probably Las Madres de la Plaza de Mayo, the group of mothers who have marched around the independence monument outside the Presidential Palace in Buenos Aires every week since 30 April 1977, demanding to know what happened to their children who were taken by the Junta's security forces. Throughout Latin America, a diverse range of womens' groups have challenged injustice and oppression, from miners' wives committees, to groups campaigning for political reform, to literacy programmes in poor communities.

I asked Hermana Alba Stella if men were prohibited from becoming consejeras in Aguablanca. 'Of course not', she says. 'We don't want to exclude anyone, and we have had a few men in the past, but presently there are none.' I later ask Elodia Nieves why the original male members left, and why they had not been replaced by new male members. 'They say they don't have time', Nieves told me. Does she believe this, I asked. 'No', she said, smiling and shaking her head: 'Our women have three jobs: their day job, their work at home, and their work in the community as consejeras.'

In the past many women's groups in Latin America have been accused of merely reinforcing the subjugation of women by formalizing and institutionalizing unequal burdens of care. But women in Aguablanca do not see their work in these terms. To them their work gives satisfaction, purpose, and power. On one of my last mornings in Aguablanca I visited Nelly Ortega, the co-ordinator of the local gardening programme, to ask some more questions. As she and I sat talking in her small garden patio, her two daughters stood at the door of their small, two-room house, listening to us. As I got up to leave, I asked Nelly's eldest daughter what she thought of her mother's work. 'I like it *muchisimo*. I have seen my Mum grow as a person. She used to think that all she could do was wash and iron other people's clothes—now she realizes she's got all these abilities and that's she's a powerful woman.' While she was speaking I glanced across at Nelly, who was smiling at her daughter with tears in her eyes. Moreover, the consejeras see their work as providing a vehicle for transforming womens' positions within the community. As Elodia Nieves put it, 'Men say "we need to rest, and watch TV", but for the woman—this is a mission. We're beating the men.'

The political dimension of the consejeras' work is clearly evident in their role as advocates for restorative justice in

Colombia. In other words, for these women there are no clear distinctions between the personal and the political. Work with families is seen as part of larger political change, and political advocacy is intended to benefit families. This characterization of their work is not unique to the consejeras. Womens' groups throughout Latin America (Stephen, 1997), and indeed, around the world, link 'their struggle, and their oppression, to their everyday lives. They see their transformation of their condition in the family as connected to their intervention in the public sphere' (Castells, 1997: 201).

The consejeras do not, though, describe themselves as a feminist organization, nor acknowledge the label when others seek to apply it. Again, this is a tendency they share with many womens' groups in the developing world, especially in Latin America (Kuppers, 1994). Women in Aguablanca prefer to talk in specific, practical terms about the services they provide. It appears that this is done partly because women wish to avoid the alienating and confrontational connotations of the term '*feminista*'. While feminism and religion may, to varying extents, provide the motivation for individual consejeras, the women have been careful to construct a group identity based in less divisive and controversial ideas such as community-based governance, and restorative justice, on the basis that this sort of identity is more likely to gain widespread acceptance in the immediate community, and beyond.

Consejeras must both attend weekly meetings and be available to help families. Women are reluctant to complain, and, the sense of purpose and pride they gain from their work is palpable. Nevertheless, their commitments as consejaras clearly have the potential to conflict with their other commitments. This pressure is reflected in the attrition rate for the consejeras. Elodia Nieves, the co-ordinator of the consejeras programme and one of the original consejeras, says that at times the consejeras have numbered almost 150 people but currently there are 125. Most leave, she says, because it is too time-consuming to stay. Using money given to her charitable foundation, *Paz y Bien*, Alba Stella can afford to pay the women who take on the additional responsibility of co-ordinating one of the many programmes. This, however, provides a minimal salary and then only to three or four people. Most of the money is used to subsidize the cost of the consejeras' activities (for example, to provide transport and refreshments for weekly outings organized for community residents).

Remunerating all consejeras would help curb the attrition rate, but among restorative justice advocates there is some resistance to paying community participants on the basis that it is precisely the voluntary nature of their work that makes it effective and them legitimate (Braithwaite, 2001; Roche, 2003). However, it is possible that women can be paid without destroying the community ethos of the programme. Other programmes elsewhere provide some funding. For example, in South Africa community members receive money for sitting in peace-making gatherings (Roche, 2002: 516). The programmes are funded through a combination of local, and international, governmental, and private money. A portion of the money goes to the community members themselves, while a portion is earmarked for the community. This can be used for a wide range of purposes, from funding playgrounds, to providing micro-credit. In Aguablanca there are additional complexities to accepting money. Accepting funding has the potential to erode their precious independence. One possible option being considered by Hermana Alba Stella is to assist all consejeras to become self-sufficient by helping them establish their own micro-enterprises.

The Role of Accountability

The majority of consejeras have little or no formal education, and no experience of work in the formal employment sector, yet as consejeras they are defined by their professional approach to their work. Helmer José Montana, one of the district's two prosecutors, says that consejeras 'are well-trained, they have a clear purpose, and they know the limits to their work'. Nubia Ocampo Flórez, co-ordinator of *Bienestar Familiar*, the Colombian government's welfare agency, for Aguablanca and the surrounding area, is similarly effusive about their professionalism: 'They are a strong group, well trained and well accepted in the community.' She says that the consejeras provided a blueprint when she was working out how to implement a national initiative to use community members as family educators. 'I wish that all my educators had their (consejeras') skills and dedication!', Florez says.

The first fundamental principle that governs their work is that consejeras must first address the problems within their own family before they attempt to assist other families. As Elodia Nieves, co-ordinator of the consejeras, puts it 'If you're going to help others, you need first to be in good shape yourself.' For many of the women, the most important lessons they have learnt have been about how to avoid violence within the family. Nelly Ortega, one of the most experienced consejeras, explains to me that one of the first things she learnt was that she used to hit her daughter far too much. 'I used to think that *garrote* was the right way to discipline kids, hitting them and verbally mistreating them, but now I've learnt that there are other, better ways of disciplining your kids—you don't always have to be negative for a start.' Nelly says she now enjoys a close relationship with both of her daughters, aged sixteen and six.

When they are ready to help others, the women are encouraged not to stray beyond their field of competence. They emphasize that their primary responsibility is simply to listen, 'small mouth, big ears' is their slogan. Elodia tells me that sometimes families plead with them, 'just tell us what to do'. But consejeras resist, saying that is not their job. To this end, Hermana Alba Stella suggests that in hindsight a better name for the consejeras would have been orientator (*orientadores*) or companions (*acompañantes*). They also emphasize the importance of referring serious cases to experts, and will accompany women to the *fiscalía* (the Prosecutor's office).

In keeping with their professional approach, the consejeras practice a carefully developed form of self-regulation. Meetings provide a vital role in quality control by providing an opportunity to consider the difficult cases that consejeras have encountered. One of the women explains to me their processes by likening their meetings to those used by doctors to discuss difficult cases. These meetings also provide a form of ongoing training. In these meetings, Hermana Alba Stella says 'we clear many things up'. She explains that 'meeting together becomes a form of training—discussion of cases refreshes training—Did you ask that question? Did you ask this question?' For this reason, consejeras who do not attend the weekly meetings lose their status as a consejera.

Comprehensive Governance

The number and diversity of programmes run by the women of Aguablanca is almost overwhelming. Many community programmes teach people to read and write, or help them to resolve conflicts, or give them training in how to start a business, or provide emergency food and accommodation, but few do all these things. Moreover, these programmes are designed to be interlocking. As Ortega, the co-ordinator of the gardening programme explains, the gardening programme is a way of making contact with isolated families. Ortega visits the families and asks them if they wish to join the gardening programme, when in fact gardening is part of a bigger community-strengthening programme. 'If I see that families don't know how to eat, I can send them to the community pot. One programme is a bridge to another.'

Among the women the consejeras help, Laura Garces'[3] story is not unusual. Garces and her family moved to Aguablanca in 2001 after they were forced to flee their home in Porvenir, in the Putamayo region, where Garces washed clothes and cooked meals at a local army station and her husband worked as a truck driver. Garces says her family's problems started when her husband accepted a job delivering food to a local guerrilla camp. Local paramilitaries soon discovered who her husband was working for and ordered him to stop; his guerrilla bosses insisted he continue and, before long, Laura says, they had made themselves targets for both the paramilitaries and the guerrillas. In the end, the paramilitaries gave them twenty-four hours to leave. With the assistance of the Colombian National Army, Garces, her husband, and their eight children, the youngest of whom was only eight days old, fled to Aguablanca, where they arrived with nothing more than a couple of hens and a rooster, which they sold as soon as they arrived so they could buy some food.

Garces learnt about the consejeras after one of her neighbours told her about the food parcels and weekly lunches provided by consejeras. Garces heard about the other services provided by the consejeras when she went to collect food for her family.

---

[3] This is not her real name.

Three-and-a-half years on, she reflected on the help the consejeras have given her: 'They've pointed me in the right direction. They have helped me get food and clothes for my family as well as sensible advice. For example, I've attended workshops on how to live with your family, how to raise children. They've shown me how to manage my debts and how to budget.' Life remained difficult for Garces, who said it is stressful bringing up kids in Aguablanca, among gunfights and kids using drugs. And although she has found work as a cleaning lady and her husband as a bus driver, their work is neither secure nor well-paid. Nevertheless, Garces was optimistic about the future, and had aspirations of starting her own small sewing business: 'I've learnt to sew—I made this t-shirt (stretching out the front of her own embroidered t-shirt) and I'm now going to learn how to run a business.'

Much of the consejeras' work consists of educating women about their basic rights. Ortega says she has learnt that, 'As a human, I have the right to talk and protest, and say if I don't agree with something.' Dispelling popular rumours and misinformation is another important aspect of their work. One morning I meet a local woman who tells me how the consejeras helped saved her life. Carmen Santos became convinced she was cursed after drinking tap water from a local graveyard. After becoming so distraught that she was losing weight and unable to sleep she confessed her fears to one of the consejeras (a woman she knew from the local café) who was able to convince her that she was not in fact under a spell.

Restorative Justice in Aguablanca

The Monday meetings are the occasion for introducing the women to new ideas. One such idea that has become important to the consejeras' work is that of restorative justice. In recent years the restorative justice movement has become perhaps the largest criminal justice reform movement in the world, advocating the use of informal dispute resolution, and a move away from punitive punishment towards reparation (Braithwaite, 2001). Hermana Alba Stella says she first learned about restorative justice when she joined a number of Colombians on a fact-finding trip to Europe sponsored by a Latin American bank: 'I hadn't heard of this concept before, but it made sense immediately—it [restorative justice] provided a way of repairing the social tissue in Aguablanca.' She also realized that in the family advisors she had a ready-made structure for implementing restorative justice. Upon her return to Aguablanca she immediately began conducting training in restorative justice in the Monday afternoon meetings.

Six years on, restorative justice now influences the work of consejeras in a number of ways. The consejeras employ the concepts of restorative justice when counselling residents in conflict with one another. They seek to mediate minor conflicts themselves using principles that they learnt in the course of their restorative justice training. For example, mediators emphasize the need to give both sides a chance to speak, and look for outcomes that both de-escalate the conflict, and repair the victim's harm.

A number of the consejeras are also trained as Justices of the Peace (JPs). JPs are a nationwide initiative of the Colombian government designed to encourage the resolution of conflicts at a local level without formal prosecution. Consejeras refer more serious matters to one of their fellow consejeras who has also been trained as a JP. After notifying and consulting with one of the Prosecutors, the JP then seeks to negotiate a settlement between the parties drawing on the skills she has learnt both as a JP and as a consejera.

Doris Campo is one of the consejeras who acts in this dual capacity. In early 2004 she was called upon to assist after an argument between two neighbours ended with one man stabbing and seriously injuring the other. The victim had been taken to hospital and the assailant's family feared retaliation. Neighbours told the young man's mother to contact Campo, telling her that Campo could help. Campo arranged for a local young man whom both families trusted, and who was trained in restorative justice, to begin mediating between the families, at first indirectly. She also contacted the prosecutor to obtain his approval to mediate. The victim admitted that he had provoked the young man, while the young man donated blood for the victim. The young man and his victim and their families eventually met face-to-face at the hospital, when the offender's family agreed to pay half the victim's hospital costs and all agreed to cease hostilities.

Restorative justice has become an important tool not only in mediating conflicts but also in other aspects of the consejeras' work. In 2000, the consejeras helped establish Casas de Francisco Esperanza, centres for local youth from Aguablanca. Working with trained psychologists, counsellors, and educators, the consejeras work with more than 120 children between the ages of seven and twenty, many of whom were formerly *bandidos*, gang members, or *bandidas*, young children in training to become gang members. Meeting two or three times a week, the young people participate in a range of activities, including a programme called '*Proyecto de Vida*' ('Life Project') which, through workbooks and activities, teaches children to reflect on their lives, and the consequences of their choices, and to live healthily and safely, and how to restore relations with the community. John Murillo, twenty-eight years old, is one of the original members from the youth centre: 'when we started, relations with the community were totally broken. We knew things had to change, so we started to do things that benefited the community. We started by cleaning up the parks, and some of the local streets. People started to respect us, whereas before they just were scared of us, and hid behind their doors when they saw us. But after a while, after cleaning the streets, people who used to hide from us, came out of the homes and offered us breakfast. We got breakfast from almost every house', Murillo joked.

The houses' work is not easy: gangs continue to exert strong pressure on some of the young people, and there have been a number of serious setbacks along the way. Four members of the original cohort of ten have been killed in gang fights in the last three years. However, the programme is continuing to grow, and has recently acquired its third centre, which allows it to reach children in other parts of Aguablanca. On the day I visited the most recently opened house, Campo and some of the children were working to prepare the exterior of the house for repainting. She explains that when they took possession of the disused house, the children were put off by the bullet holes that peppered the garage door, so restoring the building as well as the park behind the house, has become a major project.

Restorative justice has previously been promoted in a wide range of settings, from the criminal justice systems of developed countries to political transitions such as in South Africa, following the dismantlement of apartheid. It has been used to describe a wide range of processes, from victim–offender conferences, through to truth commissions. While it would be a mistake to assume that there is a single model of restorative justice that could work across such a broad range of settings and crimes, the consejeras' approach to restorative justice reflects and develops a number of important principles that have widespread application.

Restorative Justice Lessons

The most cited definition describes restorative justice purely in terms of process: restorative justice is a process whereby all the people with a stake in an harmful incident come together to discuss the implications of the offence for the future (see Roche, 2003). Much of the research in restorative justice has been devoted to comparing the relative strengths and weaknesses of the different processes that have been used in different parts of the world.

The consejeras programme enlarges our understanding of restorative justice by shifting the focus away from the particular process to the aim. As it is applied in Aguablanca, restorative justice is first and foremost about repairing broken relationships. The pedagogical device the consejeras use to explain restorative justice to community members is a triangle, with the three points of the triangle representing the victim, the offender, and the community, and the sides of the triangle depicting the various relationships in need of restoration. From this it follows that restorative justice can take a number of forms. It is as much about teaching young people skills that will allow them to live as law-abiding members of a community, as it is about mediation after a conflict. Restorative justice, in the hands of the consejeras, is not a just an approach to conflict resolution, but a framework for advancing social justice.

Some of the most creative restorative justice activity is occurring not in developed countries such as the United States, Canada, New Zealand, and Australia where restorative justice first became well known, but in developing countries, and countries seeking to make the transition from war to peace (Shearing, 2001; Roche,

2002). Programmes in these places are not following a template but seeking to respond to the needs of their communities, using whatever resources they can muster, either locally, or internationally, through non-government agencies. Moreover, in these contexts the resources of the state are stretched. This means there are fewer obstacles, in terms of competing bureaucracies or intrusive regulation, to establishing creative, holistic programs such as exist in Aguablanca.

The consejeras' approach has potential lessons for any programme seeking to establish restorative justice, whether in Colombia, the United Kingdom or elsewhere. Their approach also arguably has some relevance for national debates about restorative justice in Colombia. In recent years the language of restorative justice has appeared with increasing frequency in these peace negotiations. Paramilitary leaders, politicians, and the High Commissioner for Peace have all embraced the concept. Human rights groups, including Human Rights Watch, the United Nations High Commissioner for Human Rights, and Amnesty, have expressed concerns about the way in which restorative justice is being used in this context. Their concern is that restorative justice has become the latest way to disguise what is really impunity for criminals. At a national level there is a concern that wrongdoers will interpret restorative justice as implying that all offenders should simply be forgiven for their crimes. This perception is reinforced by the impression in some minds that the South African Truth and Reconciliation Commission, often described as a form of restorative justice, was nothing more than a forum for handing out amnesties.

But advocates argue that restorative justice is not just about forgiveness and reconciliation. On the contrary, first and foremost restorative justice is about getting offenders to take responsibility for their actions (Braithwaite and Roche, 2001). This can be seen in the work of the consejeras, whether mediating in the aftermath of a serious crime or in attempting to prevent less serious problems from escalating. (On a visit to one of the programme's youth centres, I witnessed a conference convened to address the recent disruptive behaviour of one of the teenage girls in the group.) For big and small incidents alike, wrongdoers are encouraged to accept their wrongdoing and devise ways of making amends, in consultation with their victims and the community.

Many advocates argue that accepting responsibility for one's wrongdoing is an essential element of restorative justice. Even in the South African Truth and Reconciliation Commission, which dealt with severe human rights abuses, the Commission only provided amnesties to individual applicants who satisfied strict conditions (to qualify, applicants had to make a public confession, and demonstrate that their crime was political in nature). Some of the commissioners also felt that the offenders should have been expected to make reparation, and commissioners who asked victims to forgive their offenders were criticized for exacerbating victims' suffering (Wilson, 2001).

The consejeras' work also contributes to debates about the scope of restorative justice. Consejeras do not consider restorative justice a complete answer to crime. They also see the need to combine restorative justice with other more conventional approaches. They seek to deploy restorative justice wherever possible, but they are always prepared to escalate to more formal modes of dispute resolution. So, for example, a consejera will accompany victims to the *fiscalía* to assist in the prosecution of more serious cases. The insight here, then, is that restorative justice does not have to exist in a vacuum but can be combined with other approaches. In fact, restorative justice may work best when it operates against the background of a more coercive threat. This was the idea behind the South African model, where prosecution was threatened against those wrongdoers who did not obtain an amnesty (although the policy was undermined by a lack of resources). This mix-n-match approach throws down a challenge to many restorative justice enthusiasts who argue that restorative justice provides a complete framework for responding to crime and that participation must be voluntary. However, it is consistent with the regulatory theory of responsive regulation (Braithwaite, 2001), which advocates the use of informal regulatory approaches but against the background threat of more formal, tougher sanctions in the event that informal approaches fail. Such an approach provides a principled basis for deciding how to allocate scarce funds for formal prosecutions and imprisonment.

Conclusion

The Colombian peace puzzle is a large and complicated one. Most accounts of Colombia tend to focus almost exclusively on the country's considerable problems, and many also stop at a national level, focusing on the state of negotiations between the government and armed groups. There is relatively little attention given to the creative ways in which local communities survive and adapt to their social and economic contexts. The women of Aguablanca show how even in the poorest and most violent of communities, it is possible to nurture a culture of peace and justice, and furthermore, that these efforts can be led by the most disadvantaged and marginalized members of the community. But, perhaps contrary to first impressions, this is not simply a small and isolated band of women; on closer inspection, it is clear that the consejeras employ the techniques and forms characteristic of successful modern social movements (Castells, 1997), consciously developing and expanding decentred networks of expertise, support and finance.

Finally, it is difficult fully to appreciate the work the consejeras do without understanding the sense of hope that underlies their work. Most accounts of how societal change is accomplished ascribe little importance to the role of hope. Hope, it is generally thought, clouds the critique and realism needed to bring about institutional and structural reform. However, these women show that it is possible to be realistic *and* hopeful. And while it is true that hope by itself accomplishes little, when it is combined with institutional and structural change, it is an important ingredient in change (Braithwaite, 2004). South Africa's transition from apartheid state to democracy under the leadership of Nelson Mandela demonstrated clearly that this was the case. In Aguablanca, Cali, women are hopeful that their work can contribute to building peace and justice, not just in their immediate neighbourhood, but, through their example, elsewhere in Colombia. As Hermana Alba Stella puts it: 'For a long time Aguablanca has had a negative reputation—but now Aguablanca is offering something positive to Cali—Now there is a light coming out from Aguablanca.'

Bibliography

Amis, M. (2005), 'Authors in the Front Line: Martin Amis', *Sunday Times Magazine*, 6 February (available online at <http://www.timesonline.co.uk/article/0,,2099-1458940_1,00.html> (last accessed 17 April 2006)).

Bannon, I. (2004), 'Colombia: The Role of Land in Involuntary Displacement', Social Development Notes No. 17: Conflict Prevention and Reconstruction (The World Bank, March 2004).

BBC (2001) 'Colombia: Kidnap Capital of the World.' BBC News Online. <http://news.bbc.co.uk/1/hi/world/americas/1410316.stm> (last accessed October 2005).

Braithwaite, J. (2001), *Restorative Justice and Responsive Regulation* (Oxford University Press: Oxford).

—— (2004) 'Emancipation and Hope' 592 *Annals of the American Academy of Political and Social Science* 79–98.

—— and Roche, D. (2001), 'Responsibility and Restorative Justice' in Schiff, M. and Bazemore, G. (eds.), *Restorative Community Justice: Repairing Harm and Transforming Communities* (Anderson Publishing: Cincinnati) 203–20.

Castells, M. (1997) *The Power of Identity* (Blackwell Publishers: Oxford).

Freire, P. (1972) *Pedagogy of the Oppressed* (Sheed and Ward: London).

Hill, J. (2004) Testimony of General James T. Hill, United States Army Commander, United States Southern Command, before the House Armed Services Committee, US House of Representatives, 24 March 2004, available online at <http://www.house.gov/hasc/> (last accessed October 2005).

Interpol (2005) <http://www.interpol.int/Public/Drugs/cocaine/default.asp> (last accessed October 2005).

Kane, L. (2001), *Popular Education and Social Change in Latin America* (Latin America Bureau: London).

Kuppers, G, (1994), Introduction in Kuppers, G. (ed.) *Companeras: Voices from the Latin American Women's Movement* (Latin American Bureau: London) 1–3.

Putnam, R, (1993), *Making Democracy Work: Civic Tradition* (Princeton University Press: Princeton).

—— (2000), *Bowling Alone: The Collapse and Revival of American Community* (Simon and Schuster: New York).

Roche, D. (2002), 'Restorative Justice and the Regulatory State in South African Townships' 42 British Journal of Criminology 514–33.

—— (2003), *Accountability in Restorative Justice* (Oxford University Press: Oxford).

Shearing, C. (2001) 'Transforming Security: A South African Experiment' in Strang, H. and Braithwaite, J. (eds.) *Restorative Justice and Civil Society* (Cambridge University Press: Cambridge) 14–34.

Stephen, L. (1997) *Women and Social Movements in Latin America: Power from Below* (University of Texas Press: Austin).

UNHCR (2004) '2004 Global Refugee Trends' (Geneva: UNHCR, available online at <http://www.unhcr.ch>).

Wilson, R, (2001). *The Politics of Truth and Reconciliation in South Africa: Legitimizing the Post-Apartheid State* (Cambridge University Press: Cambridge).

World Health Organization (2002) 'Reducing Risks, Promoting Healthy Life' (World Health Report 2002) (available online at <http/www.who.int/whr/2002/en/index.html>).

11
Neither Honesty nor Hypocrisy: The Legal Reconstruction of Torture
Stanley Cohen

This chapter highlights some changes in official, legal, and public discourses about torture over the past five years; that is, following the Ur-date of '9/11', 11 September 2001. I concentrate on the internal negotiations within the United States about justifying the use of torture to combat the terrorist threat against national security. This is a discourse generated by the mass media and by government, security services, and their lawyers talking to each other or replying to their political, legal, and human rights critics.

This is an important and troubling episode in itself. But I select only those features that illustrate more general problems in the legal model of human rights violations—especially problems that arise from paradoxes in the success of the human rights movement. In criminology, the concept of success has a rather dubious status. Yes, there is the banal empirical sense in which debates about 'nothing works', or 'prison works' address questions of success and failure. But criminology as a whole cannot readily be evaluated in these terms. Indeed much of British criminology from David Downes' cohort onwards, has tried to deconstruct any simple congruence between academic criminology and the aims of the criminal justice system. Human rights scholars, however, find it natural to accept the same criterion of success used by the human rights system: something like 'the advancement of human rights'.

The reconstruction of diverse sets of cultural values, ethical intuitions, and religious commandments into a common, uniform, and universal set of standards created a new language to describe the minimum norms of human dignity. Part of the wider critique of this 'legalization of human rights', ('... the practice of formulating human rights claims as legal claims and pursuing human rights objectives through legal mechanisms')[1] deals with the particular mechanisms of the criminal law and crime control. Most of this debate is pragmatic ('What works?') despite the fact that no one seriously believes that mass atrocities such as genocide can be conceptualized, let alone be prevented by the criminal law model. Other criticism focuses on the related matters of boundary-setting and historical truth-telling. Legal truths (the 'findings' of 'guilty' or 'not guilty') are seen as partial and misleading; deep political conflicts are converted into a series of discrete legal events, the legal dialect and testimonies of individual moral culpability. Another line of criticism is more relevant to the torture debate: the danger that legal and human rights talk may blunt our moral and emotional sensitivity and distort our political judgements.

In the end, these criticisms are easily and inevitably absorbed into a qualified liberal support for the institutions of criminal law as the only fair way to pursue justice and accountability.[2] This is the spirit of Woody Allen's restaurant criticism: the food is lousy—and the portions are too small. That is: the law is all we have and despite its flaws, we want it to be implemented more rather than less seriously. This will be a continuing theme in my case study of torture. But there is another more meta-theoretical problem about the use of the metaphor of crime control in the human rights discourse. It sounds strange to mention this. Terms like 'Crimes Against Humanity' and 'War Crimes' are part of popular discourse; the logic of the 'International Criminal Court', has become known through the International Criminal Tribunals dealing with the former Yugoslavia and

---

[1] Jack Donnelly, 'The Virtues of Legalization' in Saladin Meckled-Garcia and Basak Cali (eds.), *The Legalization of Human Rights* (London: Routledge, 2006) p. 68.

[2] For a well-documented and spirited defense, see Mark Osiel, *Mass Atrocity, Collective Memory and the Law* (New Brunswick: Transaction Publishers, 1997).

Rwanda; 'Crimes of the State' is an established social scientific, if not public term.

And for most of the time and for most purposes (theoretical or practical) a legalistic model of human rights violations and a sociological model of crime are compatible: they use the same mechanisms and language (trial, punishment, evidence, responsibility, guilt, etc.) or else the differences are indeed only linguistic: instead of offender or criminal, we have 'perpetrator'; instead of crime or offence, 'violation'. But while 'violation' in the human rights discourse can mean violation of a rule or prohibition (that is, deviance or rule-breaking) it can also be interchangeable with *abuse*. This applies not to abuse or violation of a rule, but of a particular (putative) *right*—a meaning completely absent from the crime control model. Furthermore, human rights students would not routinely use some sociological ways of viewing torture as a crime: first, through notions of prohibition, ban and abolition; second, through the processes of moral enterprise, construction, definition, and negotiation.

My case study of the current reconstruction of torture is designed to explore these comparisons.

Talking about Torture
Pre-history
The history of torture, in the obvious sense of 'history', has not yet been written: neither a chronology of the actual practices that have constituted or been designated as torture, nor the social contexts in which they were used. Two other histories are more familiar. The first deals with social reaction: the oscillation between the extremes of tolerance and prohibition. In the standard narrative: the Enlightenment sees the disappearance of judicially approved torture; one European nation after another abolishes the practice; by the end of the nineteenth century, public figures proclaim that torture has ceased to exist, that the word would not appear in future dictionaries. This story ignores the continued practice and tolerance of torture as the European powers established their colonial empires. But at the domestic level, there was little practice and no public interest. By the mid-twentieth century, the era of human rights declarations and prohibitions had signalled victory for the abolitionist case: the

ban was supposed to be universal and absolute. There were no circumstances whatsoever in which torture could be justified. Or at least not if the torturers and their masters were—as they obviously were—Bad People doing these Bad Deeds.

This was just the time (1949) of Orwell's famous warning in *1984* about Good People doing Bad Deeds. He did not mean the micro-sociology of torture: the situational pressures (later explored in the Milgram and Zimbardo tradition) which induce ordinary people to conform because of obedience to authority. He obviously meant the grand narratives of patriotism, liberty, freedom, and democracy. Long-abandoned practices like torture, Orwell wrote, would not only become common again, but would be '... tolerated and even defended by people who considered themselves enlightened and progressive'.

This is why there has to be a second history of torture, a chronicle of justifications. This draws on the accounts of individual perpetrators; wider cultural texts and—most important of all—the official discourse used by governments.[3] Bad Deeds committed by Good Societies (enlightened, progressive, liberal, democratic) require—at the very least—justifications that other like-minded societies and 'the international community' could accept. These justifications have to be crafted within the special dialects and rituals of liberal legality. This calls for something far more remarkable than learning how to talk legal language ('Does this correspond with Article 23, Clause (b) of the VP Convention?'). Democratic leaders who authorized the violation, had to learn voodoo talk: 'yes, we understand and affirm that a total prohibition on torture means just that: there can be no exceptions, not under any circumstances. But what we are doing isn't really torture and anyway is morally justifiable under the special circumstances we find ourselves (in these terrible times).'

By the third quarter of the twentieth century, three emblematic cases of this type appeared—each generating a rich list of items to be used in future lexicons of *Democratic Justifications For Torture*. First, there were the 'special procedures' (probably the most brutal violence ever used on this scale) used by France

---

[3] I will not repeat here my analysis of the discourse of official denial: Stanley Cohen, *States of Denial* (Cambridge: Polity Press, 2001), ch. 4.

to defend its 'civilizing mission' in Algeria; second, Israel's not so moderate 'moderate physical pressure' used against Palestinians in the occupied territories. And finally the slow, but long-running story of the British in Northern Ireland, with its repertoire of 'depth interrogations'.

Torture was a prominent feature of the Latin American military dictatorships, notably Argentina, Chile, Uruguay, and Brazil. But the justificatory language of divine violence, purge, salvation, cleansing, and 'national security' (in its fascist, rather than democratic, version) needed no fancy legal manoeuvres, certainly not at the time. Only after the collapse of these regimes and the subsequent 'transitions' to democracy in Latin America, South Africa, and the Soviet Empire, was there some attention to the legalistic prohibition of torture. In two particular cases, Argentina and South Africa, a combination of national considerations and international interest gave special importance to torture in the overall quest for truth and justice.

In the aftermath of 11 September 2001, the launch of a new global war against terrorism and then revelations about the abuse of detainees in Guantanamo and Abu Ghraib, the issues of torture and detention became objects of media and public attention, marked by new revelations, vivid imagery, and extreme political positioning. As these dramas played out in the public arena so (as we were to learn later) were various legal satellites of the Bush administration reconstructing a 'new paradigm' for torture.[4]

Guantanamo and Abu Ghraib: Public Revelations and Justifications

I will comment on four processes at the public level: *media saturation, everyday normalization, mock honesty*, and *ethical populism*.

Media saturation refers to the sheer amount of space devoted over this three-year period to news items, talk shows,

---

[4] All my sources—documents, reports, letters, memoranda—appear in the two excellent collections, Mark Danner, *Torture and Truth: America, Abu Ghraib, and the War on Terror* (New York: New York Review of Books, 2004) and Karen Greenberg and Joshua Dreitel (eds.), *The Torture Papers: The Road to Abu Ghraib* (Cambridge: Cambridge University Press, 2005).

documentaries and debates on the subject. As the *New York Times* detected: 'Torture Seeps Into Discussion by News Media' (5 November 2001). The horrors of 9/11 gave this discussion a sense of urgency, of being long overdue. Integral parts of the war against terror were information-gathering, risk analysis, early warnings, reliable intelligence. It was unfortunate that these methods might need some degree of torture; but it was better to debate all this in the open. 'Time to Think About Torture', said *Newsweek* (5 November 2001). A subject previously seen as too squeamish, arcane, and remote should now enter the agenda of ordinary thinking. A discussion of torture is not melodramatic; it should be normalized into everyday routines and settings, like family dinners. In responding to criticism about the lack of news coverage of torture, Jim Murphy (the executive producer of Dan Rather's CBS *Evening News)* agued that speculation about torture and its merits was for now best left to talk shows and columnists, not the news: 'It's like the conversation you or I would have at dinner: "I wonder if we should torture?"'

Media saturation also demands more pictorial images. Orwell pointed out that the euphemism, question-begging and 'sheer cloudy vagueness' of political language is needed '... if one wants to name things without calling up mental pictures of them'.[5] Phrases like 'stress and duress' were as blandly non-pictorial as 'moderate physical pressure'. 'In this autumn of anger', wrote Jonathan Alter (*Newsweek*, 5 November 2001) 'even a liberal can find his thoughts turning [to?] torture. OK, not cattle prods or rubber hoses, at least not here in the USA, but something...'

But what is this 'something'? 'All appropriate pressure' was hardly pictorial, although 'inappropriate' is the Clintonesque term for designating something as vaguely wrong. Pictorial images and exact descriptions of techniques now started appearing. This was *mock honesty* in that it was never clear whether these techniques were actually being used now. But the drift of the public message was clear: there are some coercive forms of interrogation that fall short of being 'real torture'.[6]

---

[5] George Orwell, 'Politics and the English Language', in *The Penguin Essays of George Orwell* (London: Harmondsworth, 1984) p. 362.

[6] Joseph Lelyveld, 'Interrogating Ourselves', *New York Times Magazine*, 12 June 2005.

These methods were variously designated as 'C.I.D' (for 'cruel, inhuman and degrading treatment'); 'H.C.I.' (highly coercive interrogation); then, in blander Pentagon-speak 'counter-resistance strategies'; or in Porter Goss, the Director of the CIA's postmodern reference to 'waterboarding' as 'professional interrogation techniques'. The term that stuck in the public discourse was the excellent ad-agency phrase invented by Wayne Madsen (a former US navy intelligence officer), 'torture lite'.

The techniques of torture lite were listed with some pictorial clarity; as an adult audience, folks, you are ready to hear this: hooding...withdrawal of painkillers...beating and shaking ...sleep deprivation...harsh lights...loud noise...sensory deprivation...'position abuse'. 'None of them', Leyleveld comments, 'would be remotely legal in an investigation of an American on American soil.' If this term does cover these techniques, then there is clearly something wrong with international definitions of torture. 'Torture lite' may be used in all innocence but it usually requires the same bad faith as 'diet Coke' or 'fat free cheese cake'. It is difficult to imagine, even harder to incorporate into legal and public discourse, anything like a clear definition of 'justified' torture: this amount of pain; using this technique; to these parts of the body; over a certain time. This is not an aesthetic or descriptive problem but overcoming the taboo about being too explicit about what your culture does not permit. This task required the moral authority of a Harvard University Law Professor. Confronted on prime-time TV with the accusation that 'civil rights lawyers' like himself never think about what coercive interrogation methods they would permit, Alan Dershowitz assured viewers that 'we' at Harvard (the Law Faculty?) were indeed working on finding a solution—then gave a graphic and pictorial description of inserting sterilized needles under fingernails until the detainee screamed with pain, and surrendered with no serious physical damage.

By *Ethical Populism* I mean the spread and popularization of liberal-legal justifications. None of these was new but they were once more confined to legal settings: United Nations diplomatic deals, first-year university ethics courses or ritual exchanges between human rights organizations and offending governments. Audiences became primed to neutralize any scruples by two disarming arguments: we urgently need something new and this is what we do anyway. Thus: (1) The September 11th disaster and the birth of Islamic fundamentalist terrorism caught us by surprise; it might have been prevented and must be prevented from happening again. Only the inflexibility and absolutism of liberals, human rights organizations, and the United Nations gets in the way. (2) We can assure you that nothing radical or even new is coming up for your approval. You must have known that all this stuff has been used already? So smart up, get wise, be as cynical as Alan Dershowitz: 'If anybody has any doubt that our CIA over time has taught people to torture, has encouraged torture, has probably tortured in extreme cases, I have a bridge to sell you in Brooklyn.' (Dershowitz, January 2001). These are the three most important and farreaching justifications:

1. The ticking bomb story is the best known: you have captured a terrorist who knows where and when a bomb is about to explode; surely you have the right, indeed duty, to torture him to extract this information to save fifty lives (or whatever number is proposed)?
2. This is part of the state's broader right of self-preservation: the doctrines of security, necessity, and self-defence are self-evident in both immediate terms and the long run. This is merely living up to the slogan 'the constitution is not a suicide pact'.
3. The doctrine of the lesser evil: the defenders of democracy are entitled to do something wrong in fighting terrorism. We must keep ourselves in close control; this is why have a set of restraining democratic values and internal checks and a commitment to human dignity. But democracy is special and fragile: precisely because we are a democracy, we have to protect this in ways that might stray from our foundational commitment to dignity.[7]

All these principles are embedded in the logic of regulation. However complicated its jurisprudential status might be, the logic of regulation is comprehensible and appealing to the wider public. Its best-known version—cited approvingly by some

---

[7] An important and subtle example is Michael Ignatieff, *The Lesser Evil: Political Ethics in an Age of Terrorism* (Princeton: Princeton University Press, 2004).

American jurists—is the 1987 Israeli judicial commission on torture (the 'Landau Commission').[8] I will explain its solution. Note though, that the Commission did *not* condemn the long record it uncovered of brutal interrogation methods; on the contrary, these methods '... are largely to be defended, both morally and legally'[para 1.8]. The object of 'utter condemnation' was false testimony and perjury. It is permissible to use pressure but it is 'painful,' 'tragic' and 'deplorable' to lie about this (especially to your 'own' judges). So the problem—very much like the one faced by the White House lawyers nearly twenty years later—was how to find the bad faith needed to permit the impermissible to be carried out in good faith. This is the path of the Third Way.

1. The first way was tolerance and *laissez-faire*. We give the security services a free hand to operate in a twilight zone outside the realm of law. This means coming right out to acknowledge that torture had indeed been used in this situation (however reluctantly), and that all decisions about when it was appropriate would be left to the security services. But that is not a viable solution. No Israeli government then or now, nor any other present democratic government could abandon all political or legal control over such matters. This would be the road to fascism, 'the despotism of a police state', '... sliding towards methods practiced in regimes which we abhor' [para. 4.2].
2. The second possibility was to deny completely that it (or anything like it) was happening at all; to keep confirming your total commitment to the prohibition; and to keep on saying, whatever the evidence, that something that was prohibited couldn't exist. We repeat the absolute ban ... but turn a blind eye to what is going on beneath the surface. This was in Landau's words: 'the way of the hypocrites'.
3. Now we arrive at the third way: interrogation is regulated and supervised by judicial bureaucrats. This means

---

[8] Report of the Commission of Inquiry into the Methods of Investigation of the General Security Service (GSS) Regarding Hostile Terrorist Activity ['The Landau Report'] (Jerusalem: State of Israel, 1987).

regulation, control, restrictions, guidelines, lists, and explicit limits. Neither total prohibition nor total discretion to the agent on the ground. In Alan Dershowitz's version, authorities apply to the judge for a 'torture warrant' on a case-to-case basis: 'I'm not in favour of torture, but if you're going to have it, it should damn well have court approval... If we have torture, it should be authorized by law' (*Los Angeles Times*, 8 November 2001). The question becomes whether it is worse for that torture to be conducted in secret and then publicly denied, as the French did in Algeria, or for the government to acknowledge that it is making an exception to the general prohibition against torture in this case. The Landau solution was as elegant as it was ugly: locate a grey area of practices that are coercive enough to give the security service what it needs; give these another name ('moderate physical pressure' or the more honest 'torture lite') and have their use legally regulated.

This is appealing, because—like all Third Way solutions—it appears as a voice of reason, a pragmatic compromise between two extremist, absolutist positions: uncontrolled trust in the security services ('do what you have to do, but don't tell us too much about it') versus total prohibition ('no coercive force under any circumstances'). The case is particularly strong because it assumes an instrumental rationality: the arguments for and against regulation seem to be purely about effectiveness and prevention. When the policy can hardly even pretend to be utilitarian, then regulation makes no sense at all. This was precisely why the infamous Abu Ghraib episode was so important. When the first words and images about Abu Ghraib appeared in May 2004, much of the initial shock came from sheer surprise. None of us had ever seen anything like this. Now, after seeing so much analysis and exegesis, the novelty fades but the revulsion is deeper: the hooded, naked, manacled men huddle by cell gates; the grinning American soldiers point at the prisoners' genitals; the off-stage photographer obsessively records each move; dogs are about to attack naked men in their cells; detainees are punched, kicked, and forcibly arranged in various sexual positions for photographing; naked male detainees are forced to wear women's underwear and masturbate on camera; a female officer holds a dog chain round a naked detainee's neck. What was going on? The humiliation and sadism did not seem to correspond to serious physical pain—yet they didn't fit the vague notion of 'torture lite'. The techniques of degradation were not totally improvised—yet surely did not appear in standard training courses and manuals. And nothing called for legal change—whether a looser or tighter criminal law, whether state regulation or ticking-bomb justified torture. Most observers evaded questions of legal and moral responsibility, advancing instead some imaginative (and alas, plausible) theories (of the 'cultural studies' type) about causes or precedents: reality television, lynch-mob racism; violent internet pornography.

The New Paradigm

The Bush administration argued that the threat posed by stateless terrorists who draw no distinction between military and civilian targets was so profound that it required new rules of engagement. This change was described by Albert Gonzalez (then Whitehouse general legal counsel, later Attorney-General) in early 2002, as the 'New Paradigm': a high premium on the ability to get quick information from captured terrorists while giving less weight to the rights of subjects and the niceties of international law.

The evolution of the Paradigm can be traced in a sequence of memoranda, nearly all unintended for public dissemination but exposed in 2004/5. Many internal documents from this period have been leaked or declassified, but we must assume that many others have remained secret. Some of these internal documents referred to the US military, while others to the CIA; some to activities in Guantanamo and others to Iraq; some are advisory opinions and others operational orders. They were composed by various teams of lawyers working for the Justice Department, the White House, the State Department and the Defense Department. Reading through these memos is, as Lewis comments, a strange experience: 'The memos read like the advice of a mob lawyer to a mafia don on how to skirt the law and stay out of prison.'[9]

[9] Anthony Lewis, 'Making Torture Legal', *New York Review of Books*, 15 July 2004, p. 4.

Looking at the New Paradigm in criminological terms, we see changes in the *legal status of the victim; the act* and *the perpetrator.*

Legal status of victim

The Defense Department described the first detainees to arrive at Guantánamo Bay, on 11 January 2002 as 'unlawful combatants', thus automatically denying them possible status as prisoners of war. Later practices used in Guantánamo were said to have 'migrated' to Iraq where—even according to the US administration—the Geneva Conventions did apply. Gonzales, in a 25 January 2002 memorandum to President Bush famously called the Geneva Conventions 'quaint'. He urged the president to declare the Taliban forces in Afghanistan, as well as al-Qaeda, as being outside the coverage of the Conventions; he wrote that the war against terrorism, 'in my judgment renders obsolete Geneva's strict limitations on questioning of enemy prisoners'. The Geneva Convention was 'outmoded' because it dealt only with state parties and al-Qaeda was not a state; Afghanistan under the Taliban was a 'failed state' whose territory had been overrun and held by violence. Taliban prisoners were hence all 'unlawful combatants'.

Legal definition of torture

Perhaps the most important internal document to be revealed, was the 1 August 2002 memorandum from the Justice Department to the White House Counsel (signed by Assistant Attorney-General Jay Bybee and written by his assistant, Professor John Yoo). The standard definition of torture, as it appears in the International Convention against Torture (1984) and reiterated in numerous other instruments, is 'any act by which severe pain or suffering, whether physical or mental, is intentionally inflicted on a person...' (article 1). The Bybee memo took a deliberately narrow view of which acts might constitute torture. The pain inflicted (and intended) by interrogation procedures had to pass a demanding threshold before it could count as torture. 'For an act to violate the torture statute, it must be equivalent in intensity to the pain accompanying serious physical injury such as organ failure, impairment of bodily function or even death.' The memo referred to seven practices that US courts have ruled to constitute torture: severe beatings with truncheons and clubs, threats of imminent death, burning with cigarettes, electric shocks to genitalia, rape or sexual assault, and forcing a prisoner to watch the torture of another person. It then advised that 'interrogation techniques would have to be similar to these in their extreme nature and in the type of harm caused to violate law.'

This memo was disavowed by some members of the administration a few months after it was leaked in 2004. But the principle was clear—and exactly the opposite of the frequent claim that Gonzalez had tried to '...stretch the definition of torture, which can be rather elastic'.[10] On the contrary, the point was to shrink the definition. The corollary was to expand the definition of torture lite. The memo pointed to the 'significant range of acts that though they might constitute cruel, inhuman or degrading treatment or punishment, fail to rise to the level of torture'. These include stress positions, hooding, excessive tightening of handcuffs, subjection to noise, and sleep deprivation.

The memo suggested that 'mental torture' really only included acts that resulted in 'significant psychological harm of significant duration, e.g., lasting for months or even years'. Just to be sure on this point, a few months later (October 2002) Diane Beaver (Staff Judge Advocate of the Defense Department) wrote that the severe mental pain or suffering had to be '...prolonged mental harm caused by or resulting from the intentional infliction or threatened infliction of severe physical pain or suffering'. She was particularly vexed by the requirement of intentionality. It was permissible to use 'scenarios designed to convince the detainee that death or severely painful consequences are imminent', *but* only if there was: 'a compelling government interest and it is not done intentionally to cause prolonged harm'; *but*: 'caution should be utilized with this technique because the torture statute specifically mentions making death threats as an example of inflicting mental pain and suffering'. A moral maze, indeed.

A 2002 memo by John Helgerson, the CIA inspector general, listed eight interrogation procedures falling short of torture—all

---

[10] Ian Buruma, *Financial Times Magazine*, 5 February 2005, p. 18.

approved internally by the CIA after 9/11. The agency was now seeking legal guidance about how far it could go. The list included waterboarding (feigned drowning). In 2004, the list was reduced to eight; a year later it had gone up to twenty. While there was a core of 'enhanced' interrogation techniques—hooding; prolonged isolation and sensory deprivation; use of dogs; stress positions—others were added and deleted in a prolonged game of pass the parcel.

Perpetrator
The guiding objective of legal talk was to secure some advance indemnity for ordinary working interrogators and their immediate superiors. Gonzales had warned that US officials involved in harsh interrogation techniques could potentially be prosecuted for war crimes under US law if the Conventions applied. 'It was difficult,' he said, 'to predict with confidence' how prosecutors might apply the Geneva Conventions' strictures against 'outrages against personal dignity' and 'inhuman treatment' in the future. But declaring that Taliban and al-Qaeda fighters did not have Geneva Convention protections 'substantially reduces the threat of domestic criminal prosecution'. The prohibition, that is, already excludes CIA interrogations because they take place overseas (Guantánamo is under Cuban sovereignty and hence outside the jurisdiction of United States courts) and people (like Al-Qaeda and the Taliban) who are not citizens of the United States nor lawful combatants from any real state.

The President also has to be protected from prosecution. The August 2002 Bybee/Yoo memo expressed an extremely broad position on the powers of the US President in 'war time'. Thus, even though US law makes it a criminal offence for anyone in an official position to commit or attempt to commit torture against a detainee outside the United States, and even though the United States has ratified treaties prohibiting torture, the US President's authority as Commander-in-Chief could override these laws. The Justice Department advised that torturing al-Qaeda detainees in captivity abroad 'may be justified', and that international laws against torture 'may be unconstitutional' if applied to interrogations conducted in the war on terrorism. The president can *lawfully* order torture, without regard to federal criminal laws or international law. Any measure 'that interferes with the president's direction of such core war matters as the detention and interrogation of enemy combatants would thus be unconstitutional'. An attempt by Congress, for example, to interfere with the President ordering torture, would be unlawful. The memo added that the doctrines of 'necessity and self-defense could provide justifications that would eliminate any criminal liability' on the part of officials who tortured al-Qaeda detainees.

In summary, the new paradigm consists of 'a continuing, collective effort to find a minimalist definition of torture' plus 'a carefully constructed anticipation of objections at the domestic and international levels', plus 'a legal justification based on considerations of failed states, non-state actors and the national security interests of the United States'.[11]

In what looked like the first reverse of this trend, in December 2005 the US Senate passed the McCain amendment, which states that 'no individual in the custody or under the physical control of the United States Government, regardless of nationality or physical location, shall be subject to cruel, inhuman, or degrading treatment or punishment', and that 'nothing in this section shall be construed to impose any geographical limitation on the applicability of the prohibition against cruel, inhuman, or degrading treatment or punishment under this section'. However, even the language of the amendment leaves open some potential interpretation and definitional questions. Moreover, if the doctrine regarding the power of the US President in wartime to override all existing legislation is to remain intact, the amendment by itself will not suffice to end policies of torture.

Honesty and Hypocrisy

In 1964 Graham Greene wrote a letter to the press about photographs of South Vietnamese soldiers torturing Vietcong captives.[12] For twenty years before, he began, the French had

---

[11] Karen Greenberg, 'From Fear to Torture', in Greenberg, K. and Dratel J. (eds.), *The Tortune Papers: the Road to Abu Ghiraib* (Cambridge: Cambridge University Press, 2005).

[12] Graham Greene, *Daily Telegraph*, 6 November 1964. Reprinted in *New York Review of Books*, Vol. 3, No. 9, 17 December 1964. I am grateful to Ron Dudai for drawing my attention to this reference and for his other help in preparing this paper.

practised torture in Indo-China, but at least in the old days of the war, 'hypocrisy paid a tribute to virtue by hushing up the torture inflicted by its own soldiers and condemning the torture inflicted by the other side'.

The strange new thing about the photographs of torture now appearing in the British and American press is that they have been taken with the approval of the torturers and are published over captions that contain no hint of condemnation. They might come out of a book on insect life... Does this mean that the American authorities sanction torture as a means of interrogation? The photographs certainly are a mark of honesty, a sign that the authorities do not shut their eyes to what is going on, but I wonder if this kind of honesty without conscience is really to be preferred to the old hypocrisy.

At first glance, Greene's rhetorical question seems not only perceptive but also uncannily prescient. He could surely be talking about the United States forty years later. But whatever the historical consistencies, Greene's contrast between 'honesty without conscience' and the 'old hypocrisy' is not as convincing as it looks. And this is not the choice given to democratic societies today. Let us return to the Abu Ghraib photos. Despite their vividness, hyper-reality and public availability, their disclosure and massive public dissemination were not at all examples of honesty. The administration certainly did not want these scenes exposed. This was, indeed, a peculiarly postmodern type of scandal. As Danner argues, in both the Abu Ghraib and Weapons of Mass Destruction stories, the heart of the scandal was revealed right from the beginning.[13] Unlike the classic Watergate scandal narrative—revelation, investigation, official version, punishment, expiation—we are stuck at step one: everything about the wrongdoing is exposed, nothing much more can be revealed, but there is no follow-up.

If this was not 'honesty', it certainly was 'without conscience'. The lack of conscience takes different forms, depending on the motivational accounts accepted by those at different levels of the hierarchy. We must visualize the highly fragmented scene that characterizes modern warfare, atrocities, and political violence.

---

[13] Mark Danner, 'Humanism and Terror', *New York Review of Books*, 23 June 2005.

Take the simple contrast between the central command and the micro-systems of power at the periphery, such as the Abu Ghraib detention centre or inside a US military installation in Afghanistan.

At the centre, is the calculating, amoral, and instrumental reality of the Bush administration and the Neo-cons. At the periphery, is the carnival; the spectacle of unrestrained ludic sexuality; trick shop horrors; atrocity tourism; an unnerving lack of shame; the narcissism and cruelty of reality television. Much of the Abu Ghraib cruelty was spontaneous and improvised; it seemed gratuitous, redundant, or even counter-productive. But even if every step was not planned, it was planned for. This does not mean that every move was choreographed and co-ordinated from the centre, but clearly that CIA and the Defense Department intended a programme of humiliation, including sexual humiliation like this, if only to intimidate detainees into informing on each other. And, like old-fashioned conspirators, senior officials, civilian and military, took pains to cover their tracks.[14] What went wrong was using the cam-recorders. Visual recording was an absolutely integral part of the theatre of cruelty. But looking from the outside, even a minimal political sensitivity would have realized that allowing mass reproductions of such visual images to leak out would be utterly stupid.

So with neo-liberal rationality in the centre and madness at the multicultural edges, there is little room for *conscience*. Neither project is strong on moral justifications. The periphery is not even interested in the subject. As Bourke first described the Abu Ghraib scene: 'There is no moral confusion here: the photographers don't even seem aware that they are recording a war crime... There is no suggestion that the scene is morally skewed; the aesthetics of porno protects them from blame.' *Guardian* (7 May 2004).

The ruthless core of the Bush Administration had to make a more conscious calculation: either ignore even the façade of legality or rely on its own lawyers to construct a new voodoo talk—about torture lite, constitutional overrides of international taboos or failed states. On 20 May 2003, in a remote stretch of

---

[14] See Seymour M. Hersh, *Chain of Command* (London: Penguin, 2005).

desert near Faluja, west of Baghdad, an American Marine Division attacked a group of Iraqis who said that they were guests at a wedding. Some twenty 'military aged males' were killed. Major General James Mattis, commander of the 1st Marine Division, was scathing about suggestions that these could have been *bona fide* wedding guests. Why would so many people go into the desert for a wedding? Reporters then asked him about footage on Arab TV showing a child's body lowered into a grave. This was his reply: 'I have not seen the pictures but bad things happen in wars. I don't have to apologise for the conduct of my men.'

'Bad things happen'—the polite form of 'shit happens'—is not just a radical denial of accountability. It refuses to see the salience of human rights principles at all. It reveals an amoral world governed by the application of standard military considerations and the presence of ideologies (free market, social Darwinism, utilitarianism) lacking a vocabulary of internal constraints. It should be clear now why delegating to the security services operational freedom without constraint (the Landau report's first option) is not permissible, nor is the result–honesty, though it might be 'without conscience'.

But what about Greene's supposed opposite, legal hypocrisy? Many participants to the current torture debate have indeed adopted the so-called 'hypocrite's way': proclaiming the righteousness of a prohibition while knowingly evading it and strenuously denying these evasions. While this solution seems to at least acknowledge the existence of a moral problem, it has four flaws, each fatal in very different ways:

1. The term 'hypocrisy' can only make sense if the political authority (or else at least some influential weight of public opinion) does indeed believe in the morality of the prohibition. This is by no means clear anymore.
2. As the Landau Report pointed out, legal hypocrisy is perfectly designed to ensure that the prohibition is safely violated (that is, torture continues), leaving the state's machinery of justice diverted entirely to the question of whether (and which) perpetrators (at all levels, from the commander in chief to the lowest recruit) can get away with lying.

3. The solution depends on a strong bifurcation between 'real' torture which is defined in the narrowest possible way (like pain severe enough to cause 'organ loss') and something like 'enhanced interrogation' whose use, following the logic of the Landau Report, is regulated (the 'torture warrant').
4. The obvious moral defect of hypocrisy is true by definition: the gap between belief and action. If the action is not admitted but denied (lied about) then any move towards regulation exposes a less obvious defect: if we claim not to be doing what others claim we are doing, then why bother to support (or resist) a legal move to restrict what we are surely not doing?

In Greene's contrast between honesty and hypocrisy, there is no mention of regulation—the heart of the 'new paradigm'. But the logic of regulation *always* depends on defining some feature (intensity, gravity, repetition, context) of the undesirable action as permissible. By definition—and this is its whole point—regulation undermines the original intended prohibition. Think what it would look like to propose the 'regulation' of slavery or incest. By analogy, this is just the role played by the most influential parts of the US legal establishment in the recent story of torture.

And by 'legal establishment' I mean not just the house lawyers of the Bush administration. In 2004 an academic task force gathered at Harvard University, under the sponsorship of the Kennedy School of Government and the Harvard Law School. True, this was partly underwritten by the Department of Homeland Security and true, most of the participants had some government experience, many on security issues. But this was clearly an academic project: to discuss the balance between security needs and civil freedoms. The conclusion: a proposal for new rules regulating the use of coercive force; a code with declared limits; a process of oversight and accountability; in other words '... a tightly supervised highly qualified license for the application of torture lite'.[15]

---

[15] Lelyveld, p. 6.

The Harvard guidelines were found too permissive by human rights groups—but too restrictive by the administration for submitting its authority to outside review. There is clearly a continuum of legal opinion on such matters. And there is space for a straightforward debate about whether the record of law in any particular episode like this, is to strengthen or undermine the protection of human rights. But this debate assumes the liberal starting-off point that the human rights project must be judged only in terms of law's own claims.

To accept this criterion of success would be to view this episode as another case of good intentions going wrong—benevolence undermined by bureaucratic compliance, professional interests, servitude to power, greed, political expedience. Surely just another story of lawyers 'playing cute with the law'. And this is indeed what happened—which is why oppositional human rights lawyers (from Amnesty, the Lawyer's Committee, Human Rights Watch, the ICRC) spent so much time crafting their criticisms: this interpretation of the Geneva Convention is tendentious; this memo is misleading about Article 14(b). But the problem is that the Bush lawyers *did* play within the rules of the (or 'a') legal paradigm. It just turns out that at the heart of liberal legality lies a little problem that lawyers condescendingly tell us is no secret at all: when the law says 'no' it nearly always means 'maybe' and 'sometimes under some circumstances'.

This flaw is neither inherent in the law, nor purely contingent on the special features of this case: there is nothing special about the torture prohibition compared say to the genocide prohibition; nothing especially barbarian about Bush, Rumsfeld, and Cheney. The problem is that trusting the criminalization model of prohibition will always be a Faustian bargain if the perpetrator of the prohibited act is not the individual citizen (who smokes, uses drugs or alcohol, gambles, is cruel to animals, pollutes the environment) or corporation but is the government itself acting against its own or other citizens.

In the cases of judging previous regimes after transitions or (in the international arena) other regimes, then we have no choice but to support legality according to the Allen principle: there are problems (the food is lousy) but this is all we've got and we need more of it (the helpings should be bigger). Indeed, our dependence on coercive legal control on the international level is the most dependable and desirable way of enforcing truly universal values and riding against the power of the sovereign state. The discourse about torture that I have discussed is largely the product of the current US government and its domestic public. But wider matters are at stake. These go beyond the case of torture and beyond the political jurisdiction of the United States. The United Nations administered Tribunals for Rwanda and the former Yugoslavia and the future International Criminal Court allows for notions of truth, justice, and legality to be tested in a realm theoretically untouched by considerations of domestic politics, national identity, modes of governance, or 'national security'. Here—the protocols of a cosmopolitan order and not internal memos by CIA lawyers—is where to look for the rule of law instead of rule by law.

Bibliography

Cohen, S. (2001) *States of Denial: Knowing About Atrocities and Suffering* (Polity Press: Cambridge).
Danner, M. (2004) 'Torture and Truth: America, Abu Ghraib, and the War on Terror' (*New York: New York Review of Books*).
—— (2005) 'Humanism and Terror', *New York Review of Books*, 23 June.
Donnelly, J. (2006) 'The Virtues of Legalization', in Meckled-Garcia, S. and Cali, B. (eds.), *The Legalization of Human Rights* (Routledge: London) p. 68.
Greenberg, K. (2005) 'From Fear to Torture', in Greenberg, K, and Dreitel, J. (eds.), *The Torture Papers: the Road to Abu-Ghraib* (Cambridge University Press: Cambridge).
—— and Dreitel, J. (2005) (eds.), *The Torture Papers: The Road to Abu-Ghraib* (Cambridge University Press: Cambridge).
Hersh, S. M. (2005) *Chain of Command* (Penguin: London).
Ignatieff, M. (2004) *The Lesser Evil: Political Ethics in an Age of Terrorism* (Princeton University Press: Princeton).
Lelyveld, J. (2005) 'Interrogating Ourselves', *New York Times Magazine*, 12 June.
Lewis, A. (2004) 'Making Torture Legal', *New York Review of Books*, 15 July.
Orwell, George (1984) 'Politics and the English Language', in *The Penguin Essays of George Orwell* (Harmondsworth: Penguin) p. 362.
Osiel, M. (1997) *Mass Atrocity, Collective Memory and the Law* (Transaction Publishers: New Brunswick).

Index

Abu Ghraib 301–7, 312–13
academy ambassadors, establishment and role of 100
accountability
  Cali, Colombia, governance in 285–6
  constitutional standards 213
  penal system 213
  police power 217
  torture 314
actuarial justice 31–2, 164–5
administrative criminology 149–50, 156–7
administrative offences 219–21
Aguablanca programme *see* Cali, Colombia, governance and restorative justice in
Algeria 300–1
Al-Qaeda 308, 310–11
anomie theory 14
anti-social behaviour policy, New Labour and 92–109
  academy ambassadors, establishment and role of 100
  Anti-social Behaviour Act 2003, provisions in 99
  anti-social behaviour orders 98, 100–1, 104–9
    breaches as criminal offence 98–9, 107–8
    civil measure, as 98
    statistics 101–2, 107
  Anti-social Behaviour Unit 99–101
  ASBO Concern consortium 108–9
  Basic Command Units (BCUs) 101–2
  burden of proof 98
  Casey, Louise 99–100, 108
  Communities First Partnerships, Bridgend police use of 106–7
  European Convention on Human Rights 98
  evidence-based policy 102–9
  family support 100
  name and shame schemes 102
  parenting orders 99–100
  research, lack of 102–9
  Straw, Jack 97
  TOGETHER campaign 99–105
  young people 102, 105–9
Ashworth Special Hospital 54, 59, 64–72
  Blackburn, Ronald 68–70
  Blom-Cooper Inquiry 64–6, 68–70, 79
  Fallon Inquiry 59, 61, 64, 66–71, 79–80
  leadership, lack of medical 67–70
  Personality Disorder Unit 66–9, 79–80
  psychiatrists 65–6, 70–1
  psychologists 65–6, 68–70
  Responsible Medical Officer (RMO) 66, 68
  treatability test 70–1
  treatment 64–6, 69–71
  untreatable disorders, persons with 69–71

barbarism, social democracy and 37–40
behavioural economics 162–3
Blair, Tony
  deviance, sociology of 153
  New Labour's law and order agenda 91–3, 96, 109–10
  risk 81–2
  tough on the causes of crime 153
Blunkett, David 91–2

Boateng, Paul 57–8, 61–2
British Crime Survey 22–3, 94–6
Bush, George 110, 310–11

Cali, Colombia, governance in 271–96
  see also Cali, Colombia, restorative justice in
  accountability 285–6
  barter 278
  church, role of 282
  community-based governance 277–9
  comprehensive governance 287–8
  conditions in Aguablanca 272–3, 276
  consejeras de familia 274–96
  credit scheme 278
  crime problems 273, 275
  displaced people 275
  education and learning 277–8, 281, 285–8
  families, addressing problems in own 286
  family advisers (*consejeras de familia*) 274–96
  feminism 284
  funding 285
  leadership, role of 280–2
  men, role of 283
  networks, role of 279–80
  police, distrust of 273
  political dimension of work 283–4
  population, composition of 273
  refugees 275
  remuneration 285
  rumours and misinformation, dispelling 288
  self-reliance 277–8
  self-regulation 286
  services, delivery of 274–5, 284, 287–8
  social capital 278
  state prosecutors 272–3
  sustainability 281
  ungoverned spaces 275–6
  women 271–2, 274–7, 282–8, 294
Cali, Colombia, restorative justice in 288–93
  agencies, cooperation with 290
  aims of 291
  consejeras de familia 274–96
  conventional approaches, combined with 293
  family advisers (*consejeras de familia*) 274–96
  forms of 291
  gangs, young people and 290
  Justices of the Peace 289
  Life Project 290
  mediation 289–90
  settlements 289
  training 289
  young people, working with 290, 292–3
Canada 83–4
capital punishment 239–41, 248, 252–4, 258–9, 264
capitalism
  contrology 28–9
  critique of 15–16
  East London, delinquency in 139
  economic factors and crime 16
  free market systems, problems with 15
  global 139
  social democratic criminology 15–16
causes of crime see also economic factors, causes of crime and
  deviance, sociology of 152–4
  root causes 157–8
  tough on the causes of crime 153
class
  dissociation concept 118, 121, 125, 127–8, 130–1, 136
  East London, delinquency in 120, 125
  justice 19
  social democratic criminology 19
Colombia see Cali, Colombia, governance in
communism 8, 11–12

Index

community law and order
  programmes 93–4
comparative criminology 173–95,
  197–200
  categories of comparative
    criminologists 182–3
  corruption 182
  Council of Europe, data held by 189
  Crime in Europe conference 179
  cross-cultural research 183, 189
  culture of control 198, 227–70
  data collection 188–90
  development 173–95
  Downes, David, *Contrasts in
    Tolerance* 173–81, 190–1,
    197–9, 208, 221–3, 264–5
  ethnocentricity 181–2
  European refugees from Nazis,
    experiences of 184, 185–6
  European Union, data collected
    by 189, 190
  explorers 187–8
  globalization 198
  historical criminal justice
    studies 201–2, 221–3
  International Crime Victimization
    Survey 188–9
  international criminology 177–9
  *International Journal of
    Criminology* 179–80
  Netherlands
    co-ordinated market economy 209
    Downes, David, *Contrasts in
      Tolerance* 173–81, 190–1,
      197–9, 208, 221–3, 264–5
    pillarization 208–9
    penal policy 197–8
    penal reformers as comparative
      criminologists 188
    penal system 213–15
    policing 186–7, 217–18
    policy transfers 177, 191
    publications 173–80
    rendez-vous-ers 186–91
    research 222–3

September 11, 2001 attacks on the
  United States 189, 190
stranger, idea of 181, 183–8, 190
taxonomy 181–4
terminology 175–84
terrorism 190
transnational crime, increase in 190
transnational criminology 177–80
UN Interregional Criminal Justice
  Research Institute, data held
  by 189
United Kingdom 227–70
United States 187–8
  culture of control 227–70,
    238–58
  exceptionalism 188
  penal policy in 197–8
  regional variations 238–58
  United Kingdom compared
    with 188
women
  penal treatment of 186
  police officers 187
consejeras de familia 274–96
consequentialist theories 213–14
Conservatives 23–6, 34–5, 92, 95
constitutional settlements, police
  power and 218
consumerism 30, 35
Contrasts in Tolerance see also
  Downes, David
  comparative criminology 173–81,
    184, 190–1, 197–9, 208, 221–3
  cultures of control 227
  Netherlands 264
control *see* cultures of control in the
  United States and Britain
contrology 21–3, 27–30, 34
co-ordinated market economies
  209–11
correctional supervision, increase
  in 231–2
corruption 182
crime rates 39–40 *see* increase
  in crime rates

Index

Crime Reduction Programme (CRP) 103–4
cruel, inhuman or degrading treatment, torture as 303, 309–11
culture *see also* cultures of control in the United States and Britain
  change in 27, 35, 37
  comparative criminology 183, 189, 198
  continuity 122–3, 134–5
  cross-cultural research 183, 189
  cultural capital 140
  East London, delinquency in 122–3, 134–5, 140
  increase in crime rates 27, 35, 37
  social democratic criminology 27, 35
  United States, political culture in 250–1, 255–8
cultures of control in the United States and Britain 227–70
  capital punishment 258–9
  comparative criminology 227–70
  contrasting cultures of control 229
  correctional supervision, increase in 231–2
  denial, policies of 230–1
  Downes, David, *Contrasts in Tolerance* 227
  expressive justice 230–1
  historical criminal justice studies 227–9
  late modernity, shift to 230, 233
  mandatory minimum sentencing 261–2
  mass incarceration 231
  Netherlands 227–8, 233
  penal policy 234–5, 259, 264–5
  police forces and agencies, number of 234
  political culture, changes in 232–3
  pragmatic or adaptive approaches 230
  prison population, increase in 231–2, 259–61
  punitiveness 231–3
  sentencing policy 261
  three strikes policy 261–2
  tough on crime 232–3
  vote, removal or restriction of right to 262

dangerous severe personality disorder, persons with 51–89 *see also* Ashworth Special Hospital
  automatic life sentences 62
  Boateng, Paul 57–8, 61–2
  Boyle, Mike 59–61
  Butler Report 57, 71
  Canada 83–4
  civil proceedings 62–3
  Department of Health 56–8, 65–6, 73–4, 77
  detention 55, 59–63, 76–7
  discretionary life sentences 62
  DSPD orders 62–3
  Fallon Inquiry 71–2
  Giddens, Tony 81
  Home Office 56–7, 61, 73–7, 82–3
  Italy 84–5
  Jones, Dilys 59
  just deserts 52
  Mental Health Act
    protections in 52
    revision of 79
    treatability test 57, 62–4, 71, 76–7
  New Labour 51–89
  numbers of persons with 55–6
  prison system 71, 82–3
  psychiatrists 74–9
  psychologists 79, 83
  reviewable sentences 57, 71–2
  risk 55, 80–3
  special hospitals 71
  Stone, Michael 53, 58, 60, 64, 71–80
  Straw, Jack 57, 76–7
  third way system 62–3, 81
  treatability test 57, 59–64, 71, 76–7

Index

United States, sexual psychopath statutes in 78–9
untreatable disorders, persons with 53–4, 57, 59–64, 71–8
death penalty 239–41, 248, 252–4, 258–9, 264
degradation
  hypothesis 205–7, 209, 211
  police power 216–17
  punishment 216–17
  torture 306–7, 309, 312–13
  United States 205–6, 209, 211–12
  Whitman, James Q, *Harsh Justice* 205–6, 209, 211–12
democracy and equality 17–18
demographic changes, reduction in crime and 39
demonization of offenders 25
denial, policies of 230–1, 305–6
Department of Health 56–8, 65–6, 73–4, 77
detection, fear of 165
detention *see also* penal system, prison population
  dangerous severe personality disorder, persons with 55, 59–63, 76–7
  fear of crime 78
  New Labour's law and order agenda 109
  terrorists without charge, detention of 109
  United States 78
deviance, sociology of
  Blair, Tony 153
  causes of crime 152–4
  irrationality of human behaviour 162
  National Deviancy Conference 151–2
  New Labour 153
  norms 157
  opportunity theory 149, 151, 168
  rational choice theory 162
  root causes 157–8
  social problems, addressing 152–3
  tough on the causes of crime 153
discretionary life sentences 62
disintegrative shaming 263
dissociation concept 118, 121, 125, 127–8, 130–1, 136
Downes, David *see also* East London, David Downes and delinquency in
  career of 1–6
  Contrasts in Tolerance 173–81, 190–1, 197–9, 208, 221–3, 264–5
DSPD *see* dangerous severe personality disorder, persons with
Dubber, Markus Dirk, *The Police Power* 202, 213–21

East London, David Downes and delinquency in 117–46
  Canary Wharf 130, 133, 140
  City of London 123–4, 138
  cultural capital 140
  cultural continuity 122–3, 134–5
  dissociation concept 118, 121, 125, 127–8, 130–1, 136
  docks, death of London 122
  Downes, David, *The Delinquent Solution* 117–46
  drug trade 127–8
  education, rejection of 120
  gangs 119–20, 139
  global capitalism 139
  house prices 129–30, 132, 138
  immigration 123
  industry, decline in 121–2, 139
  informal observation 119, 126
  middle-class culture, rejection of 120, 125
  Muslim population 127–30
  organized crime 124–5, 128
  political economy 136
  South Asian population 127–30, 136–9
  Spitalfields 123–38
  statistics 119, 126
  Stratford, Olympics and 130, 134

East London, David Downes and delinquency in (*cont.*)
  street corner groups 118–19, 139
  unemployment 121–2, 129
  United States, gangs in 119–20
  work opportunities 130–2
economic factors, causes of crime and
  capitalism 16
  ethics 13–14
  increase in crime rates 18, 27, 30, 33–9
  opportunities, expansion in criminal 33–4, 150–1, 158, 160–8
  policy implications 163–9
  poverty, measures of 33
  reduction in crime 39–40
  social democratic criminology 13–14, 18, 30, 32–9
  socio-economic change 27, 35, 37
  unemployment 33, 34
  United States 160
economics *see also* economic factors, causes of crime and
  behavioural economics 162–4
  co-ordinated market economies 209–11
  exclusion 212
  liberal market economies 209–12
  Netherlands 209
encouraged egoism 37
environmental criminology 158
equality and democracy 17–18
ethics
  Communism 11–12
  economic factors 13–14
  family values 11
  free market 37
  Golden Rule 12–13
  legitimate means 13
  materialism 14
  populism 303–4
  primacy of 11–14
  religious Right in United States 11
  risk 31
  socialism 8–9
  social democratic criminology 11–14
  torture 303–4
Europe
  prison population 258–60
  torture 299–301
  vote, removal of right to 262
European Convention on Human Rights 98
European refugees from Nazis, experiences of 184, 185–6
European Union 189, 190
explorers 187–8
expressive justice 230–1

Faluja massacre in Iraq 314
family values 11
fear of crime 24–5, 78
fear of detection 165
Ferri, Enrico and dangerous offenders 84–5
France 300–1, 311–12
franchise *see* vote for offenders, removal or restriction of right to
free market 15, 37

gangs 119–20, 139, 290
general election 2005 92, 94
Geneva Conventions, torture and 308, 310, 316
globalization 38, 139, 198, 212
governance *see also* Cali, Colombia, governance in
  culture of control 250–1, 255–6
  United States, regional variations in 250–1, 255–6
gradualism 16–17
Guantanamo Bay 203, 301–8, 310

historical criminal justice studies 200–1
  comparative criminology 201–2, 221–3
  co-ordinated market economies 210–11

culture of control 227–9
degradation hypothesis 205–7, 209, 211
Dubber, Markus Dirk, *The Police Power* 202
globalisation 212
liberal market economy 209–12
Netherlands 207–10
status-based punishment 203–6
United Kingdom 206–10, 227–9
United States 202–12, 227–9
Whitman, James Q, *Harsh Justice* 202–12
Home Office 56–7, 61, 73–7, 82–3, 91–3, 149
Not Rocket Science 159
house prices 129–30, 132, 138
human rights
  anti-social behaviour policy, New Labour and 98
  torture 297–301, 303, 309–11, 316
humiliation, torture and 306–7, 309, 312–13

immigration 123
impunity for criminals 292, 310–11
increase in crime rates
  1960s liberal, social consensus, blaming the 36
  British Crime Survey 22–3, 94–6
  Conservatives 26
  consumerism 30, 35
  cultural change 27, 35, 37
  economic factors 18, 27, 30, 33–9
  encouraged egoism 37
  globalization 38
  interpretation of 22
  mass consumerism 35
  materialism 30
  opportunities, expansion in criminal 33–4
  permissiveness 36
  reporting, increase in 22, 35
  socio-economic change 27, 35, 37
  statistics 22
  unemployment, 33, 34, 36
  violent crime 34
Indo-China 311–12
International Crime Victimization Survey 188–9
international criminology 177–9
International Journal of Criminology 179–80
international law, torture and 308, 310–11, 316
Interregional Criminal Justice Research Institute (UN), data held by 189
interrogation techniques, torture and 303–6, 309–11
Iraq, Faluja massacre in 314
Israel 301
Italy
  dangerous offenders 84–5
  Ferri, Enrico 84–5
  positivism 84–5

just deserts 52, 83
justice *see also* restorative justice
  actuarial justice 31–2, 164–5
  class 19
  dimensions of 18–19
  expressive justice 230–1
  state as instrument of 18–20
justification
  penal power 221
  punishment 214–15
  torture 300–7, 313

labelling 28
Labour 23–4, 26–7 *see also* New Labour
Las Madres de la Plaza de Mayo 282–3
Latin America 301
left idealism 17
Left Realism 2, 17, 29–30
lesser evil, doctrine of 304
liberalism
  liberal consensus in 1960s, blaming the 36, 91–3

liberalism (cont.)
  liberal market economies 209–12
  neo-liberalism 8, 155–6
  penal systems 213
life sentences 62
London see East London, David
  Downes and delinquency
  in 117–46
lynching 253

managerialism 156
mandatory minimum sentencing
  244–5, 261–2
Marxist or radical criminology 2, 17
mass consumerism 35
materialism 14, 30
media
  demonization of offenders 25
  punitiveness 25, 35
  torture 301–3
mediation 289–90
mental disabilities see Ashworth Special
  Hospital, dangerous severe
  personality disorder, persons
  with
mental torture 309
modernism 21
Muslim population of East
  London 127–30

name and shame schemes 102
National Offender Management Service
  (NOMS) 93–4
national security, torture and 301, 304,
  311, 315
neo-liberalism 8, 155–6
Netherlands
  comparative criminology 174–8,
    184, 191, 197–8, 208–9
  co-ordinated market economy 209
  criminal justice system, reform
    of 214–15
  culture of control 227–8, 233
  Downes, David, *Contrasts in
    Tolerance* 174–8, 191,
    197–8, 208–9, 264–5

historical criminal justice
  studies 207–10
pillarization 208–9
prison population, growth in
  228, 223
United Kingdom, comparison
  with 207–10, 227–8, 264–5
New Consensus 92–7
New Labour see also anti-social
  behaviour policy, New Labour
  and, New Labour's law and
  order agenda
  1960s liberal, social consensus,
    blaming the 36
  Crime and Disorder Act 1998 26
  dangerous severe personality
    disorder, persons with 51–89
  deviance, sociology of 153
  Giddens, Tony 81
  permissiveness 36
  police powers, increase in 27
  reduction in crime 39
  third way 62–3, 81
  toughness policy 26–7
  zero tolerance policing 27
New Labour's law and order
  agenda 26–7, 91–115
  1960s liberal consensus 91–3
  Blair, Tony 91–3, 96, 109–10
  Blunkett, David 91–2
  British Crime Survey 94–6
  community programmes 93–4
  Conservative Party 92, 95
  general election 2005 92, 94
  Home Office Five Year Plan
    91–3
  Manichean approach 110–12
  National Offender Management
    Service (NOMS) 93–4
  New Consensus 92–7
  Old Labour 91–7, 110, 112
  prison population 94
  punitive populism 94–5, 111
  reduction in crime 94–5
  respect agenda 97–102

Index

terrorists without charge, detention of 109
victims and offenders, relationship between 112
young offenders as victims and offenders 111–12
new liberalism 8
New Paradigm, torture and 307–11
norms 157
Northern Ireland 301

offenders
  demonization of 25
  impunity for criminals 292, 310–11
  National Offender Management Service (NOMS) 93–4
  New Labour's law and order agenda 112
  restorative justice 291–4
  risk averse 160, 163
  targets and, interrelationship between 166–7
  torture, indemnities for 310–11
  victims and, relationship between 112, 166–7
  vote, restrictions on right to 241, 243–5, 262–3
  young people 111–12
opportunity theory 147–72
  actuarial justice 164–5
  administrative criminology 149–50, 156–7
  behavioural economics 162–3
  deviance, sociology of 149, 151, 168
  discounting 163
  displacement of crime 148–9
  economic analysis of 33–4, 150–1, 158, 160–9
  environmental criminology 158
  Felson and Clarke, *Opportunity Makes the Thief* 147–9
  imprisonment, costs of 164
  increase in crime rates 33–4
  managerialism, politics of 156
  neo-liberalism 155–6

Home Office, *Not Rocket Science* 149
  offenders, victims and targets, interplay between 166–7
  rational choice theory 150, 157–62, 165
  research 156
  risk assessment 164–5
  routine activity approach 166
  situational control theory 160–1, 168
  situational crime prevention 165–8
  young offenders 163
organized crime 124–5, 128

Palestine 301
penal policy
  comparative criminology 197–8
  culture of control 234–5, 259, 264–5
  dangerous severe personality disorder, persons with 71, 82–3
  United States 197–8, 234–56, 260–1, 264
penal system *see also* penal policy, prison population
  accountability to constitutional standards 213
  comparative criminology 213–15
  liberal democracy 213
  penal power, justification for 221
  risk 82
  United Kingdom 206–10
  United States
    conditions in 203
    privatized prisons, growth in 241–3, 258–60
    vote, restrictions on right to 241, 243–5, 262–3
  women 186
permissiveness 36
personality disorders *see* dangerous severe personality disorder, persons with
pillarization 208–9
police *see also* police power
  Cali, Colombia, governance in 273
  Communities First Partnerships, Bridgend police use of 106–7

police (cont.)
  comparative criminology 186–7
  culture of control 234
  policy 25–6
  United Kingdom 234
  United States 234
  women 187
  zero tolerance policing 27
police power
  accountability 217
  comparative criminology 217–18
  constitutional settlements 218
  criminal justice system 216–21
  degrading punishment 216–17
  Dubber, Markus Dirk. *The Police Power* 202, 213–21
  increase in 27
  New Labour 27
  political power 215–17
  regulatory or administrative offences 219–21
  status distinctions 216
  United Kingdom 216, 219–21
  United States 217–20
policy *see also* penal policy
  economic analysis 163–9
  opportunity theory 163–9
  police 25–6
  politics 25–6
  social democratic criminology 25–7
  three strikes policy 261–2
politics
  Cali, Colombia, governance in 283–4
  Conservatives 23–6, 34–5, 92, 95
  culture 232–3, 250–1, 255–7
  East London, delinquency in 136
  individualistic political culture 255–6
  Labour 23–4, 26–7
  moralistic political culture 255–6
  New Labour 26–7
  police power 215–17
  policy 25–6
  social democratic criminology 23–4, 34–7

Thatcher, Margaret 23, 25–6
toughness policy 23–4, 26–7
traditionalist political culture 255–6
United States, political culture in 250–1, 255–7
populism
  ethics 303–4
  New Labour's law and order agenda 94–5, 111
  punitiveness 94–5, 111
  torture 303–4
positivism 20–1, 83–5
poverty, measures of 33
pragmatic or adaptive approaches 230
President, protection from prosecution of 310–11
prison *see* penal system, prison population
prison population
  African-American population 249–50
  costs of imprisonment 164
  culture of control 231–2, 259–61
  Europe 258–60
  mass incarceration 231
  Netherlands 22, 228
  New Labour's law and order agenda 94
  United Kingdom 228, 231
  United States 231, 238–9, 248, 250–1, 258–61, 263
  African-American population 249–50
  privatized prisons, growth in 241–3, 258–60
proportionality 213
psychiatrists
  Ashworth Special Hospital 65–6, 70–1
  dangerous severe personality disorder, persons with 74–9
psychologists
  Ashworth Special Hospital 65–6, 68–70

dangerous severe personality
disorder, persons with 79, 83
public discourse 24–5
public disorder, increase in 23
punishment
consequentialist theories 213–14
degradation 216–17
historical criminal justice
studies 203–6
justification 214–15
police power 216–17
proportionality 213
status-based 203–6
three strikes policy 245, 247–8,
251–2, 258, 261–2
United States, regional variations
in 263–4
Whitman, James Q, *Harsh
Justice* 202–6
punitiveness
culture of control 231–3
media 25, 35
New Labour's law and order
agenda 94–5, 111
populism 94–5, 111
public discourse 24–5
United Kingdom 94–5, 111,
231, 233
United States, regional variations
in 263–4

radical criminology 2, 17
rates of crime 39–40 *see also* increase
in crime rates
rational choice theory
capacity 165–6
decision-making, norms and 158
detection, fear of 165
deviance, sociology of 162
marginal benefits and costs 158–60
norms 158
opportunity theory 150, 157–62, 165
risk averse offenders 160, 163
signalling 159–60
situational control theory 165–6

reduction in crime rates
British Crime Survey 94–5
causes of 39
demographic changes 39
disbelief in 95
economic factors 39–40
New Labour 39, 94–5
refugees from Nazis, experiences of
European 184, 185–6
regulatory offences 219–21
rehabilitation 28
religious right in United States 11
rendez-vous-ers 186–91
reporting, increase in 22, 35
respect agenda 97–102
restorative justice *see also* Cali,
Colombia, restorative justice in
aims of 292–3
concerns over 292
developed countries 291
impunity for criminals 292
responsibility, accepting 292–3
South African Truth and
Reconciliation Committee
292–3, 294
war to peace, transition from 291–2
risk
actuarialism 31–2
assessment 31–2, 164–5
Blair, Tony 81–2
dangerous severe personality
disorder, persons with 55, 80–3
ethics 31
imprisonment 82
opportunity theory 164–5
social democratic criminology 30–2
routine activity approach 166

science 20–1
self-preservation 304
sentencing
automatic life sentences 62
culture of control 261–2
dangerous severe personality
disorder, persons with
57, 62, 71–2

sentencing (*cont.*)
  discretionary life sentences 62
  mandatory minimum
    sentencing 244–5, 261–2
  reviewable sentences 57, 71–2
  United Kingdom 261–2
  United States, regional variations
    in 244–5, 261
September 11, 2001 attacks on the
  United States 109–10, 189, 190
sexual psychopath statutes in United
  States 78–9
shaming 263
signalling 159–60
situational control theory 160–1,
  165–6, 168
situational crime prevention 165–8
slavery 204–5, 235, 237, 256–7
social democracy *see also* social
    democratic criminology
  barbarism 37–40
  ethical socialism 8–9
  history of 8–9
  meaning of 8–9
  new liberalism, association with 8
  Rawls, John, *Theory of Justice* 8–9
  Soviet communism, association
    with 8
  'third way' 8
social democratic criminology 7–40
  anomie theory 14
  capitalism, critique of 15–16
  class 19
  contrology, rise of 21–3, 27–30, 34
  cultural change 27, 35
  economic factors 13–14, 18,
    30, 32–9
  equality and democracy 17–18
  ethical, primacy of the 11–14
  gradualism 16–17
  ideal-type 9–30
  justice
    dimensions of 18–19
    state as instrument of 19–20

Left Realism 29–30
meaning 7–8
modernism 21
optimism 18
policy shifts 25–7
politicization of law and order
  23–4, 34–7
problem of crime 9–11
public discourse 24–5
risk society 30–2
science 20–1
socio-economic change 27, 35
state 19–20, 38–9
white collar crime 10–11
wrong, whether social democratic
  analysis of crime is 32–4
socio-economic change, increase in
  crime and 27, 35, 37
sociology of deviance *see* deviance,
  sociology of
South African Truth and Reconciliation
  Committee 292–3, 294
Soviet communism 8
Spitalfields 123–38
status distinctions 203–6, 216
stereotyping 24–5
Stone, Michael 53, 58, 60, 64, 71–80
stranger, idea of 181, 183–8, 190
Stratford 130, 134
Straw, Jack 57, 76–7, 97
street corner groups 118–19, 139
symbolic gestures 247–8, 251

Taliban 308, 310
terrorism
  Al-Qaeda 308, 310–11
  criminal criminology 190
  detention without charge 109
  Iraq, invasion of 110
  New Labour's law and order
    agenda 109
  September 11, 2001 attacks on the
    United States 109–10, 189, 190
  torture 297, 301, 307–11
  war against terror 109–10
Thatcher, Margaret 23, 25–6

'third way' 8, 62–3, 81, 305–6
three strikes policy 245, 247–8, 251–2, 258, 261–2
TOGETHER campaign 99–106
torture in United States, legal reconstruction of 297–317
  abolition 299–301, 306
  Abu Ghraib 301–7, 312–13
  accountability 314
  Algeria 300–1
  Al-Qaeda 308, 310–11
  conscience, lack of 312–14
  cruel, inhuman or degrading treatment 303, 309–11
  degradation and humiliation 306–7, 309, 312–13
  denial 305–6
  ethical populism 303–4
  Europe 299–301
  Faluja massacre, Iraq 314
  France
    Algeria 300–1
    Indo-China 311–12
  Geneva Conventions 308, 310, 316
  geographical limitations on prohibition of torture 311
  Greene, Graham 311–12, 314–15
  Guantanamo Bay 203, 301–8, 310
  Harvard guidelines 315–16
  human rights 297–301, 303, 309–11, 316
  hypocrisy and honesty 311–17
  Indo-China 311–12
  international law 308, 310–11, 316
  interrogation techniques 303–6, 309–11
  Israel, moderate physical pressure against Palestinians in 301
  justification 300–7, 313
  judicial bureaucrats, supervision by 305–6
  Latin America 301
  legal definition 308–11
  lesser evil, doctrine of the 304
  McCain amendment 311
  media saturation 301–3
  mental torture 309
  moderate physical pressure 301, 302
  national security 301, 304, 311, 315
  New Paradigm 307–11
  Northern Ireland, use of torture in 301
  perpetrators, indemnities for 310–11
  pre-history 299–301
  President, protection from prosecution of 310–11
  regulation, logic of 304–6, 315
  self-preservation 304
  special procedure 300–1
  Taliban 308, 310
  terrorism 297, 301, 307–11
  third way, path of 305–6
  ticking bomb story 304
  tolerance and laissez-faire 305–6
  torture lite 303, 307, 313–14
  unlawful combatant status 308
  victim, legal status of 308, 310
totalitarianism 19
tough on crime 23–4, 26–7, 153, 232–3
transnational crime, increase in 190
transnational criminology 177–80
Truth and Reconciliation Committee 292–3, 294

UN Interregional Criminal Justice Research Institute, data held by 189
unemployment
  East London, delinquency in 121–2, 129
  economic factors 33, 34
  increase in crime rates 33, 34, 36
United Kingdom *see also* United Kingdom, culture of control in
  liberal market economy 209–10
  Netherlands compared with 207–10, 227–8, 264–5
  Northern Ireland, use of torture in 301

United Kingdom (*cont.*)
  penal system 206–10
  police power 216, 219–21
  prison population, growth in 228
  torture 301
  United States, comparison with 188
United Kingdom, culture of control in
  mandatory minimum sentences 261–2
  police forces in, number of 234
  prison population, increase in 231
  punitiveness 231, 233
  three strikes policy 261–2
  vote, removal or restriction of right to 262
United States *see also* torture in United States, legal reconstruction of, United States, culture of control in
  comparative criminology 187–8, 197–8
  degradation hypothesis 205–6, 209, 211–12
  detention of sexual psychopaths 78
  economic analysis 160
  exceptionalism 188
  fear of crime 78
  gangs 119–20
  Iraq, invasion of 109–10, 314
  opportunity theory 180
  penal policy 197–8
  police power 217–20
  prison conditions 203
  punishment 202–6
  religious right 11
  September 11, 2001 attacks on the United States 109–10, 189, 190
  settlers 204–5
  sexual psychopath statutes in 78–9
  slavery 204–5
  status-based punishment 203–5
  terrorism 109–10
  United Kingdom 188
  war against terror 109–10
  weak and strong states 297, 210–11
  Whitman, James Q, *Harsh Justice* 202–12
United States, culture of control in
  see also United States, regional variations in culture of control in
  correctional supervision, increase in 231–2
  mass incarceration 231
  penal policy 234–5
  political culture, changes in 232
  prison population, increase in 231
United States, regional variations in culture of control in 235–58
  African-American population 249–50
  agency, political structures and 257–8
  capital punishment 239–41, 248, 252–4, 258–9, 264
  comparative criminology 238–58
  disintegrative shaming 263
  exceptionalism 263–5
  federal government 234
  governance, types of 250–1, 255–6
  lynching 253
  mandatory minimum sentences 244–5, 261
  Midwest 235, 237–58
  migration 255–7
  national culture of control, existence of 238
  Northeastern states 235, 239–58
  penal policy 234–56, 260–1, 264
  police agencies in, number of 234
  political culture 250–1, 255–7
    individualistic 255–6
    moralistic 255–6
    traditionalist 255–6
  political participation, levels of 250–1
  political structures 257–8
  prison

Index

population rate 238–9, 248, 250–1, 258–61, 263
privatized, growth in 241–3, 258–60
punishment, punitiveness of 263–4
sentencing policy 244–5, 261
slavery, 235, 237, 256–7
South 237–58
states, differences in criminal justice system amongst 229–38
symbolic gestures 247–8, 251
three strikes policy 245, 247–8, 251–2, 258, 261
vigilantism, death penalty and 253
vote, removal or restriction of right to 241, 243–5, 262–3
welfare, level of 249–50
Western states 235–58
unlawful combatant status, torture and 308
utilitarianism 12

victims
New Labour's law and order agenda 112
offenders and, relationship with 112, 166–7
targets and, interrelationship between 166–7
torture, legal status of victims of 308, 310
unlawful combatant status 308
young people 111–12
vigilantism 253
violent crime, increase in 34
vote for offenders, removal or restriction of right to
culture of control 262
Europe 262
United Kingdom 262
United States, regional variations in 241, 243–5, 262–3

war against terror 109–10
white collar crime 10–11
Whitman, James Q, *Harsh Justice* 202–12
degradation hypothesis 205–6, 209, 211–12
Guantanamo Bay 203
historical criminal justice studies 202–12
prison conditions 203
punishment system in 202–6
settlers 204–5
slavery 204–5
status-based punishment 203–5
weak and strong states 207, 210–11
women
Cali, Colombia, governance in 271–2, 274–7, 282–8, 294
comparative criminology 186–7
Las Madres de la Plaza de Mayo 282–3
penal treatment of 186
police officers, as 187
working class *see* East London, David Downes and delinquency in

young offenders *see also* East London, David Downes and delinquency in
anti-social behaviour policy, New Labour and 102, 105–9
Cali, Colombia, restorative justice in 290, 292–3
gangs 290
New Labour's law and order agenda 111–12
opportunity theory 163
restorative justice 290, 292–3
victims, as 111–12

zero tolerance policing 27

Printed in Great Britain
by Amazon.co.uk, Ltd.,
Marston Gate.